Guide to Cretan Antiquities

GUIDE TO CRETAN ANTIQUITIES

by

Costis Davaras

Ephor of Antiquities
Director of the Archaeological Institute of Crete

Forth Edition

EPTALOFOS S.A.

ATHENS - GREECE

Published in the United States by
NOYES PRESS
Noyes Building
Park Ridge, New Jersey 07656

Forth Edition
EPTALOFOS S.A.
Ardittou str., 12-16,
Athens 116-36, Greece
e-mail: info@eptalofos.com.gr
www.eptalofos.com.gr

Davaras, Costis,
    Guide to Cretan Antiquities

    Bibliography: p.
1. Crete-Antiquities. 2. Crete-History. I Title.
DF901.C82D38   949.98'003   76-4600
ISBN: 0-8155-5044-8

PREFACE

The purpose of this book is to give the reader, through alphabetical entries, an outline of all important cultural, natural, social and technological elements, artistic tendencies, individual works of art, and historical happenings in Crete during several millenia, from the arrival of the first settlers in the island to its liberation in the beginning of this century. The entries were compiled with special care to include essential information in a brief way. Entries about the great Minoan civilization, art, religion and monuments are, of course, by their own right far more numerous. On the other hand, the extremely interesting Dorian Crete, with its aristocratic society, rich mythology, fine art, and connections to the Minoan culture, has been not neglected.

An asterisk following a word indicates a separate entry under this word. Thus, the reader has a reference available and by use of parallel information may explore his subject more deeply. This book can, of course, serve as a summary guide for every worthwhile site or monument on the island. The author has tried to choose the right entries and to compile them in the right proportions.

January 1976

Costis Davaras
Director of the Archaeological Museum
in Hagios Nikolaos and Ephor for Eastern Crete

TABLE OF CONTENTS

LIST OF FIGURES

Acknowledgements

Figs. 8, 31, 59, 60, 73, 79, 81, 84, 99, 106, 121, 123, 133, 150, 167, 170, 172, 174: Venetian maps after Francesco Basilicata.

Figs. 3, 4, 9, 11, 107, 112, 159, 166, 189: Drawn by Thomas Phanourakis, Herakleion.

Figs. 2, 6, 7, 12, 13-21, 26-28, 33-36, 38-40, 42, 44-46, 49-53, 55, 58, 61-62, 65, 68, 76-77, 80, 85, 88-89, 93-95, 98, 100-105, 107, 111, 113, 115-118, 120, 128, 131, 135, 137-139, 142, 143, 145-147, 149, 152, 155, 156, 159, 161, 173, 175-178, 181, 188, 195, 198: Photographs by George Xylouris, Herakleion.

Figs. 87, 122, 154, 157, 160, 162, 168: Photographs by M. Androulakis, Herakleion.

Figs. 144, 192: Photographs by Dr. A. Zois.

Figs. 22, 23, 29, 30, 47, 56, 74, 114, 184-186: Photographs by the author.

INTRODUCTION

Crete is an old and beautiful island, a bridge between three continents charged with history. In the second millenium B.C. Crete became the cradle of one of the great civilizations of mankind and specifically the first major civilization in Europe. Minoan Crete was indeed unique in antiquity, in many ways astoundingly modern, and it left works of art of an unsurpassable beauty. Minoan culture at its later stages was Hellenized and formed an entity with the Greek Mycenaean civilization of the Mainland, which was in turn an adaptation of Greek immigrants to Minoan prototypes. Minoan-Mycenaean civilization disappeared from the scene of history towards the end of the second millenium B.C., but left behind it a precious cultural heritage, which influenced profoundly the next great civilization: Classical Greece.

Crete played a major role in the creation of early Greek civilization and especially of its religion and mythology, being evidently the place where the Greek alphabet was first introduced, the first written laws developed, and Greek monumental sculpture was born. After a long period of internal strife and social conservatism which led to stagnation, Crete became a flourishing Roman province for several centuries. This prosperity later enabled it to develop an important Early Christian culture and to become—with a short interval of occupation by some Arab adventurers from Spain—a rich and active province of the Greek Byzantine Empire.

In 1204—two and a half centuries before the fall of Constantinople—the island was detached from the Empire by the Crusaders and sold to the great Mediterranean naval power of the time, Venice. Under its exploiting but rather mild rule, which lasted until the middle of the seventeenth century, long after the rest of Greece had fallen into Turkish hands, Crete was again able to create a civilization of its own. The Creto-Venetian era was in fact a Renaissance culture, faithful to Greek Byzantine tradition but at the same time enriched with Italian elements.

This evolution, which achieved a rather high artistic level of architecture, painting, theater and literature, was abruptly and violently interrupted by the Turkish occupation. This period, which lasted until the end of the nineteenth century, was a sad time of exploitation, revolts and repressions, massacres and violent attempts at Islamization. Consequently the economy decayed, the population dropped by half, and any higher form of civilization ceased to exist. Crete, as well as the rest of Greece, almost lost its European personality, but it fiercely persisted in its religious, national and linguistic nature. The coming of the twentieth century saw Crete become an integral political and cultural part of Greece, the destiny of which it has since followed.

Alphabetical Entries

Achaians. *Achaioi* is the name most commonly applied to the Greeks in the poems of Homer. They must be the people called *Aqaiwasha* by the Egyptians, and *Ahhijava* in the records of the Hittites, a mighty people of Anatolia and a world power of the time, whose king addresses the Achaian king as "brother." It is obviously the name of the Mycenaeans, the people ruled by the kings of Mycenae. During the second half of the fifteenth century B.C.—about 1450-1400 B.C. or a little later—an Achaian dynasty probably ruled Knossos, and controlled Crete, perhaps taking advantage of the disasters which befell the island and weakened Minoan authority (see Destructions of Palaces*).

These Achaians in Knossos influenced Minoan art to a certain extent, giving a sense of formalism, monumentality and tectonic composition, which can be seen in the so-called Palace Style* pottery* or some late frescoes* like the Griffins* of the Throne Room. A military spirit quite new to Crete was introduced, which can best be distinguished in the Warrior Graves near Knossos, where a number of excellent weapons* were found. The Minoan Linear A script* was adapted to the Greek language,* thus forming the Linear B script,* recorded in clay tablets.* Mainland ideas in architecture* seem to have influenced the megaron-type buildings that arose at Gournia* and on the ruins of Hagia Triada,* which served as a palatial center, perhaps in place of the partially reoccupied palace at Phaistos.* The palace at Knossos* was spared and seems to have been slightly modified to the new rulers' tastes.

In the next century and after the final destruction of the Knossian palace, the island probably was no longer organized as a Mycenaean kingdom, but Achaian settlers had evidently already colonized most of its more fertile parts. Originally, the chief area of Achaian occupation was obviously Central Crete, as the Cretan towns named in the Catalogue of Ships in the Iliad are from this area (see Idomeneus*). The Achaians were linked together by ties of friendship and even of kinship, and spoke a Greek Mycenaean *koine* ("common") language. The same term is applied to the common standardized pottery and almost uniform civilization of the late Bronze Age, which can be seen in most parts of the Aegean, including Crete, although the island during the Late Minoan III period* clearly shows a nonconformist spirit owing to the great Minoan legacy (see Pottery*).

Administration (Minoan). During the first half of the second millenium

B.C., the time of maturity of the Minoan civilization, Crete may have been a loose federation of the sort of "city-states" found in Syria or Mesopotámia, unlike Egypt which was under the strict centralized rule of the Pharaoh. Although details are not known, we may assume that Knossos held first place, enjoying some kind of religious and political hegemony—probably connected with the "priest-king"*—or sharing one without any apparent political rivalry with the other palaces.* It has been suggested that the kings might not have been absolute monarchs but were perhaps assisted in their functions by some sort of senate or council of elders or priests, or even by popular assemblies. The local governors lived in smaller "palaces," such as the one dominating the town of Gournia,* or in villas.* Evidently the central authorities formulated and administered the laws, which probably were based on tribal customs as well as on the interests of the ruling classes. Economy* was centralized on a large scale, while overseas relations and regulation of exports* or imports* were surely for the most part among the duties of the central authorities. As Renfrew has said, "the systematic hierarchical organization documented in the records, and illustrated on the map, demanded and brought a measure of peace and internal security. Clearly one of the secrets of Crete's stable settlement growth was an absence of defensive problems, facilitated by the existence of ample non-coastal arable lands and probably by an adequate control of the sea."

Agelai. The training bands known as *agelai* ("herds") in Dorian Crete were an old important institution of the educational system of Cretan youth, corresponding to the Spartan *bouai*, where the training and education of the youth were very similar. These bands were in fact a survival of older tribal customs and depended upon the system of age-grades. They were supported by the state and organized by sons of the most distinguished aristocratic families, depending on their patronage. Each *agela* tried to draft as many members among the boys as possible. The initiation ritual was considered a very important happening. The *archon* ("ruler") of the *agela* usually was the father of the organizer. A boy had to attend one of the *agelai* probably at the end of his seventeenth year. There he was fed at public expense and received his education,* mainly physical and military training. On certain days the *agelai* had to meet each other in combat, both armed and unarmed. They fought to music* as in real war. The great Greek geographer Strabo is our main source of information about the *agelai:* he reports that young boys were obliged to participate in the *syssitia* ("common meals"), sitting together on the ground to eat under the charge of a supervisor (*paidonomos*), and always to wear the same poor garments. All the young men promoted from the *agelai* dined at public messes called *andreia* ("Men's Houses," corresponding to the Spartan *phiditia*) and had to marry at the same time and start a family.

Agia; Agios see **Hagia; Hagios.**

Agriculture. The first Neolithic* settlers of Crete were apparently food producers on a relatively advanced scale. In the Bronze Age* agriculture developed further, although cultivable land was, and still is, scarce. Nevertheless the climate* favours agriculture. The inhabitants of the various settlements practised mixed farming. Of course an agrarian economy* was the base of society. A variety of bronze tools* was used. The plough was probably entirely of wood* and no example has survived; its form, with stilt, pole and share beam, is shown by sign 27 of the Minoan Hieroglyphic script.* Its introduction allowed the cultivation of larger tracts of land and must have started a revolution in man's diet. Grain was cut by bronze sickles, threshed by means of a wooden sled and stored in large pithoi* and granaries (see Kouloures*), then crushed, ground in hand querns and sieved. Sickles, sometimes found in excavations, usually were hafted by a tang fastened with rivets. Bread was made from wheat and barley, and perhaps from millet. On a famous relief scene (see Stone Vases,* *Harvester Vase*) winnowing forks are shown.

There was a large variety of fruit. The cultivation of the olive* and the use of olive oil* are well attested for Minoan times. Almond seeds—evidently used also for the manufacture of perfumes*—have been found in Neolithic* and later levels. There is also some evidence of the cultivation of the carob tree and the fig tree, while date palms, although not native to Crete and probably introduced from Egypt, are represented in Middle Minoan art. The date palm was evidently considered sacred, as some representations permit us to deduce. Pears and grapes were perhaps indigenous, while apples were introduced before the end of Minoan times. The alcoholic fermentation of various sugary fruit juices was probably known. Beer also, known in Egypt as early as the fourth millenium B.C., may well have been brewed in Crete. Sinclair Hood believes that quinces were probably native to the island, as the name Kydonia* suggests.

Beans, lentils and peas occur in Middle Minoan levels. Pistachio nuts were also known. Garden vegetables, wild forms of lettuce, asparagus and celery, and plentiful supplies of edible or medicinal herbs, including the scented ones such as thyme, basil, oregano, mint, sage, cumin and marjoram, abundant and very popular in the island today, were certainly used by the Minoans, perhaps some of them for drinking in a tisane, as is done today (see also Flora*). Honey* was known and wine* was made from the grapes of the vine.

Aigagros see **Animals (Wild).**

AKAKALLIS. The nymph Akakallis or Akalle was a daughter of Minos* and Pasiphae.* Her name with the reduplication of the first syllable betrays its pre-Hellenic origins; in Cretan Greek it meant "narcissus." Akakallis was considered the mother of the founders of five Cretan cities. She became the first love of Apollo in the house of the seer Karmanor at Tarrha* in Western Crete, when the god came there for purification. From this union were born the twins Phylakis and Philandros, who were suckled by a goat in Elyros.* This story reminds us of the twins Romulus and Remus (see Amaltheia*). Minos was vexed and banished Akakallis to Libya. Among her children were also Kydon,* son of Hermes or Apollo, who later became the eponymous hero of Kydonia,* modern Chania,* as well as Miletos and Oaxos, founder of Axos.*

Alabaster see **Alabastron.**

Alabastron. Alabastron (alabaster), a white and slightly translucent stone, has been used since the fifteenth century B.C. to make squat jars with a curved profile. The shape of these low bulbous vessels, evidently of Egyptian origin, is also named by modern scholars "alabastron" after the stone. This shape was also imitated in clay, usually with three miniature handles on the upper shoulder, and decorated with paintings. These vases were designed for perfume* or fine oil. Egyptian alabastra were imported both to Crete and to the Mainland. Some large examples of Cretan manufacture with elaborately decorated lids and mouths have been recovered from the Throne Room of the palace at Knossos.* In later Greek times a pear-shaped alabastron vase, often copied in clay, bears the same name.

Alphabet. The use of an alphabet for writing is one of the most decisive historical achievements of mankind. Slightly adapted for the pronunciation, the North Semitic script became the model for the Greek, from which came at a later date both the Latin and Cyrillic (Slavic) alphabets, the latter in the ninth century A.D. The earliest of the extant Greek inscriptions go back as far as perhaps 775-750 B.C. The Cretan alphabet is the closest of all to the Semitic Phoenician. It has long been acknowledged that Crete was one of the places in which the Greek alphabet was received and developed, if it did not actually originate here, as some scholars believe. With its introduction, society became again literate after the extinction of the Linear B script* and the long centuries of illiteracy of the Dark Ages.* As in the Semitic model, the earliest Greek inscriptions began from right to left, but with an important innovation: after the first line the inscription did not continue in this direction but at the end of the line returned in the reverse direction, from left to right. The third line was again from right to left and so on. This system was called *boustrophedon*: as the plough-ox turned at the end of a furrow. The famous Code of Gortyn* was written in this way (see figure 32), from which eventually developed the system of writing from left to right. This was later copied by the Latin alphabet. The Greeks were very careful about the aesthetic form of the characters and the whole arrangement of the inscription. The archaic alphabet of the Code has 18 letters, including the F (*digamma*), instead of the 24 of the standard Greek alphabet.

Altars. The Minoan cult used a variety of altars. Some of them were permanent and regularly built; among them are one in the middle of the Central Court and two in the West Court of the palace at Knossos,* of which the rectangular bases survive. Other fixed altars have been discovered at Phaistos,* Hagia Triada* and the first tholos tomb* at Apesokari;* the first of them was stepped. In the middle of the central court of the palace at Malia* stood a sunken altar for burnt sacrifice. Cave sanctuaries also had altars, as the constructions in the caves* of Eileithyia* and Psychro* show. Altars were sometimes crowned with sacral horns,* as we see on representations on stone vases* from Knossos* and Zakros.* The altars on pictorial representations were often heraldically framed by lions, powerful attendants of the divinities.* A small square altar from Knossos has on each side double axes* in relief, evidently with painted shafts, standing above sacral horns.* The scenes on the sarcophagus* from Hagia Triada* show on one side a square altar of ashlar masonry with three steps in front, while on the other side a bowl for libations rests on an altar between a pair of double axes.* There were also clay models of such fixed altars as well as small portable round altars or libation tables of stone with incurving middle parts, probably used as receptacles for offerings, and sometimes imitated in clay.

AMALTHEIA. The Cretan nymph Amaltheia, daughter of the Ocean or the Cretan King Melisseus, nursed the infant Zeus* in the Diktaian Cave.* According to authors of the Hellenistic period* she was a goat-nymph. Zeus was grateful to her and later set Amaltheia's image among the stars as Capricorn. He also borrowed one of her horns, which became the famous Cornucopia, or horn of plenty. Legends about exposed babies being suckled by animals are very old, and are common in folklore, especially in Crete. The children of Akakallis,* a daughter of Minos,* were nursed this way by various animals such as goats, bitches or wolves, like the famous twins Romulus and Remus. All these animals must be considered as totemic survivals (see Praisos*).

Amber. Baltic amber is uncommon in Minoan Crete in contrast to the Mycenaean Mainland, where it is found in abundance. This is characteristic of the existing commercial relations with northern European countries. The "amber route" seems to have passed through the Adriatic corridor to the Alpine passes and Central Europe. Another possible source of amber was the Red Sea. Some Cretan tombs of the early Iron Age* contained amber beads or jewels with inlaid amber.

Amnisos. A fine villa of Late Minoan IA date was excavated beginning in 1932 by Marinatos and further explored by Platon at Amnisos, on the shore east of Herakleion.* It was a two-storey building with massive ashlar masonry in the more important parts (figure 1). Some of the blocks, in spite of their size, had been toppled out of position, perhaps by an earthquake or even a strong tidal wave (see Thera*). The main reception room of the villa (7) had columns off its center; the walls of the upper floor were adorned with excellent frescoes* representing formal gardens with inlaid white lilies on one wall, (figure 2) red irises on another, and on the third other plants in stone vases.* A large room (1) had a five-bayed pier-and-door partition opening on to a terrace with a fine view of the sea. This villa was interpreted as the dwelling of a "Naval Officer", as Amnisos is considered a special harbour* of the palace at Knossos.* As the geographer Strabo informs us, Minos* used Amnisos as a seaport.

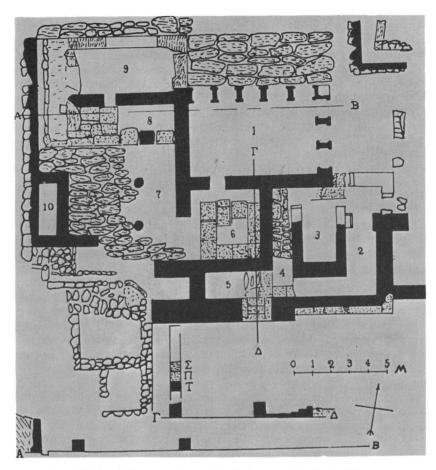

1. Provisional plan of the Villa at Amnisos (*after Marinatos*)

Beyond the low hill west of the villa, near the shore, a smaller Minoan building and an open-air early Greek sanctuary dedicated to Zeus* Thenatas, according to the inscriptions found here, was excavated together with the villa. Thenai was a town near Knossos. A large round altar and a wall were found along with two limestone life-size sitting eagles. The cult continued into Roman times, as the numerous votive offerings revealed. A large Minoan wall discovered here has been interpreted as having belonged to the harbour. Not far to the south lies the well-known cult cave of the goddess Eileithyia* mentioned by Homer.

Amulets. Amulets evidently played an important role in popular religion* of the Bronze Age* Cretans. They were made of different materials such as ivory,* bone, steatite, and bronze or copper, and show a variety of shapes including small size human or animal figures, human limbs, mini-

2. White Lilies Fresco from the Villa at Amnisos

ature tools* and shields,* or even simple smoothed shells* or pebbles. Their magical protective qualities were derived mainly from their materi-al, but also from their shape or the motifs engraved on them. Rock crystal bird pendants of the Early Minoan period* may have been amulets. A most common type during early times was the foot-amulet, which may have been worn to provide protection from snakebites; perhaps they were modelled on the Egyptian leg-amulets.

A large class of seals* is considered to have possessed value as amu-lets or talismans; those inscribed in the Minoan Hieroglyphic script*

3. Cuttle fish on a seal from Elounda

surely must be counted among them, as well as many seals representing double axes,* marine life (figure 3) and ships,* libation jugs (figure 4), birds,* shrines,* or the motif known as the lion's mask. Red carnelian seems a favourite material for talismanic stones, while the most frequent shape was the amygdaloid (almond shape). Surely the most remarkable Minoan amulet is one of gold recovered from a tomb at Hagia Triada:* it has the shape of a miniature heart with attached figures of a spider, a scorpion, a snail, a hand, and a snake (figure 5).

Angarathos Monastery. This Medieval monastery east of Herakleion, already mentioned in sixteenth century manuscripts preserved today in Venice and in the British Museum, has probably been the most important of all Cretan monasteries. It honoured the Dormition of the Virgin. A center of Greek and religious education, it was the school of many priests such as Meletios Pigas and Kyrillos Loukaris, who later became patriarchs and erudite scholars. The monastery today preserves very few of its original elements.

Animals (Domestic). Domestication of animals presupposes a social

4. Libation jug on a seal from Siteia

medium. From deposits of the Neolithic period* there is evidence of the existence of domestic sheep, goats *(Capra hircus)*, swine *(Sus domesticus indicus)* and cattle, including the Cretan short-horns *(Bos creticus)* (figure 6). Cretan cattle—probably descended from the giant *Bos primigenius* with long horns—undoubtedly served as draught animals in agriculture* and transport.* Some of these animals must have been brought by the first Neolithic settlers. Bulls were kept for bull-games.* The Cretan hunting hound *(Canis creticus)* is sometimes represented in Minoan art.* On two Early Minoan* stone vase lids, one from Mochlos* and the other from Zakros,* are handles shaped like long and lean dogs, reminiscent of those seen in present day Cretan villages. In other representations dogs, evidently the first animals domesticated by man, are wearing collars. A colossal collared mastiff with two attendants can be seen on a seal from Isopata near Knossos.* Both Minos* and Europa* were associated with a legendary hound. The hounds guarding the Greek temple of Diktynna* near Kydonia* were famous.

Other domestic animals of the Minoans were asses and later horses,*

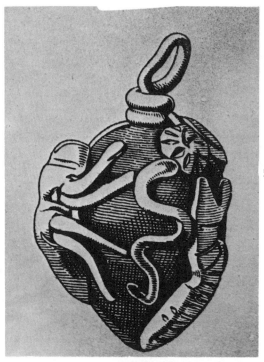

5. Gold amulet from Hagia Triada
(*after Evans*)

while the domestic fowl was possibly introduced during the Bronze Age;* in Greece chickens, known as Persian birds, appear from the eighth century B.C. onwards. Minoan art* has depicted several kinds of domestic animals; well-known are the various clay models found in peak sanctuaries,* or the charming clay model of a large flock and its shepherd inside a bowl from Palaikastro.* Cats appear on Middle Minoan* seals; those depicted on the splendid naturalistic Cat Fresco from Hagia Triada,* are not native wild cats but domesticated ones introduced from Egypt, where they were trained to help in hunting wild fowl in the marshes. Monkeys* were also introduced from Egypt.

At present the mountainous areas of the island, denuded of their forests,* support sheep and goats, which are kept more for milk and its products than for meat.

Animals (Wild). Palaeontological evidence shows that among the fossils dating to remote times are some belonging to hippopotami and pigmy elephants. The Cretan fauna is European. It appears that in prehistoric times there were in Crete various wild beasts which are now extinct, such as wolves, foxes, bears, wild boars whose tusks were used for the manufacture of helmets (see Armour*), great oxen and even lions, the memory of which survived in Greek legend. Lions are so often seen on seals* (figure 157) that it is difficult to believe they were not at home in Crete at one time. Hunting them surely was an important operation.

6. Middle Minoan clay cattle from the peak sanctuary of Traostalos

Often they appear as powerful attendants of the divinities, and sometimes they heraldically frame an altar.*

A characteristic feature of the Cretan fauna is the *aigagros* or *agrimi* (figure 7), a splendid kind of wild goat, the Cretan ibex *(Capra aegagrus cretensis)*, often depicted in Minoan art* (figures 112 and 146). This proud animal lives today in very limited numbers in practically inaccessible areas of the White Mountains of the West; the Greek State protects it from extinction. In Minoan times the ibex probably offered abundant prey (evidently also useful for providing the raw material for horn bows), along with deer, stag, hare *(Lepus cretensis)*, rabbit (these species shown by evidence of deposits as early as Neolithic), pigeon, pheasant, partridge, hoopoe (depicted in the fine fresco of the Caravanserai*), quail and other

7. Late Minoan wild goats of bronze

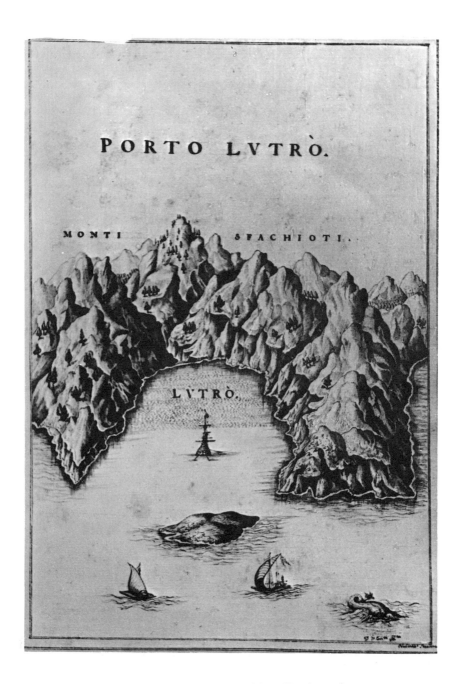

8. Loutro of Sphakia in 1615 (*after a Venetian map*)

birds.* Probably fur bearing animals such as weasels, badgers, martens and wild cats were also trapped.

Minoan seals* often show hunting scenes. Familiar figures in Minoan art* and later are the Master and the Mistress of Animals, perhaps hunting deities, appearing in the middle of a group of wild animals and exerting power over them as well as over the forces of nature; occasionally demons* take the place of the animals in the group.

Anopolis. The Classical Greek city-state of Anopolis was situated near the modern village of the same name on an upland plain at Sphakia* in Western Crete. Anopolis was one of the thirty-one Cretan cities which made an alliance with Eumenes II, king of Pergamon in Asia Minor, in 183 B.C. Parts of its strong fortification walls are preserved. The site is still unexplored. The port of the city was Phoinix, today the fishing village of Loutro (figure 8), on a splendid section of the south coast, still unspoiled by man. Phoinix is mentioned in the Acts of the Apostles.

During the Venetian occupation* Anopolis was a center of the resistance movement under John Kallergis and was subsequently destroyed in 1365. Resettled later, it was again destroyed by the Turks in 1770 during the uprising of Daskaloyannis, who was captured and skinned alive.

Apanosiphis Monastery. The rich monastery of Apanosiphis near the village of Metaxochori in the district of Herakleion* was probably erected in 1600, in honour of St. George. The monastery was burned down during the uprising of 1821 and later rebuilt. Its treasury includes some interesting gospels and crosses.

Apesokari. On a knoll west of the modern village of Apesokari in the Mesara Plain* lie two important tholos tombs* of the Early and Middle Minoan periods.* The smaller and later one was excavated by the Germans during the war. It shows several interesting features, such as a rectangular complex of rooms joining the tholos itself. One large room had a wooden pillar* on a stone base, in fact a pillar crypt like those of the palaces* and villas* employed for the cult. Two altars* are associated with this complex, indicative of some sepulchral ritual. A natural concretion of rock resembling a cult image (see Caves*) was found on one of the altars, which was built inside a niche to the right of the entrance. The other altar was built in the open, surrounded by a paved area.

The second tomb, at some distance east of the first, was excavated by the author. The large circular chamber had been plundered but not the numerous rectangular side rooms, which yielded several interesting finds, including some seals* (figure 9), an oval larnax, a minature stone double axe,* and some pottery,* including several dozen cups. A Minoan settlement has been located on a hill to the south.

Aphrati see Arkades.

Apodoulou. Near the village of Apodoulou on the southwest slopes of

9. Scorpion on an Early Minoan seal from the Mesara Plain

Mount Ida and not far from the Libyan Sea, in the prefecture of
Rethymnon,* Sp. Marinatos explored a rather large country mansion of
the Middle Minoan III period.* Among the finds were an inscribed libation vessel of stone and a miniature double axe* of gold. By the road just
outside the village the author excavated a plundered Late Minoan tholos
tomb,* which still contained four upturned clay larnakes,* one of them
now in the Chania Museum, depicting lamenting figures with upraised
hands.

The church of St. George with its fresco-paintings belongs to the fifteenth century.

Apollonia. Apollonia, besides being an alternative name for Kydonia*
and Eleutherna,* and a small town on the south coast in the area of
Lappa,* was a small city-state in central Crete. In 171 B.C. it was attacked
and captured by Kydonia,* although both cities were bound by treaty
under oath to the Idaian Zeus. The Kydonians killed the men and divided
among themselves the land, the women and the children. Then Gortyn,*
the powerful city-state of the Mesara Plain,* in support of Apollonia
attacked and almost captured Kydonia, which in turn had invoked the aid
of King Eumenes of Pergamon, who sent troops to protect his allies. The
whole matter, very characteristic of the incessant strife among the Cretan
cities during the Hellenistic period,* was settled by treaty, and Apollonia,
which in the meantime had fallen into the hand of Knossos, was transferred to Gortyn (168–166/5 B.C.).

Recently St. Alexiou was able to identify Apollonia with modern Hagia Pelagia on the north coast near Rogdia, to the northwest of Herakleion.* The whole area, which offered a number of good anchorages, was known as Panormos. The Greek scholar excavated here, among other ruins, a rectangular civic building of great importance of the fourth or third century B.C., which included two axial hearths and a sunken *bothros* for libations. This building, 15 by 6.3 metres (50 by 21 feet), seems to have combined the functions of an *andreion* ("Men's House") and a *prytaneion* (town-hall) of a Dorian city. The site had already been settled by Minoan times.

Aptera. One of the strongest Greek city-states of Western Crete, Aptera was situated on a plateau on a high hill enjoying a fine view over the Suda Bay,* east of Chania.* According to tradition, the city was named for the Sirens, who became wingless after losing at a musical contest with the Muses. The victorious Muses plucked out the feathers of the Sirens, who then threw themselves in despair into the sea. The name of Aptera seems to be attested in the Linear B* tablets* from Knossos.* The city possessed a temple of Artemis, where the goddess was worshipped as Aptera, "Wingless Artemis." Pausanias tells us how Aptera helped Sparta in 668 B.C. in the Second Messenian War, sending troops of archers.* In the war against Lyttos,* Aptera, which usually remained neutral, was an ally of Knossos, but later turned against it after the intervention of the Macedonians. The city was damaged in the seventh century A.D. by a severe earthquake,* and in 823 A.D. was completely destroyed by the invading Arabs.

The strong fortification walls—almost four kilometres (two and a half miles) long—surround a large flat area. On this plateau several ruins are scattered (figure 10). There are a number of large, impressive, barrel-vaulted cisterns in ashlar masonry, some excellently preserved, dating to the times of the Roman occupation.* Several temples have been excavated; one of them belonged to the goddess Demeter.* A wall contained a number of inscriptions. To the south, the ruins of a theater are barely visible. More recent constructions inside the fortification walls are the small and almost abandoned monastery of St. John, and the Turkish fortress Izzedin. The place, resettled during the Byzantine period,* was the seat of a bishop.

Arab Occupation. The Byzantine Emperor Nikephoros I, a good financier but a poor amateur general, lost Crete to a band of Arab invaders, emigrants from Cordoba in Spain to Alexandria in Egypt, who occupied the island in 823 A.D. under the leadership of Abu Ka'ab. During this period Sicily was also subjugated by the Arabs. The invaders conquered Crete little by little and destroyed most of the existing cities. However, they founded a fortress, *Chandax* ("moat"), later known as *Candia*, at the site of ancient Herakleion.*

The Saracen invaders, who did not share the fine contemporary civilization of their compatriots in Spain, tried to impose their religion on the Cretans and turned the island into a base for pirates, who endan-

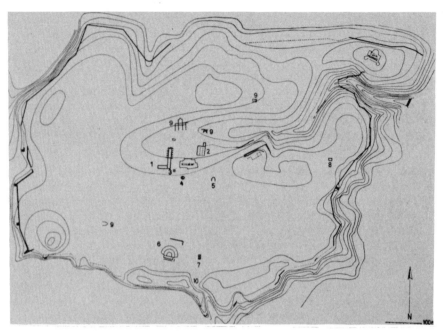

10. Plan of Aptera (*after Matz*)

1. Roman Cistern	6. Theater
2. Roman Cistern	7. Dorian Temple
3. Shrine	8. Temple with Bull Statues
4. Inscriptions Wall	9. Byzantine Buildings
5. Roman Apsidal Building	10. Rock-Cut Tombs

gered the seas and plundered the Aegean islands and coastal areas. The Byzantines made efforts to regain this important province in 826, 902 and 949, but they failed. In 826 the Byzantine general Karteros, after an initial success, was defeated near Chandax and executed on the cross. In the year 961 the Byzantine general and later Emperor Nikephoros Phokas, who commanded a strong army which included Scandinavian and Russian mercenaries, came with 3,300 ships and landed near Chandax, winning a battle. After a siege which lasted a winter, Chandax fell into his hands and the whole island with it. The losses of the Arabs were enormous, estimated at 200,000 dead or taken prisoner. It seems that almost no one was left on the island.

Many of Nikephoros Phokas' soldiers settled in Crete. In 1182 the Emperor Alexios II Comnenos sent his son Isaakios together with twelve noble Byzantine families known as the Archontopouloi, and a number of settlers.

This short occupation of the Arab adventurers, who were merely intent on plunder and the slave market, left almost no traces except for some coins which their "emirs" had struck.

Araden. This small city-state was situated near what is now the modern village of Aradena at Sphakia* in Western Crete, overlooking the south coast. Araden was among the thirty-one Cretan cities which made an alliance with Eumenes, King of Pergamon, in 183 B.C. Some unimportant ruins are preserved. In fact, the city still is unexplored.

The village of Aradena has the Byzantine church of St. Michael with its fresco-paintings, built in the fourteenth or fifteenth century on the ruins of an Early Christian basilica. An impressive gorge separates the Araden area from that of Anopolis* to the west.

Archaic Period see **Orientalizing and Archaic Periods.**

Archanes. A major Minoan site was located by Evans* at Archanes (ancient Acharna), a large village south of Knossos,* not far away from Mount Jouktas.* Archanes produces the best grapes of Crete today. The site includes a small palace, possibly a summer palace for the "priest-king"* of Knossos, as Evans suggested. Evans excavated here a monumental circular well-house or reservoir of massive ashlar masonry, having a diameter of over five metres (about sixteen feet) and five descending steps.

The Greek archaeologist John Sakellarakis, who has conducted regular excavations here for a number of years, has discovered antiquities of great interest at Phourni, near the village. A large burial complex, replacing an earlier collective tomb or ossuary with rectangular rooms, was built to the east of it after 2000 B.C. and was used for a considerable length of time, more than half a millenium, showing an exceptional continuity of burial customs.* Noteworthy among them was a bull sacrifice. The complex comprises a circular burial chamber, in fact a tholos tomb,* with a bench running along the wall, and several rectangular compartments including a pillar* to the south. A flight of steps led up to a second storey, evidently also used for burials. Eventually the entrance to the circular chamber was blocked, the floor raised and a new and shorter entrance opened to the east side, according to the customary orientation of the early tholos tombs. A tholos tomb was found to the north of the burial complex, with a rock-cut side-chamber which yielded an amount of fine jewellery.* It has been suggested that a princess was buried here shortly before the final destruction* of the palace of Knossos.* Another interesting tholos tomb was explored to the south of an extensive complex of rectangular rooms.

The excavation of the cemetery at Phourni brought to light such objects, as several fine seals,* especially early ones of ivory,* a number of larnakes,* bronzes, stone vases,* some fine ivory plaques with representations in relief, figurines,* pieces of gold jewellery* and a considerable amount of excellent pottery.* The jewellery includes a gold ring representing the goddess and a griffin.* A bone comb is considered the oldest one of the whole Aegean region. Extremely important is the clay model of an elaborate house datable to the Middle Minoan period* (see Houses*), which turned up in the village itself during an excavation by A. Lembessi.

11. Archers on a Dedalic bronze girdle from the Knossos area (*after Davaras*)

In the vicinity of Archanes are two Byzantine churches* with fresco-paintings, Hagia Triada* and Hagia Paraskevi.

Archers and Archery. According to Greek legend, archery was a Cretan invention: the mythical Kouretes* first invented the bow and showed people how to hunt. Cretan archers of Greek times (figure 11) enjoyed a great reputation and were much sought after to serve outside the island as mercenaries* of the great powers, especially during the Hellenistic period.* They were also recruited for the armies of Alexander the Great.

Archery was practiced in Crete early in the Bronze Age.* The bow seems to have been a simple type, identical with that of early Egypt and Libya, with bone, wood, or rarely obsidian* arrowheads. Even in the Neolithic period* arrows tipped with hard wood or leaf-shaped bone may have been used. Bronze arrowheads with sockets are known in the Early and Middle Minoan periods. In the next period an almost spindle-shaped tanged type was introduced from the Near East, while hollow-based or tanged arrow-plates of a flat barbed Mycenaean type were recovered from tombs of the Late Minoan period.* A great number of bronze arrowheads and one of flint were found inside decayed wooden chests in the Armoury building at Knossos, together with carbonized debris of the shafts and a clay tablet of the Linear B script* listing 8,640 arrows.

The composite bow, manufactured partly of wood, partly of horn and sinews, possibly introduced from Anatolia not later than the Late Minoan I period* and occasionally appearing in art,* probably never superseded the simple bow in Crete. This composite bow, described by Homer, was strengthened with keratin from the Cretan ibex horns. On the Knossos tablets* we sometimes see representations of these horns, which have been interpreted as denoting the raw material for the manufacture of bows. A fragment of a stone vase represents a Minoan archer with a pointed beard mounting some steep conventional rocks and shooting upwards.

Architecture (Cretan Popular). This term refers to the architecture from the last years of the Venetian occupation* until the beginnings of the twentieth century or later. Not much could survive the destruction under the Turkish occupation,* the subsequent Cretan revolts and, especially, the often severe earthquakes.* Older houses, such as town houses in Chania* and Rethymnon,* show certain Italian influences in their facades. The same can be said about the churches, which very often have two naves, each honouring a different saint. Village houses are of the unpretentious masonry-built Aegean type with a flat roof and are strictly limited to the necessities and technical abilities of the peasants, being simple and austere constructions with no decorations. Arched openings are often used. Important elements are the court and the oven. Very often bottomless jars are used as chimneys.

Architecture (Minoan). Minoan architecture finds its highest expression in the construction of the palaces,* which share a common plan around a central court, originally owing certain features to Oriental prototypes but after a long experimentation evolving into a form characteristically Cretan, showing the creative spirit of the Minoans (see Palaces*). The central courts* were the focal points of the palaces, which faced inward toward them rather than to the outside. There were also large private town and country villas* repeating the architectural features of the palaces in more modest proportions, as well as smaller houses,* solitary or clustered in hamlets, villages or towns. These can be seen at places such as Tylissos,* Malia,* Zakros* and Vathypetro.*

A concern for stability is always apparent. The basis of measurements seems to have been a unit known as the Minoan foot, 30.36 centimetres long, very similar to the modern foot, which is 30.48 centimetres long. The facades and some other important parts of the palaces and the larger houses—which often reached a height of several storeys—were built in ashlar masonry with large blocks of various stones (see Building Stones*), carefully dressed and fit together, and worked with a variety of tools.* These fine facades were not covered with plaster.* The blocks, for the first time employed in the earlier palaces,* presented a smooth front face with straight edges, while the back surface was roughly worked and the interior of the wall between two blocks was filled with rubble.

The lowest course (*orthostates* or *"stander"*) rested upon a low projecting plinth, a levelling course (*euthenteria*). The use of an *orthostates* had been taken over from Syria or Northern Mesopotamia. Courses differed in height within the same wall, but in some cases they were almost identi-

cal, without being absolutely so; thus, true isodomic masonry was unknown in Minoan Crete. As Shaw wrote, "instead of being guided by
elaborate structural and aesthetic principles like those that characterize
Classical architectural design, the Minoan mason simply aimed at producing a reasonably attractive sturdy masonry with a minimum of material and effort. As a result, once the technique of cutting and laying the
blocks was established in the early palatial period, the appearence of the
walls seems to have remained basically unchanged." Much of the upper
walls consisted of sun-dried mud-brick. The walls and floors were often
coated with plaster* and the more important rooms had gypsum* dadoes
or bright frescoes.*

Columns* of a peculiar shape and square pillars* were often used in
larger buildings, arranged in porticoes—sometimes in alternation, in
rythmical change—by way of allowing a view over the landscape, or
decorating monumental entrances, stairways and light-wells.* The existence of a great number of light-wells shows the Minoan affinity for air
and light. Lustral basins* and especially the "inverted" column are
among the features of Minoan architecture, as well as pier-and-door partitions, doorways with recesses for the accommodation of the doors,
which could be folded back especially during fair weather, or could be
closed, completely isolating the rooms. Porticoes, also much favoured in
Greek and Roman architecture, provided open gathering places protected from heat or rain. On the other hand large corridors were probably
unroofed. Doorways often were two-leaved and had window-like openings above, probably for the passage of light and air when the doors were
closed. Fixed hearths were practically unknown, portable braziers* of
plaster having been used instead.

The Minoan architect had the eye of a painter and gave much
thought to the impression of a building as a whole, as well as to the view
from the inside of the building outwards. Flow and flexibility are ever-
present features. Although gradual growth can be observed in most of
the buildings, the irregularity is rather willful; it is clear that the end result
is a deliberate composition, exhibiting considerable freedom of design
and adaptation. The existing space has been skillfully organized and the
various parts beautifully coordinated, but in quite a different way from
the unity of plan used in Classical Greek architecture.

The Bronze Age* Cretans were also the first builders of open "theatral
areas" and large engineering works in Europe. They created aqueducts
and piped water supplies, and built networks of roads, irrigation channels and harbours.* Technical facilities such as the elaborate drainage
systems* and the indoor toilets show a liking for cleanliness and represent
astounding progress for this early time, thereafter forgotten for several
millenia. Although the splendid Minoan palaces* clearly had a monumental character, which found its expression chiefly in the west facades
where we see a number of recesses or set-backs, Minoans did not strive to
create a wholly monumental exterior in their best buildings, as did the
Greeks. This fact, together with the absence of monumental stone
sculpture,* explains why Minoan rulers had no desire to underline their

might through mere civic monuments, as was the custom in other countries or times.

Argyroupolis see **Lappa.**

ARIADNE. Ariadne ("Very Holy Maid"), daughter of Minos* and Pasiphae* according to the Greek tradition, was once a vegetation goddess who had emanated from the Mother-Goddess. According to the myth, she left Crete with the hero Theseus* after helping him with a sword and a clue by which he was able to escape from the Labyrinth* after killing the monstrous Minotaur.* In the Homeric account, she was killed by Artemis in the island of Naxos. In other versions, she was deserted by Theseus in Naxos and hanged herself on a tree, or was rescued by Dionysos, who married her. With him she had three sons, Staphylos, Thoas and Oinopion, who later became king of the island of Chios.

The first literary reference to her occurs in the Iliad, where Homer records that the skilled craftsman and architect Daidalos* prepared a fine dancing place for her: "In broad Knossos Daidalos wrought a dancing place for Ariadne of the lovely tresses." Ariadne was perhaps a goddess in whose honour a ceremonial dance* was performed. According to one interpretation, this dance was part of the ritual of collective marriage, following on the graduation of the initiates, virgins and bachelors. The goddess had close associations with Britomartis* and also with the moon and fertility. Nilsson thinks that no other heroine suffered death in so many ways as did Ariadne; this can be explained as originating in a cult in which her death as a goddess of vegetation was celebrated annually with sorrow and lamentations, and her resurrection with joy and exultation. According to the Swedish scholar, this is a purely Minoan religious conception. Ariadne was worshipped in Amathus in Cyprus as Aphrodite Ariadne.

Arkades. Arkades or Arkadia near modern Aphrati in the prefecture of Herakleion* was an important inland Greek city-state. In 221 B.C. the city took part in the war between Knossos* and Lyttos* and was consequently ruined. It was one of the thirty-one Cretan cities to make an alliance with Eumenes II, king of Pergamon. The city was destroyed by invading Romans and abandoned, but later was resettled.

At Arkades a number of tombs of the Geometric* and Orientalizing* periods containing an abundance of interesting pottery* of a rustic character were excavated by the Italian Doro Levi (figure 122). Of special interest is the palm capital of a column of the seventh century B.C. found at Arkades, which copies an Egyptian model and is unique in Crete.

Arkadi Monastery. This Byzantine monastery south of Rethymnon,* founded before the fourteenth century by the monk Arkadios amidst a picturesque mountainous landscape, was one of the largest and wealthiest monasteries of the island. In 1587 the church which we see today arose in the court of the strongly fortified monastery. The facade of the church shows one of the most interesting Baroque constructions in Crete. The monastery had a rich library where ancient Greek manuscripts were copied, but this was destroyed in 1645 by the Turks. In 1700 the monastery had 300 monks and 200 huge wine jars. During the uprising of 1866 the monastery became a center of revolt. Almost a thousand men, women and children were besieged by a Turkish army 15,000 strong. After a heroic but vain resistance the monastery was about to fall to its besiegers. As the Turks stormed into it, the desperate defenders exploded their gun powder magazine, killing themselves and many of their attackers. Thus, Arkadi Monastery became a symbol of independence.

Arkalochori Cave see **Caves.**

Armenoi. The name of this village near Rethymnon*—like another near Siteia*—originated with the Armenians who settled it after the liberation of Crete from the Arab occupation* by Nikephoros Phokas in 961 A.D. A large cemetery of the Late Minoan period* was excavated in recent years by Tzedakis. Its exceptionally elaborate chamber-tombs* have yielded a series of excellent painted larnakes* with religious symbols or hunting scenes, and a number of seals,* today exhibited in the Chania Museum.

Armour. The traditional defensive armour of the Minoan warrior shows the characteristic figure-of-eight shield.* There is no direct evidence that the armoured corselets and grieves of the Mycenaeans had been introduced into Crete, although metal armour may have been developed here in connection with chariot* warfare.* Corselets and "breast-plates" are among the ideograms of the Linear B* Armoury tablets* of Knossos,* often drawn alongside the chariot's signs, and probably recording the military equipment issued to the chariot's personnel. Only scraps of bronze armour have been found in tombs at Phaistos,* while a small vase of mottled stone in the shape of a corselet with shoulder-protecting pieces turned up in Knossos. Corselets of leather also seem to have been used during Late Minoan times. On the other hand the existence of conical helmets is well attested: on a sealing* we see one with earguards, a chinstrap and a spike on top, presumably for the attachment of a plume or a tufted crest. Very characteristic is the boars' tusk helmet (figure 12), known from Homer's description, where horizontal rows of split tusks are applied on a cap, obviously of leather; each row has the tusks' curves in the opposite direction to those of the rows above and below it. This type goes back well into the Middle Minoan period.* The tusks, probably originally trophies of the chase, both protected and at the same time decorated the helmet.

A few warriors' helmets, more characteristic of the Mycenaean Mainland, have been illustrated on vases and elsewhere, as well as having been found in excavations. But the only metal helmet we possess from Minoan Crete, dating to the Late Minoan II period, has turned up in the Achaian* Warrior Graves near Knossos; this is bell-shaped with a perforated knob on top for a plume, with cheek-pieces riveted on (figure

12. Reconstruction of a boar's tusk helmet from a tomb near Knossos

13). The metal is thin, and was originally attached by holes on the edges to a lining of leather. Similar helmets with waving plumes are depicted in art. Sometimes horns of different animals, perhaps a symbol of power

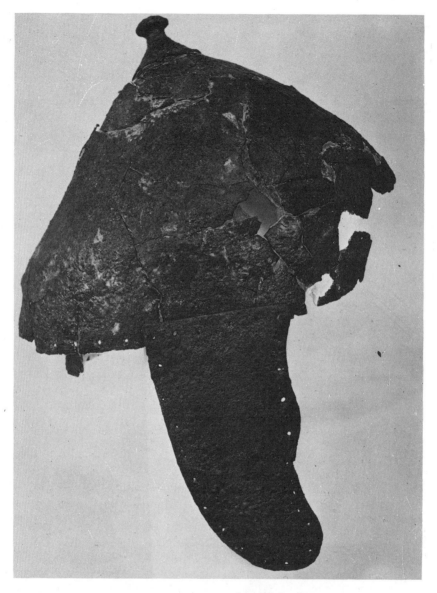

13. Bronze helmet from a Warrior Grave near Knossos

and originally hunting trophies, were fixed to the helmets, which we see illustrated on seals* or clay sealings* or converted into signs of the Linear A script.* Heavy helmets with cheek-pieces of a different shape and probably of metal, reminiscent of the Classical Corinthian type of helmet, are worn by the boxers on the stone relief Boxer Vase from Hagia Triada.*

The armour of the Iron Age* in Crete does not differ greatly from that

14. Archaic bronze *mitra* from Axos

in the rest of Greece. A special Cretan feature of early times seems to be the bronze *mitra*, a crescent-shaped plate attached below the breast-plate and protecting the abdomen, rarely inscribed but usually finely incised and embossed in a way that makes it a work of art. A number of *mitrai* came from Axos (figure 14). An example from Rethymnon* has two borders round the edge and a phallus and tree in the middle; above the tree two youths followed by two others hold a wreath. Among early bronze helmets the sixth century example from Axos* is a masterpiece, decorated in relief with horses* and rosettes, and having eyebrows above the eye-sockets (figure 15).

Art (Minoan). The zenith of art in Bronze Age* Crete, closely bound to the life and economy* of the palaces,* is characterized by a fortunate combination of stylization and spontaneity, abstraction and true "impressionistic" naturalism, quite different in spirit from its contemporaries in the Near East. The Minoan artist is open to foreign models and influences but he reacts with flexibility and creative power, managing to transform everything into a personal creation, an artistic world of his own. From the beginnings this art, although ruled by conventions, avoids stiff forms and dullness of any kind, often transcends anatomical realism and instead is fond of movement, fluidity, colour, dynamism and vitality, elements which are the essence of nature. Minoan art is delicate, sophisticated and joyful throughout its evolution. Its prevailing features are grace, elegance and lightness. The severeness of life and the agony of death, so common in other contemporary civilizations, are here unknown, replaced by youthful *joie de vivre*.

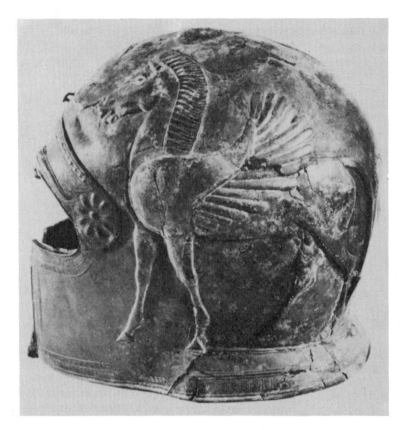

15. Archaic bronze helmet from Axos

The painter is under the spell of colours and has an acute sense of the organic, creating splendidly alive forms, even when they are simple non-representational patterns. The architect (see Architecture*) has a painter's eye and disposition. The sculptor (see Figurines;* Sculpture*) has little taste for large creations in stone but prefers to express himself in small spirited figures, exquisite studies rendered in an impressionistic way, which record instantaneous movement with an emphasis on gesture. The painter of pottery* and frescoes* and the cutter of seals,* who creates masterpieces in a tiny scale, begin from abstract over-all patterns and intricate designs based on natural forms to achieve later a brilliant expression of a forthright naturalism.

A basic principle of Minoan surface decoration in early times is the principle of torsion, where twisted motifs are used. No historical events are ever represented among these lively compositions. Minoan art has been considered the "first occidental feeling for life and nature" or "the first really European effort." A certain inherent stylization and religious formalism do not hamper the astounding originality and versatility of the artist but lend a special flavour to his works. One should bear in mind that freedom was an essential feature of this art, as no strict religious rules were imposed and no spirit servile to authority was shown.

Art (Popular) see **Popular Art.**

ASKLEPIOS. The cult of the god of health Asklepios was prominent in Crete as in the rest of Greece. As Willetts remarked, the respect shown to his cult in later antiquity,with its combination of superstition, miracle cures and genuine medical lore, together with the growing scepticism towards the traditional Olympian hierarchy, made him as Saviour and Healer the chief opponent of Christ. In Crete the prominence of his cult is attested to by many insciptions but especially by his great sanctuary at Lebena* on the Libyan Sea. Another less important sanctuary has been excavated at Lisos* in Western Crete. The god had temples at Knossos* and Olous.* In the sanctuaries of Asklepios (*Asklepieia*), like that at Epidauros in the Peloponnese, the patients entered the temple and "incubated," after purifying themselves and offering sacrifices. The god appeared to them in their sleep or in a vision and recommended treatment or healed the disease. Numerous inscriptions contain the sincere thanksgivings of healed patients. The attribute of Asklepios was the snake, a familiar element in the Minoan religion (see Snake Cult*). This symbol still survives today in the caduceus, emblem of the medical profession.

ASTERIOS see **MINOS, RHADAMANTHYS, AND SARPEDON.**

Axes. The axes of the Neolithic period* were of various well-polished stones, such as serpentine, greenstone, jadeite or schist, with the edge parallel to the handle,usually either large with roughened butt to facilitate hafting, or of a small trapezoidal type (figure 117). They were made with great skill and care, and a lot of labour was necessary for their manufacture. Stone axes probably were used into the Early Minoan period.* Double axes* of bronze were a very common tool* and not regular weapons.*

Battle-axes of the ceremonial type from the second millenium B.C. which have been found scattered all over Europe are extremely rare in Crete. A splendid example of brown schist was found in the palace at Malia* (figure 16). This ceremonial weapon, perhaps the ornament of a sceptre among the royal regalia, had one end in the form of a leaping panther or lioness with inlaid eyes and a collar round the neck and the other shaped as an axe, and was covered with an elaborate design of interlocking spirals.

Axos. Axos, near the present inland village of the same name west of Rethymnon,* was one of the strongest city-states of Classical Greek times in Western Crete. Its seaport to the north coast was Astale, situated at modern Bali. The mythical founder of the city was Oaxos, a son of Akakallis* and grandson of Minos* and Pasiphae.* Herodotos tells us that Vattos, who founded the Greek colony of Cyrene in Libya in 631

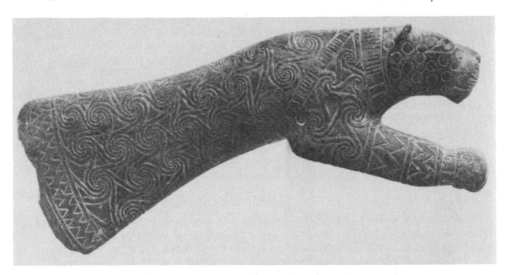

16. Ceremonial schist axe-head from the palace at Malia

B.C., was a grandson of Etearchos, king of Axos. Among the divinities worshipped here was Demeter.* The city continued to flourish during Roman and Byzantine times. The elegant Byzantine church* of Hagia Eirene was built early in the Venetian period and shows the influence of Italian architectural prototypes. In 1899 the Italian Archaeological Institute explored some archaic ruins and found several figurines* of the Dedalic style.* A number of archaic bronze *mitrai* and a fine bronze helmet, all of them with a splendid decoration, as well as several inscriptions, have turned up at Axos (see Armour*).

Bali see **Axos.**

Barbotine Ware. The so-called Barbotine Ware of some Middle Minoan IA vases and later usually consists of elaborate thin strips of clay applied to jugs in a torsional way. In other vases the surface is worked up with a tool to form prickles resembling thorns, not unlike the shell of a sea urchin. This curious type of fabric, very common in the Mesara Plain,* is usually combined with polychrome decoration in black, white and buff. Sometimes this ware shows an excess in the application of the fabric and becomes heavy and rather unpleasant.

Bathrooms (Minoan) see **Lustral Basins.**

Biannos. Biannos, a city-state of Classical Greek times, has preserved its name in the modern village and province of Viannos, in the southeast part of the prefecture of Herakleion.* As an independent city, Biannos was among thirty-one Cretan cities which made an alliance with Eumenes II, king of Pergamon. Later Biannos seems to have been dominated by its mighty eastern neighbour, Hierapytna.*

The city itself has not yet been explored, but several neighbouring Minoan sites of importance were excavated by N. Platon, including the Late Minoan III settlement at Kephala Chondrou, a large complex of houses which had been destroyed by fire, and two Middle Minoan III–Late Minoan I houses at Galana Charakia and Rouses. At the former place were also discovered thirty burial pithoi.* On top of a hill, Platon brought to light an elaborate fire-signal tower.

At Kato Symi an important sanctuary of Hermes and Aphrodite, probably dating mainly to the early Iron Age,* has been recently discovered by the Greek archaeologist A. Lembessi. The sanctuary includes a temple, an altar, three terraces and other buildings, where great numbers of horns were recovered. Among the finds are many excellent bronze figurines of the Dedalic style,* both human and animal, clay figurines,* bronze cut-out plaques of outstanding artistic merit, and fragments of tripods. The beginnings of the sanctuary are at least as early as the Middle Minoan IIIB period, when a small shrine was built. Among the rich Minoan votive offerings are bronze figurines, three long swords with fine incised decoration, chalices of the sacred communion,* stone tables of offerings with Linear A* inscriptions on two of them, and an abundance of pottery.*

In Viannos are several Byzantine churches,* such as Hagia Pelagia at Plaka, dating to 1360, with fine frescoes, St. George with frescoes (1401), St. Michael and St. Marina.

Birds in Religion. In Crete birds were associated with religion long before the arrival of Christianity. Birds played an important role in Minoan religion* as representations or embodiments (epiphanies) of the divinity. This conclusion can be securely drawn from several representations in art, where birds are seen perching on sacred symbols such as boughs placed between the sacral horns,* or on double axes,* like those on the cult scenes on the sarcophagus from Hagia Triada.* The presence of the divinity is clearly indicated in representations of birds perching on shrines* or on the heads of a number of idols. In other cases birds are seen hovering over a cult scene.

These birds were directly associated with the Household Goddess in a number of cases including the minature model of a shrine at Knossos,* or several late shrines like those at Gournia* and Karphi.* The Knossian model, from the so-called "Dove Shrine Deposit," shows three pillars having beam-end capitals with three dove-like birds perching on them. Perhaps the existence of clay libation vessels (see Rhyton*) in bird form, known since the Early Minoan period,* is indicative of the sacral character of the bird, as are a number of dove amulets.* An Early Minoan I vase from Lebena* is perhaps the earliest example of a bird in a ritual context. Clay models of birds are among the regular furnishings of the shrines* of the Household or Snake Goddess,* and usually are considered as representing doves. The species of all these birds has been a subject of long discussions among scholars.

It is clear that many bird figures in Minoan art,* as in later pottery*

17. Lid of a Late Minoan larnax with birds pecking a flower

(see Pachyammos*), including representations of waterfowl imitating
Nilotic scenes, have a mere decorative character, being a favoured subject of Minoan nature painters (figure 17). Birds also appear as signs in
the Hieroglyphic script.* A series of libation vessels of a characteristic
bird form with no wings and standing on three short feet are usually
known as "duck-vases" (figure 18). These vessels, often with a spout
in the place of the bird's head, are assignable to the Late Bronze Age.*
Their shape is considered to have derived from a wineskin.

In later times Greek divinities inherited from the Minoan goddess the
custom of having a bird as their attribute. Well-known are Zeus's eagle,
Athena's owl and Aphrodite's doves. It is noteworthy that in the poems
of Homer the gods sometimes change themselves into birds. In Greek
and Roman religion birds also had a religious significance as predicting
the future.

18. "Duck-vase" from Eastern Crete

Boxer Rhyton see **Sports; Stone Vases.**

Braziers (Minoan). This characteristic Minoan clay vessel shows a long saucepan handle with the lip bending up near the single handle, in order to protect the hand of the person holding it from heat. Some of these vessels have been found still containing burnt remains of charcoal and resin. They were used instead of fixed hearths, which were practically unknown in Minoan Crete. Occasionally they served as lamps,* ritual fumigators or incense-burners, evidently being indispensable in the Cretan ceremonies as in almost all religions. To these categories belong some luxurious specimens with polychrome decoration, such as those found inside the great Temple-Tomb* near the palace at Knossos.* Undoubtedly the best brazier ever found in Greece comes from the palace at Zakros:* its wooden handle was held by a bulbous bronze tube, while the bronze vessel was decorated with a band of ivy leaves. Some small round tripod hearths made of clay or plaster and usually associated with the cult (see Gournia*; Nirou Chani*; Shrines*) possibly were also employed as braziers.

BRITOMARTIS. The goddess Britomartis was a close companion of Artemis and hunted with her, or was partly identified with her. According to a late myth, the virgin was pursued by Minos* for nine months over craggy mountains and level plains and finally escaped by throwing herself in desperation into the sea, from which she was hauled to safety by the nets (*diktya*) of some fishermen. Artemis made Britomartis a goddess under the name of Diktynna.* In another version of the myth she escaped by disappearing into a grove at the island of Aigina near Athens, where she was later worshipped as Aphaia.

Britomartis had a temple at Chersonesos* and another at Olous,* which contained a wooden statue of her (*xoanon*), made by the famous Daidalos* himself. Here, at Olous, a festival was named for her, the *Britomarpeia*. She was represented on the coinage* of both these cities, possibly copies of actual cult-statues. This virgin goddess with a Minoan name, meaning "Sweet Maid," was obviously a survival of a Minoan divinity.

Bronze see **Metallurgy.**

Bronze Age. This term encompasses the period of antiquity during which common tools* and weapons* were made of bronze or copper. The Bronze Age comes after the long Neolithic period* as a real revolution which leads to a higher form of civilization, and precedes the Iron Age,* during which bronze was but sparingly used for weapons* and tools.* In Crete the Bronze Age or Minoan Era covers roughly the third and second millenia B.C. and is divided into the Early,* Middle* and Late* Minoan periods (see Chronology*). This age together with the Neolithic is sometimes also called Prehistoric, as the division between history and prehistory is based upon whether or not a culture possesses written documents, or whether such written documents can be read. Of course the Minoan civilization,* or rather its later Hellenized part, has written documents in the Linear B script,* which can be now read rather satisfactorily. This is not yet the case with the Minoan scripts proper, the Hieroglyphic* and the Linear A.* Thus, Minoan civilization* as a whole is still a prehistoric one.

Bronze Casting see **Sculpture (Minoan).**

Building Stones. The Minoans used a variety of stones for their buildings, all locally available. The soft porous limestone which exists in rich supplies especially near the two largest palaces,* was the most favourite stone for ashlar masonry, followed by crystalline gypsum,* a very decorative material. There are several varieties of limestone—yellowish or brownish white, greyish, and bluish—including a hard one, known as ironstone (*sideropetra*). Schist, also known as slate, which occurs naturally in flat slab-like layers, was much sought after mainly for pavements but also for column or pillar bases. Blocks were also cut in friable sandstone. Other stones, being hard to work, played a lesser role in Minoan architecture.* Among them were conglomerate and more rarely marble, a fine decorative material used in certain places, a hard-veined limestone, gabbro, serpentine (also known as opheiolite and resembling steatite or soapstone), and phyllite.

The mason had at his disposal a variety of bronze tools,* much more efficient for cutting blocks than the earlier copper ones. J. Shaw, who recently made a thorough study of the subject of Minoan building materials, has suggested that the clay model of a wagon found at Palaikastro* (see Transport*) perhaps copies an ox-driven wagon used for the transport of heavy stone blocks.

Bull-games. The famous Minoan bull-games, obviously an exciting and dangerous sport, are often represented in art. They demanded a long and vigorous training as well as exceptional acrobatic agility: a "toreador," for instance, ran towards a charging bull, seized the horns near their tips, turned a full somersault over its head and was then projected over the back of the animal to the ground behind to be caught by another performer. No weapons* were involved in the game—which was not a fight—and the bull was not hurt. Perhaps the bull-leaping was performed to music.* Maidens as well as youths participated, as the existing evidence shows; the girls wore male attire for this purpose. These games seem to have involved some kind of ritual contest or ordeal, or may have been connected with magic or fertility rites. It has been suggested that the games took place in the central courts* of the palaces,* probably fenced for the purpose. Some scholars consider them as mere secular sports, probably practised on days of religious festivals. These bulls seem to have been of a domestic breed but not tamed, and their capture was quite an adventure, as the famous Minoan golden cup from Vapheio shows. It is not known whether these bulls were sacrificed afterwards, but this seems very probable (see Religion*).

The game was often illustrated in Minoan art,* in frescoes* as well as

19. Bull-game on the Boxer Rhyton from Hagia Triada

on seals,* sealings* and bronze figurines.* The famous stone Boxer Rhyton* from Hagia Triada* gives a good example (figure 19). Perhaps the earliest representations, with tiny human figures clinging to the bull's horns, might be seen in some Early Minoan clay libation vessels (figure 20) in the form of figurines* from the tholos tombs* at Koumasa and Porti in the Mesara Plain.* Bull figurines from other similar tombs are painted with something resembling a leather harness. Nevertheless, there is no clear evidence for the practise of bull-games before the peak of the Minoan era. The best representation of the game is seen in the Toreador Fresco from Knossos* (figure 21): a girl deftly grasps the horns of the charging bull at full gallop, preparing to vault over the animal backward; a youth is just accomplishing this feat while another girl with outstretched hands stands ready to catch him or to steady him when he alights the right way up.

It has been tried unsuccessfully to trace the *corridas* of Spain, which were a local outgrowth of the Roman arena, to Minoan Crete. Bull-games have survived in later times in Greece; better known are the *"taurokathapsia"* held in Thessaly, mostly a horseback performance.

20. Libation vessel in form of a bull from the Mesara Plain

Burial Customs. Like all peoples, the Minoans believed in an after-life. Perhaps the blissful heaven ruled by the Cretan Rhadamanthys,* a brother of Minos,* and known to later Greeks as Elysion or Isles of the Blessed, in contrast to gloomy Hades with its pale shadows, is a survival of a Minoan conception. Major sources of information are the representations on the sarcophagus* from Hagia Triada,* evidently connected to some sepulchral ritual. The usual burial method of the Minoans was inhumation during the Neolithic period* and later, in caves* or rock shelters, overhanging ledges of rock with the front roughly walled in. Cremation,* a rule for later Greek times, was a very rare exception in the Bronze Age.*

During the earlier part of this age, tombs were collective, used for centuries, often containing hundreds of burials belonging to many generations of the dead of a single clan or large family. These tombs were built above ground like houses.* These built tombs usually were large tholos tombs,* like those found in the Mesara Plain* at Platanos,* Aspesokari* and other sites (see figure 185). In Eastern Crete house-tombs, family ossuaries of a rectangular plan imitating the houses of the living, were also used during the Early Minoan period,* like those at Mochlos* (see figure 114), Palaikastro* and Gournia* (figure 22). The dead seem perhaps to have been buried separately, and their bones later transferred

21. Toreador Fresco from the palace at Knossos

to these ossuaries, which could comprise several rooms, evidently added when needed. Other tombs were cut in the soft limestone, usually in an irregular shape. At Hagia Photia* we see a type of grave which can be called a primitive chamber-tomb, used for a limited number of burials. A rare type is the cist grave.

A popular method of burying, especially during the Middle Minoan period,* was to put the dead trussed tight, knees to chin, into pithoi,* as in the cemetery of Pachyammos.* These large jars were then inverted and buried.

An interesting burial complex is the so-called Temple-Tomb* at Knossos* (see figure 183), while others have been found at Malia* (Chrysolakkos) and Archanes.* The rectangular complex at Chryso-lakkos, to the northeast of the city of Malia, a large Protopalatial enclosure 39 by 30 metres having no entrance, was divided into many chambers or ossuaries accessible from above. A portico ran in front of the east side of this monumental building, looking on to a paved court. This intricate tomb, famous for the jewellery* found in it, may have been the burial ground for the royal family. Today this interpretation is challenged.

After about 1450 B.C., burial was limited to a group of three or four rel-atives or even a single person in a small tomb, a fact interpreted as illus-trating the growth of individuality in the framework of the clan after the loosening of the clan ties, as a consequence of the increasing wealth and the subsequent differentiation of the financial status of the clan's mem-bers. These more exclusive burial places were either tholos tombs* or the far more common and widespread chamber-tombs* cut underground in the soft limestone and approached by a sloping narrow open passage (*dromos*). Bodies were placed in clay coffins (*larnakes**), or rarely in wood-en coffins, especially in Western Crete, or in pits dug into the floor, or even on the floor itself. The dead usually were placed on their backs with

22. Early Minoan ossuary at Gournia during its excavation (1972)

their knees drawn up. In the case of a new interment the tombs were
opened afresh for a while, usually by removal of only part of the dromos
fill and the entrance blocking. Sometimes the tombs were fumigated. In
some cases, according to the custom of the Mainland Mycenaeans, the
remains of previous burials were simply pushed aside, or were heaped
inside one of the coffins (figure 23), in order to create room for the new
interments. This custom demonstrates the utter disregard of the Minoans
for the remains of their forebears, a disregard which had been already
exhibited in earlier cemeteries like the one at Pachyammos.* On the other
hand, fresh burials were always accompanied by a variety of grave-
goods.* Some splendid graves containing a whole armoury of fine

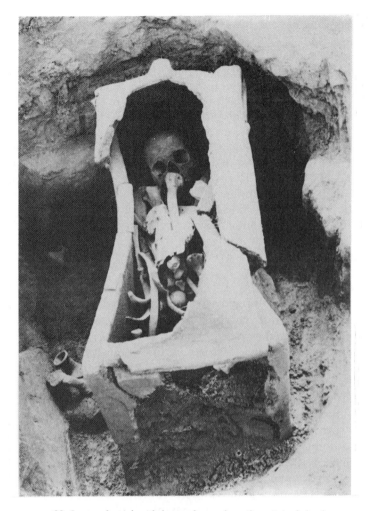

23. Larnax burial with bones heaped on the original dead

weapons* and perhaps belonging to Achaian* warriors have been excavated near Knossos.*

A certain cult of the dead seems to have been practised throughout the Bronze Age.* Some early tombs have yielded evidence concerning the existence of funerary or post-funerary rituals (see Sarcophagus from Hagia Triada;* Tholos Tombs*). One common custom was a farewell toast drunk outside the tomb, after which the cup was smashed. Perhaps the cemeteries were considered as sacred areas.

Byzantine Churches. The highly sophisticated art of Byzantium, which can be seen all over the Empire including Crete, found its best expression in the building of churches. This art is rather homogeneous and dominated by certain principles. During the Early Christian period basilicas such as those at Gortyn,* Olous,* Chersonesos* and other places, often adorned with mosaics, were common. Later, a typical Byzantine form evolved, quite different from its counterparts in Western Europe, which became traditional and which has survived in many variations of shape and size to the present. The ground plan is square, usually inscribing a cross. The sanctuary is always at the eastern end, screened by the gilded iconostasis, which conceals it together with the part of the service performed here in front of the altar. Along the western end there is usually a vestibule, the narthex. The whole edifice is compact and well-proportioned, displaying a harmony and unity of mass. A monumental characteristic is the dome, resting on a system of internal buttressing upon the square below. This essential feature gives distinction to the building on the outside, while on the inside the dome seems to float above the people, symbolizing the vault of Heaven. It has been remarked that the dome has the quality of the infinite.

The frescoes are closely associated with the architecture of the church. These paintings are arranged according to a usual iconographic scheme, which was didactic and met the dogma, according to the decisions of the General Councils in the first eight centuries of the Christian era, to which the Orthodox Church held fast. An outline of this scheme is followed in accordance with the size of the building. Various scenes occupy definite positions in the interior of the church. In the dome is portrayed the majestic figure of the Christ the Pantocrator ("Ruler of All"), holding the book of the Gospels and blessing the devout below. This heavenly place often is surrounded by a rainbow while the four pendatives, which connect the dome to the vaults below, are meaningfully occupied by the evangelists. The walls of the sanctuary above the altar are often reserved for the scene known as the "Divine Liturgy," where we see the Christ among angels bearing candles and instruments of the Passion. The focal point of the sanctuary, like the dome symbolizing Heaven, is the conch of the apse, normally reserved for the Virgin framed by the archangels, or Christ the Pantocrator, when a dome is absent as it often is in the small Cretan churches.

The sanctuary includes the solemn figures of the "Fathers of the Church," represented as bishops. The twelve Great Festivals of the Church, the Gospel events, are unrolled upon the vaults and upper walls of the nave in a certain order—the Annunciation, the Nativity, the Presentation in the Temple, the Baptism, the Transfiguration, the Raising of Lazarus, the Entry into Jerusalem, the Crucifixion, the Resurrection (usually shown as the Descent into Hades), the Ascension, and the Death of the Virgin. The lower zones of the walls are reserved for the miracles and parables of the Gospels, and below them are figures of saints imposingly standing with earnest expressions, gazing solemnly at the worshippers with inward looking eyes. All these pictures are painted flat in pure un-blended colours put one above the other. Colours often had a symbolic inference. It has been remarked that everything combines to create a sense of mysticism and transcendentalism, as the Orthodox Church has always felt intensely the reality of the unseen world. The Byzantine painter, with his introspective attitude, is considered to be a contrast to the Baroque artist: he brings heaven down to earth and the eternal into the temporal.

There are several hundred painted Byzantine and post-Byzantine churches in Crete, usually village or country chapels of a small size scattered all over the island from the east to the west, and as a rule rather difficult to reach. An outstanding early painter was Pagomenos, who decorated some churches from 1314 to 1328. Later the island was to be the birthplace of the famous Cretan School of Painting.*

Byzantine Period. When the partition of the Roman Empire occured in 324 A.D., Crete became part of the Eastern Roman or Byzantine Empire under Constantine the Great, the first Christian Roman Emperor. The island, controlling the East Mediterranaean sea routes, was of distinct importance, both commercially and strategically. Already in the Early Christian period Crete had become a flourishing self-governing community under a *consularius*, again with Gortyn as its capital. Its prosperity is revealed by the existence of a great number of dioceses and also of several splendid basilicas, often decorated with bright mosaic pavements, such as those excavated by various Greek scholars at Olous,* Chersonesos,* Goulediana, Visari, Metropolis, Panormon and Syia.* The large basilica of St. Titus at Gortyn* is especially important. Remains of the important iconoclastic period, during which the iconoclastic Emperors detached Crete from the jurisdiction of the Pope of Rome and placed it under the Oecumenic Patriarch of Constantinople (732 A.D.), can be seen in the fragmentary frescoes of the small church of St. Nicholas at Hagios Nikolaos.* Nevertheless, these aniconic frescoes are now dated to the tenth or eleventh century.

After being occupied by the Saracens (see Arab Occupation*), Crete was retaken by the Byzantine general and later Emperor Nikephoros Phokas in 961 A.D. and lost again to the Empire for the last time in 1204, when it was captured by Crusaders and sold by them to Venice (see Venetian Occupation*). The Byzantine period in Crete was marked by a relatively high degree of prosperity and cultural development. The island had tight links with Constantinople, and Imperial art could be easily transplanted and flourish: a number of churches dated to this period are good examples of Byzantine architecture and often preserve fine frescoes, such as those at Chromonastiri (see Byzantine Churches*).

Under Venetian rule, Crete, although outside the limits of the Byzantine Empire, continued to be a part of it from the point of view of religion, language and art. A considerable number of small but fine churches and chapels scattered about the country testify to the flourishing of Byzantine tradition in art. In architecture some foreign elements, such as the ogival frames of doors and windows, are often seen incorporated in an otherwise purely Byzantine building. In painting, Byzantine tradition continued to evolve untouched by Italian examples. Fine frescoes were created, such as those in Kera Church at Kritsa.* During the fifteenth century, the last of the thousand-year old Byzantium, its influence was even stronger in Crete, owing to the fact that many artists fleeing the invading Turks found a refuge here and contributed to the creation of the Cretan School of Painting.*

Calendar. As the Minoan economy* basically depended upon agriculture,* the observation of the seasons and the regulation of the calendar were of the utmost importance. Of course, since observation of the moon is the oldest method of reckoning time, the first calendar universally was the lunar one, with the month as the basic unit. In later Greek times, in order to reconcile the discrepancy of almost eleven days between the solar and the lunar year, a thirteenth month was intercalated in three years out of every eight, giving an octennial cycle, known as the *oktaeteris*. It has been suggested that the Greek calendar, including this octennial cycle, may have derived from Minoan Crete, where the "priest-king's"* tenure of office was probably restricted to an octennial period. The ultimate origin of the Greek calendar seems to have been Mesopotamia, transmitted through the Minoans. The main figure of the Minoan divinities,* the Mother Goddess, as a moon deity was especially associated with fertility and time-reckoning.

The independent city-states in Dorian Crete as in Greece had—along with an individual coinage*—an individual calendar on a common basis, ruling the cycle of festivals. Our knowledge about the Cretan months, resting on epigraphical evidence, is extremely fragmentary. The new year began with the autumnal equinox.

Candia see **Herakleion.**

Capitals see **Columns.**

Caravanserai. South of the palace at Knossos* and in front of it there is a small building named by Evans the Caravanserai (a word meaning in Arabic and Turkish "inn for caravan-travellers"), which lies near a monumental viaduct with stepped channels and a roadway connecting the palace with Southern Crete and the Libyan Sea. The Caravanserai (figure 24) may have been used by travellers visiting the palace. With two elegant main rooms approached by stepped passages, it possesses a spring and a large stone public bath for washing the feet, where water still runs. Nearby is a small underground spring chamber containing two ledges and a niche for lamps* besides the basin and its overflow pipe. The border

24. Restored view of part of the Caravanserai (*after Evans*)

slab of this basin near the entrance has been much worn away by use, like
the two steps leading to this much visited place. Finds, which include
offertory vessels and a clay model of a little round hut-shaped urn containing a figurine of the Minoan Goddess with upraised hands, visible
through the open door, reveal that this spring chamber was later used as a
shrine.

   An important feature of the Caravanserai is an attractive fresco, a
colourful strip with a natural scene around the top of a high black wall: a
continuous frieze of red-legged partridges and hoopoes (figure 25), with
polychrome balls probably not representing eggs but river pebbles of
breccia. Parts of the background are conventionalized foilage, water and
rocks. Evans thought that the subject had possibly been chosen in order
to give "an anticipatory assurance of good cheer" inside a room perhaps
designed as a refectory.

Cauldrons. Among the finest achievements of Minoan metallurgy* are
the cauldrons; several of them, legless and of a huge size, were found
inside a room of one of the villas* at Tylissos.* The largest of them is over
4 feet (1.4 metres) in diameter, weighs 114 pounds (52 kilograms), and
consists of four bronze sheets, three for the sides and one for the bottom,
and a rim, made also of three sheets, with three handles attached
horizontally. The several parts were joined with rivets, the heads of

25. Restored drawing of hoopoe and partridge (*after Evans*)

which were also decorative. These cauldrons were possibly used for boiling must or for drenching olives, or, of course, for boiling a sheep or a goat whole.

The Idaian Cave* has proved to be a major source of bronze tripod cauldrons dating to the Geometric period and later.

Caves. The island of Crete, possessing a limestone karst, is dotted with almost two thousand caves of various sizes and shapes. Caves and rock-shelters (see Neolithic period*) are generally considered the earliest dwelling places of man as well as the earliest shrines.* Even after the people had moved to houses,* the dead continued to be buried there (see Burial Customs*). The cave at Pyrgos near Nirou* contained bronze objects, stone idols, an abundant pottery covering the Early Minoan period* (see Pyrgos Ware*), and hundreds of burials. Some of the dead were buried in larnakes.* Of the same character was the cave of Trapeza near Tzermiado on the plateau of Lasithi,* explored by the British. Their suggestion that the cave was a dwelling-place during the Neolithic period has recently been challenged.

Several caves in Crete had a sacred character, lasting from the Neolithic period until historical times or even late antiquity. The use of caves as cult-centers was a characteristic feature of Cretan religious conceptions. It is clear that primitive man was deeply impressed by these large, awe-inspiring subterranean places, which had dark winding galleries and stalagmite formations of fantastic form. The strong religious associations of the caves persisted for centuries, even millenia. There is evidence that some of the stalactites and stalagmites as well as other rock formations inside the caves were regarded and worshipped as cult images. Some of them were slightly fashioned to give them more resemblance to human or animal forms. Sometimes similar rocks were brought into sacred buildings, such as those found at the shrine of the Little Palace* of Knossos* or

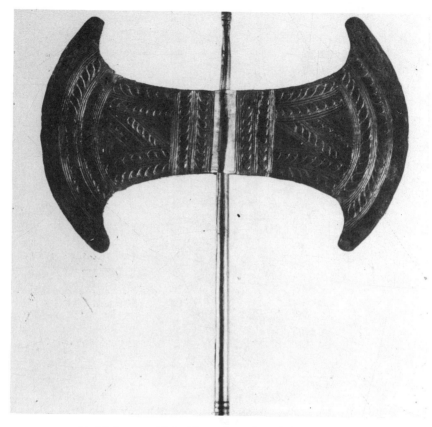

26. Miniature gold double axe from the Arkalochori Cave

at the cult chambers which joined the smaller tholos tomb at Apesokari.*
On the other hand some altars* have been recovered from caves, although in most cases natural rocks served as such. We may assume that
the pilgrimages to the cult caves took place at certain festival times. The
nature of the divinities* worshipped here is not exactly known, but they
must have had a chthonic or underworld character.

Some sacred caves warrant special mention. The cave at Miamou,
not far from Phaistos,* explored by the Italian Taramelli, yielded interesting Neolithic material together with hearths and remnants of meals, including shells and claws of crabs and lobsters. The cave at Arkalochori, a
village near Herakleion,* was an important cult-center during the whole
Bronze Age.* Its excavation brought to light a great quantity of important
votive offerings including swords and a series of double axes* of gold,
silver or bronze, some of them with a splendid incised decoration (figure
26). The impressive cathedral-like cave at Skoteino at some distance east
of Herakleion, which reaches a depth of some 160 metres (528 feet), with

27. Bronze votary from the Skoteino
Cave: frontal view

stalagmitic columns and winding galleries, was assumed to be either the
sacred cave of Knossos—according to Evans* who explored part of the
cave—or even the real place of the Labyrinth;* the author found here
three fine bronze statuettes of votaries (figures 27 and 28; see Sculpture,
Minoan*).

   The well-known cave of Eileithyia* at Amnisos,* where the goddess
was born to Hera according to the Greek tradition mentioned in the

28. Bronze votary from the Skoteino
Cave: side view

Odyssey, has been identified and explored by Hazzidakis, and later by
Marinatos, who found pottery in abundance and was able to conclude
that the cult persisted from Neolithic times into the fifth century A.D. In
the middle of the cave two smooth stalagmitic formations vaguely resembling human forms are surrounded by enclosures. One of these stalagmites has obviously been smoothed by the fingers of the pilgrims who believed it to possess miraculous powers.

Mount Ida* has two famous sacred caves, the Idaian cave* and the cave of Kamares, at an altitude of 1524 metres (5029 feet), which has given its name to Kamares ware,* a splendidly decorated pottery first found here. Perhaps the best known sacred cave of the island is that of Psychro.* In Western Crete some important caves have been explored, including Arkoudiotissa and Lera (see Gouverneto Monastery*). All these cave sanctuaries had practically no structures except sometimes an altar or an enclosure around the holiest spot inside the cave, as in the case of Psychro* or the Eileithyia Cave.

During the times of trouble in the long Cretan history, especially during the Turkish occupation,* caves also played an important role as natural places of refuge, often easily defended. Sometimes the concentration of refugees resulted in tragedy, as was true of the cave at Milatos* and the one at Melidoni near Rethymnon,* in which 3,700 women and children were massacred in 1823 by the Turks. In recent years, hundreds of caves about the island have been explored and catalogued by a tireless French scholar, Paul Faure.

Central Courts of Palaces. A characteristic feature of the plan of a Minoan palace (see Palaces*) is its large rectangular central court, which occupies a considerable part of its whole area and constitutes its focal point, running precisely from north to south. It is almost a standard length, slightly over fifty metres (165 feet), although the court at Zakros* measures only about one third of that. At Knossos* the width is almost thirty metres (100 feet) while at Phaistos* and Malia* it is more than five metres (16 feet) narrower. At Knossos,* its dimensions match those of the Parthenon. The palace faced inward toward the court rather than to the outside, and grew from the center outwards. These courts, which follow prototypes of Oriental palaces but without being restricted by surrounding rectangular rooms and corresponding outer walls, serve as the organizing nucleus of the palace plan, which thus developed from within. Some scholars believe that the bull-games* took place here, a sensible idea but difficult to prove. There is no doubt that the central courts were important for the everyday life of the palace and further for various ritual activities and ceremonies observed at the appropriate times of the year, dances* and entertainments. Indicative of the cult practises were the altars* placed here. The courts were surrounded by shrines,* verandas, porticoes and galleries.

Chamaizi. The Middle Minoan IA house excavated in 1903 by St. Xanthoudides, at the top of a high hill in the vicinity of the village of Chamaizi west of Siteia,* is a unique oval building (figure 29). The site is not easily accessible but enjoys a splendid view. The rooms are set around a small open court with a deep circular rock-cut cistern lined with masonry in its upper part. It has been suggested that the shape of

29. View of the oval house at Chamaizi

the house was fortuitous, determined by the lay of the ground at the crest of the hill; also that it was not a simple house but a peak sanctuary* shrine.

In 1971 the site was further explored by the author in order to clear up some of the questions. A second entrance to the north was unexpectedly discovered, as well as some steps leading down to the various rooms, a pillar, the pavement of the court, an overflow drain connected to the cistern, and several other new elements, which radically modify the previously accepted plan. An important finding was the location of earlier houses* beneath the oval building, with walls showing a tendency to curved lines. These new discoveries proved that the oval shape of the house was for the most part deliberate, a fact with some implications for the history of Minoan architecture.* Also, the building was proved to be

30. Typical Late Minoan chamber-tomb

a secular one – a rich isolated country manor house probably including a
shrine but with no connection to a peak sanctuary.

Chamber-tombs. These underground tombs, a widespread type which
belongs mainly to the Late Minoan period,* were cut deep in the soft limestone, preferably on slopes. A long, narrow, open passage (*dromos*), the
sides of which were sloping inward, led down to the chamber (hence the
name chamber-tombs), which had an oval, circular or usually almost rectangular shape. The narrow entrance, usually hewn in the rock and
shaped as a doorway (*stomion*) with slightly inclined jambs, was closed by
a blocking wall of rough stones, taken down and rebuilt for every new
burial. The *dromos* was filled with earth, to be redug for each interment.
This type of tomb, usually well-hewn and provided with some larnakes*
in the chamber (see Burial Customs*), spread rapidly after the Late Mino-

31. La Canea (*after a Venetian map*)

an II phase. Chamber-tombs closely resemble tholos tombs* except for
the masonry-lining of the walls and the roof. These tombs—several hundreds are extant—were distributed all over Crete (figure 30), and were
used over a long period. Well known are those of Mavro Spilio, cut in the
slopes of a hill opposite the palace of Knossos.* A series of elaborate
chamber-tombs has been found at Armenoi* in the west.

Chania. Chania, the second largest city of Crete (more than 40,000 inhabitants) and capital of the westernmost prefecture of the island, is situated
on the site of ancient Kydonia.* The town flourished during the Byzantine* and Venetian* periods; during the latter period it was named by the
Italians *La Canea*, after the Greek *Chania*, a name which was probably
another form of *Alchania*, a locality known from an ancient incription. The
wall surrounding the inner town, known as Kastelli, the *Castello vecchio* of
the Venetians, is believed to be a work of the Byzantines with some later
additions. In 1266 Chania was captured and plundered by the Genoese,
great rivals of the Venetians. The town was fortified in 1336 and again in
1536, in accordance with plans of Sammicheli, who also designed the
walls of Herakleion,* but the fortification, which possessed four bastions
and 319 cannons, was unable to resist the attack of the Turks, who
captured Chania in 1645 after a short siege.

During the Creto-Venetian era, a time of prosperity and cultural development for Chania, a number of notable buildings were constructed
(figure 31). Some of them survive today, such as the large cathedral of St.
Francis (Hagios Frangiskos), later converted into a mosque, which today
houses the Archaeological Museum of Western Crete; the fountain

known as Sandrivani; the lighthouse (Pharos) reconstructed by the Egyptians during their short occupation (1830–40); and the elegant small church of St. Rocco, under reconstruction by the Archaeological Society of Western Crete. The old town preserves some very interesting traces of Creto-Venetian architecture mixed with Turkish elements, but the remarkable character of these houses, often severely damaged during the last war, is unfortunately being extensively obliterated by modern constructions.

At the entrance of the small Medieval harbour, which includes some Venetian ship sheds, is the Fortress Firkas, where the Greek flag was raised in 1913 for the first time in Crete. A Naval Museum has been housed here. The harbour includes the mosque of Hassan Pasha, a fine building obliterated by a modern pavilion.

Chariots. The chariot is supposed to have been basically introduced during the Late Minoan II period (1450-1400 BC), perhaps by the Achaians,* although chariots drawn by horses* appear already on sealings* during the previous period. This light and swift spoke-wheeled vehicle, which revolutionized warfare,* seems to have been an Oriental military invention. The chariots were drawn by a pair of horses,* as the yoke system shows, which was attached over the horses' withers. A stay ran from the top edge of the chariot to the junction of shaft and yoke. Of course bridles and bits were used. Chariots were employed in hunting and religious processions, perhaps for transport* but mainly in warfare,* operating ahead of the main force. The wheels were large and four-spoked. A shallow leather or wicker body was stretched over a light bentwood frame, which was designed to carry a normal complement of two warriors, one to drive and one to fight. The sides of the chariot sometimes were lengthened at the back by means of semicircular wings covered with leather, evidently to give additional protection.

Sometimes chariots are represented on seals:* one of them, a signet ring carved out of a solid piece of banded agate, assigned as early as the Late Minoan I period, shows a chariot drawn by two magnificent ibexes. Such animals could actually have been trained to draw a chariot. The elaborate harness is decorated with tassels. The principal person, obviously armed with a sword, sits behind the driver, who holds the reins and a forked whip. These figures may be divine, or may be mortals taking part in a ceremonial pageant.

The Knossian army had numerous chariots: it is estimated that more than four hundred are listed on the clay tablets* of the Linear B script* found in the palace; it has been suggested that the chariot may have helped the Mycenaean dynasty of Knossos to acquire supremacy in Crete. These tablets inform us that chariots were decorated with ivory and crimson colouring. It is obvious, however, that considering the rugged nature of the surface of Crete, chariot driving, especially for passenger transport, must have been limited to constructed tracks.

Chersonesos. The location of modern Chersonesos ("peninsula"), a village on the north coast east of Herakleion,* was occupied in Classical

Greek times by a city of the same name. Traces of a Minoan settlement have been located here. The settlers of Chersonesos were, according to the legend, descendants of the Tyrrhenians. With them they brought a wooden statue (*xoanon*) of Britomartis,* who became the main divinity of the city. The geographer Strabo mentions the temple of the goddess.

At one time Chersonesos was a seaport of Lyttos,* about 15 kilometres (10 miles) inland from it, but later it also had an independent existence, as it was allowed to issue its own coinage.* The city flourished especially during the Roman occupation.* It possessed a number of fountains adorned with mosaics, a theater with an oval peristyle court in front, and an acropolis, which perhaps stood on the peninsula. The defense walls which surrounded it are dated to the Late Roman or Byzantine period,* as their masonry, which uses concrete, indicates. The ruins of the Graeco-Roman town occupy an extensive area in the fields to the west and south of the peninsula. The remarkable engineering works at its harbour (see Harbours*) are today below sea-level (see Geography*) and suggest the importance and prosperity of the city.

In later times two large Early Christian basilicas with fine mosaic floors arose, testifying to the importance of the diocese of Chersonesos, which was founded by St. Titus, a disciple of St. Paul.

Chieftain Cup see **Stone Vases.**

Chromonastiri. In the vicinity of this village near Rethymnon* is the isolated single-nave church of St. Eutychios, which is adorned with fine fresco-paintings dated to the eleventh century, perhaps the best example of Byzantine painting in Crete. The figures are flat and strongly outlined, with large inward-looking eyes and a hieratic immobility. These clearly drawn figures show the influence of the imperial art of Constantinople.

Chronology. An impressive body of evidence has been built up on pottery* and its ubiquitous and readily preserved sherds, which, according to their shape and style, form a system of relative chronology for the prehistoric cultures of the Aegean, including Crete. Other objects of the material culture play a secondary role to this scheme. On the other hand, absolute chronology—that is, dating in terms of years B.C.—of the Aegean archaeology can be fixed only by correlations with the well-known Oriental civilizations.

Radioactive carbon (carbon 14) dating offers only indirect and partly satisfactory chronological suggestions. This promising process, discovered by the American, W. F. Libby, is still in an experimental stage and gives date ranges too wide to be really useful. We must bear in mind that the carbon 14 date of a sample applies to the date at which the organic material—a piece of wood or a bone—to which the sample belongs had ceased to live, and its constant proportion of carbon 14 had gradually begun to diminish at a known rate.

Some of the earliest Minoan seals* resemble those of the VIth Egyptian Dynasty and the subsequent period (from about 2400 B.C. onwards).

Fragments of imported Minoan pottery and other objects were recovered in Egypt, and on the other hand Egyptian objects* have been found in Knossian deposits. A cylinder seal of the period of the famous Hammurabi of the First Dynasty of Babylon buried some time during the 19th century B.C. was found in one of the tholos tombs* at Platanos.*

Evans* and Mackenzie worked out a dating system based on stratigraphy: they divided the Bronze Age* sequence into three periods, Early,* Middle* and Late* Minoan, each with three subdivisions (I, II, and III). A Sub-Minoan period is added. These periods of Minoan history roughly correspond with those of the Early, the Middle, and the earlier part of the New Kingdom in Egypt. This division, based chiefly upon differences of style in the local pottery of Knossos,* presents some restrictions and difficulties, and has been criticized; for instance Middle Minoan II and Late Minoan II are not chronological divisions but merely pottery styles. Nevertheless the system works and is still accepted in general, because we are dealing with only a single culture. On the whole, the three periods correspond with the Early, Middle and Late Bronze Age periods.

An alternative dating system has been proposed by N. Platon, based on major events in the history of the palaces,* focal points of Minoan civilization and economy, thus sensibly dividing the Bronze Age into Prepalatial, Protopalatial (or period of the First or Early Palaces*), Neopalatial (or period of the Second or Later Palaces), and Postpalatial (or the period after the final destruction of the palace at Knossos* in the beginning of the fourteenth century B.C.).

After the coming of the Dorians* and the subsequent beginning of a new era, the Iron Age,* chronology follows in general the divisions which are standard for the Greek civilization: the Geometric period,* which covers roughly the three first centuries of the first millenium B.C.; the Orientalizing period,* which covers the end of the eighth and most of the seventh century; the Archaic period, until about the beginning of the fifth century; the Classical period, which includes the fifth century and most of the fourth, until the death of Alexander the Great in 323 B.C.; and the Hellenistic period,* which lasts until the Roman occupation* of Crete in 67 B.C. The long Roman, or more exactly the Graeco-Roman period, covers almost four centuries (67 B.C.—324 A.D.), until Crete becomes part of the Byzantine Empire.

Chrysolakkos see **Burial Customs/Jewellery.**

Chrysoskalitissa Monastery. This nunnery on the west coast of the island derives its name from one of the ninety steps leading to the top of a nearby rock; according to legend this step is made of gold but looks like an ordinary stone step to the eyes of the sinner. The monastery lies among a splendid scenery of rocks of fantastic shapes on the shore. In its vicinity a small settlement of Middle Minoan times was located.

City-states see **Dorians.**

Climate. The climate of Crete in Minoan times was probably very similar to its typically Mediterranaean climate today: the heats of summer are tempered by cool winds and, because of a generally very low degree of humidity, not unpleasant; the winters, which begin about the middle of December, are mild with many days of sunshine. Crete is considerably warmer during the winter months than the French Riviera, Sicily or the Balearic Islands, without being hotter during the summer. The Cretan climate is considered to have a bracing quality, promoting the energy and vigour of the population. Of course we must bear in mind that the forests* in antiquity were very abundant and the soil uneroded, and rain must have been more abundant. The plains have a dry, pleasant climate, with practically all the rain falling in short, heavy showers between October and March, and even these are only occasional and are succeeded by warm sunshine. The time between May and September is practically rainless, causing agriculture problems.

The temperature rarely falls below the freezing point; snow is common in the mountains, even until mid-summer, but rare in the lowlands. Owing to the variation in altitude, the large mountainous masses and the gorges, climate is not uniform in all parts of the island: the south shore is warmer than the north one; the east is much drier than the west, much windier and also warmer. Crete has fewer cloudy days than any other part of Greece.

The major characteristic element of the island clearly is the wind. During the summer, wind blows steadily with some force from the northwest, a fact which creates a most favourable climate. These regular Etesian winds, called "meltemia," cool the atmosphere so that during even the hottest period of the year air temperatures are lower in Crete than in other European locations farther north.

Cloth. An important Minoan household craft (see Industries*), evidently established since the Neolithic period* and playing an important role in economy,* has been the spinning and weaving of cloth. Already in the Early Minoan settlement at Myrtos* a complex of rooms was probably used for the fulling and dyeing of textiles. Looms of the upright type common in every period in antiquity and later, were made of wood, so that they could be more easily housed indoors, and have consequently perished. Only the weights survive, which were attached to the lower ends of the vertically hanging warp threads to hold them under tension. Loom-weights show a variety of shapes and sizes: perforated flat discs, and later solid globes with three or four outside grooves for the thread of the warp, or cubes perforated at the four corners. Loom-weights of later Greek times had a high pyramidal or conical shape perforated horizontally below the top, with eventually a potter's mark incised on the wet clay.

Hand-spinning was done by the same method which has survived until today: the mass of raw wool was held on the distaff; part of it was pulled and twisted with right hand and forefinger so that a continuous thread was formed; a spindle-whorl hanging from its end was necessary to keep it turning. Many Minoan stone and clay spindle-whorls have survived in various places. At Myrtos* a probable wool workshop was

32. Section of the Code of Gortyn (*after Comparetti*)

found. Wool is considered to have been the staple material used for making cloth in the Bronze Age,* since it was evidently one of the main Cretan exports,* its production must have been considerable. The Knossian tablets* record an annual census of flocks, the total number of animals being about 100,000.

About the lost woolen artifacts we know practically nothing, but we can get an indirect glimpse of the variety of their intricate patterns through the painted decoration on the dress* of some figurines.* The art of weaving brocade in over-all patterns must have been splendid in these times,as we can guess from existing frescoes.* Linen, perhaps imported from Egypt, seems also to have been in use, as well as some varieties of silk, like the one made in Kos, near Eastern Crete, in Classical times. A purple dye (*porphyra*) obtained from the *murex* shell-fish, often found in excavations, was evidently extensively used for woollens, in Minoan as well as in Classical times.

Code of Gortyn. The Law Code of Gortyn is a splendidly inscribed, well-preserved, ordered and self-contained collection of statutes of the fifth century, perhaps earlier than 450 B.C. (figure 32). The Code reveals the survival of an old tribal system as well as several Minoan elements. It is the first European law-code and the only complete one which survived from ancient Greece. The "Queen of Inscriptions," as this unique document is sometimes named, is over 600 lines long and divided into twelve columns. It is inscribed in the *boustrophedon* system (see Alphabet*): one line is read from left to right but the next inversely from right to left, and so on. This important legislation, written in Doric Greek (see Greek Language*) and in a beautiful archaic alphabet upon the facade of a long concave wall incorporated in the back of the Roman Odeum at Gortyn,* is a major source of information and an extremely important social document.

The Code clearly contains older law material and reveals the tradition of the past centuries. This body of law has been considered as the dividing line between the end of primitive law and the beginning of mature law, this beginning being especially emphasized by the increase in its procedural technicalities. R. F. Willetts, leading authority on the subject, observed that the topics covered by the Code are arranged, not by reference to legal principles, but by the need to group together statutes covering like or similar circumstances.

Thus there are regulations relating to suits which concerned the ownership of actual or alleged slaves (see Slavery in Dorian Crete*); such matters as seduction, rape and adultery; marriage and the rights of property; the division of property among heirs; the sale and mortgaging of the family property; the repayment of ransoms for prisoners; the duties and functions of judges; the children of mixed marriages; the responsibility for the acts of a slave; a most important and highly interesting series of regulations about the division of property among the children, including the special case of adopted children, and the marriage of an heiress and the disposal of her property; the procedure for adoption; the legality of gift giving; as well as a variety of provisions in certain special cases. We give here a characteristic table, as compiled by Willetts, showing the scale of fines for rape and adultery as detailed in the Code, considered not as criminal offences, but as matters to be settled by private monetary compensation:

A. For rape:
   1. Against a free person ....1,200 obols
   2. Against an *apetairos*..120 obols
   3. By a slave against a free person ....2,400 obols
   4. By a free person against a serf...............................30 obols
   5. Against a serf by a serf ....60 obols
   6. Against a household slave ....24, 1 or 2 obols
                                          depending on circumstances

B. For adultery:
   1. With a free woman....................................600–1,200 obols
   2. With the wife of an *apetairos*.................................120 obols
   3. A slave with a free woman........................slave pays double
                                                    (1,200–2,400 obols)
   4. Slave with slave...60 obols

Codpiece see **Dress; Keftiu.**

Coinage. During the Bronze Age* evidently no standard of value was used. Coinage was introduced to Greece from Asia Minor. At the begin-

ning small pieces of metal were stamped to guarantee by state authority
that they were of the weight specified, a process which later led to a real
art. An engraved die was set in an anvil and a metal blank on it was strick-
en with a punch. The island of Aigina near Athens was the first city-state
to strike a coinage; Crete followed some 150 years afterward (at the beginning of the fifth century B.C.), accepting the Aiginetic system—the drach-
ma and the didrachm or stater being the main denominations. This
system was gradually replaced by the Attic standard after the time of
Alexander the Great and during the Hellenistic period.*

Later, after 200 B.C., many Cretan cities issued imitations of the Athenian tetradrachm, using of course their own symbols and names. The
autonomous issues of about forty Cretan cities—always a sign of political
independence—ceased after the Roman conquest. Coins were of silver or
bronze. Silver was used in a form much purer than that found in modern
coins. Some of the Cretan silver coins are outstanding for their artistic
quality; their symbols are varied: coins from Knossos* show among other
subjects the traditional Labyrinth* and the running Minotaur;* those from
Phaistos* show Europa* riding on the bull; those from Itanos* show Triton and impressive figures of sea-serpents; from Kydonia,* a bitch suckling the infant Kydon;* from Lyttos,* a flying eagle and a boar's head, (see
figure 110) and later a prow; from Chersonesos* and Olous,* a figure of
Britomartis;* from Gortyn,* Europa* in the tree; from Axos,* a tripod or a
thunderbolt; from Aptera,* a warrior saluting a tree; from Hierapytna,* a
palm tree and eagle; from Rithymna,* Apollo, a trident or a pair of dolphins; from Elyros,* a bee; from Hyrtakina,* the head of a wild goat.

It has been remarked that the Cretan coins show a great interest in nature, which is probably the emergence of the old Minoan love of scenery
visible on seals* and rings, of which these coins are in a way the true descendants. Some coins show countermarks—small stamps which are
overstruck on a coin without attempting to deface the whole of it. Coins
symbolizing the alliance between Knossos* and Gortyn* were issued
about 220 B.C., with subjects belonging to both cities, the Labyrinth* and
Europa* on the bull. During the Roman occupation* cistophoros coins
were struck. Later the inscription *Koinon Kreton* or *K.K.* (see Koinon*) appears. Several important hoards of coins have been found in the island.

Columns (Minoan). Minoan columns, except very short ones, were made
of wood, usually of cypress wood, as some carbonized remains show. Being basically made of inverted tree trunks, they characteristically tapered
slightly to their base, as pictures of them in frescoes* or seals* show, the
wider end being at the top to support the capital and the large wooden
beams. The diminution was about one-seventh or less. This inverted arrangement prevented the eventual sprouting of the unseasoned trunk
and allowed the capital to throw drips of water clear of the base, thus preserving it better from rain and the danger of rot. Whatever the original
practical purpose of this peculiar shape, it soon developed into a characteristic feature of Minoan architecture,* as it expressed the Minoan taste
for flexibility, lightness and grace, denying heaviness. Later columns

showed a tendency to have their shafts of an even diameter.

The columns rested on stone bases, which at the beginning were drum-shaped and proportionally rather tall but later took the shape of a flat disc. A rare type tapered towards the top, while some other bases, found more often, had their lower part roughly worked and embedded. Sometimes round columns rested on rectangular or square bases, while an oval base denotes the existence of oval columns, evidently a rarity. Earlier examples were of variegated stones, and later ones of limestone or gypsum.* To prevent the column from slipping, the upper surface of the stone base, which rested on wide deep foundations, was often roughened, or had a shallow socket corresponding to a tenon of the column.

Capitals of various types—sometimes ornate—can be seen in illustrations. They were made of separate blocks of wood. They had mouldings, both convex and concave, including a cushion-like full spreading one, the echinus, and were crowned with a projecting square block, the abacus. The early Doric capital is generally considered to have derived from this Minoan ancestor, modelled by artists of the Archaic period* in the seventh century B.C. after examples which survived from the Bronze Age.* One type of Minoan capital imitates the Egyptian palm column.

Minoan columns were normally plain but in some exceptional circumstances were concave or convex, fluted or ribbed (see Little Palace*). Egyptian influence is shown in these columns with cannellated or fluted shafts. Sometimes columns were copied on a smaller scale by some elaborate pedestalled lamps* of stone. The wood was plastered and usually boldly painted in red or black with a counterchanged capital, often picked out in yellow or white. Some examples show a dark band just above the base.

Columns were ranged in porticoes—alternately with pillars*—and peristyle courts thus allowing a free view over the landscape, or placed in light-wells* and formal entrances, mainly because of their decorative value. Another type of column, as depicted on frescoes* and stone vases,* tapered upwards and supported an oblong block decorated with discs, probably the ends of beams. Columns were of all sizes, the largest at the palace of Phaistos* having a diameter of three and one half to four feet (over a metre). They sometimes had a religious character and were related to the tree and pillar cult.* On some representations of columns a bird* is perched on top, denoting the presence of a divinity.

Communion (Sacred). The transmission of the sacred communion to the devout was one of the more solemn moments of the ritual of the Minoan religion.* The existence of this ceremony is well attested in scenes painted in frescoes* or cut on seals.* Especially instructive is the so-called Campstool-Fresco from Knossos (see Frescoes*), a large composition in which is pictured the maid known as the "Parisienne." The communion was transmitted in special vessels such as tall chalices, of which four have been recovered from the palace at Zakros.* The best example was carved in spotted obsidian.* The ingredients of the holy liquid perhaps may be inferred from later examples such as the well-known *kykeon* used in the

33. Late Minoan cinerary urn from Kritsa

Eleusinian Mysteries. It has been suggested that the Minoan communion liquid mainly consisted of milk, honey* and the blood of the sacrificed bull. The use of bull's blood would account for the existence of libation vessels (see rhyton*) in the form of a bull's head. Similar religious and magical conceptions can be found in many religions. According to the dogma of many Christian churches, the wine in the Holy Communion is the transubstantiated blood of Jesus Christ.

Couretes see **Kouretes.**

Cremation. Cremation of the dead was one of the rarest burial customs* during the Bronze Age* in Crete, perhaps reserved for foreigners married into local clans. The earliest cremations, dated to the end of the Middle Minoan III period, were found by Sinclair Hood in the Ailias cemetery near Knossos.* After a long period with no examples of cremations, this burial custom was really introduced during the latter part of the Late Minoan III period and gradually became an established practise, prevailing over inhumation, with which it often indiscriminately coexists in the same cemeteries. Cremation became the rule from the tenth century B.C. onwards, with the ashes of the dead put inside various types of closed vases (figure 33). This burial custom probably had its origins in Anatolia and not in Central Europe. Most of the early cremations were found in Eastern Crete, in places like Zakros,* Vrokastro,* Praisos,* Olous* and Kritsa.*

34. Jesus Christ and St. George, Cretan School of Painting, 16th-17th century

Cretan School of Painting. This term especially encompasses the art of several generations of Cretan painters, from the second half of the fifteenth century, that is after the collapse of the Byzantine Empire, until the end of the seventeenth century, corresponding with the beginning and consolidation of the Turkish occupation,* when all important cultural life became extinct. After the fall of Constantinople in 1453 which caused a diaspora, a considerable number of artists found in Crete—especially at Herakleion*—a refuge from the Turks and favourable conditions for work under the relatively milder Venetian occupation.* These artists were mostly of Cretan origin and led the art of the island to a true renaissance of Byzantine painting (see Byzantine Churches*), enriched with contem-

35. Jesus Christ by Manuel Tzanes

porary Italian influences, as Crete was in close touch with Italy, particularly Venice.

The Cretan School became the heir of the long Byzantine tradition, which expressed the mysticism of the Orthodox Church (figure 34). Acquiring charm and intimacy, it surpassed the limits of the island, spreading over to the Greek Mainland and Cyprus, where it created excellent wall-paintings in places such as Meteora in Thessaly, Macedonia, and especially the great monasteries at Athos. Outstanding among these painters was Theophanes "the Cretan," who decorated among others the refectory of the Lavra on Athos. His splendid compositions are calm and well balanced. Later remarkable artists were Michael Damaskenos, born in about 1550, whose icons can be seen inside the chapel of St. Menas (see Herakleion*), and Emmanuel Tzanes (figure 35). The Cretan School is better represented in icons than in wall-paintings. These icons are to be distinguished by their brilliant colouring and excellent quality. This School gave birth to the art of a great master, Domenicos Theotocopoulos, the famous El Greco, himself a Cretan (see Fodele*).

CRETE. Crete was a nymph who gave her name to the island. There is a variety of traditions in Greek literature about her origin and life. Crete usually was considered the mother of Queen Pasiphae* by Helios (the "Sun"), or the daughter of one of the Kouretes,* or of King Asterios and one of the Hesperides, and further as a wife of Minos* or of the Egyptian god Ammon.

Cross. The cross is a religious symbol much older than Christianity and of a far wider geographical distribution. As a secondary symbol it was used in Minoan religion.* The most astounding example is the large marble cross of the equal-armed type—the so-called Greek cross—found in the western cist of the Temple Repositories* of the palace at Knossos.* This cross, 22.2 centimetres (almost nine inches) wide but very thin, originally was set in some other material, as is suggested by its rough underside, in contrast to its finely polished face. The veined marble has white and dark grey undertones. Significant in the origin of the symbol perhaps is the representation of a rayed disc of the sun with four cruciform spokes on a stone mould from Siteia,* together with other religious symbols like the double axe.* The cross is a regular character of the Linear A* and B* scripts. Another cruciform symbol is the "swastika" or *crux gammata*, occuring on many clay sealings.* This special form of cross occurs later as a decorative pattern in the pottery of the Geometric period.*

Currency see **Coinage; Ingots.**

Daggers see **Weapons.**

DAIDALOS. According to Greek tradition there was a legendary engineer and craftsman Daidalos, who had worked for King Minos,* and a much later artist, the mythical (or historical?) prototype of Greek sculptors and founder of the famous Daidalid School. He was the eponymous hero of all "cunning artificers" and had the reputation of being extremely ingenious and versed in many techniques. Named after him, in modern terminology, is the Dedalic style* of Archaic Crete and some other areas outside it. Several Cretan cities such as Olous* and Chersonesos* boasted the possession of a *xoanon* (wooden statue) made by him.

Daidalos, son of Metion and Iphinoe, was reputedly a native Cretan, but the later political propaganda of Athens made an Athenian of this father of sculpture, the first creator of figures "in motion," clearly for reasons of prestige. In fact, the fame of the Bronze Age* Cretan craftsmen is reflected in the legends about Daidalos, as well as the general consensus in Greece, that Greek sculpture was first created in Crete. The Minoan Daidalos had fashioned at Knossos a dancing place for the Princess Ariadne,* and had made a simulacrum of a cow for the Queen Pasiphae,* who was enamored of the bull sent by Poseidon. To hide the Minotaur,* born from the union of the Queen and the bull, Daidolos built the Labyrinth* similar to one he had built in Egypt. He was forced to flee from Minos' displeasure and wrath at his aid to Pasiphae, and designed artificial flying wings for himself and his son, Ikaros*. They flew out over the Aegean Sea, where Ikaros was drowned. Daidalos escaped to Sicily, where he was hospitably received by King Kokalos (see Minos*) and lived there until the end of his days.

DAKTYLOI. While Rhea was bearing Zeus,* she pressed her fingers (*daktyloi*) into the soil to ease her pangs and up sprang the Daktyloi: five girls from her left hand and five boys from the right: Herakles, Paionios, Epimedes, Iasios and Akesidas; the names of the girls were a closely-guarded secret. Other legends consider the nymph Anchiale as their mother; their number also varies. These lesser divinities, closely associated with Mount Ida,* played some role in the popular religion of Dorian Crete. According to tradition, the forging of iron* was invented by them. Some of their characteristics coincide with those of the Kouretes.*

Dance. Dancers are often depicted in Minoan art,* in frescoes* such as the lively *Girl Dancer* and the miniature *Garden Party* from the palace at Knossos* and elsewhere. On a stone vessel, the famous Harvester Vase* from Hagia Triada,* men are singing and dancing at harvest time. A pottery group of three female dancers with outstretched hands forming part of a circle and facing a lyre player in their center which dates from the Late Minoan period* from Palaikastro* (figure 36), possibly illustrates the Classical Cretan dance called *hyporchema* (see Figurines*). Another group of dancers dancing in a ring comes from the great tholos tomb at Kamilari.*

Dance performances played an important role in the court life, as the above miniature fresco revealed. Perhaps religion* was also involved. Ritual dancing—perhaps sometimes of an ecstatic nature—seems to have been a religious custom in cases such as the cult of the dead or the veneration paid to the sacred tree.* Probably the Mother Goddess could be induced by ritual dance to appear. A fragment of a poem of Sappho perhaps reflects the memory of such dances: "Thus once upon a time the Cretan women danced rhythmically with delicate feet around a beautiful altar, treading upon the soft, smooth flowers of the meadow."

In Dorian Crete the cult of the Kouretes* probably was associated with some Cretan armed dance of a ritual nature, such as the *epikredios*, the *tel-*

36. Group of dancers and lyre-player from Palaikastro

esias and the *orsites,* answering to the Greek pyrrhic dance. The *prylis* was a funeral dance performed by men in armour. The *pentozalis,* the vivid modern folk-dance with a "five-beat" rhythm, where the performers form a circle and grasp each other's shoulders in the way of the dancers from Palaikastro,* is possibly a descendant of the *hyporchema,* as has been suggested. This lively rapid mimetic dance, said to be invented by the mythical Kouretes,* was a combination of dance, song, pantomime and instrumental music, with flute or lyre (see also Music*). It was mainly performed in the cult of Zeus* and Apollo, but originally it was connected with the cult of Kronos, Leto and the Cretan Zeus.

Famous was the *geranos* (crane dance), which Theseus* was said to have seen the Cretan maidens dancing, and himself to have introduced in Delos, dancing it around the Horned Altar. This dance imitated the circuits and exits of the Labyrinth* from which he had escaped. This "maze" dance is said to have been performed with labyrinthine convolutions, trod with measured steps to the music of harps on an area marked with sinuous lines to guide the steps of the dancer (see Labyrinth*). Cranes notoriously do perform a sort of dance. The dances of the Labyrinth were later connected with the Roman Game of Troy, performed by armed riders. In the Iliad Homer describes a dance or rather a dancing arena "such as Daidalos once made for Ariadne in broad Knossos" with the maidens and youths hand in hand dancing "so lightly with cunning feet" in a circle or in two lines facing each other (see also Ariadne*).

Of Cretan origin were the Classical Greek dances such as the solemn processional *paean*, performed to the accompaniment of lyres and flutes, the *nomos* (for both see also Music*) and the vigorous and lewd *skinnis*, used in the satyr play. According to Lucian, an author of the second century A.D., among the Cretan dance-themes were the Labyrinth, the Bulls, Daidalos, Ariadne, Glaukos and Talos.

Dark Ages. The period which succeeded the Bronze Age* was named the Dark Ages because it was marked by a real decay of civilization. This period began about 1100 B.C., after the arrival of the Dorians* and the introduction of iron* to Crete, and lasted perhaps slightly more than three centuries, or two centuries according to other opinions. During this period cremation* replaced inhumation as a burial custom. The Dark Ages, which comprised the earlier part of the Geometric period* preceded by a short Sub-Minoan phase, was a long and painful transition between the collapsed great civilizations of the Bronze Age* in Greece and the rising Classical world. Crete suffered a considerable loss of population: with piracy* being unchecked most of the coastal sites and a number of inland towns had been abandoned. Their inhabitants fled to mountain refuges such as Karphi* and Vrokastro.* Of the main sites only Knossos* survived as an important center. Probably trade* became much limited and the self-sufficiency of the island increased. The Dark Ages is a period which has certain affinities with the Middle Ages in Europe and marks an age of cultural, social and national fermentation, of which history has nothing to tell us.

Dedalic Style. Dedalic style, named after the legendary artist Daidalos,* was a Doric style of sculptures and figurines,* which flourished in approximately the seventh century B.C. The style is believed to have originated in Crete, where it found its best expression, but rapidly spread over a part of the early Doric world in Greece, such as Laconia and Rhodes, affecting other non-Doric areas and becoming a pan-Hellenic movement. It is closely connected with Oriental models and with the birth of Greek sculpture.

Dedalic figures are symmetrical, spare, and rigidly frontal, and are best regarded from the front, since the third dimension, depth, was only gradually conquered. The figures form a sort of block, with the volumes of the body exactly rendered. The hair is usually treated like a conventional wig divided in horizontal layers, clearly influenced by Egyptian models. There are also long braided locks. The top of the head is rather flat. In early examples, the features of the face were rather roughly modelled, with sharp chins, and the outlines of the cheek forming two straight lines set at an angle to one another.

37. Late Dedalic goddess from Eleutherna

Most Dedalic figures represent women, usually clad in a tight long garment known as a *peplos*, a broad and ornate girdle, and a broad *epiblema* over the shoulders and the back. There are also statues and figurines of the nude goddess. The Dedalic style, which produced the only great Cretan sculpture, affected not only large stone statues such as the goddesses from Prinias,* Gortyn* and Eleutherna* (figure 37), and the recently found imposing goddess from Astritsi, the earliest colossal statue of

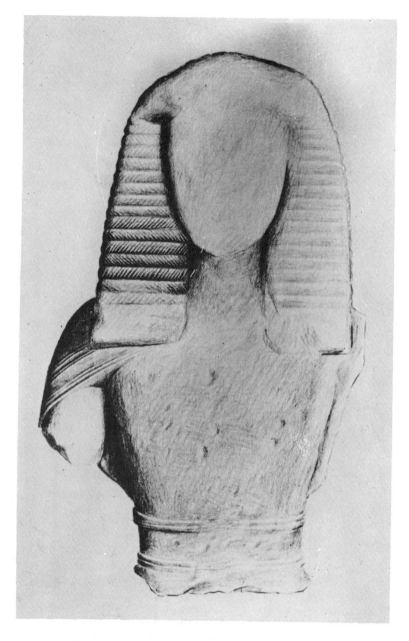

38. Colossal Dedalic goddess from Astritsi *(after Davaras)*

Greek sculpture, which perhaps represents Athena Tritogeneia (figure
38), but also small stone figures like the famous "Dame d'Auxerre," now
in Paris, and bronze statuettes like the splendid *kouros* ("youth"), a Cre-

tan work found at Delphi, as well as an extremely rich series of clay figurines and plaques. The latter include subjects such as warriors, griffins* and sphinxes. A nude goddess type with her hands at her side is very popular. Dedalic jewellery and pithoi* with moulded figures arranged in zones on the neck and shoulders were also made. The inspiration for creating large stone statues came from Egypt, a country with a very long tradition and technical skill in producing colossal works. Thus Egyptian canons of proportions were originally followed, but later abandoned.

DEMETER. The goddess Demeter of the Olympian pantheon was believed to have reached Greece from Crete. She had associations with Oriental fertility goddesses and was probably a survival of some aspect of the Minoan goddess, sharing with her some attributes such as the snake (see Snake Cult*), the tree and the poppy. The title "Demeter and the Maid (Persephone)" brings to mind the double aspect of the Minoan goddess as Mother and Maid. According to the myth the goddess made love with a mortal, Iasion (see Ida, Mount*). In Greek times Demeter was worshipped at several cities of the island, including Knossos,* Gortyn,* Olous,* Axos,* Hyrtakina* and Hierapytna.* A temple of the goddess was found at Aptera.* Of high importance is the fact that the Eleusinian Mysteries were undoubtedly introduced into Greece from Crete, as Diodoros and the Homeric Hymn to Demeter inform us. The important sanctuary of the goddess at Knossos was situated on the lower slopes of Gypsades Hill. The ruins of its temple, excavated in recent years by the British School of Archaeology, include three terrace walls. The sanctuary yielded an amount of clay figurines* and small plaques with flat backs, mainly of the seventh century B.C.

Demons (Minoan). Minoan demons, often seen on seals* and rings, form a class uniform in type and must be distinguished from the more varied and fantastically combined monsters,* which perhaps in many cases were depicted merely for decorative purposes with no religious associations. Demons walk upright and behave exactly like human beings, but their heads are like those of asses, lions, or horses,* their hands are formed like paws, and their backs seem to be covered with loose skin which ends in a point similar to a wasp's stinger. They are always depicted as ministers of the cult performing some ritual act, such as pouring libations on to altars* or sacred boughs, or bringing offerings in their uplifted hands to the divinities,* to whom they seem to be subject. Sometimes they are leading an animal. Their origin is obscure. They are sometimes considered hybrid monsters derived from Ta-urt, the Egyptian fertility or hippopotamus goddess, known in Crete, or from Babylonian demons, but, according to Nilsson, they were created by Minoan fancy and manifestly belong to some Minoan belief, perhaps to a popular one. It is also possible that they may represent human attendants masked with the heads of some animal servants of the divinities,* and dressed in animal hides, like some priestly figures in other Minoan representations.

Destructions of Palaces. The successive destructions of the Minoan palaces* and towns are among the few historical events we know something
about from Bronze Age* Crete, which otherwise possesses no useful literary or figurative evidence. The Early Palaces,* founded ca. 1900 B.C.,
were destroyed perhaps by violent earthquakes* or even possibly by internal warfare* about 1700 B.C., although perhaps not all at the same
time. After those major disasters new palaces rose more splendid than before. It is basically the excavated ruins of these later palaces which can be
seen today at various sites, although parts of the early palaces remain. It
has been suggested that an early immigration of Greeks, or of Luwians
from southern Asia Minor, a people related to the Hittites and the later
Lycians, took place during this time, but these suggestions were rather
unconvincing. Probably earthquakes* caused severe damage, especially
at Knossos,* after the beginning and before the end of the sixteenth
century B.C. This is the point—ca. 1575 B.C.—at which Evans has placed
the division between Middle* and Late* Minoan, a time which coincides
with a major historical event in Egypt, the expulsion of the Hyksos rulers
and the beginning of the New Kingdom.

The new palaces were finally destroyed about 1450 B.C. or slightly
earlier, but the catastrophe spared Knossos,* which suffered less serious
damage. There is proof of a violent major destruction including burning,
occurring throughout the island on a tremendous scale, which is marked
by deposits containing pottery of the Late Minoan IB period. All the
towns were destroyed, and the ruins of some of them such as Pseira,*
Mochlos* and the palace at Zakros* were afterwards abandoned and
never reoccupied. The palace at Phaistos,* which had been already restored after minor damage perhaps from an earthquake, was now completely destroyed by fire. This great desolation of the island was perhaps
the result of an invasion from the Greek Mainland and a subsequent large
scale war. It has been suggested that Knossos was spared by the invaders,
because in the following period the Achaians were installed there and
ruled the whole island.

Recently it has been considered that the volcanic eruption of Thera
may have been the cause of the destruction (see Thera*). The palace at
Malia* was not restored, but that of Knossos was, and stood as the sole
major palatial center, controlling affairs all over Crete. The palace at
Phaistos* may have still been partly used, though perhaps not as a palace.
Finally, the last Knossian palace was destroyed by fire, about 1400 according to Evans, or probably a little later, about 1375 B.C.

The final destruction was again caused either by earthquakes* or,
more likely, by a war, possibly waged by the ascending power of this
time, Mycenae. Knossos was never rebuilt or reoccupied again as a palace. With its fall the ruling Achaian dynasty and its apparatus of state in
Crete seems to have ceased to exist. It has been assumed that very small
parts of the Knossian palace—and perhaps also of the other palaces—
remained in use in a way, reoccupied by "squatters," and finally abandoned before 1200 B.C.

DEUKALION see **IDOMENEUS.**

Diktaian Cave. Zeus* was reputedly born in the Diktaian Cave on Mount Dikte in Eastern Crete. He was either nourished by a goat (see Amaltheia*) or a pig, or bees and doves, and was entrusted to the Kouretes.* The site of the Diktaian Cave is not unknown, although, according to Hellenistic* traditions, it is located east of the isthmus of Hierapetra.* This cave has been identified with the Psychro* Cave on the plateau of Lasithi,* obviously correctly, although there are some sceptics. Zeus was known as Diktaian in Classical times, and is so called on a Knossian tablet. Diktaian Zeus, like Welchanos,* was represented as a beardless, youthful god.

Other stories are attached by legend to the Diktaian Cave. There the famous seer Epimenides* slept for several years and had visions; Minos* used to descend into the cave to receive and return with the laws of Zeus. According to a tradition, the cave was the scene of Zeus's union with Europa.*

DIKTYNNA. The name Diktynna means "she of Mount Dikte" or "she who is worshipped on Mount Dikte"; a fanciful Greek etymology derived her name from the word *diktyon* ("net"). Diktynna was a huntress and a goddess of the wild countryside and mountains. She was worshipped in various cult-centers in Greece including Athens and Sparta, and outside it as far as Marseille. Especially venerated in Western Crete, she had a temple at Lisos,* and another, more famous, at the end of the rugged promontory of Spatha west of Kydonia* (see figure 99, right), the Diktynnaion. This sanctuary was guarded with hounds, which the Cretans boasted to be as strong as bears, as we learn from the account of the visit of the famous Apollonios of Tyana. The sanctuary was under the control of Kydonia,* but later, after the Roman conquest, the control was assumed by Polyrrhenia.* The revenues of the temple were used for public works such as the construction of roads.

The Diktynnaion was explored in 1942 by the Germans, Welter and Jantzen. The temple stood inside a large court surrounded by porticoes. The whole complex included two terraces. Several Ionic and Corinthian columns as well as an elaborate marble sima are visible. Diktynna was portrayed in the coinage* of various Cretan cities including Kydonia,* Polyrrhenia* and perhaps Phalasarna,* and later by the Roman province of Crete. In the calendar of Aptera* there was a month named after her (*Diktynnaios*). Diktynna, an obvious survival of a Minoan divinity, the Mistress of Animals, is closely related and sometimes identified with Artemis and especially Britomartis.* She kept for centuries her character as mountain-mother and guardian of initiates.

Disk from Phaistos see **Phaistos Disk.**

Dittany see **Flora.**

Divinities (Minoan). The main divinity in Minoan religion* and its central feature was an anthropomorphic female divinity, the Mother Goddess, in fact a version of the Great Goddess of Fertility which dominated the Oriental religions in early times (Isis of Egypt, Ishtar of Mesopotamia and the corresponding Astarte of Syria), and survived in later beliefs (Magna Mater). The question as to whether the Minoan religion* was monotheistic is immaterial, since this term reflects a theological conception rather than an actual religious belief. In any case, the question is considered unanswerable. Despite the fact that this appears contradictory to our modern principles, the goddess seems to have been at the same time both many and one. She evidently was worshipped under various manifestations dominating all spheres of existence; it has been assumed that a group of goddesses of a similar nature which survived in later Greek times, existed but were worshipped under different names, such as Diktynna,* Britomartis* and Ariadne.*

The goddess as Mistress of Trees and Mountains (Mother of the Mountains) and Lady of the Wild Animals (*Potnia theron,* called later by the Greeks, Mistress of Animals) is portrayed variously associated with animals, birds* and snakes (see Snake Cult*), perhaps revealing herself in their form, and further with the sacred tree and pillar (see Tree and Pillar Cult*), the poppy, the lily and especially the double axe,* her omnipresent symbol. In Classical Greek times her attributes were divided among several goddesses who in a way continued her cult: Athene took her snakes, Aphrodite her doves, Artemis her stags. She dominates the whole of nature: earth, sea, mountain, sky. She is at the same time a huntress and a household goddess (see Snake Goddess*), a goddess of sports and vegetation, Mother and Maid. She dominates life, but also death as Lady of the Underworld. Very important is her marine aspect (see Shells;* Ships*). Her prominence evidently reflected the important social position of woman* in Minoan times. When represented in seals,* rings, and figurines,* the goddess, intimately connected with palace life, wears the latest fashion of the contemporary women's dress; sacral robes are offered to her (see Temple Repositories*).

With her is closely associated a subordinate god, who is considered her consort or son. A youthful god of vegetation, dying and resurrecting annually and connected with agrarian magic, is related to her. As a male being he personified the seed, following the vegetation cycle and the seasonal death and rebirth of nature. This god often appears armed. In later times the Greeks conceived of this god as the youthful Cretan Zeus,* son of Rhea. By the end of the Bronze Age,* under the influence of the Achaians,* there is an increasing tendency to give the male gods a superior status, a fact reflecting the corresponding social changes in the status of men and women. Nevertheless, the chief divinity is still a goddess, now portrayed with upraised arms, as we see her in some late shrines.*

Diodoros, the Greek historian who lived in the first century B.C., noted that many of his contemporaries thought that the main Greek gods came from Crete.

Dorians. After they had moved to the south of the Greek Mainland at the end of the second millenium B.C., infiltrating in small clans during a succession of invasions over a number of years, the Dorians finally overcame the crumbling Mycenaean states and their diminished populations, and established their rule in the late twelfth century B.C. In fact, being themselves Greeks like the Achaians,* the Dorians were not really alien conquerors but a fresh wave of Greeks speaking a different dialect. The Greeks recognized three branches of their race, according to their three chief dialects: the Dorians, the Ionians, and the Aeolians. Some of the Mainland Dorians extended overseas into Crete and other islands, and established themselves there, completing the downfall of the local political power.

Tektamos, son of Doros and grandson of Hellen (the "Greek"), with a mixed band of Dorians, Achaians and Pelasgians, is the legendary founder of the first Dorian dynasty in Crete. This was associated in the Greek tradition with the Return of the Herakleidai, the "sons of Herakles," possibly an Achaian tribal group. Tektamos was succeeded by his son Asterios. Homer describes the island as having ninety cities and many languages (dialects?) mingled one with another. Five peoples are mentioned—Eteocretans,* Kydonians, Pelasgians, Achaians* and Dorians.

The Dorians were customarily organized as a league of three tribes, the Hylleis, descended from Hyllos, a son of Herakles; the Dymanes, who adored Apollo; and the Pamphyloi, "men-of-all-tribes," whose divinity was Demeter.* The Dorians preserved their tribal customs and institutions for many centuries; in fact, here were the roots of the Cretan social institutions of the Classical period. Their language (see Greek Language*) was Doric Greek. Of course we must bear in mind that *Dorian* or *Doric* is a linguistic term denoting a dialect, not a national tongue. The Dorians dispersed over Crete and established their supremacy. Eventually city-states emerged, self-governing political units with their own traditions, laws, cults, calendar* and coinage,* occupying a closely settled area, separate independent communities usually protected by hilly frontiers against their neighbours (see map 1). A minority of the older population took to the mountains in order to escape from trouble and preserve their independence, and founded cities of refuge on high inaccessible places such as Karphi* and Vrokastro.*

The coming of the Dorians almost coincides with the beginnings of the Dark Ages.* The Dorians did not introduce iron,* with which they managed to overcome the bronze armoury of the Achaians,* as some early scholars thought, neither is the Geometric style* their artistic expression in vase-painting.

Doric Style See **Columns.**

Double Axe. The bronze double axe is the most common Minoan tool, a heavy affair of solid-cast metal well balanced for swinging. Possessing two blades it did not have to be sharpened as often as a single axe, as there was a sharp spare blade at hand. It is often found in palaces* and houses*

39. Functional double axe with incised decoration

or even in the fields and quarries. The axe has been mistaken by several scholars as a weapon, mainly because in later times it was the traditional weapon of the legendary Amazons. Nevertheless, in Crete and the Mycenaean Mainland the double axe was undoubtedly a woodsman's, carpenter's, shipbuilder's and mason's tool, and a very efficient and popular one. Minoan double axes of a functional shape (figure 39) have a round shaft hole, which in later examples, influenced by the Mainland, becomes oval, a technical improvement which keeps the wooden handle from turning in the shaft. The sacrifice of the bull (see Religion*) was perhaps done at first stage with a double axe (figure 40), as was the custom in Classical Athens.

The double axe in a purely ceremonial, non-functional form is intimately related to religious beliefs, being the ubiquitous symbol of Minoan religion,* evidently a cult object representing the Mother Goddess her-

40. Bull's head incised on a functional double axe

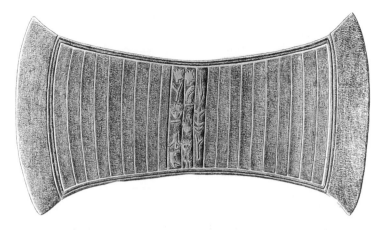

41. Inscribed votive double axe from the Arkalochori Cave (*after Bouphides*)

self. The interpretation of it being a thunder-weapon of the subordinate male god (see Divinities, Minoan*), based on later Anatolian examples, is today obsolete, as the evidence does not support it. The original association of the female divinity with this tool is still a matter of conjecture.

Votive or ceremonial axes with curved blades, of sizes varying from the huge to the miniature, are often recovered from shrines* and sacred caves* or even villas* like that at Nirou,* where the largest existing examples were found. From the Arkalochori cave come a considerable number of gold (see figure 26), silver, and mainly copper or bronze axes of a nonutilitarian shape made of a hammered sheet of metal and engraved with various linear or spiral designs. One of them is inscribed with fifteen hieroglyphic signs (figure 41). A magnificent large axe of bronze with redoubled edges to emphasize the shape, covered with intricate foliage patterns, was recovered from the palace at Zakros.*

Ceremonial axes are often seen in pictorial representations between the sacral horns,* or handled by ministers of the cult (figure 42), or

42. Cult double axes handled by a priestess on a Late Minoan III mould

mounted on stone bases in a prominent position, as in the religious
scenes on the sarcophagus* of Hagia Triada,* which has divine birds*
perching on the axes. A number of such stepped stone bases have been
found in several cult rooms. The axes were often combined with other
symbols such as the sacral knot.* Very often they were painted on vases
or pithoi* and larnakes,* or engraved on talismanic seals,* or carved in
miniature examples in various stones. One of the Knossian frescoes*
shows a columnar shrine with sacral horns* and three wooden columns*
with pairs of double axes stuck on each side of the capital. A shaft tomb
near Knossos has been cut in the form of a double axe, evidently for the
protection of the dead it contained.

   The double axe in a simplified rectilinear form also figures among the
signs of the Linear A* and B* scripts, as well as among the masons' marks*
incised on walls and pillars.* The famous Labyrinth is considered as "the
dwelling of the double axe" (see Labyrinth*). The tradition created by this
sacral symbol was so strong that we find small clay or bronze examples
among the votive offerings of early Iron Age* sanctuaries, not only in
Crete (see Eileithyia*) but also in the Mainland, in places such as Olympia
and Delphi.

Drainage Systems. In Minoan buildings and roads, covered drains and
open channels of clay and stone conducted away waste and rain water.
The well-known drainage system of the palace at Knossos,* a further development of the earlier period, was complex and highly advanced. Clay
pipes of an average length of seventy-five centimetres (30 inches), with
collars and stop-ridges, neatly fitting into each other and with their joints
tightly cemented, were found beneath the floors sometimes over three
metres (about 10 feet) deep. Evans* thought that they had supplied running water into the palace from springs outside. Such refinements show a
high degree of engineering ability, astonishing for this early time, indeed
an achievement of Minoan architecture.* It is considered that a pressure
system was probably used at Knossos, as each pipe section tapered
sharply toward one end, thus increasing the speed of flow and preventing the accumulation of any sediment. On the other hand a series of stone
ducts arranged in ramifying systems dealt with the problem of surface
waters. Some stone-lined drains provided with manholes and shafts
were large enough to admit a man to descend and enter the drain. Indoor
latrines provided with wooden seats and facilities for flushing the basin
were connected with these drans(?) As Evans* wrote, "as an anticipation
of scientific methods of sanitation, the system of which we have here the
record has been attained by few nations even at the present day".

   Clay pipes brought down the rainwater from the flat roofs. At the palace of Zakros* and other places the elaborate network possessed short
narrow U-shaped clay drains. A stone conduit had the shape of a trough.
At Gournia* and Palaikastro* the streets had stone-built channels. Drains
can be also seen at Myrtos* and Vrokastro.* It is clear that the existence of
these public drainage systems implies a communal organization under a
central authority. One of the storehouses of the "palace" at Gournia*

characteristically contained a supply of new water pipes.

Dreros. Dreros, a city-state of Classical Greek times, is near modern Neapolis.* Like the neighbouring Lato,* it was erected on a saddle between two peaks, on the slope of Mount Kadistos. This archaic city had an *agora* (market-place) about 30 by 40 metres (99 by 132 feet) in size, including some bordering steps along the southern side and a retaining wall of the eighth century B.C., and further a huge open cistern eight metres deep, and probably a *prytaneion* ("town-hall"), the ruins of which are of the same date. The contemporary temple of Apollo is one of the earliest known temples to survive in the whole of Greece. The excavation of Marinatos brought to light a single rectangular room of small stones about 11 by 7 metres (36 by 23 feet) in size, with a vestibule but with no obvious entrance, as the north corner had been destroyed by a modern kiln. Perhaps it was entered through a porch. In the center is an *eschara*, a sort of sunken hearth in the form of a square pit lined with stone slabs which was found filled with ashes. It was flanked by two axial columns supporting the flat roof. These columns, being of wood, have disappeared, and only one round stone base was found at its original place. Beyond, but more to the west corner, was a table of offerings. Against the wall stood an altar filled with young goat horns, reminiscent of the altar at Delos, where Theseus* celebrated the Crane Dance (see Dance*). In the southwest corner a ledge or shelf about one metre high held the famous sphyrelaton* statuettes of Apollo (see figure 173) and two smaller female figures. A bronze *gorgoneion* was found nearby. The features of this temple remind us of the little shrines* of Minoan times.

A famous Dorian inscription, containing an oath taken by youths, is an important social document dating to ca. 220 B.C.; among other things we learn that the young men swore loyalty to their own city and to the allied Knossos,* and enmity to Lyttos,* its dangerous neighbour. Another inscription contains the oldest constitutional law of Greece, and another one is bilingual, with a Greek and an Eteocretan* text, written in the Greek alphabet.* In 228 B.C. and later, a considerable number of Drerians emigrated to Miletos in Asia Minor, and the city lost its importance.

Dress (Cretan). The peculiar features of Minoan dress* disappeared with the Bronze Age. During Classical times the dress of the Cretans was similar to that of other Greeks, as it was later during the Byzantine period* (figure 43). The Turkish occupation* brought a total change of fashion to the Cretan dress, the style of which lasted until the first years of the twentieth century, and was then gradually abandoned by the majority of the peasants; it is worn today only by performers of folk-dances or by a few old men in villages. The dress, which is considered as showing a great sense of style, consists of blue baggy breeches (*salvari* or *vraka*, today usually abbreviated into simple riding breeches) embroidered with black or golden cords, common all over the Aegean islands; a waistcoat; a head-

43. Medieval Cretan from Sphakia (*after Dapper*)

cloth (traditionally black as a sign of mourning for the Turkish occupation*) often with a fringe hanging in front; a long broad silk belt; and well-
cut riding boots of white or black leather. Traditional also is a silver-
sheathed dagger with a handle of a peculiar shape, carried in the belt, a
feature which can be seen in the Minoan attire. Winter dress comprises a
heavy, hooded cloak of unbleached wool.

Dress (Minoan). The basic garment of the Cretan man in Minoan times—
as depicted in frescoes,* seals* and clay or bronze figurines*—was a loincloth folded around the waist or kept in place by a large girdle or belt of
metal or leather, occasionally with a dagger thrust into it (figure 44).
Tight waists were very fashionable, but looser belts were occasionally
worn by elderly men (figure 45). The loincloth, of various shapes according to fashion, might be worn as a kilt, often embroidered and sometimes
rather long, or folded under the groin. Above the waist men normally
went bare. A characteristic feature of the Minoan male dress is the codpiece, which could be worn with a belt alone and no loincloth. The loincloth, in turn, could be worn without the codpiece. The early codpiece is
straight and narrow, but later becomes wide and very prominent.
Occasionally a kind of apron was worn over the loincloth.

A change of fashion appears in the dress of the Keftiu* pictures—a
precious source of information—in Egyptian tombs. Curious scaled
cloaks or cuirasses, animal hides (a characteristic survival of earlier times,

44. Clay figurine from the peak sanctuary of Petsophas

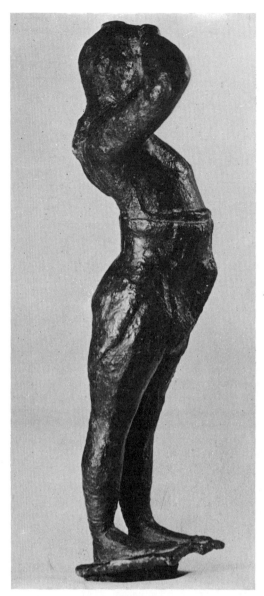

45. Bronze statuette of an elderly
worshipper from Tylissos

when they were surely men's first garments), probably the skins of sacrificed animals, and long single-piece robes, perhaps taken over from the
Orient, are some of the various special male garments of a religious character appearing in ritual scenes.

Highly sophisticated and gorgeous was the dress of the Minoan woman.* Early representations of votaries from peak sanctuaries* show long
flaring skirts with tight girdles wound double round the waist, and short-
sleeved, very low-cut bodices leaving the breasts bare, with collars rising

46. Head of a worshipper from Mochlos

in a high triangular peak at the back of the neck, reminiscent of some Italian Renaissance dresses. An excellent representation of the female court dress with all its details in form and colour can be seen on the well-known faience* statuettes of the Snake Goddess* (see figure 169). Together with them, some votive robes have been found in the Temple Repositories* at Knossos.* Skirts were often depicted with flounces, attributed to Mesopotamian inspiration; sometimes they show an elaborate decoration, representing patterns woven into the woolen cloth* or with the more elaborate designs probably embroidered. Some of the later skirts seem to have been divided but probably were not; others have a marked V in front. Short skirts were also worn, as elaborate garments were obviously suitable for certain occasions only, such as court meetings and ritual ceremonies. We may even assume the existence of some very elementary dress for everyday life and work. Maidens wore male dress when taking part in the bull-games.* Some figurines* show peaked hats or wide disk-like caps (figure 46). Capes offered protection against sun or rain, and heavy wool cloaks against rain and cold. Men and women usually went barefoot. Occasionally boots and sandals, both often with turned-up toes or high ankle straps, are seen, probably worn outdoors. The Greek word *sandalon* is of pre-Greek origin and has been considered as possibly Minoan. Jewellery* was freely used.

Early Minoan Period. In the course of this vigorous period (ca. 2800 until 2200-2000 b.c.: see Chronology*), the first one of the Bronze Age,* which succeeds the Neolithic period* and a transitional "Sub-Neolithic" phase, the population of Crete seems to have been joined by fresh waves of immigration of uncertain provenance, probably from Anatolia. Prosperous proto-urban settlements were erected in Eastern Crete. Renfrew has calculated 111 sites and 5.1 sites per thousand square kilometres for this period, during which Crete made a brilliant entry into the circle of the civilized world of antiquity (see map 2). The main social unit seems to have been the clan. Metallurgy* was introduced, the economy* developed rapidly, and foreign relations were maintained, especially with the Cyclades, Kythera (where a colony was founded before the end of the period), and the Near East. Specialized craftsmen such as metal-workers, jewellers reaching a high degree of perfection in the art of jewellery,* and lapidaries creating for the first time elegant stone vases* appeared, along with very skilled cutters of seals.* The architecture* of this period is well illustrated in the houses* at Vasiliki* and Myrtos* in Eastern Crete. The inhabitants of this latter settlement probably felt rather insecure, for their building complex was defined by a continuous outer wall with only two easily defended entrances.

The ossuaries at Palaikastro,* Gournia* and Archanes,* the house-tombs at Mochlos,* the primitive chamber-tombs* at Hagia Photia* and chiefly the circular or tholos tombs* in or around the Mesara Plain* such as those at Platanos,* Apesokari* and Lebena* represent the funerary architecture (see Burial Customs*). Based on the 111 known settlements and their estimated size, Renfrew has calculated that the approximate population of the island was 75,000 with a density of 9.18 per square kilometre, but of course many more sites will be discovered.

Pottery* was still handmade and varied considerably in different areas. Characteristic of this time are the burnished and incised Pyrgos ware* with the impressive chalice shape (see figure 149), the painted Hagios Onouphrios ware* (see figure 80), and the mottled Vasiliki ware.* Rich collections of vessels come from Kanli Kastelli, Lebena* and Hagia Photia.* At the beginning a dark-on-light decoration dominates, to be substituted at the end of the period by a reverse conception, the light-on-dark decoration. Human figurines* were generally not essentially different from those of the Neolithic period,* while stylized Cycladic figurines of marble were imported and imitated. Crete had many links with the Cyclades, at first taking an active part in a kind of common South Aegean civilization, but soon became more clearly differentiated. Weapons* of the time were chiefly copper or bronze triangular daggers, while tools* were surprisingly rare. Religion* and cult probably took a more concrete form, while social organization became more centralized, leading to the succeeding period which saw the emergence of the palaces.*

Early Palaces. The First or Early Palaces arose about 1900 B.C. or a little earlier, at the end of the Middle Minoan IA phase, roughly marking the end of the Early Minoan period* and the beginning of the zenith of Minoan architecture* and civilization.* Their plan owes certain limited features to Oriental models (see Palaces*). Their founding was the result of the evolution of the Early Minoan society and the expansion of its economy.* These palaces suffered a severe destuction* and were replaced by the Second or Later Palaces after about 1700 B.C.

At Knossos a small section of the Early Palace can be seen in the northeast quarter of the site, where all remains of the Later Palace have been lost by erosion. The general plan consisted of a large rectangular court (see Central Courts*) surrounded by a number of isolated blocks of buildings, often with rounded corners, which Evans named *insulae*. The north entrance had in front a long paved court and was flanked by two strongly walled towerlike blocks; the western one, built of large masonry with rounded corners, had deep foundations enclosing small cellars known as the "dungeons" (see Palace at Knossos,* *North Keep*). These semi-independent *insulae* had open passages between them, many of which probably later became corridors. To the west another court was approached by means of a ramp (see Palace at Knossos*, *West Court*). Here as at Phaistos and Malia, the Early Palace seems to have been similar to the later one in the main outlines of its plan. Even architectural details such as the set-backs or recesses of the facades are similar. The great Stepped Portico* was built during this period.

At Phaistos* the ruins of the Early Palace (see figure 130) were levelled after a great destruction by fire. A section of it, in excellent preservation, has been excavated deep below the level of the later one. Behind the facade of the palace on the West Court was a three-roomed shrine, of which the central room was larger and rose higher than the side ones, as often occurs with such tripartite shrines.* In this shrine stood a low rectangular table of offerings with a hollow in the middle for collecting the liquids offered; other cult objects including a triton-shell were found. The middle room contained a bench for cult objects and a small rectangular trough. Behind the north room, which included a stone bench with a grinding slab for corn, was a place of sacrifice with a sunken altar.* The ruins of this shrine were covered by the floor of the raised and enlarged West Court of the later palace. A branch of the ceremonial causeway of the court ran toward a propylon with a central column. The adjoining wing of the Early Palace included ramps and a tower-like structure.

At Malia* the palace seems to have consisted of groups of rooms which were functional parts of a building conceived as an architectural unit, and not of isolated blocks like the Knossian *insulae*.

Several remains of the older palace were found also at Zakros.*

Earthquakes. The only active volcano in Greece is that of Thera* in the Cyclades, not far from Crete, but earthquakes affect many parts of Greece. Crete, being on very unstable ground, shows a peculiar liability to violent seismic shocks. Statistics prove that Crete suffers two severe earthquakes every century with minor harmless seismic activities every year.

It is supposed that earthquakes caused the destruction of many of the Minoan palaces* and cities. The clearest evidence is that of two small private houses at Knossos* adjacent to the palace and separated from each other by a narrow paved street, the so-called House of the Fallen Blocks and the House of the Sacrificed Oxen. These houses were destroyed by great blocks hurled from the neighbouring wall of the palace itself, some of them weighing more than a ton and measuring over 20 feet (6 metres) in length. The first house, perhaps belonging to a stone cutter, included an L-shaped room with a large window on the west wall, while the second one, slightly larger, with four rooms, yielded the heads of two large-horned oxen and some fragmentary tripod altars. According to a daring suggestion by Evans, the inside of the pillar crypt of the great Temple-Tomb* near Knossos* gives evidence of earthquake victims.

Great earthquakes and consequent catastrophes were recorded in Nero's time (66 A.D.) and later (251 A.D. and 375 A.D.). Herakleion* has been ravaged many times during the last 500 years. The earthquake of 1508 is vividly described in a letter of the Venetian ruler of the island, who wrote that "the earth gave forth hideous roarings which accompanied the crash of the falling houses. These were tossed like ships in a storm and not only moved sideways, but seemed to leap up." The earthquake of 1856 had 1200 victims; out of 3620 houses only 18 were left standing.

Economy in Minoan Crete. Bronze Age* economy was basically dependent on agriculture.* The economy of the Neolithic period* was continually developed throughout the Early Minoan period* and later. Transport* evolved along with navigation (see Ships*), industries* were created. Metallurgy* developed rapidly as did other technologies, since specialized workers could be maintained from the surplus agricultural production. The economy advanced peacefully along with arts and crafts, without internal strife or threat from overseas, where trade* was expanded. Farming settlements grew into larger communities and palace economies emerged. Production of luxury goods increased. A form of money was necessary long before coinage* was introduced, but copper ingots* do not seem to have played this role as it was believed, although eventually they could have been employed as a unit in transactions, weighed out against other commodities. Goods were consigned by the use of seals* and clay sealings,* and registered in magazines* by means of inventories. The economic expansion led to a splendid flourishing of architecture:* the construction of public engineering works, such as aqueducts, bridges and roads, and mainly of great palaces,* which became redistributing economic centers and focal points of centralized organization and authority. Social structure* took a definite form and economy a marked bureaucratic character.

After the arrival of the Achaians* wealth was increasingly concentrated in the hands of ruling groups who controlled the technical resources, and the economy became extensively centralized, militarized and lopsided, as Willetts observed. The absence of any change, the expansion of the system to other territories by conquest, and the application of technology to warfare* led to downfall and eventual collapse, which coincided with the arrival of the Dorians* and the general decay of the Bronze Age societies of the Mediterranaean.

Education. Virtually nothing is known about education in Bronze Age* Crete. It seems certain that literacy was very limited, although probably not restricted to a class of professional scribes (see Writing*). Nevertheless we may assume that children received some kind of education or training, probably of a practical and religious nature.

On the other hand many literary sources are very informative as to the education in Classical Greek times. Youths were compelled to join one of the training bands known as *agelai.** The education was of a traditional kind: besides reading, writing and music* there was chiefly physical training: hunting, exercise, unarmed combat, archery,* in which the Cretans reputedly excelled, armed fighting to music,* and especially military training and the practise of hard living. Thus youth learned to value arms above everything and their education was drawn up with a view to war. An *apodromos* was a young man, probably under twenty years of age, who still did not have the right to participate in the public athletic exercises of the gymnasium, the *dromos,* and be trained there, in contrast to the *dromeus* ("runner") who had acquired this right.

A kind of mock-marriage by abduction of a younger boy, presumably of some 14 to 16 years of age, chosen by an older boy, called a *philetor,* was customary. The abduction took place at an appointed day and after a mock-resistance made by the relatives, who had already given their consent. The abduction was followed by two months of seclusion, feasting, hunting, and ritual giving of presents and sacrifices. The abducted boy returned to the city, was taken to the *andreion* ("Men's House") of the abductor, and was given more presents, including military equipment, a drinking-cup and an ox which was sacrificed to Zeus.* He was called by a special name, *parastathens* ("one placed beside"), which marked his new distinguished position, and was allowed to dress better than the others, in garments which were presented by his lover. These boys received special favours and honours in races and dances.* It was considered a disgrace for boys who were handsome or of distinguished family to fail to obtain lovers. This custom, according to Willetts, may hide a perverse reminiscence of the Minoan sacred marriage beneath its idealization of sodomy. In any case, according to Plato,* the myth of the abduction of Ganymedes by Zeus* was said to have originated in Crete.

Eggshell Ware see **Kamares Ware.**

Egypt (Relations with). Crete was in contact with Egypt as early as the third millenium B.C. These two great civilizations of antiquity were geographically near enough to be mutually influenced by each other—especially Crete by Egypt—yet they were separated by the Mediterranean basin far enough from each other so that Crete, much smaller in territory and population, could avoid being culturally and politically dependent on Egypt, and was allowed instead to develop its own magnificent culture. The shapes of some of the stone vases* of the Early Minoan period* seem to have been influenced by Egyptian prototypes, as well as some early seals.* Of course, part of the Egyptian influence might have been exerted indirectly through Syrian and Palestinian ports.

The early centuries of the second millenium B.C., corresponding to the Middle Kingdom in Egypt, show an extensive intercourse with Crete. Several signs of the Minoan Hieroglyphic script* seem to have been modelled on Egyptian hieroglyphics. Fragments of Minoan pottery* found in Kahun and Hagareh may reflect the presence of Cretan artisans there, engaged in the construction of a pyramid for Pharaoh Senusret II (1906-1888 B.C.). There is ample evidence of extensive trade,* including both exports* and imports.* A visit of Egyptian ships to Crete is mentioned in a text of the Middle Kingdom. Several Egyptian objects* have been recovered in Crete. Minoans were known as Keftiu* and elaborately depicted in Egyptian tombs, while Late Minoan I vases turned up in other tombs.

This intercourse resulted in a considerable Egyptian influence in art* and perhaps in religion.* Very characteristic is the Egyptian Ankh sign, the symbol of life, often found in Crete in association with the double axe* and the sacral knot.* Egyptian painting conventions were reflected in Cretan frescoes.* Minoan jewellery* displays several techniques probably learned from Egypt or from Syria. Motifs inspired by Egyptian plants such as the papyrus, or by waterfowl or water backgrounds, depicting typically Nilotic scenes, found their way into Cretan vase-painting and jewellery.*

Minoan designs also influenced Egyptian art. It has been assumed that Minoan painting influenced the Egyptian painters of the New Kingdom, and especially the nonconformist artists of the Amarna period (ca. 1372-1354 B.C.). Another possible Cretan influence concerns the spiral decoration, especially the rapport designs and quadruple spirals. After the coming of the Iron Age,* Egypt once more came into close contact with Crete and Greece and its influence became decisive in early Greek art (see Dedalic Style*).

Egyptian Objects in Crete. A considerable number of imported Egyptian objects have been recovered in Crete, a fact demonstrating long relations with Egypt.* The earliest—apart from some Proto-Dynastic pieces found in sub-Neolithic levels at Knossos—are fragments of a faience* bowl and a faience necklace recovered in Early Minoan tombs at Mochlos.* Egyptian scarabs* of various dynasties are not rare. Two ivory* boys from Palaikastro* may be of Egyptian manufacture, unless they were excellent local imitations. Other imported pieces are an ivory* sphinx of the XIIIth Dynasty from Malia* and a few faience* and stone vases,* several inscribed with royal names, which may have been presents from Egyptian Pharaohs or nobles. Some of them are of earlier date than the Minoan

47. Couple in a vessel from the sanctuary of Eileithyia at Inatos

context in which they were found and, unless they were acquired as antiques, they might represent a Cretan heirloom, as has been suggested. A statue inscribed for User, wezir of the Pharaoh (XIIth Dynasty) and an alabaster* lid with the name of the Hyksos Pharaoh Khyan of the XVIIth Dynasty, one of the more important Hyksos kings of Egypt, have been found in the palace at Knossos.* From a Late Minoan IIIA tomb of the harbour-town of Knossos at Katsambas comes a fine alabaster* jar bearing an incised inscription referring to the great Pharaoh Thotmes III, whose reign had ended about fifty years before the pottery of this tomb was manufactured. From a tomb at Hagia Triada* comes the circular seal of Queen Ty, wife of Amenhotep III. Pieces of lesser importance were found all over the island in Minoan deposits.

The intercourse with Egypt again became extensive during the Orientalizing period.* The excavations of the sacred cave of Eileithyia* at Inatos* have yielded a considerable number of Egyptian objects including scarabs and figurines, dated to the Saitic period.

EILEITHYIA. Eileithyia, a daughter of Zeus and Hera, was the patron goddess of childbirth. Homer calls her *mogostokos*, "goddess of the pains of birth." She attended Leto when Apollo was born in Delos, where Leto took the kneeling position to give birth to the child, a position seen in several Greek figurines. Her cave at Amnisos* is mentioned by Homer (see Caves*). Her other cave in Crete, at Inatos* on the south coast, known from inscriptions referring to her as Eileithyia Inatia, has been identified and excavated by N. Platon and the author. Among the rich votive offerings, mostly belonging to the Geometric and Archaic periods,* were bronze vases, ivory* objects, clay double axes* demonstrating the survival of this holy Minoan symbol in later Greek times, models of boats, a figurine representing a man riding an ass, a considerable number of female figurines* in a state of pregnancy, and figurine couples represented in vivid scenes of lovemaking (figure 47). Evidently people would ask the goddess to be blessed with children. Notable are several Egyptian objects. A rare find was a wooden plaque, evidently once bearing an inscription or picture.

According to Willetts, the name Eileithyia is not Indo-European, a fact which strengthens the assumption of a direct descent from a Minoan goddess of childbirth, who in turn would have had an obvious origin in the midwife. Offerings of honey* to her are mentioned in the Knossos tablets* in the Linear B script,* if the reading *e-re-u-ti-ja* as Eleuthia (Eileithyia) is correct. The cult of the goddess was widespread all over Greece but especially in Crete, in cities such as Lato,* where she was the chief divinity, and Eleutherna,* which was probably named after her. The calendar* of Olous* included a month named Eleusynios or Elousinios.

Ekdysia see **Phaistos (City of).**

Eleutherna. Eleutherna, near modern Prines east of Rethymnon,* was one of the inland city-states of Dorian Crete. Its harbour on the north coast was perhaps called Pantomatrion. The city was probably named for the goddess Eileithyia.* It was also named Apollonia, and Apollo, whose cult here enjoyed prominence, was portrayed on the city's coinage,* as was Artemis, who was depicted as a huntress shooting with a bow and accompanied by a hound. Eleutherna was strongly fortified and could be approached from a single narrow passage protected by a high tower. Diogenes Apolloniates (ca. 460-390 B.C.), a philosopher and disciple of Anaximenes, was born here. He taught in Ionia and wrote about human physiology. His books attracted the attention of Aristotle.

Eleutherna was on various occasions either an enemy or an ally of Knossos.* In 220 B.C. it declared war against mighty Rhodes because of the murder of its citizen, Timarchos. After many adventures during the Lyttian War (see Lyttos*), Eleutherna was annexed by Polyrrhenia.* Later it strongly resisted the legions of Quintus Metellus (see Roman Occupation*). The town flourished also in Early Christian times and became the seat of a diocese. Eventually it was destroyed by the invading Saracens.

The ruins of the city include an aqueduct, a high tower, several huge and impressive pillared cisterns, forty metres deep, cut in the rock, and

48. Ancient bridge at Eleutherna

two bridges built without an arch (figure 48). An important female torso of the Dedalic style* was found in Eleutherna (figure 37).

EL GRECO see **Fodele.**

Elounda see **Olous; Spinalonga.**

Elyros. Elyros was a great city-state of Classical Greek times in Western Crete, founded by the mythical Phylakis and Philandros, children of Apollo and Akakallis,* and grandchildren of Minos* and Pasiphae.* It was situated near modern Rodovani, not far from the south coast, where it had two seaports, Lisos* and Syia.* It was among the thirty-one Cretan cities which in 183 B.C. made an alliance with Eumenes II, king of Pergamon. Elyros was included in the monetary union of Lisos,* Hyrtakina* and Tarrha.* The city flourished during the Roman and Early Christian periods and was eventually destroyed during the Arab conquest. Its ruins are still unexplored. Elyros was one of the Cretan cities which claimed to be the birthplace of the famous archaic poet Thaletas (see Music*).

EPIMENIDES. The Cretan Epimenides was surely the most famous of mystic seers, poets and miracle-priests of Archaic Greece. Although a semi-legendary figure, he is considered a historical person. According to tradition he slept for several years in the Diktaian Cave* and had visions. He was associated with Apollo and purificatory activities. A poem of an

Orphic character was ascribed to him (see Zeus*), but it has not survived. Epimenides was summoned to purify Athens after the murder of Kylon's followers in 632 B.C., and to introduce reforms and purificatory rites, as the Cretan Thaletas (see Music*) did for Sparta. According to legend he was associated with the great Athenian lawgiver Solon, as Thaletas was with Lykourgos.

Erimoupolis see **Itanos.**

Eschara see **Dreros.**

Eteocretans. The Eteocretans ("true Cretans") according to the Greek tradition were the reduced elements of the original pre-Greek population of Crete which survived into Classical times. They are first referred to by such an authority as Homer. They survived chiefly in the eastern part of the island, centered around the city of Praisos,* probably occupying the entire modern province of Siteia.* The Praisians notoriously had close links with the old Minoan stock. Other areas of refuge of the pre-Dorian population seem to have been the mountainous regions south of Chania* and those surrounding the plateau of Lasithi.* It seems that the Eteocretans continued to speak their own language and preserved their identity in historical times until the third century B.C., as attested by a few fragmentary inscriptions in which the "Eteocretan" language is written in the Greek alphabet.* Most of these inscriptions were found in the Praisos* area and belong to the sixth, fourth and third centuries B.C.; one of them was recovered at Dreros.*

Etia. At the hamlet of Etia near Armenoi in the the center of the province of Siteia* are the ruins of a fine Venetian villa, which is considered one of the best of the period of the Venetian occupation* in Crete. The manor, erected during the end of the fifteenth century, belonged to the nobleman De Mezzo. During recent years extensive reconstruction work has been done on it. One can enjoy a fine view from the terrace of the second floor. On a nearby summit to the south, Etiani Kephala, the remains of a Minoan peak sanctuary* were explored by the author.

EUROPA. According to Greek mythology, this Cretan heroine, who gave her name to the continent of Europe, was originally a Phoenician princess, daughter of Phoinix and Perimede, and sister of Kadmos and of the elder Minos. Her father, King Phoinix, was of divine origin as a son of Poseidon. Her name means "the wide-or dark-glancing one." Zeus* fell in love with Europa when he happened to see her collecting flowers with her playmates on the shore. Zeus transformed himself into a handsome bull and approached her in a friendly manner. Europa played with him and finally climbed upon his back; then suddenly the bull plunged into the sea and carried her off to Crete. The sacred marriage of Zeus and Europa was said to have taken place under an evergreen plane-tree (see Flora*) near a stream at Gortyn,* or inside the Diktaian Cave.* (We know from Theophrastos that in his time the famous plane-tree still survived, and it never shed its leaves, unlike others in the neighbourhood.) Europa then gave birth to Minos.*

Europa is perhaps connected with a moon-divinity (see Pasiphae*). The coinage* of Phaistos* and Gortyn* show her sitting in a willow tree; a bull or bull's head is also depicted. Other coins illustrate her riding on the bull; this remained one of the main types of coins of the Roman province of Crete.

EVANS. The discovery of the palace at Knossos* and, in a sense, of the Bronze Age* civilization of Crete was the achievement of Sir Arthur John Evans (1851-1941). Evans, Keeper of the Ashmolean Museum at Oxford, was a wealthy Englishman of immense learning, inventiveness, and strong if somewhat tyrannical character, according to Alsop. Evans, interested in primitive scripts, first went to Crete in 1894 in order to collect and study a fascinating class of ancient stones, which were inscribed, he believed, in a mysterious language (see Seals*). Evans began travelling around Crete, and in 1897 obtained a permit to continue the preliminary excavations begun at Knossos in 1878 by Minos Kalokairinos, an antiquarian from Herakleion.* In 1900 he was sole owner of the site of Knossos and he raised funds in England for continuing the work.

The main excavations were accomplished from 1900 to 1905 but were continued annually until 1914 and again after the First World War until 1932. His main collaborators were Duncan Mackenzie, a pottery expert, and also Theodore Fyfe, Piet de Jong, and, later, John Pendlebury. Evans' discoveries and interpretations were elaborately published in his great, richly illustrated work, *The Palace of Minos at Knossos* (1921–35). Other of his important works are *Cretan Pictographs, Scripta Minoa, Tree and Pillar Cult, The Prehistoric Tombs of Knossos,* etc. His terms concerning Minoan archaeology are so firmly established that they are not easily changed. Some of his reports and theories have since been challenged, but his pioneer work deservedly holds a high place in the history of archaeology.

Exports (Minoan). The main exports of Minoan Crete, a peaceful country evidently active in trade* and possessing its own ships* and a flourishing palatial economy,* were undoubtedly products such as olives and olive oil;* timber—probably chiefly cypress—from its rich forests,* exported to wood-poor Egypt; good wine;* and perhaps honey,* dried grapes and other surplus produce of agriculture.* Among the exports we must count textiles such as woolen cloth,* perhaps dyed with purple made from *murex* shell-fish, beans, dried herbs, wax of superior quality, and lichens used in Egypt for breadmaking. Pine and cedar resin, a material necessary in embalming, was also probably exported to Egypt, brought there by the ships of the Keftiu* (Cretans), as Egyptian sources inform us. The decorative Minoan vases were exported to various parts of the Mediterranean; perhaps the best known being the splendid Marine Style* jug now in Marseille, which had turned up in Egypt. Minoan vases have also been found at Troy and other parts of Asia Minor, and in Syria, Egypt and

49. Faience goat or antelope with her kids from the Temple Respositories

Cyprus. As Sinclair Hood remarked, Cretan pottery* was exported in response to a demand for it overseas, since it was the finest pottery in the civilized world of its day, as the pottery of the great trading cities like Corinth and Athens was to be later.

Faience. Faience, made by a technique apparently invented in W. Asia and extensively used in Egypt since the fourth millenium, was probably introduced to Crete before the end of the Early Minoan period.* Faience, which is a silica composition, consists of a core of quartz, covered with an alkaline vitreous glaze, which is, in fact, glass. The glaze was formed over the core during the process of firing. The objects were made by means of moulds. Faience was used for jewellery* such as beads and pendants, as well as for relief plaques, vases and statuettes, mostly brightly coloured. These artifacts, except the simplest, were made in the palace workshops. Not much has been found, since faience is a very perishable material. A good idea of the exterior appearance of Minoan houses is given by the so-called Town Mosaic, consisting of colored plaques (see Houses*).

The Temple Repositories* of the palace at Knossos* of about 1600 B.C. have yielded the richest existing collection of faience objects, including the appliqué reliefs of a cow suckling her calf, and a goat or antelope with her kids (figure 49), both extremely sensitive animal studies, marine creatures such as argonauts and flying fish; miniature models of votive robes and girdles adorned with floral designs; flower and fruit; and the famous statuettes of the "Snake-Goddesses" (see Snake Goddess*) or, later, priestesses entwined with snakes. In the palace at Zakros* a remarkable faience vase in the shape of an argonaut was discovered. Some inlays from Knossos and Phaistos* are inscribed with signs on the back. Some seals* and beads of solid glass were manufactured during the Late Minoan period.*

Fauna see **Animals** (Domestic); Animals (Wild).

Fibulae see **Metallurgy**.

Figurines. Among the earliest types of figurines in Crete is the well-known "Cycladic" type, made of marble in a very stylized form, usually with the arms folded across the waist and almost always representing women with the pubic triangle emphasized. This type, found in an area extending from Western Asia Minor to Malta, has been interpreted in a variety of ways. Other Cycladic examples were copied in bone. Another early type of figurine with close parallels in Egypt shows a very abstract body tapering down to a point. There are very few clay figurines of the third millenium (see Neolithic period*), but after 2000 B.C. they become common, recovered in great numbers from the peak sanctuaries,* almost always broken. Some were found in the early tholos tombs* of the Mesara Plain.*

These small hand-made figurines were coloured, but the colours have by now mostly disappeared. The custom, derived from Egypt, was to paint male flesh in dark colours (reddish merging to blackish) and female flesh in white; the same convention can be observed in fresco-painting (see Frescoes*). These Middle Minoan figurines are humble offerings in a simple but often extremely spirited style with a high degree of abstraction, which includes the face (figures 50 and 51). They always keep to a strictly frontal position. Very often these charming figures illustrate the elaborate female and simple male dress* of the time. Women usually show fantastic hairdresses and headwear (figure 52), whereas the men wear only a loincloth. The men are lithe of form with powerful shoulders and wasp waists, the Cretan ideal which is also illustrated in several frescoes.* Anatomical reality and body proportions are, as a rule, transcended by an impression of instantaneous movement, which is usually expressed only by various gestures of adoration.

Of special interest are the figurines representing various deformities caused by illness which were offered in order to obtain a cure from the divinity (see Peak Sanctuaries*). Whole herds of clay animals—usually cattle—were also recovered; some large oxen are hollow and were used as libation vases (see Rhyton*). After the decline of the peak sanctuaries,* figurines become much less popular. Two bull-shaped vases from Pseira* are remarkable because they are mould-made, unique for Minoan times. Much discussed is the interpretation of the so-called "sheep bells," with horns and a loop handle. Perhaps they were stylized models of votive robes.

In the Late Minoan III period a type of female figurine evolved, the so-called Household Goddess: the body above the waist, in a frontal

50. Worshipper from the peak sanctuary of Traostalos

mode of presentation, rests on a hollow wheel-made cylinder, a support which forms at the same time a long flaring skirt or a tubular crinoline. Such statuettes have been found at various shrines (see Gournia* and Karphi*). The goddess usually has both arms raised in a gesture of blessing. One of these statuettes from Gazi west of Herakleion,* over 2 feet 6 inches (75 centimetres) tall, has three opium poppy-heads on her crown, a fact with several possible religious implications (figure 53). Another example comes from the Shrine of the Double Axes (see Shrines*) at Knos-

51. Worshipper from the peak sanctuary of Traostalos

sos.* The goddess wears a sort of decorated jacket. Jewellery* is indicated by dots. The upraised hands are enormous, the palm of the right hand being turned outwards, that of the left inwards. The breasts are placed high, just below the throat. A bird perches on the head.

There are also small solid hand-made figurines, but we do not see among them the typical Mycenaean shapes. Sometimes figurines are combined in groups representing scenes, such as three women from Pal-

52. Worshipper from the peak sanctuary of Traostalos

aikastro* dancing with linked hands round a central figure playing a lyre (see Dance*). Some of the Minoan figurines rival in artistic value the bronze statuettes and must be counted among the most sensitive creations of Minoan art.*

After the coming of the Iron Age,* in the eighth and seventh centuries B.C., we find small solid handmade figurines of a coarse but interesting type, as well as larger, hollow, wheel-made figurines. Crete sees the rise and flourishing of the excellent Dedalic style,* the principles of which are the same in either stone or terracotta sculpture, including small figurines, (figure 54). There are also figures moulded in front but with a flat back forming a small plaque, dating to the seventh and sixth centuries. The mould, extremely rare in Bronze Age* Crete, was introduced ca. 700 B.C. from Syria or Cyprus and revolutionized the coroplast's art.

In Classical and later times, after Crete had lost its leading role in Greek art, Cretan figurines show no special value or originality, and copy artistic standards set in other parts of the Greek world such as Rhodes, Corinth and Attica, while after 425 B.C. local types evolved. In the fifth and fourth centuries the mould was in general use. The figurines are ei-

53. Household Goddess with raised hands from Gazi

ther solid with their backs flat, or hollow with a handmade back. In order
to avoid cracks during the firing, vents were left at the back of the hollow
figurines to let the hot air escape; these vents were sometimes rather large
and normally of a rectangular shape. In the Hellenistic period* there is
quite a different process: the principal and more difficult parts of a figurine—including the head, limbs and trunk—were made separately by
means of a mould, while the other parts were handmade; the whole was
assembled together and finished by hand. These figures are normally hollow and belong to the well-known Tanàgra Style which, originating in
Attica, can be found all over Greece from ca. 320 until 200 B.C. This style,
with its complete naturalism, illustrating standing, draped women and
girls and many other figures, is more artistically valid than the earlier
forms. The finds come mainly from Knossos* and Axos.*

54. Proto-Dedalic goddess from Gortyn

Filigree see **Jewellery.**

First Palaces see **Early Palaces.**

Fish and Fishing. Fishing must have contributed on a large scale to the
food supplies of the Bronze Age* Cretans. Smoking was certainly known,

55. Votive model of fish from the peak sanctuary of Traostalos

as well as drying and salting of the surplus catch. The offshore waters of the island yielded at least all the modern varieties of fish (figure 55), probably in an abundance unknown today, when one considers our pol-

56. Rock-cut fish tanks at Siteia

luted and exploited sea. Among these varieties are mullet, sea bass, sole, sargue, mackerel, parrot wrasse or scaros fish (*scarus cretensis:* a gold bead from Knossos* has its shape), tunny, lobster, eel, crab, sea perch, sprats, cuttle fish and of course delicacies like octopus, so prominent in later Minoan art.* Already from Neolithic deposits we find *murex* shell-fish, probably exploited more for its precious purple dye than for food. A variety of other shells* was also known. Sponges were also collected and used for different purposes, including the application of paint to walls and pottery.*

A variety of fishing methods was probably employed. A copper two-pronged fishing harpoon with midribs of Early Minoan date has been recovered at Hagios Onouphrios* near Phaistos* and a net-mending copper implement at Platanos.* Evidently fish-harpooning was not difficult in the clear coastal waters of Crete. At Hagia Photia* the author found a series of bronze fish hooks, probably the earliest examples in Crete. Lead and stone weights of a later date for the nets are also known. The famous Marine Style* in pottery* vividly depicts various sea creatures, as do some frescoes. Representations of flying fish on frescoes,* seals* (figure 158), and bronze inlays are rather impressive.

In regard to later times, of interest are some large rock-cut compartments at Mochlos,* Chersonesos* and Siteia* (figure 56), as well as the monumental one recently found near Hierapetra,* which were used as fish-tanks connected by an elaborate system of channels to the sea. These tanks date to the times of Roman occupation,* when people became extremely fond of seafood, a passion which developed into a positive mania, as many ancient anecdotes relate.

Flora. Cretan flora (see Agriculture*; Forests*) is among the most varied in Europe; it is, in fact, much richer than that of the Greek Mainland. There are 139 native plant species. A limited number of specimens of the evergreen plane-tree *(Platanus orientalis L., var. cretica)*, known in mythology (see Europa*) and referred to by authors such as Theophrastos and Varro, still exist in Crete; it is now a protected species. The island is famous for its unending variety of herbs and wild flowers, of which a list is given by Pliny. Some of them were depicted on Minoan frescoes* and vases (figure 57), such as the *Iris cretica*, the saffron flower, the beach narcissus and the white lily *(Lilium candidum)*, the Minoan sacred flower (see fig. 2). The goddess often appears in a field of lilies and is variously associated with them as well as with the poppy, a symbol of fecundity and an opium-producing plant, which perhaps was used in some ecstatic ritual. We may assume that in Bronze Age Crete as elsewhere in antiquity some form of herbal magic was practised, evidently by priestesses (see Woman, position of*), but no information about it was survived.

The Cretan dittany (today called *diktamnos, diktamos* or *erondas*, the true *Dictamnus creticus*) is a medicinal herb of great literary celebrity, referred to by authors such as Pliny, Aristotle and Theophrastos, the author of the first methodical treatise on botany. Virgil relates that when Aeneas was wounded by an arrow, his mother Venus (Aphrodite) went to Crete

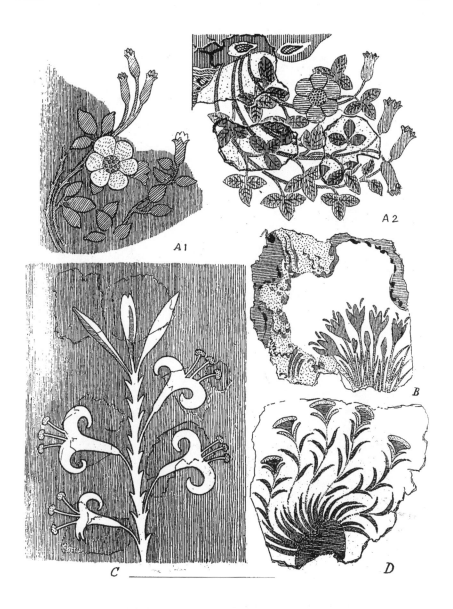

57. Floral types from the House of Frescoes at Knossos (*after Evans*)

to bring him this wonderful herb. According to Greek legends, it was eaten by wild goats to help them to eject poisoned arrows. The statues of Diktynna* were wreathed with dittany by women to help ease the pangs of childbirth. In fact this herb, steeped like tea, not only produces a pleasant drink, but when taken in large quantities at an early stage of preg-

58. Floral Style jug from the palace at Phaistos

nancy is an abortifacient, as Hippocrates informs us. Other plants of Cretan origin are *Lotus creticus, Althaea cretica* (hollyhock), *Eryngium creticum, Ophrys cretica* (mirror orchid) and many others.

Floral Style. The so-called Floral Style of Late Minoan IA pottery (ca. 1550-1500 B.C.) shows the Cretan love of purely natural subjects and marks the triumph of a forthright naturalism, which had been introduced during the previous period (see Pottery*). A black paint, often glossy, was used in an over-all decoration on a yellowish background. The motifs stemmed from contemporary frescoes.* Several forms of plants were represented gracefully, such as branches, leaves and flowers, or tangling grasses and reeds, rising from a line representing a rocky ground and sometimes arranged over the entire surface of the vase (figure 58). They perfectly adapted themselves to the vessel's form, which showed a new elegance. The papyrus plant was a motif taken over from Egypt.

Fodele. This picturésque village on the north coast west of Herakleion* was probably a harbour of Axos* in later Greek times (figure 59). According to a tradition the painter Domenicos Theotocopoulos, the famous El Greco, was born here in 1545, although Herakleion seems the more likely birthplace of this great European master, who, although he later emigrated to Spain and became a Roman Catholic, had his roots in the Cretan School of Painting* and never forgot his origins, signing his works in Greek.

Folk-art see **Popular Art.**

Forests. In antiquity Cretan hillsides and mountain slopes, today rocky and barren over extensive areas, were heavily forested with cypress, plane, fir, the Cretan maple and oak. Cedars are today almost extinct, but their existence in antiquity can be considered as sure, as place-names (*Kedros*) suggest and as ancient authors like Hippocrates, Pliny and Vitruvius explicitly attest. Even in Early Minoan houses* evidence was found that wall timbers had been used. During the Palatial era timber was much used in architecture* for columns,* wall timbers and roofing beams. Of course timber was used for the construction of ships* and carts. Still in Pliny's time the island was the very home of cypress. Even in more recent times Cretan cypress wood was extensively used to build ships for the Venetian navy as late as the sixteenth century.

During the Turkish occupation* and later the woods were felled and burned and the saplings ravaged by goats. Gradually erosion of soil followed upon deforestation. Unfortunately, very little has been done about it. As Pendlebury wrote, "the wanton destruction of the forests has altered the whole aspect....Crete, which was once one of the most fertile and prosperous islands of the Mediterranean, is now one of the rockiest and most barren." Indeed, the island is the victim of gross mistreatment by man. Nowadays most of the remaining wooded area is near Chania:* scrub, consisting of pine, chiefly *Pinus haricio* or *Pinus halepensis*, especially near Araden,* and chestnut, which appears at altitudes between 600 and 1000 metres (about 2000 to 3300 feet). Other parts of the island have small forests of oaks, carob, conifers, and *prinari* (evergreen oak). Vai,* near Itanos* in the extreme east, has a grove of wild palms (see Agriculture*).

Fortetsa see **Geometric Period; Orientalizing Period.**

Francocastello. This fine Venetian fortress was erected in 1371 at an iso-

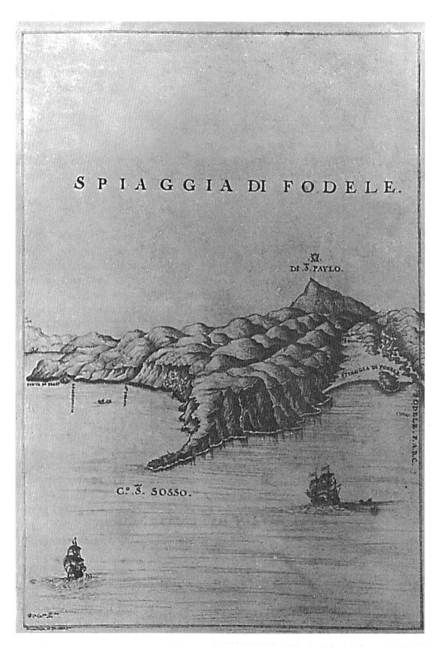

59. Fodele in 1615 (*after a Venetian map*)

lated place on the south coast of Sphakia* in Western Crete with a splendid view (figure 60). The fortress, a rectangular building with towers at the corners, was known as Castel Franco ("The Valiant Castle") to the Venetians. It had no settlement around it. In the revolt of 1828 the fortress was captured by the Cretans but shortly afterwards recaptured by the Turks after a fierce battle.

According to a persistent legend, at a certain time of the year and early in the morning there appears near Francocastello a procession of ghosts, the so-called *drosoulites* ("Dew Shadows"). The subject has often been investigated and various interpretations suggested, such as a mirage of a caravan from the African coast (which is impossible) or a mass self-hypnosis.

Frescoes. In the Early Minoan period* walls of houses* were coated with plaster* painted red (see Vasiliki*). From about 1700 B.C. walls of palaces* and villas* were colorfully adorned with true frescoes. Wall-painting was a major art especially patronized by the palace; its very existence depended upon it. The pictures were painted when the plaster was still moist, sometimes with the use of guiding outlines sketched by means of a blunt point or impressed with taut string, without the use of any medium except water. Thus fresco-painting was a rapid process requiring a quick and sure hand. The pigments in general use were white, black, red, yellow, green and deep blue, later of a brilliant cobalt hue. All of them were of excellent durability and of a mineral origin, such as silicate of copper, haematite, hydrate of lime, and carbonaceous shale or slate.

Sometimes the colours were painted on figures moulded in a very low relief in the plaster to give a three-dimensional effect. Limestone and gypsum* being unsuitable materials for reliefs, the painted plaster relief was substituted. This technique, applied to life-size figures of men, women and animals, is an Egyptian influence. The same can be said about the custom of painting male figures in dark, brownish colours—interpreted as denoting a healthy outdoor tan—and female figures in white. This convention was later inherited by the Greek painters. The objects are not rendered in their natural hues but in a willful, free choice of colours, for which the artist always had a keen sense. Figures vary from life-size or even larger to only an inch in height in the miniature frescoes.

Wall-paintings, originally simple geometric designs, often spiraliform, evolved later into vividly coloured scenes of ceremonies and of everyday palace life. The painters had no feeling for historic or simply narrative scenes. A special taste for the beauties of nature was shown: gardens with stylized or imaginary flowers, trees, charming studies of birds and animals, either wild or domesticated or even fabulous like griffins,* sea creatures and other subjects. Sometimes the artist created the impression of an outlook over a park view. The scenes were always graceful, original and pleasant in the extreme. There are also several remarkable miniature frescoes with lively crowds of people represented, a subject which art did not attempt again until the Roman Imperial times. In Minoan frescoes we see a fortunate combination of stylization and true natural-

60. Francocastello (*after a Venetian map*)

ism with a lightness of touch and a vivid manner. Anatomical realism is transcended by the effect of fleeting movement and elasticity. As Matz wrote, the peculiarity of Minoan pictures lies in the ability to conjure up an appearance of life, a vision, and not in an attempt to recreate existence. This quality marks a fundamental difference between the character of Minoan and Oriental painting, giving the former its unique personality in world art.

The murals disintegrated into fragments when the walls collapsed. Most have been heavily restored, according to the conceptions about total restoration which were current during the first quarter of this century. Thus, the whole picture is very often influenced more by the work of the modern restorer than of that of the original artists.

The pictures were in one plane without perspective, with definite limits around each scene, or in narrow frames. Humans and animals were usually shown in profile as in Egypt, the former usually walking in a slightly unstable way on the base lines. Landscapes were conventional but treated in a strange way, as Hood remarked, somewhat as if seen from the air, with rocks and plants projecting from the sides and top of the picture as well as from the bottom, like stalactites and stalagmites in a cave. This treatment, very different from Egyptian conventions, may reflect the hilly character of the Cretan countryside which affords a background for almost every view. As we know, little interest in landscape painting was displayed until the Hellenistic period.*

Some of the best-known frescoes come from the palace at Knossos* and its dependencies, while the other palaces possessed practically none. Other fine frescoes have been recovered at Pseira,* Amnisos,* Tylissos* and Hagia Triada* (see these entries for their frescoes). The whole heritage of this great and purely palatial Minoan art*—mostly made between 1550-1450 B.C.—is kept in the Herakleion Museum. Probably the earliest existing example is the **Crocus-Gatherer,** a figure in a field of saffron crocuses surrounded by a fantastic landscape of many-coloured conventional rocks on a general red background. The creature is represented plucking crocuses and putting them into vases. The head is missing and Evans interpreted the figure as a boy, but N. Platon proved it to be a monkey, evidently a pet, wearing a red leather harness and painted conventionally greyish-blue as in Egypt, much like the monkeys who pick flowers on a later fresco from the so-called House of the Frescoes. The charming **Girl Dancer** from the Queen's Megaron is whirling around in a quick dance with her long curls flaring out. Her right arm is thrown forward and her left bent. From the Caravanserai comes the frieze of **Partridges and Hoopoes** (see Caravanserai*).

A string of life-size youths and maidens bringing gifts to Minos—in fact a version of an Egyptian theme reproducing an actual Cretan procession—adorned the walls of the Corridor of the Procession. The number of these figures, depicted in serried ranks in two superimposed friezes, has been estimated to many hundreds. Some youths, perhaps playing music,* wear long priestly robes. The central figure, clad in a long dress, was either a priestess or goddess. The best surviving figure is that of the **Cup-**

Bearer, an attractive, solemn youth with curly hair, powerful shoulders and slim waist, often considered as the representative type of the Minoan. The figure wears a brilliantly embroidered kilt and a lentoid gem of banded stone on the left wrist. The youth tends back to counterbalance the heavy stone rhyton* he is carrying. The figure has movement but is flat and two-dimensional; the artist did not attempt to render the volumes of the body and its muscular and bone structure. The background consists of blue and yellow zones and conventional rocks.

The **Captain of the Blacks** (figure 196) shows a Minoan officer wearing a black goatskin cap with the horns attached, dressed in a short yellow tunic, holding two spears and leading off at the run some well-drilled black troops (see Warfare*). The background is blue. Interesting and solemn but also formal and stiff in its conception of monumentality is the late heraldic fresco of the confronted **Griffins*** of the Throne Room; the body is a pale yellow hue; a rudimentary shading obtained by cross-hatching can be distinguished on them. As Pendlebury remarked, this is the first appearance of any such attempt since the days of Altamira. These griffins are wingless. The back wall of the Throne Room was similarly adorned. The griffins apparently were tied to sacred columns.

A colossal relief of a fierce **Charging Bull** stood in a portico above the North Entrance of the palace. A nearby olive tree shows the colours of autumn in its leaves. Only part of a human figure is here preserved; the picture includes a formal rocky foreground. It has been supposed that the scene represents the bull-game or the capture of a wild bull in nets set between trees. The picture of the enormous bull communicates great power. The pupil of the eye is very prominent, the tongue protrudes. A similar subject is painted on the **Toreador Fresco** (see Bull-games*).

Well-known is the large relief which is supposed to represent the **Priest-King;*** this late fresco is also known as **"The Prince of the Lilies"** or **"The Prince with the Feather Crown."** This splendid dignified figure wears a crown with formal lilies rising above, with three long peacock's plumes falling back, and a collar of lily-like beads round the neck. His torso in frontal view is bare. The fresco is extremely fragmentary (figure 61): in fact several scholars think today that the restoration of the picture from various fragments is completely erroneous: the head should originally face to the right, the lower part of the body should belong to another figure walking to the left, and the feather crown to a sphinx! The figure has an attitude characteristic of both Minoan and Egyptian art: it is represented in profile but with the upper part of the body facing frontwards.

The delicate **Blue Bird Fresco** shows a roller, with red spots on its breast, rising from behind a rock. A small fragment with the fingers of a hand holding a necklace from which hang pendants in the shape of negroid heads is all that remains of the **Jewel Fresco.**

The exquisite maid with large eyes, perky nose and curly dangling locks known as the **"Parisienne,"** enthusiastically so named at the time of the "belle époque" by the workers of the excavation, is the most charming of all surviving Cretan paintings. The characteristic essentials of her face

61. "Prince of the Lilies". Erroneously restored fresco from Knossos.

are vividly rendered, with details suppressed. Evans remarked that "her elaborate coiffure and suspiciously scarlet lips are certainly marks of a highly artificial social life." The girl is wearing a sort of scarf tied behind perhaps with a sacral knot.* This painting belongs to a larger composition heraldically organized, the so-called **Campstool-Fresco,** where vivacious pairs of young people are seated on campstools and passing tall communion* chalices. The boys are wearing long, feminine-looking

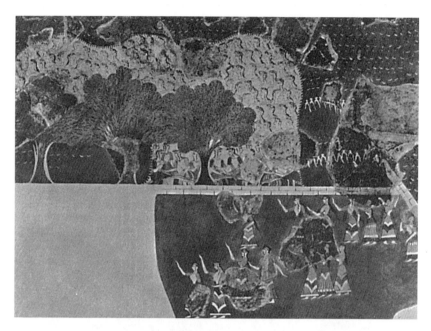

62. Miniature "Garden Party" Fresco from Knossos

robes reaching to the feet. One of them has a red glove(?) tucked into his belt. The fresco was composed of two superimposed friezes. The girl, together with a twin figure, was considerably larger than the boys and perhaps represented a goddess presiding at the ritual scene.

A large scale fresco known as **The Ladies in Blue**, in a very fragmentary condition but heavily restored, depicts in natural size several seated court ladies, who are probably attending some spectacle, elegantly toying with necklaces and conversing with each other. They wear blue, short-sleeved, richly embroidered bodices which leave their breasts bare. Another very fragmentary fresco shows a **Lady in Red.**

The restored **Dolphin Fresco** from the Queen's Megaron (see figure 126) showing dolphins playing in the sea surrounded by flying fish is also on a large scale. The dolphins have white bellies and deep blue upper parts and tails, while a double yellow band runs along their sides. Some details of this picture are remarkable, such as the sea-spray and bubbles flying off the fishes. The fresco had a coralline border.

Among the more important miniature frescoes, which evoke the court and social life, is the **Garden Party** or **Sacred Grove and Dance**, with ladies (priestesses?) sitting in the shadow of olive trees,* watching along with serried crowds of other spectators a number of ceremonially dancing girls. Several men seem enthusiastic, as we see their hands flung up in the air (figure 62). About one third of the original fresco is preserved, containing as many as 350 men and 120 women. The conventions of the picture have a certain naivety. Inside the brown mass of the tiny faces of the men we see a large patch of white for the women.

A fragment found inside one of the storehouses of the palace, showing a crowd of male spectators, is executed in a kind of artistic "shorthand," a convention usual for the representation of crowds in a small scale, a technique comparable to that of modern line drawing. Among other fragments there is one depicting some warriors hurling javelins upwards, perhaps to battlements above. Another gaily painted miniature fresco is the **Palace Feast:** one easily recognizes the Tripartite Shrine (see Shrines*) of the palace, round which the whole composition is centered. The courts of the palace are densely crowded, mostly with men. Those of the upper row are pointing excitedly at some spectacle below. Some eminent court ladies are sitting in a veranda, not very absorbed in the spectacle, conversing in a lively manner with each other and displaying their fine coiffures and the fashion of their brightly coloured dresses,* which have flounced skirts and sleeves to the elbow. The artist took care to distinguish the old ladies from the young ones by the forms of their breasts, which are bare.

Furniture (Minoan). The furnishings of Minoan palaces* and houses,* being of perishable material, have mostly not survived. In any case furniture must have been minimal. In frescoes* (see Frescoes: Campstool-Fresco) we see folding stools with legs that must have been of metal work supporting pieces of leather. Among the ordinary household furnishings we may assume the existence of foot-stools, chairs, wooden beds, low stands and small tables, sometimes depicted in art* and often appearing among lists of furniture on tablets* of the Linear B script* from the Greek Mainland. On a seal we see a stool with angle braces at the legs and a crosspiece. Inlaid decoration was applied to the more luxurious furniture.

The gypsum* chair in the Throne Room at Knossos* clearly imitates a wooden model; the upper surface of the seat is carefully hollowed to shape for comfort, a modern feature indeed. The high back has an undulating outline and slopes slightly backwards; its inner surface was once painted. The front legs are fluted and arched, with a swag between. The design of the throne is at the same time dignified and graceful. The existing stone example was once covered with a thin plaster* coating, coloured white and red.

Stone benches are very often found along the walls of rooms from early times. There were also cists set into the floors (see Magazines*) and cupboards let into the walls. Various wooden boxes might be highly prized objects painted or inlaid with materials which survived, such as ivory* and faience.* Large wooden chests—often decorated—were employed for storing clothes and textiles. We can guess their shape because in imitation of them clay boxes and chests were also made, often used as coffins (see Larnakes*). The clay bathtubs also found the same use. Lamps,* braziers* and portable clay hearths on three legs are among the regular furnishings. Mats and cushions of wool and leather-work* were evidently used in abundance.

63. Left-hand upper corner of draught-board (*after Evans*)

Gaidouronisi see **Islands of Crete, Satellite.**

Games. The clearest evidence concerning games is given by a draught-board from Knossos,* almost one metre or three feet long, datable to the end of the Middle Minoan period.* Perhaps it imitates an Egyptian game. This magnificent piece was made of ivory* plated with gold and inlaid

64. Draught-board, diagramatically shown (*after Evans*)

with faience* and rock crystal plaques backed by silver plates or blue paste. On the outer border there are ivory daisies with rock crystal bosses. In two corners are a pair of argonauts (nautiluses) in relief with a central boss of crystal on a background of blue paste (figure 63). Below is a group of four elaborately made large medallions set in crystal bars backed by silver plates. The central part of the board consists of six ribbed bars of rock crystal backed with silver alternating with five of gold-plated ivory. Below these is a group of ten medallions surrounding similar bars of crystal and ivory (figure 64). The framework was probably supported by a wooden panel. Four large ivory cones elaborately carved were found nearby; Evans,* who made several suggestions about the nature of the game, considered them as draughtsmen for it. Perhaps dice were also used.

A die consisting of a knuckle-bone marked with numbers from one to four and two sets of two men each turned up in a tomb at Katsambas by the harbour town of Knossos in a Late Minoan context. Another die in a clay goblet—obviously the dice box—has been found in the Early Palace* of Phaistos,* together with two ivory gaming-pieces imitating a lion's head and a bull's leg. Evans* suggested that the prism seals* which show different numbers of circles and dots on each side may have been dice. A number of small cups on the surface of a pavement slab of the Knossian palace probably represents some kind of game played on the pavement.

Gaudos. This small island near the south coast of Western Crete is the southernmost point of Greece and Europe. The island has been inhabited since the Neolithic period.* According to a legend, Gaudos was the famous island of the nymph Calypso, who kept Ulysses here in captivity for six years. In Classical Greek times *Kaudos* was a dependency of Gortyn* and paid a tithe on all their products but enjoyed a certain degree of independence of self-government. Among other things, the island produced juniper berries. As *Klaudos* the island is mentioned in the Acts of the Apostles.

Gazi see **Figurines; Shrines (Minoan).**

Geography. Crete is an island of great natural beauty. As Homer says, it was the land "in the midst of the wine-dark ocean, fair and rich, with the waters all around." It is also named "broad Crete." The island, lying between parallels 23°30' and 26°60' east and 34°50' and 35°4' north, is about 245 kilometres (156 miles) long from east to west, and about 58 kilometres (36 miles) wide from north to south at its widest point. Its area is almost 8300 square kilometres (3240 square miles). Its coastline, one of its most interesting and beautiful features, is 1056 kilometres (656 miles) in extent, but offers only a small number of harbours.* There are also some small satellite islands, all uninhabited except Gaudos* (see Islands of Crete, Satellite*). Its central position in the Eastern Mediterranean forms a sort of bridge between Europe, Asia, and Africa. As Evans* wrote "a half-way house between three continents, pointing East and West and barring both the Aegean and the Libyan seas, this 'mid-sea land' had sufficient territorial extension to permit the growth of a distinct and independent national life. Insular, but not isolated, it was thus able to develop a civilization of its own on native lines and to accept suggestions from the

Egyptian or the Asiatic side without itself being dominated by foreign conventionalism."

Crete, lying across the entrance to the Aegean basin, may have been connected with the Mainland by a land bridge, but no trace of that remains today. A string of islands—the Dodecanese—joins Crete to Asia Minor, and another one, including Kythera, to the Greek Mainland. On the other hand there are about 200 miles of open sea between Crete and Africa. It is the largest Greek island and the fifth largest in the Mediterranaean.

A rib of mountainous country mainly of gray limestone straddles the island. These massive chains of mountains (see map 3) have peaks which reach as high as 2452 metres (8000 feet) in the White Mountains, or Madares, to the west, which dominate the scenery and come very near to the south coast (fifty-seven peaks are higher than 2000 metres or 3300 feet), and are separated by lower ground from Mount Ida* in the center of the island (2456 metres or 9056 feet high); around them are lower mountain systems, today mostly barren (see Forests*). The Ida (Psiloritis) range is separated from the Dikte massif by a hillside and the fertile Mesara Plain.* East of Dikte lies the flat isthmus of Hierapetra,* the narrowest point of the island, with lower mountains further to the east, toward Siteia.*

The mountains divide the cultivable area into small fertile plains, the Mesara Plain* in the mid-south being the largest. Apart from the fertile coastal areas, there are upland plains. Lasithi* in the Dikte region is the largest plateau. In the west the plateau of Omalos* is connected with the sea through the famous Samaria gorge,* the most impressive of the island's picturesque gorges. The island is dotted with caves.* There is one small lake in the northwest, Lake Kournas (160 acres). There are only five small rivers that have never been known to be dry. Generally the island is poor in water.

It is often said that the island has tilted along a north-south axis, but this is an oversimplified and rather inexact consideration. In fact, through geological disturbances the whole island was gradually uplifted in its western part as high as 8 metres (26 feet), so that the whole harbour of the Greek city of Phalasarna* now lies dry and well above sea-level. On the other hand, a general rise of sea-level, owing to a melting of the polar icecaps, in combination with a very variable vertical movement between one site and the next, has submerged certain areas of the central and eastern coastline, so that parts of ancient places such as Matala,* Chersonesos* and Olous* now lie under water.

Crete is today separated into four prefectures; from the east to the west they are: Lasithi with 66,105 inhabitants, Herakleion with 209, 652, Rethymnon with 60,156 and Chania with 119,595. The total population of the island in 1971 was 456,208.

Geometric Period. The Geometric period, covering roughly the first three centuries of the first millenium B.C., succeeds the Bronze Age* and the Sub-Minoan phase and marks the beginnings of the Iron Age* and the

Greek civilization all over Greece. Society of this period, under the rule of local kings, is known from the Homeric poems.

The pottery of the period, preceded by a Proto-Geometric phase, is characterized by abstract patterns of geometric forms—hence the name of the period—such as triangles with various forms of hatching, chequers, lozenges, meanders, chevrons, crossed squares, concentric circles and semicircles made after precise planning with the help of a compass. A world of absolute regularity and clarity was created, successfully adjusting itself to the neat form of the vessel. The Geometric vase painter had no taste for floral patterns of any kind. Birds* appear rather frequently, horses* rarely, but human figures are almost unknown. The cemeteries of Geometric Knossos* at Fortetsa and elsewhere yielded a large collection of fine vases, including peculiar cremation* urns or pithoi,* as they are called in Crete (figure 65). Some use white paint on a dark background, mostly limited to circles on the lower part of the vases. The Geometric pottery in Crete never attained the high standard and clear forms of the contemporary vases of Attica, the homeland of the style. Nevertheless, there is a diversity of interesting shapes, and the tenacious survival of a very long tradition which partly resisted the Geometric austerity is apparent. Workshops in marginal areas often show a rustic but strong and unsophisticated style. Sometimes a limited Cypriote influence is visible.

Solid hand-made figurines* of humans and animals have a high degree of abstraction, a feature making them very interesting to the modern eye (see figure 116). A number of metal objects is quite remarkable; fibulae appear now for the first time, both in bronze and iron* (see Metallurgy*). Of importance are the bronze cauldrons with attached bronze figurines.

The remains of Geometric buildings are scanty. A good example of the architecture of a temple can be seen at Dreros,* where the Minoan influence is clear. Later in date are the temples at Prinias* and Gortyn.* These early Cretan temples had rectangular plans and walls entirely of stone, in contrast to the apsidal mud brick structures of the Greek Mainland. An interesting small settlement has been excavated on a high place at Kavousi near Pachyammos* in Eastern Crete. A characteristic feature is that the entrance, in contrast to Minoan custom, was placed on one of the narrow sides of the building. The plan of the settlement is quite haphazard.

Tholos tombs continued to be built in this period but are much smaller than their Bronze Age* predecessors and usually rectangular. The door was only about one metre (one yard) high. In front of it there was often a very short unlined *dromos,* really a small pit to facilitate entrance. A number of them have been found at various places of Central and Eastern Crete. However, during this period cremation* of the dead became the prevailing burial custom. Iron tools* and weapons* gradually superseded bronze ones throughout this time and led to a revolution in economy.* At the end of the Geometric period—the young years of Greece—strong influences from the Near East led to the Orientalizing period.*

65. Geometric cinerary urn from a tomb near Knossos

GLAUKOS. Glaukos, the young son of Minos* and Pasiphae,* was playing one day in the palace at Knossos* when he suddenly disappeared. His parents, unable to find him, went to the Delphic Oracle, and were sent by it to the diviner Polyeidos ("he who knows many things"), son of Koiranos, the Argive. Polyeidos, commanded to go in search of the boy, after seeing a night owl driving away bees, wandered through the labyrinthine palace, until he found Glaukos drowned head downward in one of the huge pithoi* containing honey.* Following the command of the king, the diviner was shut up in a tomb together with the lifeless body and a sword. A snake suddenly appeared and Polyeidos promptly killed it with a sword. Another snake approached in search of the first, saw that it was dead and brought a magic herb, with which it restored its mate to life.

Polyeidos then applied the herb to restore life to the boy. It is clear that the snake in this Greek myth is a symbol of resurrection (see Snake Cult*). A similar life-restoring herb is mentioned in the story of the well-known ancient Mesopotamian hero, Gilgamesh.

Later Glaukos led an expedition westward and demanded a kingdom from the Italians; he introduced into Italy the Cretan military girdle and shield.*

Gold see **Jewellery.**

Gonia Monastery. The monastery was founded in the "corner" (Gonia) of the bay of Chania* in 1618. After 27 years the Turks invaded Crete with an army 50,000 strong at the coast near the monastery, which was then destroyed. Although it was rebuilt, its rich library was destroyed in 1866 by the Turks. The monastery today possesses a collection of fine post-Byzantine icons. Near it is the Orthodox Academy, a remarkably progressive religious and cultural institute, founded in recent years.

Gortyn. Gortyn, in the Mesara Plain* and between the modern villages of Hagioi Deka and Metropolis, was one of the mightiest city-states of Classical Crete. Its beginnings go back to Minoan times, to which belongs a villa of the sixteenth century B.C. explored by the Italians at Kannia. Gortyn was the legendary place to which Europa* was brought by Zeus.* The great Plato in his *Laws* shows himself an admirer of the conservative institutions of Gortyn. The well-known Code of Gortyn is an extremely important social document.

Homer refers to Gortyn as a walled city. This wall was later demolished; Ptolemy Philopator tried in 220-205 B.C. to rebuild this long wall—according to Strabo, Gortyn had a diameter of almost ten kilometres (six miles)—but succeeded in finishing only a part of it. The city had two harbours on the south coast, Lebena* and Matala;* the latter was captured together with Phaistos* in the third century B,C. During the long Hellenistic period* Gortyn was often a rival of Knossos* and sometimes at war with it. Hannibal came to Gortyn as a refugee after his defeat by Antiochos. Gortyn helped the Romans to conquer Crete and was consequently spared by Quintus Metellus, who destroyed many resisting cities such as Knossos.* During the Roman occupation* the city became the provincial capital of Crete and Cyrene (Libya) and flourished as the largest Cretan city, with a population perhaps as high as 300,000 persons. In Gortyn was installed St. Titus, a disciple of St. Paul, who appointed him the first Bishop of Crete. The city flourished again during the first Byzantine period* but was destroyed by the Saracens in 824 A.D. and was never rebuilt.

The site was explored by the Italian Archaeological Institute and a clay Dedalic statuette was found there (figure 66).

The ruins are scattered over a large area (figure 67). The acropolis **(1)** with many archaic remains and rich finds is on top of a hill. The grandiose

66. Clay Dedalic statuette from Gortyn.

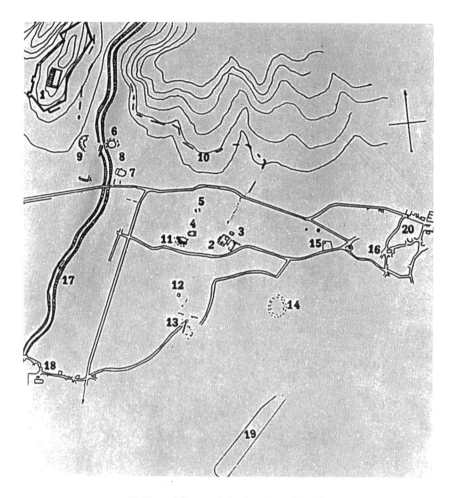

67. Plan of Gortyn (*after Pernier and Banti*)

1. Acropolis
2. Roman Praetorium
3. Northeast Public Fountain and
   Nymphaion
4. Temple of Pythian Apollo
5. Sanctuary of Egyptian Divinities
6. Odeum and Code of Gortyn
7. Church of St. Titus
8. Market Place
9. North Theater
10. Aqueduct

11. South Theater
12. Southwest Public Fountain and
    Nymphaion
13. Great Baths ("Thermae")
14. Amphitheater
15. Modern Antiquarium
16. Modern Church of Hagii Deka
18. Modern Village of Metropolis
    and Early Christian Basilica
19. Stadium
20. Modern Village of Hagii Deka

Praetorium **(2)** was the official seat of the provincial Roman administrator; it was built during the second century A.D. and rebuilt 200 years later. The building included the Basilica with one row of columns and eight statues of eminent citizens, a hall with three apses, and a peristyle court to the north, which is connected to a public bath.

West of the Praetorium lies the chief temple of the city, that of Pythian Apollo **(4)**, an important monument remodelled several times. The temple served also as the state treasury. The simple original cella, of the latter part of the seventh century B.C., was almost square. The outside walls were covered with inscriptions. At their base two steps ran around the temple, which was entered by a door in the middle of the east side. It has been assumed that the interior of the walls was perhaps faced with bronze plates, while two inner columns must have supported the flat roof. In 200 B.C. a pronaos with six Doric half-columns was added to the cella, which was later divided into three naves by two Corinthian colonnades of four columns each. There is also an altar and an apse of the third century B.C. at the west wall.

North of the temple of Apollo is a small temple of Isis, Serapis, and other Egyptian divinities **(5)**, whose cult was introduced into the Roman Empire. Two theatres **(9)** and **(11)**, two public fountains and shrines of the Nymphs **(3)** and **(12)** (see Springs, Sacred*), the amphitheatre **(14)**, great public baths **(13)**, a market place **(8)** with a temple of Asklepios,* a stadium **(19)**—all show the splendour of the city.

The Odeum **(6)** was erected in the first century A.D. at the place of an earlier building. On its northern side was incorporated the earlier wall, the surface of which was inscribed with the famous Code (see Code of Gortyn*). The Odeum had two entrances at the north side. The orchestra was paved with black and white marble slabs. The southern wall of the Odeum was provided with rectangular niches which were used for statues.

An important monument of the Early Christian period in Crete is the Church of St. Titus **(7)** which has a cross-in-square plan, built of large ashlar masonry (figure 68). This was the church of the martyrdom of the saint, constructed in the late sixth century. The bema had niches and side chambers. The ends of the south and north arms of the cross had apses. Better preserved is the east part of the church with three apses and a barrel vault. The capitals of the church bear the monogram of the Byzantine Emperor Justinian.

Gortyn Code see **Code of Gortyn.**

Gournia. The industrial Minoan town known to us as Gournia lies on a knoll near the coast of the Gulf of Mirabello in Eastern Crete, close to a good anchorage. The town was destroyed at the time of the disasters of ca. 1450 B.C. At a small distance to the east lies Pachyammos,* a modern village known for its Minoan cemetery. Gournia, occupying an area of

68. Church of St. Titus at Gortyn

15,000 square metres, (about 18,000 square yards) was excavated by the American Harriet Boyd-Hawes, of the University of Pennyslvania, and her collaborators at the beginning of the century (1901–1904).

The earliest traces of a settlement at Gournia, this Minoan Pompeii, are datable to the Early Minoan period.* To the same time belong some ossuaries just outside the settlement, near the modern guard house (see figure 22). On the other hand, an early cemetery on the slopes of a nearby hill toward the sea, Sphoungaras, yielded a great number of burials inside pithoi* and larnakes,* accompanied by many vessels and a very important series of seals.*

The town (figure 69) flourished late in the Middle Minoan III period, when a small "palace" enjoying a fine view was erected on the crown of the hill in obvious imitation of the great palaces.* Its area covers about one-tenth of that of the palace at Knossos.* It was probably the residence of a local governor (figure 70). Its portico facing the large rectangular central court of the town had alternate pillars* and columns,* and its principal facade with massive limestone blocks or orthostates faced west on a small

69. Plan of Gournia (*after Boyd*)

west court, showing small recesses or setbacks, typical of the west palace facades. The central court is rather a court-yard of the palace than a real central court* as seen elsewhere, accessible from at least two public roads. There is also a tiny "Theatral Area" vaguely reminiscent of those at Knossos* and Phaistos,* with a low flight of steps forming an angle facing the court. A pair of limestone sacral horns* has been found nearby. There is

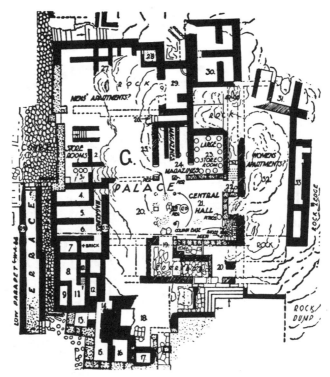

70. Plan of the "palace" at Gournia (*after Boyd*)

also a small room paved with a large block possessing a hole, which has been interpreted as a sacrificial platform for the bull. The internal arrangements of the palace are rather obscure, since the building, probably destroyed by an earthquake,* seems to have been reoccupied in the Late Minoan IA period. Along its south front are distributed a number of magazines,* while above them the existence of a second storey with some formal rooms has been presumed. At the northeast corner are other magazines* and a large storeroom with twelve pithoi* found in their original positions along the walls. A small cement floored room is possibly a Lustral Basin,* not sunken as usual.

A regular settlement grew up around the palace with narrow paved streets clambering up the slopes of the hill, stepped at intervals and approximately at right angles with two main ring-roads. These streets, of Middle Minoan times, unfit for wheeled traffic, included a public drainage system,* which implies a degree of communal planning and organization. The town's houses,* which belong mainly to the Late Minoan I period, are small and tightly clustered both inside and outside the major ring-road. They occupy an area of about 25,000 square metres (nearly 30,000 square yards). The road-system divides the town into six irregular, large blocks composed of several separate houses.* Block C possessed fif-

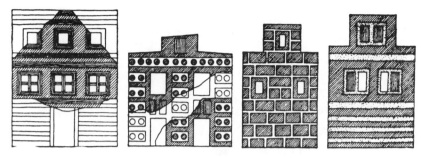

71. Minoan houses: "Town Mosaic" from Knossos (*after Platon*)

teen houses around its perimeter and several more in its center. There are
no fortification walls (see Urbanism*). What we see of the houses today
must be mainly the storeroom basements usually entered from above,
while the living rooms must have been chiefly on the first floor reached by
short flights of steps which led up from the street (figure 71). The largest
of these houses measure about 5 by 5 metres (16.5 by 16.5 feet) at the outside. Limestone thresholds flush with the street and paved courts are
found. These houses were built in groups and not as free-standing buildings. From these houses have come a considerable number of objects illustrating the paraphernalia of everyday life as well as the industrial character of the settlement, such as eight potter's wheels* found in the southern part of the town, a complete set of eight tools belonging to a carpenter's workshop, three metal-workers' shops and a factory for processing
olive oil* or wine.*

North of the palace, at the end of a well-worn cul-de-sac lay the ruins of
a small single-roomed civic shrine* built during the Late Minoan I period
(although its furniture probably belonged to the Late Minoan III period at a
time when parts of the destroyed town were reoccupied). Here the cult of
the Household or Snake Goddess* was practised. The finds (figure 72) include a tripod altar,* two bird* figurines,* three snake tubes and the fragment of a fourth (see Snake Cult*), a sherd with a double axe* in relief,
and cult images with arms raised in blessing, almost featureless faces and
a bell-shaped skirt, evidently standing on the benches of the shrine, and
an arm and a hand belonging to such images, with snakes attached to
them.

An interesting example of a building erected during the time of reoccupation is the partly excavated Mycenaean house which can be seen at
the southern end of the settlement beyond the court.

During recent years the Greek Archaeological Service undertook extensive consolidation and cleaning work on the site, which produced several finds.

Gouverneto Monastery. This isolated and fortified monastery, not very
far from the Hagia Triada monastery* east of Chania,* was founded during the Venetian occupation* in honour of Mary, "Lady of the Angels."

72. Finds of the Civic Sanctuary at Gournia (*after Boyd*)

The monastery was destroyed by the Turks in the uprising of 1821, and reconstructed later. In its immediate vicinity is the large cave of Arkoudiotissa or Arkoudia, an important sacred cave of the goddess Artemis, who was venerated here in the form of a bear (*arkouda* in modern Greek). Indeed a large stalagmite formation is strongly reminiscent of a bear. A chapel of Mary the Arkoudiotissa inside the cave, consecrated to the Purification of the Virgin, demonstrates the survival of the ancient cult in another form. The cave was explored by the author.

To the north of the cave lay the ruins of the monastery of St. John the Hermit, perhaps the oldest monastery in Crete locally known as *Catholico* and reached over a bridge. The grave of the saint is at the end of an exceptionally impressive deep cave, originally the bed of an underground river.

Grambousa. On this small and steep uninhabited island—ancient Korykon—near the northwest coast of Crete (figure 73) was built in 1579 a strong Venetian fortress (''fortezza delle Garabuse''), which became an important naval base controlling the sea-routes (see figure 99, left). In 1692 the fortress, then among the last possessions of Venice in Crete, fell into the hands of the Turks due to the treason of its commander. Grambousa later became a pirate lair (see Piracy*).

Grave-goods. Burials in antiquity (see Burial Customs*) were as a rule accompanied by grave-goods (figure 74). The Bronze Age* Cretans gave their dead no extremely luxurious grave furniture as did the Egyptians; nevertheless, especially in earlier times, some important gold jewellery* might be put into the tombs of those having high social positions, as was the case at Mochlos,* or later at Chrysolakkos of Malia* and Archanes.* Seals,* which had been protective amulets* and means of personal identification during a lifetime, were also buried with the dead. The grave-goods, which invariably included a variety of pottery* filled with drinks and food, provided the departed with his needs in the after-life. The stone vases* seem to have been manufactured especially for sepulchral use. The dead person, at least until the total decomposition of the body, obviously was considered a spirit who could become beneficial or harmful. In this way a cult of the dead* was developed. Sometimes, when a tomb was reopened for a new burial, the earlier grave-goods were unceremoniously pushed aside along with the bones, or the best of them might be occasionally despoiled.

Greek Language. Greek has the longest and most complete historical record of any European language. It belongs to the large Indo-European linguistic family but not to any of the three main groups, the Latin, the Germanic or the Slavic. Several thousand of English words are Greek or have a Greek origin. The language spoken on Crete and in the Mainland before the arrival of the Greeks had distinctive possessive or locative suffixes in *-sos, -ndos,-ntha* or *-nthos*, also recorded in Asia Minor. This language left signs of itself in later Greek which survive until today in such place names as *Knossos, Tylissos, Amnisos, Parnassos, Tiryns* (gen. *Tirynthos*) and many others, as well as in common words for plants, birds etc., such as *kissos* (ivy), *olynthos* (the wild fig), *kyparissos* (cypress), *kolokynthos* (the squashy gourd), *minthe* (mint), *kerasos* (the cherry tree), *glossa* (the tongue), *plinthos* (brick), and *thalassa* (the sea). There are also a small number of mythological personal names: *Marpessa, Hyakinthos, Narkissos.*

73. Fortress of Grambousa (*after a Venetian map*)

74. Grave-goods inside a Late Minoan chamber-tomb near Siteia

Greek developed in Crete from the second millenium B.C. alongside other languages in more than a single dialect. In the Iron Age,* Cretan Doric Greek—Doric was distributed in the south and east Peloponnese, the south Aegean including Crete and Rhodes, and southwest Anatolia—was spoken all over the island, although a small minority of the Eteocretans* preserved their old language until late. Cretan forms a specific part of the Doric dialect, in fact the best known and most extensively documented part. Some of its main features are common to other dialects, but some are quite peculiar to itself. The dialect of Gortyn* and its neighbors is called Central Cretan, in contrast to East Cretan, which extends from Hierapetra* eastward, and West Cretan, from Lappa* westward. Both East and West Cretan are lacking many special Cretan dialectal characteristics.

The Medieval Cretan dialect partly survives today, constantly yielding to Mainland Greek, with which it had only a few secondary differences in vocabulary and accent. Some dozens of words are of Italian origin, and a few are of Turkish, French, and nowadays, English origin.

Griffins. These solemn fabulous animals with a lion's body and an eagle's crested head and wings have been taken over from Oriental art, probably from Syria or Egypt. Like sphinxes (see Monsters*), they are not holy beings but mere followers of the divinities and guardians of sacred places and objects. They have been inherited by Greek mythology and art, where they played about the same role as in Minoan Crete. Usually they are engraved on seals,* often heraldically on each side of the goddess or a column, sometimes tethered to it. In some cases a priestly man holds a griffin by a cord. Painted representations of griffins are better known, like the one on a larnax from Palaikastro,* or the late heraldic fresco (figure 75) on each side of the throne at the palace of Knossos* (see Frescoes*). It has been suggested that perhaps they symbolized a combination of worldly and divine power.

During the Orientalizing period* the griffin reappears as a Greek adaptation of an Oriental subject. Bronze attachments in the form of a griffin head often decorate Orientalizing bronze vessels, sometimes imitated in clay (see figure 122).

Gypsum. Crystalline gypsum, this handsome and easily worked typically Cretan stone, was much used in Minoan architecture.* It was especially employed for interior decoration and was restricted to sheltered places where there was protection from the weather, as it is slightly soluble in water. This quality makes it a problem for the archaeologist when found in excavations, for its ancient protection has somehow to be restored. This stone is calcium sulphate, which nature in the far past deposited upon the drying up of salt waters, such as inland seas. It is a highly decorative material of a white or pinkish colour, often beautifully veined. Rich local quarries existed at the hill of Gypsades at Knossos,* where gypsum slabs—sometimes huge—were cut by bronze saws and extensively employed in the later palace. This material, unsuitable for reliefs but of an elegant appearance, was used for wall blocks, benches, monolithic pillars,* flagstones for floors and thresholds, step treads and parapets, doorjambs and column bases. A contrasting effect was achieved by putting a frame of gypsum slabs around a pavement of darker stones. An architectural peculiarity of the palace at Phaistos* and the villa at Hagia Triada* is a certain partiality for gypsum dado slabs rather than for fresco decoration.

Hagia Galini see **Sybrita.**

Hagia Pelagia see **Apollonia.**

Hagia Photia. On the shore of Hagia Photia, the first village east of Siteia,* perhaps the largest cemetery of Bronze Age* Crete and one of the largest of prehistoric Greece was explored in 1971 by the author. The cemetery, of Early Minoan I/II date, consisted of 252 tombs; about fifty more tombs are presumed to have been destroyed and plundered during previous years. Some of them were simple pit-tombs, but the majority were a sort of primitive chamber-tombs; a large upright slab closed the entrance,

75. Restored drawing of Griffin Fresco (*after Evans*)

while in front a small antechamber was formed, mostly paved with irregular stones. This antechamber had no roof, being rather a pit to facilitate entrance, and playing the role of the later *dromos*. The chamber as well as the antechamber had an elliptical or an irregular round form. About 1500 vases (figure 76 and 77) of different shapes were found (see Pottery*). Among them were various kernoi.* Some of them show a rich incised decoration. The influence of Cycladic culture is very strong. The gravegoods* included a rich series of first-class obsidian* blades (see figure 120). A fine collection of bronze objects included the earliest fish-hooks and the largest known Minoan dagger of this period (see figure 197). Noteworthy were some amulets* and stone vessels.

76. Bird-vase from Hagia Photia

Hagia Roumeli see **Tarrha.**

Hagia Triada. The villa or little "palace" was found by the Italian Luigi Pernier in the vicinity of the small two-nave church of Hagia Triada ("Holy Trinity") of the fourteenth century near the palace at Phaistos* and excavated at the beginning of the century. It seems to have been erected at the end of the Middle Minoan period* and probably lasted until 1450 BC, or even 1400 BC according to some scholars, when it was burned down. The palace is much smaller than the one at Phaistos and is considered a replacement for the official residence of the king after the palace of Phaistos had been damaged and its importance largely diminished. Perhaps it was normally a pleasure or seasonal resort for the rulers of Phaistos.

Gypsum* veneering was abundantly used, and there are a number of excellent frescoes.* Notable is a marine design with an octopus and dolphins arranged symmetrically, not on a wall but on the floor of the rectangular little Shrine **H** at the extreme east of the site. This isolated shrine, built in ashlar masonry, included a bench against the back wall of the cella, which was entered through two doors, a vestibule and a portico. The walls were covered with plaster. The shrine was burned down during the Late Minoan I period but was reconstructed in Late Minoan III times.

77. Vessel from Hagia Photia with incised decoration

Another remarkable painting found inside Room **14** is the **Cat Fresco,** per-haps the finest of all Minoan naturalistic frescoes. The scene illustrates two cats stalking a pheasant-like bird, with red body and black tail, and the hindquarters of a roebuck leaping over rocks and flowers, an instan-taneously recorded impression of nature. Of course the best known fres-coes from Hagia Triada adorn the famous sarcophagus* found here.

The plan of the little palace forms an irregular L (figure 78). The south extremity comprises perhaps the servant rooms with floors of beaten earth. To the east was the long light-well **(9).** The famous Chieftain Cup (see Stone Vases*) was recovered from one of them (see figure 179). Room **15** was perhaps a pottery* storeroom. The chief residential quarter was located at the northwest corner of the palace, at the angle of the L. The paved floors with red plaster* in the interstices show the traces of the vio-lent fire of the destruction. The main hall **(3)** has two pier-and-door parti-tions: the northern one opens onto a court with an L-shaped columned portico facing a splendid view, while the eastern one leads to Room **12**

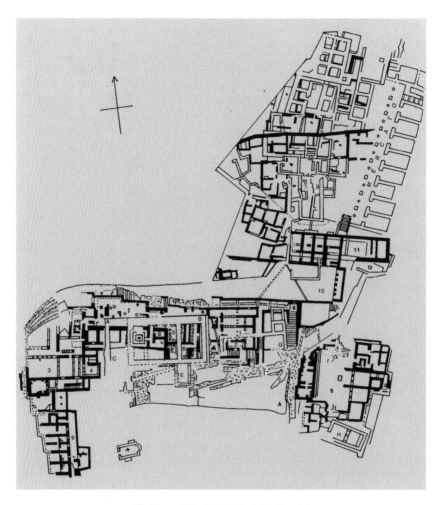

78. Plan of Hagia Triada (*after Pernier*)

1. Room with Portico
2. Room with Two Windows
3. Main Hall
4. Room with Benches
5-6. North Magazines
7. Magazine of Ingots
8. Gypsum-Veneered Room
9. Long Light-well and Personnel Quarters
10. Intermediary Portico and Area of Later Temple of Welchanos
11. Court and Porticoes
12. Room with Portico
13. Room of Sealings (Archive Room)
14. Cat Fresco Room
15. Pottery Storeroom
16. Workshop
17. Pillared Magazine
19. Pottery Storeroom
20. Room with Window
21. Main Hall of East Suite
ABCD. Late Minoan III Megaron
E. Late Minoan III Loggia
FG. Late Minoan III Building
H. Shrine with Dolphin Fresco
Mercato. Market Place

and a two-columned light-well* which has a window on either narrow side. Beyond two other wooden columns* on the west side, three doors open to Room **4**, which has a restored bench around the elaborately panelled walls. There is another door to the north. Inside the narrow magazine **(7)** were found nineteen bronze ingots,* a great wealth for this time (see figure 88). Room **13** to the west yielded a hoard of sealings.* The whole complex forms a fine architectural composition. A number of staircases led up to the second storey.

The remains of the surfaced Minoan road are still visible along the west facade. The north facade, elaborately built with ashlar masonry, shows a number of setbacks, a regular feature of Minoan architecture.* A stepped road, the Sea Ramp (*rampa dal mare),* runs along it. In the middle of the north wing and below the foundations of a later construction are several magazines* containing large pithoi.* Magazine **17** has a staircase and a central pillar.* East of these magazines lies another residential suite with small but elegant rooms. The lower parts of the walls are decorated with dadoes. Room **20** has a window on the Sea Ramp. Room **21** includes a pier-and-door partition, a colonnade and a light-well to the east. To the south of Room **2**, which possesses two windows, a staircase led up to the second storey.

South of this suite lies the Square of the Shrines (*piazzale dei sacelli),* bounded on the east by a paved road which was connected to the Sea Ramp with a large flight of steps and ultimately probably led to Phaistos. This square was contemporary with the little palace, but after the destruction of 1450 B.C. and the subsequent reconstruction of the Late Minoan III period, it became larger, occupying part of the burned down palace with a higher pavement. On this level two grandiose buildings—**ABCD** and **FG**—arose in ashlar masonry on the ruins of the buried palace. The first one was divided in three parts, bringing to mind the plan of a Mycenaean megaron and of a later Greek temple. It seems likely that this building was the palace of some Achaian* ruler. Adjoining it on the south was the small loggia **E** with a column to the east and a window to the south. The famous Boxer Rhyton (see Stone Vases*) was found near the flight of steps of the neighbouring building **I**.

North of the palace complex and the intermediary five-pillared Portico **(10)** are the remains of a settlement, mostly erected during the Late Minoan III period on the ruins of earlier houses. East of them is a vast long square. This area is limited to the east by a long portico with alternating columns and pillars and a series of eight rectangular magazines or shops behind it, possibly used as a market place like the similar structures of the Hellenistic period.* A staircase at the north end led up to the second storey. At a distance of 150 metres (about 500 feet) to the northeast the ruins of two early tholos tombs* can be seen.

Among the notable objects found at Hagia Triada, beside a great quantity of excellent pottery,* are a number of clay tablets* of the Linear A script,* three splendid stone vases decorated with scenes in relief, the Chieftain Cup, the Boxer Rhyton which we have mentioned above, and the Harvester Vase (see Stone Vases*), and of course the famous sarco-

79. Hagios Nikolaos and Fortress Mirabello (*after a Venetian map*)

phagus* from Hagia Triada. Quite remarkable is a clay model of a woman on a swing; a dove perches on each post of the swing. This clearly was a ceremonial activity, perhaps connected to a fertility rite.

In later Greek times a temple of Zeus* Welchanos* and later a Roman villa arose upon the ruins. In the immediate vicinity of the site lies the single-nave Byzantine chapel of St. George Galatas, of the fourteenth century, with its fine frescoes.

Hagia Triada Monastery. This monastery east of Chania,* not far from the Gouverneto Monastery,* was erected in ca. 1608-1620 by the brothers Tzangaroli, Venetians of the orthodox rite. The building was partly destroyed during the revolt of 1821 (see Turkish Occupation*) but reconstructed later. An important religious college was founded here in the nineteenth century.

Hagios Myron see **Rhaukos.**

Hagios Nikolaos. The small town of Hagios Nikolaos with over 10.000 inhabitants, on the west side of the Gulf of Mirabello, is the capital of Eastern Crete (Prefecture of Lasithi) and a major tourist center of the island. In antiquity the site was occupied by the harbour of Lato,* known as *Lato pros Kamara* ("Lato towards the arch"), evidently some unidentified arched structure. Some inscriptions, statues and tombs have been found here. During the Venetian occupation* the fortress Mirabello was built in the thirteenth century on the highest hill near the coast (figure 79) in order to protect the harbour, named *porto di San Nicolò* after the existing chapel of Hagios Nikolaos. The chapel (figure 79, foreground) dates not from the Byzantine iconoclastic period –eight or ninth century– as was previously thought but from the tenth or eleventh century and has an original aniconic fresco with geometric motifs, unique for Crete and very rare for Greece, under paintings with figural motifs from the fourteenth century. The entire province and the gulf were named after this fortress.

Castel Mirabello was severely damaged in the earthquake* of 1303 and burnt down by pirates in 1537 but it was later reconstructed. In 1645 the fortress was given by its commander to the Turks, but the Venetians reconquered and destroyed it completely. After the middle of the last century the existing hamlet grew to a small town and now flourishes as a tourist resort. Hagios Nikolaos possesses a picturesque lake with a funnel-shaped bottom 64 metres (198 feet) deep, now connected with the sea by a small channel. An archaeological museum was recently built to house finds from Eastern Crete.

Hagios Onouphrios Ware. This style of the Early Minoan period* was named after a site just below the hill of Phaistos,* where for the first time vessels with this type of decoration were discovered. A characteristic shape is the round-bottomed spherical jug with beaked spout. Shapes, including cups, two-handled jars and tankards, are in general well-proportioned and show a great variety, each vessel being an individual creation. The decoration, which is quite distinctive, consists of simple linear patterns usually in a red or brown semilustrous paint on a buff or cream

80. Hagios Onouphrios Style vessel

background (figure 80). The painting, of good quality, usually combines horizontal and vertical lines around the vessel, emphasizing the contour. It has been suggested that such jugs were copied from vessels made from gourds, and their decoration evidently imitates the strings with which gourd vessels were carried. Perhaps this ware was introduced from Anatolia. Many outstanding examples have been found in the Mesara Plain.*

Harbours. Minoan Crete possessed a number of safe harbours where ships* could be beached on stretches of sand, as was the custom in ancient times. Harbour installations of some elementary kind existed to allow the ships to load and unload more securely. Nevertheless, most of the very long coastline of Crete, especially the southern one, offered no protection. The difficulties of St. Paul's voyage are well described in the Acts of the Apostles. Most of the trade* and transport* of the island were conducted through its harbours. The flourishing of settlements such as Pseira,* Mochlos,* Zakros* and Palaikastro* can be accounted for by their position near some important seaway.

Mochlos* evidently possessed two harbours, one on each side of the isthmus which then joined the islet with the land. The one which was used depended on the prevailing wind. This use of an anchorage on either side of a promontory, like the harbour of the Homeric Scheria in the land of the Phaeacians, seems to have also been the case at other sites. It has been suggested that some of the satellite islands* of Crete could have played this role.

The harbour at Kommos near Matala* lay near Phaistos.* Most important was Katsambas, the harbour-town of Knossos* from the Neolithic period,* partly explored in recent years by St. Alexiou. The villa* at Amnisos,* another harbour of Knossos, is presumed to have belonged to a kind of naval officer. More to the east, Nirou* has a small port, while in the west, Souda Bay* offers the largest and safest harbourage of the whole island.

During later Greek times each important inland city-state possessed a harbour town. Of special interest were Chersonesos,* Phalasarna* and Lebena.* The spacious anchorage of Chersonesos,* dating to Roman times, was roughly rectangular and measured some 270 by 150 metres (886 by 492 feet). The existence of a lighthouse has been assumed. There are also traces of quays constructed of concrete. Massive moles over five metres (sixteen feet) wide, built of rubble and concrete, bounded it on the east and south. Today they are under sea-level (see Geography*). Outside the moles strong breakwaters of huge boulders have been observed. On the other hand the close harbour of Phalasarna* in the far west, once accessible through a channel, is today completely dry. Noteworthy is a very rare construction in the far east, near Siteia*: a rock-cut ship-shed or slipway of mounumental dimensions, gently sloping to the water, and probably made during the Hellenistic period.* The inner wooden structure has vanished.

An important Byzantine document of the sixth century A.D. is the *Stadiasmus*, a compilation giving distances and anchorages, noting at the same time the presence of water and temples, which were probably noted more as prominent landmarks than as facilities for devotion.

Harvester Vase see **Stone Vases.**

Hellenistic Period. The large empire of Alexander the Great, comprising the major part of the ancient world, gave rise to the Hellenistic civilization. After his death the empire was divided among his successors, but in all the conquered countries a common Greek civilization prevailed, with a common language *(koine)* and a cultural uniformity. Hellenistic Crete did not stand in the cultural foreground during this time, nor did it play an influential part in international politics. The history of this long period, which spans the three centuries from Alexander's death in 323 B.C. to the Roman conquest in 67 B.C., is a record of incessant strife among the Cretan city-states, in which external powers were often involved, especially Macedon and the Ptolemies, the mighty Greek monarchs of Egypt. Crete was torn by internal warfare. Major and minor wars among the strongest cities, such as Knossos,* Gortyn,* Lyttos* and their allies, led to catastrophic results for many of them as well as for Crete and its

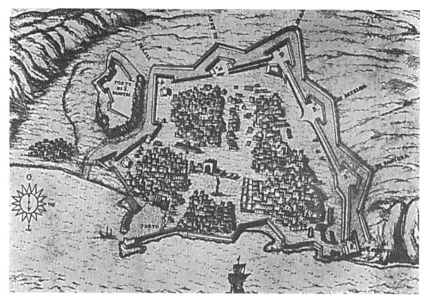

81. Candia and its fortifications (*after a Venetian map*)

population as a whole. The cities maintained their separatism (see map 1), and the existing loose, unstable federation, the *Koinon*,* never achieved unity for the island, which became a source of mercenaries* and a base for piracy.* As Willetts pointed out, the autonomous cities were plagued by the irreconcilable contradictions of their social structures. Resistant to all change, they became more and more at the mercy of forces they could not hope to control, their rivalries sharpened by the intervention of much stronger states.

Helmets see **Armour.**

Herakleion. Herakleion (or Iraklion) is the largest city of modern Crete, with some 85,000 inhabitants. Herakleion, a harbour of the city of Knossos* during later Greek times, was named after Herakles. The village survived until the Arab occupation,* when the conquerors founded there a fortified town surrounded by a large moat (*Khandak* in Arabic: hence the Byzantine *Chandax* and the Venetian *Candia*, the Medieval names of the city). The place became a major center of piracy* and a slave market. In 961 A.D., Nikephoros Phokas, a Byzantine general and later emperor, captured the fortress after a short but difficult siege. The city flourished during the Second Byzantine period.*

Later the Venetians surrounded the expanding city with new and exceptionally strong fortifications designed by Michele Sammicheli, the great architect of Verona. These walls, protected by a huge moat and provided with four arched gates, seven bastions and elaborate auxiliary networks, required more than a century to be built and still survive today,

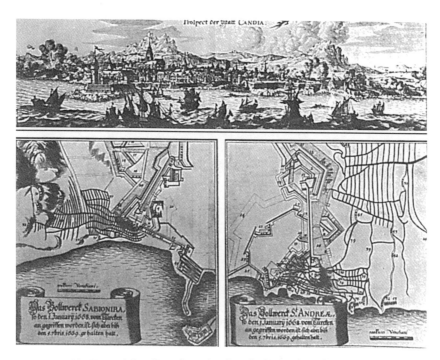

82. View of Candia and two bastions in 1668 (*after a German map*)

partly reconstructed by the Archaeological Service (figure 81). The elaborate Gate of Jesus of a Classical Doric order and the Gate of Chania are imposing, as are the Bastions of Martinengo (now including the tomb of Nikos Kazantzakis), Pantokrator ("Panigra"), Bethleem, Sabbionara and St. Andrew (figure 82). The walls were able to withstand the Turkish siege for more than twenty years (1648–69), a siege which has been considered as one of the most remarkable in the military history of the seventeenth century.

Candia, closely related to the Italian Renaissance, developed quickly into the chief center of social, political, commercial and cultural life in Crete. Several fine public structures were erected, such as the elaborate Fountain of Morosini (1628) adorned with lions, Priuli Fountain (1666), and Bembo Fountain (1588), which includes an ancient headless statue brought from Hierapetra; the Turks painted it black and held a fiesta here each May, with songs and dances. Other important buildings were the Palazzo Ducale (not surviving); the Loggia (1626-28), a two-storey masterpiece of Venetian architecture, of the well-known Palladian style, serving as a club for the nobles (now under reconstruction); the fortress Rocca al mare, today known as Koules, an imposing structure (1523) protecting the harbour; the Venetian Naval Arsenal (1584) with one ship-shed still surviving.

Also important is the Church of St. Marc, a basilica erected in 1239 and

83. Scene from the siege of Candia

rebuilt several times; its colonnades, of green stone, came from Graeco-Roman buildings of Knossos; the church was converted later into a mosque and is today used as a concert hall. It houses a permanent exhibit of copies of Byzantine frescoes. The Church of St. Titus was erected in 961, after the liberation of Crete, in honour of the patron saint of the town, and has been rebuilt several times; the church we see today was built in the nineteenth century; the relics of St. Titus were brought back from Venice a few years ago. The oldest Roman Catholic church in Crete, St. Francis, was erected at the place where the archaeological museum is now, but was ruined in 1856 by an earthquake; its magnificent doorway was the gift of Pope Alexander V, who was a Cretan. The orthodox Sinaiite School of St. Catherine was a sort of university for Greek studies, with an important library.

Shortly after the Turkish invasion and the capture of Chania the long siege of Herakleion began (figure 83). The population of the town was then 17,000. Venice tried hard to keep the capital of the island. The forces of the Venetian general Morosini were exhausted when a French contingent under the Duc de Beaufort was sent by King Louis XIV. After a vain counterattack de Beaufort was killed, the remains of the French contingent sailed away, and the defenders of the town surrendered (1669). During the Turkish occupation* most of the churches were converted into mosques. The Church of St. Menas was built in 1862 as the Cathedral of Herakleion. Just by it, in the Sinaiite Church of St. Catherine, are exhibited six fine large-scale icons of the sixteenth century, painted by Michael Damaskenos (see Cretan School of Painting*). The chapel of St. Menas nearby is interesting because of its fine woodcarvings of the seventeenth century. Herakleion possesses two important museums.*

Hierapetra. Hierapetra, at the place of ancient Hierapytna,* is the southernmost Greek and European town. It lies on the south end of the flat isthmus of the same name, which is twelve kilometres (about seven and a half miles) across, forming the narrowest width of the island (figure 84). Compared with Greece and the other parts of Crete, this area has the lowest rainfall and humidity, and also the hottest temperature in winter. Its climate* has been compared with that of the periphery of a desert. The town of 8000 inhabitants possesses the largest Cretan harbour on the south coast. The fortress by the sea was erected during the first years of the Venetian occupation,* perhaps on the ruins of a Byzantine fortress, and was renovated in 1626 by General Morosini and later by the Turks, who conquered it in 1647. The town was ruined by the great earthquake* of 1508, and after that event was reduced to a hamlet around the castle. According to tradition, Napoleon Bonaparte during his campaign in Egypt came here in 1798 for one night. The house where he was said to have slept can be seen in the old town. Hierapetra possesses a small archaeological collection in a provisional exhibition, with an important painted Late Minoan larnax (see figures 105, 145-147).

Hierapytna. Hierapytna, situated at the location of modern Hierapetra,* was one of the most important Greek city-states in Crete. In earlier times it was known as Pydna and still earlier as Kyrba, named after its mythological founder Kyrbas, one of the Telchines* who came from Rhodes. Among the divinities worshipped here were Demeter,* Zeus Meilichios (Zeus "the Kindly One") and Apollo Dekatophoros ("the Tithe-Receiver"). The city slowly expanded its territory and in the second century B.C. controlled almost the entire south coast of Central and Eastern Crete. Among others, it absorbed the neighbouring city of Larisa. At the beginning of the second century B.C., Hierapytna concluded a treaty with Priansos. Later, in 146 B.C., the Hierapytnians managed to destroy their old eastern enemy, Praisos,* occupying its territory but inheriting at the same time the rivalries of this city with Itanos.* Various inscriptions record institutions, festivals and treaties of the Hierapytnians. Rhodes managed to overcome Hierapytna and conclude a treaty with it, as well as with Olous,* in an effort to suppress the piracy* which was supported by these Cretan cities and incited by Philip V, king of Macedon and the great enemy of Rhodes.

Hierapytna stubbornly resisted Roman invasion as the last free Cretan city and was destroyed in 66 B.C. During the Roman occupation* the city flourished again. Many important public buildings were erected, such as temples, great public baths (*thermae*), aqueducts, an amphitheater and two fine theaters of which no trace remains. Both had in front of them large courts surrounded by porticoes of the Ionic order. The city remained important during the First Byzantine period* but was destroyed in 824 A.D. by the invading Saracens. Later, among the antiquities looted and sent to

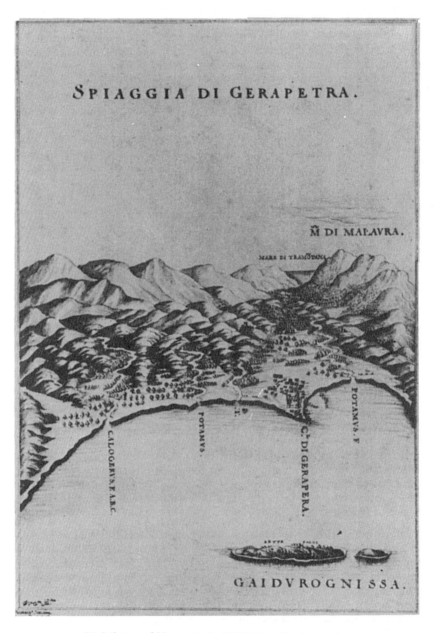

84. Isthmus of Hierapetra in 1615 (*after a Venetian map*)

85. Hieroglyphic inscription on a seal from Mochlos (*after Davaras*)

Venice, were a number of the capitals and entablatures of the small theater. In recent years a splendid, almost life-sized, bronze statue of a draped youth was found in the sand of the beach.

Hieroglyphic Script. The earliest examples of writing* in Crete belong to the Hieroglyphic or Pictographic script, which appears rather suddenly in Middle Minoan I-II times. Its signs are like pictures, some of which resemble and are most probably modelled on the Egyptian Hieroglyphic script, or are, rarely, reminiscent of the precuneiform writing of earliest Mesopotamia. Others seem to have been evolved in Crete, unless they were borrowed from some as yet unknown script of the Near East. Evans* enumerated a hundred and thirty-five signs. Many of the pictures in the Pictographic script are easily recognized actual things: an eye, a man walking, a star, a double axe,* a throne, a jug, various utensils, ships,* insects, plants and trees, a gate, two crossed hands and other limbs, an arrow, the head of various animals. The sign of eight-stringed lyre yields precious evidence about Minoan music,* while the recurrence of a bee points to honey* production. The sign of the plough with stilt, pole and share beam gives us a clear picture of the important agricultural instrument used at this time.

This script is found on stone seals* (figure 85), perhaps considered amulets* containing a magical phrase or incantation, and further on clay labels, bars and tablets* of oblong form; occasionally it appears on a double axe* or stone vessel. The Hieroglyphic script, the only one existing for several centuries (from about 2000 B.C. until about 1650 B.C.), shows a later development and becomes less naturalistic and more schematic. The

Linear A script* developed from it. Despite many efforts, this Hiero-glyphic script still evades decipherment; only some broad inferences can be made, while a few signs are understood. Evidently this script, unlike the Egyptian hieroglyphs, does not record the full extent of the language but only certain standard ideas in an abbreviated way, perhaps exclusively religious or magical.On the other hand the signs for numbers are clear: thus, units were shown by vertical or slightly curved lines, tens by dots, a hundred was represented by a long slanting line, and a thousand by a lozenge. Fractions, perhaps quarters, were indicated by a V.

Hodigitria Monastery. This monastery honouring the Virgin Hodigitria ("Indicator of the Way") was built in the sixteenth century at an isolated place in the western part of the Asterousia Mountains, which bound the Mesara Plain* to the south. Some interesting frescoes still survive here. Because of its remote position, this fortified monastery played a certain role during the uprising of 1828 against the Turks. One can see the tower of Xopateras, a valiant fighter who was killed here.

Honey. In very remote times wild honey was collected from hollow trees in the forests or in rock crevices, but later bees were domesticated and kept for their precious product, the main source of sugar in antiquity. The alcoholic fermentation of honey was known to the Egyptians and probably also to the Minoans. An important by-product was first-quality wax. The mythical Kouretes* were said to be the first to invent the art of rearing bees and to discover the making of honey. On the splendid gold pendant from Malia,* one of the highest achievements of Minoan jewellery, a pair of bees is heraldically represented (see Jewellery*). Sign 86 of the Minoan Hieroglyphic script* is the picture of a bee. Legend describes how Glau-kos,* son of Minos,* was drowned by falling into one of the huge pithoi* of the palace containing honey; it has been suggested that this might be symbolic of a possible use of honey for embalming inside the burial pithoi,* as the Babylonians did, accordingly to Herodotus. This method was used for transporting the body of Alexander the Great from Babylon to Alexandria.

Offerings of honey to Eileithyia* and other divinities are mentioned on the Knossos* tablets* in the Linear B script.* The presence of honey, a primitive intoxicant, among the ingredients offered in the sacred com-munion* had been assumed. Perhaps this is in accordance with the later Greek belief that honey, which played an important role in ritual, was the food of gods.

Horns of Consecration see **Sacral Horns.**

Horses. Horses were probably brought gradually to Greece from the east and north after 2000 b.c., a date in which they were already known in Cy-prus. Perhaps they were introduced by the immigrating Greeks. Some animals engraved on early Cretan seals have been interpreted as horses but they may have been donkeys. The first sure representations of horses

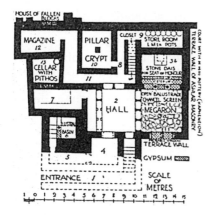

86. House of the Chancel Screen
(after Evans)

appear during the fifteenth century B.C. and their bones have been recovered in various deposits dating from this time onwards. According to many scholars the horses-in fact rather wild goats – on the famous sarcophagus from Hagia Triada,* dated around 1400 B.C., are painted in a manner showing that the artist was hesitant and inexperienced with this new motif. Signs of horses are found in the Linear B* tablets.* Often the manes of the animals are characteristically divided into knotted tufts.

Horseback riding was apparently practised in a limited way before the invention of saddles and stirrups. In any case, no horsemen are depicted in Minoan art* and no cavalry existed. The horse served mainly as a draught animal for the chariot* and probably played a minor role in transport.*

House of the Chancel Screen. This private house (figure 86), built at the southeast corner of the palace at Knossos,* includes a pillar crypt with a single square pillar* **(10)**, a Lustral Basin* **(6)** and three magazines* **(9, 12 and 13)**. Especially interesting is the hall **(2)** in the middle of the house, with another hall **(3a)**, which leads on the left to a balustrade with an opening flanked by columns.* Behind this are two steps leading up to a room with a raised stone dais, supposedly for a formal seat of honour.

House of the High Priest. This partly vanished house south of the palace at Knossos* was so named from a stone altar* flanked by stands for double axes* and set back behind a balustrade supporting two columns,* which resembles a chancel. In front of the altar a hole leads down into a stone drain; the area of the altar was closed by a grille of metal. The entrance is flanked by chests for offerings. The House of the High Priest lies near the great Temple-Tomb.*

Household Goddess see **Snake Goddess.**

House (Minoan) Minoan architecture* found its expression not only in the construction of palaces,* villas* and other larger buildings but also in that of smaller private houses. Even huts must have existed (see

Lebena*). The Neolithic settlement at Knossos* yielded ample evidence of the earliest houses (see Neolithic period*). The houses of the Early Minoan period* are well represented in the settlements at Vasiliki* and Myrtos* in Eastern Crete. Ordinary Bronze Age* houses were often several storeys high. Their roofs were flat, as is usual in the south. Little faience* inlays in the form of coloured plaques—decorating a wooden box or small chest now vanished—found at Knossos* and assigned to 1700 b.c. or earlier, depict facades or backs of private houses of two or three storeys built often of clay bricks (figure 87). Their flat roofs are sometimes surmounted by small attic rooms, perhaps summer sleeping places. Windows–two- or four- or six-panelled and often elongated—are only in the second floor. Some of them are painted scarlet, a fact interpreted as implying that oiled parchment was used before the invention of glass. It has been suggested that the houses depicted here were incorporated in the defense wall of the city. This "Town Mosaic" is indeed a precious source of information about the exterior appearance of Minoan houses and their constructive features.

The walls and floors of these houses were often coated with mud or lime plaster.* Occasionally a dado of gypsum* slabs protected and decorated the lower part of the walls. The usual houses were built on foundations of coarse rubble. Heavier walls received deep foundations, often resting on roughly coursed blocks. A stepped plinth was necessary for constructions built on a slope. The facades were often constructed of carefully coursed ashlar masonry (see Architecture, Minoan*). The walls were normally built to a certain height with rubble composed of rough, uncut fieldstones, with clay or mud mortar, and continued upwards with mudbrick. Some early walls were built entirely of sun-dried mud-brick, material regularly reserved only for thin partition walls. Sometimes an interlacing timber framework of horizontal and upright beams affixed to the stone by means of wooden pegs tied the fabric of the walls together. This was a good measure against earthquakes* and was regularly employed for the larger buildings throughout the whole Minoan Age.

Doors were normally placed on the long side of the room. No fixed hearths seem to have existed until a late period. In some late examples at Karphi* large broken jars were reused as chimneys, a custom which has survived in Cretan popular architecture.*

A great variety of Minoan private houses can be seen at the town of Gournia* and at Knossos,* Palaikastro,* Zakros* and other sites. The better-known towns of Eastern Crete show us that houses, although self-contained units, were nevertheless not free-standing structures, as a number of them formed a large irregular block confined by the road-system of the town. Characteristic of earlier times are the houses at Vasiliki,* Myrtos,* Phaistos,* Palaikastro* and Chamaizi.*

A splendid clay model twenty-three centimetres (nine inches) high of a Middle Minoan III house was recently found by A. Lembessi at Archanes,* all details are elaborately represented, including windows, a stairway and a light colonnade on the flat roof obviously supporting a thatch; the columns* characteristically taper downwards.

Hunting see **Animals (Wild); Weapons.**

87. Faience "Town Mosaic" from Knossos

HYBRIAS. Hybrias, a Cretan poet of the sixth century B.C. or even earlier, is best known for a war song belonging to the Greek lyric poetry genre and of historical value. In the poem a warrior, a Cretan aristocrat, praises his weapons as his great wealth and for the power they give him

over the serfs (see Slavery in Dorian Crete*), who dare not raise arms.
Here is the last verse of the song, translated by T. Campbell, which vividly
illustrates the existing social relations and the securely settled aristocratic
establishment in Crete:

> But your wights that take no pride to wield
> A massy spear and well-made shield
> Nor joy to draw the sword,
> O I send those heartless hapless drones
> Down in a trice on their marrow bones
> To call me king and lord.

Hyrtakina. South of modern Temenia in the Prefecture of Chania* in
Western Crete is situated the Classical Greek city-state of Hyrtakina,
which was an inland power. The city was surrounded by a strong double
fortification, the ruins of which are preserved. Hyrtakina was included in
the monetary union of its three neighbours, Elyros,* Lisos* and Tarrha.*
The Greek archaeologist Theophanides excavated a temple of Pan here. A
statue of the goat-legged god is now in the Chania Museum. Another divinity worshipped in the city was Demeter.* A temple of Hera is mentioned in an inscription. Another inscription reveals that the "common
hearth" of the city was placed in the temple of Apollo Delphinios.

Ida (Mount). Mount Ida, modern Psiloritis, thus named since at least the
twelfth century A.D., located in the center of Crete, reaches a height of
2456 metres (8058 feet) and is the highest mountain of the island. Its sum-
mits are covered with snow for nine months of every year. It includes the
Nida Plateau, which reaches a height of 1400 metres (about 4600 feet). The
mountain was named after Ida, daughter of Korybas and wife of
Lykastos.* In fact the name means "the forest," evidently in accordance
with its once heavily wooded slopes. Hesiod tells us how the goddess
Demeter* made love with a mortal, Iasion, a son of Minos* and the nymph
Phronia, in a thrice-ploughed field prepared for sowing on the slopes of
Ida. From this union was born a son, Ploutos ("wealth"). Ida is of great
literary celebrity.

The mountain has two important cult caves, the Idaian Cave* and the
Kamares Cave.* A third is situated much further to the west near the village of Patsos (see Sybrita*). In recent years the discovery of a papyrus
fragment, containing *Kretes* ("Men of Crete"), the lost drama of Euripides, reveals the possible existence of a mystic cult of Zeus* of Ida, associated with Orphism. The votaries of this cult seem to have been
recruited in the region of Axos.*

Idaian Cave. The famous Idaian Cave (*Idaion antron*), below the summit of
Mount Ida,* 1500 metres (5000 feet) above the sea, was an important cult
place (see Caves*) for more than a thousand years and until Roman times.
There is evidence that it had been used since the Late Minoan period.*
According to one tradition, this cave, not the Diktaian Cave,* was the
birthplace of Zeus.* The great philosopher Pythagoras was said to have
visited the cave after his purification by one of the Idaian Daktyloi* with
the thunder-stone. There he offered a funeral sacrifice to Zeus, saw his

throne, and inscribed an epigram with the title "Pythagoras to Zeus."

The site was explored in 1885. Beyond the entrance, where a large fallen rock was shaped into a rectangular altar with a high step all around, the cave consists of two main chambers. The floor was covered with a deep layer of ashes, charcoal, bones and rich votive offerings, which included a seal depicting a cult scene. Among the dedications in the cave most important are the famous bronze shields, dating to the Orientalizing period* (see Shields*). Notable are some imported Oriental ivories, bronze bowls, cymbals and gongs; a tambourine-like object of an Oriental style shows a god accompanied by two winged attendants with cymbals (possibly Zeus and two of the Kouretes*), striding over a bull and brandishing a lion above his head. Most of the decoration is hammered out. Other votive objects include vessels for pouring wine; tripod cauldrons;* an important bronze head-vase with a "layer-wig" (divided between museums in Oxford and Herakleion); groups in cast bronze, such as a warship with rowers; models of chariots,* and a man milking a cow; various animals in bronze, such as goats, bulls, sphinxes and snakes; and a number of clay objects. These artifacts were probably made in Knossian workshops. Even in Roman times there were inscriptions to Zeus.*

IDOMENEUS. King Idomeneus, son of Deukalion and grandson of Minos,* claiming descent from Zeus,* was the leader of the Cretan contingent in the expedition of the army of the Achaians* before Troy. The Cretan entry in the Catalogue of Ships in the Iliad seems to refer to a total of eighty ships under Idomeneus and Meriones. Seven Cretan towns are named as contributing the fleet: Knossos,* Gortyn,* Milatos,* Phaistos,* Lyttos,* Lykastos and Rhytion. Evans believed that the name Idomeneus seems to point to an early settlement round Mound Ida.* Homer says: "And of the Cretans Idomeneus the famous spearman was leader, even of them that possessed Knossos and Gortyn of the great walls,...and of all others that dwelt in Crete in the Hundred cities....With these followed eighty black ships." The Cretan contribution in the Trojan War was quite important, if we compare the hundred ships under Agamemnon, King of Mycenae and leader of the whole expedition.

Ierapetra see **Hierapetra.**

IKAROS. Ikaros, the symbol of human striving for flight, was the son of the famous engineer and craftsman, Daidalos,* and Naukrate, one of King Minos' slave girls. He was locked together with his father in the Labyrinth* by command of Minos,* who was angry because of the assistance Daidalos had given Queen Pasiphae* in coupling with the white bull of Poseidon. Pasiphae then freed them from the Labyrinth, and Daidalos, a great inventor, manufactured flying wings for himself and Ikaros that they might escape from Crete through the air, since Minos ruled both the sea and the land. The quill feathers were threaded together, but the smaller ones were held in place by wax. During their flight Ikaros disobeyed his father's strict instructions and, exhilarated by the lift of the wings, incautiously approached too near the blazing sun, which then melted the wax; Ikaros fell into the sea and drowned. Daidalos buried the body on a nearby island, called afterwards Ikaria.

Imports. In early times marble idols, imitated locally, were imported from the Cyclades; other imports were some vases, obsidian,* and Naxian emery, useful as an abrasive for making stone vases.* As a matter of fact, Crete and its palatial economy* were self-supporting for the essential needs such as food and building materials. Nevertheless, since the island was not very rich in mineral resources,* some copper may have been brought from outside, perhaps from neighbouring Cyprus, to supplement the limited local resources, while tin for alloying with copper to make bronze was obviously imported from Etruria and the Tyrrhene shores or from Central Europe. Other raw materials which came to the island must be considered luxuries which the flourishing palace economy* could afford, such as fine stones indispensable for making seals* and vases of good quality, or precious metals such as gold and silver, together with a limited number of foreign manufactures. Although Crete possesed its own ores, some silver was imported during the early periods, perhaps from Italy or Spain through the Cyclades. Gold must have been imported either from Egypt, which had access to the rich Nubian mines, or from the Pactolus area in Asia Minor, which provided Babylonia with all its needs in gold. From the south Peloponnese came stones such as *rosso antico* and *lapis lacedaemonius*, the "Spartan basalt" much favoured for the manufacture of vessels and lamps;* from Gyali in the Dodecanese spotted obsidian for stone vessels was imported, and from Egypt came various manufactured items (see Egyptian objects in Crete*) and further materials such as amethyst, veined white alalaster*, and perhaps papyrus for writing,* linen, plumes, and ostrich eggs, which were transformed into libation vases or imitated in clay and stone. Ivory* in the form of elephants' tusks was probably imported from Syria, and seals and other objects were brought from Syria, Anatolia and Mesopotamia. Lapis lazuli, the *kyanos* of the Greeks, is considered to be an import from Badakshan in far-off Northern Afghanistan.

Inatos. A harbour of Greek and Roman times at the south coast of Central Crete near the modern hamlet of Tsoutsouros, Inatos or Winatos was mainly known because of the existence of an important cave sanctuary of Eileithyia.* An Early Christian basilica arose before it in the fifth century B.C. A group of statues including Niobe was recovered from the ruins of the town. The name of Inatos is perhaps recognizable in the Linear B* tablets* as *wi-na-to*.

Industries. Nothing precise is known about the social structure* and the occupations of the Minoan population except what can be reconstructed from archaeological research and the material evidence, which are the only sources of our knowledge about Bronze Age* industries. Besides the food producers, such as the farmers, shepherds, herdsmen, fishermen and hunters, and the distributors of agricultural products (see Agriculture*), such as the merchants and the men occupied with transport,* we may assume an extensive craft specialization, as no one man could be proficient in all skills: the evidence shows the existence of various craftsmen, including masons, lapidaries, potters, coppersmiths, carpenters and shipbuilders, and other artistically specialized craftsmen, such as fresco painters (see Frescoes*), seal* cutters, ivory* carvers, scribes, makers of stone vases,* faience* artifacts and jewellery.* These men were probably supported by the palatial economy* as full-time craftsmen, working and perhaps dwelling in the palaces.*

For later times the Linear B* tablets* are highly relevant: the occupations mentioned here are various, including, besides those already mentioned, bow-makers, spinners, tailors, bronze-smiths, unguent boilers, chariot-builders, as well as huntsmen, goatherds, ox-drivers, heralds, messengers, serving women, and bath attendants. Remains of several kilns (see Terracotta*) have been excavated as well as various kinds of workshops, such as the lapidary's workshop in the royal domestic quarter at Knossos* and the carpenter's workshop and the bronze foundry at Gournia.* Spinning and weaving of cloth*—and perhaps leather-working* and perfume* making—were household industries obviously carried on by women, although they might have been further developed into real industries with a larger production.

Ingots. The standard type of Minoan copper ingot, about 60 to 90 centimetres (two or three feet) long—widely found also outside Crete—had incurving sides and projections, at first interpreted as vaguely imitating an ox-hide, a skin without head or tail. More recently it is believed that the shape was determined by the needs of transport. This type—well adapted for portage on a man's shoulder and convenient for storage—is dated to about 1500 B.C. Several ingots were recovered at Hagia Triada* (figure 88), Zakros,* Tylissos* and elsewhere. The six examples from Zakros* were perhaps of Cypriot manufacture. Some of the ingots have incised signs on them.

It has been assumed that ingots were a rudimentary form of currency to be weighed out against other commodities, with a fixed weight generally accepted, for in many cases the weight is uniform, averaging about 29 kilograms (64 pounds), perhaps the equivalent of the Homeric talent. The largest weight unit of the Linear B* tablets* probably represents the talent. A large pyramidical weight of reddish stone of 29 kilograms decorated with octopuses in relief was originally considered a sort of royal or standard talent, but later it was recognized as an elaborate anchor (see Ships*). More recently, some scholars, marking the existing differences in weight which range from 26 to 33 kilograms (57 to 73 pounds), believe that these ingots were the standard form in which the unworked copper, obtained as raw material from moulds in the smelting workshop, was primarily transported and sold, and eventually used as a unit in transactions. Smaller bun-shaped ingots were also in use.

During the late Bronze Age* the shape of the ingots changed: the deeply incurved short sides contrast to the straight long ones, while the four ends project sharply. Some of the Keftiu* figures painted in Egyptian tombs bear ingots as gifts from overseas.

88. Inscribed bronze ingot from Hagia Triada

Inscriptions (Greek) see **Writing.**

Insulae see **Early Palaces.**

Iraklion see **Herakleion.**

Iron. The oldest iron object found in Crete (eighteenth century B.C.) in the cemetery of Mavro Spilio near Knossos,* was a small cube. From Hagia Triada* comes a meteorite, polished like a stone vase, and showing traces of sawing on its surface: this example characteristically demonstrates the celestial origin of the first iron used by men, regarded as divine and laboriously shaped into an amulet;* let us note that stoneworking techniques were here applied. Although meteoric iron is quite frequently found, it is a hard alloy because of its nickel content; thus, Bronze Age* metallurgy,* with no high-temperature furnaces, was not able to make it fluid so that it could be properly worked. An iron nail with a gold head from Knossos* clearly shows how iron, then rare and precious, was used in jewellery.*

The theory that iron was introduced into Greece by the invading Dorians,* who were able to overcome the bronze weapons* of the older Achaian* inhabitants, has been shown to be incorrect by modern research, although it was generally accepted until recently. In fact, iron working, which had been at first a secret, and a monopoly of the Hittites, developed rapidly in the Near East during the last two centuries of the second millenium B.C., and was then introduced into Greece and Crete, where it was connected with the mythical Daktyloi.* If we consider the difficulties of iron smelting in early times, it is no wonder that iron came into general use about two millenia later than copper.

In Crete iron gradually replaced bronze as the chief metal for weapons* and especially for tools* such as axes,* hammers, knives, sickles, and ploughshares. This caused a sort of industrial revolution.. The earliest weapons seem to have been mere translations into iron of bronze types. Of course, fine work for figurines* and ornamental shields* continued to be done in bronze. The Iron Age era began with tremendous implications for peace and war. Agriculture became more productive and domestic industry more efficient. Local self-sufficiency increased, a fact which, among others, contributed to the formation of the Dorian city-states in Crete.

Iron objects are often found in excavations in Crete, but are always badly corroded and almost deformed.

Iron Age see **Iron/Tools.**

Islands of Crete, Satellite. Crete possesses several small satellite islands near its coasts, all of them uninhabited except the largest one, Gaudos.* The surface of these islands is about 70 square kilometres (about 27 square miles). Three of them, Grambousa* (see figure 73), Souda Bay* Island (see figure 170), and Spinalonga* (see figure 121) were fortified with Venetian fortresses controlling navigation. Others are famous because of their archaeological sites, such as Mochlos* and Pseira* (see figure 123, left). Gaidouronisi—ancient Chrysea—opposite Hierapetra,* with its subtropical climate, its all-pervading deep sand and its cedar forest, undoubtedly is the most beautiful (see figure 84, foreground). In Minoan times, here and on neighbouring Kouphonisi—ancient Leuke—to the east, sponge diving and murex-shell fisheries were probably local industries. Leuke belonged to Itanos* but was claimed by Praisos,* its rival, and after its destruction, by Hierapytna.* In 112 B.C. the matter was settled in favour of Itanos* after arbitration by the Magnesians. The large island of Dia, opposite Herakleion,* was settled during the Neolithic period.* Some of these coastal islands are preserves for *agrimia*, the Cretan ibexes (see Animals, Wild*), a protected species.

Isopata see **Tholos Tombs.**

Itanos. Itanos, today called also Erimoupolis ("Deserted Town"), the easternmost of the Greek city-states in Crete, lies north of Palaikastro*

and Vai.* Perhaps it was the *u-ta-no* of the tablets. The city was named after one of the Kouretes.* The promontory of Itanos ends at the Cape Samonion (today Cavo Sidero), where a temple of Athena Samonia was
consecrated by the Argonauts. Actual remains of an archaic temple have
been found. The city is mentioned by Herodot. A Cretan from Itanos led a
colony from Thera* to found Cyrene in Libya. The Itanian territory included the entire eastern coast of Crete. Its harbour was an important
station in the trade* between Crete and the Near East. The sanctuary of
the Diktaian Zeus, which stood in the area of the Minoan town of Palaikastro,* had a rich income. This economic expansion led Itanos to become
one of the first Cretan cities to strike a coinage.* Its coins were outstanding examples of the coin-engraver's art; among other subjects depicted
were tritons. An important decree of the third century B.C. reveals that all
the Itanian citizens were obliged to take an oath of loyalty. This document
indicates the existence of social unrest and a movement of social revolution, which was repressed with Egyptian aid. During this century Itanos
was an ally of Knossos.*

In 121/20 B.C. Itanos and Lato* became involved in a war against
Olous* and Hierapytna.* An inscription informs us how the Itanians in
146 B.C. asked for the help of their mighty ally, Ptolemaios Philometor,
one of the Ptolemies, the Macedonian kings of Egypt who had had a base
there since 285 B.C., in their dispute with Praisos.* This large inscription
is today incorporated in a wall inside the Monastery of Toplou near Vai*
(Virgin Mary of the Cape: a Medieval monastery, the character of which
has been almost totally obliterated by unchecked modern construction;
the Turkish name Toplou refers to a place equipped with cannon, probably against pirates). After the destruction of Praisos by the Hierapytnians, Itanos and Hierapytna* shared a common frontier but developed
conflicting interest. During the Roman occupation* and the Early Christian period Itanos continued to flourish but was eventually destroyed,
probably by the Arabs (see Arab Occupation*).

The site has been explored by the French School of Archaeology. The
ruins of the city are minimal. On the western acropolis is a fine terrace
wall. The houses of the Greek and Roman times have been obliterated by
a great number of Byzantine houses and a large basilica.

Ivory. Ivory may have been imported from Syria, since wild elephants of
a small-sized species survived there as late as the ninth century B.C. The
craft of ivory-carving, an outstanding achievement of the palace
workshops and one of the most sophisticated and beautiful arts the Minoans practised, originated in the Orient but the Cretans developed early
their own typically Minoan style in this attractive material. The earliest
examples date from the Early Minoan period,* especially amulets* and
seals,* some of which show excellent carvings of figured handles. Several
later ivory inlays and statuettes have survived, such as the well-known
Sacral Knot* and the astoundingly vivid statuette of an acrobat (figure 89),
obviously a bull-leaper in the Bull-games,* found in the residential quarter of the palace at Knossos.* (No trace of the bull has survived.) This
tense, slender and beautifully proportioned figure is not well preserved

89. Ivory acrobat from Knossos

but has been skillfully restored. We see here for the first time a figure moving freely in space. The muscles, the veins on the back of the hands and even the finger-nails are finely modelled. A number of tiny holes in the head denote that originally flowing locks of hair were attached, probably of gold or bronze with gold plating.

The statuettes were made in a number of separate pieces adroitly joined together by means of dowels and pins; parts of them apparently were covered with gold leaf. The largest of them must have stood about thirty centimetres (about one foot) high. An outstanding example is a statuette of a Snake Goddess* wearing a high crown. Details of the statuette are in gold. This figure is now in Boston, and has very uncertain provenance. The same is true of other statuettes, such as the goddess known as "Lady of the Sports" according to Evans,* which is now in Toronto. This goddess wears a male loin cloth and has ornaments in gold plate.

Furniture* and boxes were adorned with inlaid ivory, which was also used for spindle-whorls and for toilet articles* such as mirror handles and combs, sometimes elaborate and adorned with rosettes or sphinxes. An ivory box from Katsambas near Knossos* illustrates in relief a bull-game.* The famous inlaid draught-board from Knossos* has an ivory framework

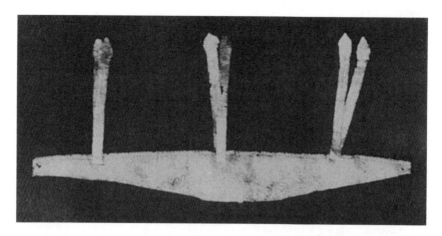

90. Early Minoan diadem from Mochlos

(see Games*). Several Egyptian objects* found in Crete are also of ivory.

Some complete elephant tusks which probably came from Syria were discovered in the palace at Zakros;* the largest and best preserved of them reached a length of seventy centimetres (over two feet). From sections of such tusks, cylindrical boxes with elaborate relief decoration and sometimes coated with gold leaf were carved during the Late Minoan period.* An ivory-worker's shop has been found at Knossos.*

Jewellery. Minoan jewellery displays an astounding grace, skill and elegance. Techniques in gold and silver work are varied: filigree and granulation (fine wires or minute grains of gold fixed to the surface of the gold; the lost secret of attaching the grains has only recently been rediscovered) were learned from Egypt or from Syria; repoussé (a technique of embossing little dots in patterns or even scenes on a thin sheet of gold by pressure from behind by means of punches or with moulds) was also known, as was inlaying with paste or stones. The invention of enameling is attributed to fifteenth century Crete. Extremely fine and delicate chains of gold were also made.

Some jewels were manufactured in stone moulds, of which a number have been found. Splendid diadems (figure 90) of gold sheet (often decorated by means of flimsy high antennae waving freely, and raised dots, sometimes representing animals or human eyes), as well as a number of sprays of leaves (figure 91), armlets with edges gripping a core of leather, delicate beads, and flowers resembling daisies set on hairpins (figure 92) have been found in Early Minoan tombs at the islet of Mochlos.* Other interesting jewels of this period and later come from the tombs of the Mesara Plain.* This early jewellery, obviously made for very eminent persons of their society, is inspired by the more stylized and elaborate Mesopotamian jewellery from the Royal Tombs at Ur.

The most famous of all Minoan jewels is perhaps the splendid bee pendant (figure 93) from the great tomb of Chrysolakkos at Malia,* datable to the seventeenth century B.C.: the confronted bees are sym-

91. Early Minoan spray of leaves from Mochlos

metrically arranged about a honeycomb which is adorned with minute granulation, as are the eyes and the abdomens of the insects; above them is a minature cage with a gold bead enclosed inside it; from the pendant hang three discs. The arts of embossing, granulation and filigree are here splendidly combined.

An excellent treasure of gold jewellery, unlikely plundered from Chrysolakkos (characteristically meaning "the Gold Hole") but known as the Aegina Treasure, was acquired in 1892 by the British Museum. This collection includes elaborate earrings and pendants, obviously worn as pectorals on the chest. An Egyptian influence is often apparent. Outstanding in the collection is the so-called Master of Animals, a purely Cretan figure, holding in either hand a water bird and standing on a field of lotuses. Another pendant consists of a curved gold plate terminating at either end in a human head. The eyes and eyebrows were inlaid, probably with lapis lazuli. Both jewels have a series of hanging discs, perhaps sun-

92. Early Minoan daisy-pin from Mochlos

symbols. There is also a series of superb finger rings, inlaid with lapis lazuli, as well as a rich collection of various beads.

Minoan jewellery included hair-pins, armlets, anklets, wristlets, earrings, and collars and necklaces of beads. Finger rings had a slightly convex oval bezel set across the axis of the hoop. In early times the bezel was left plain but later was often engraved or inlaid. Some earlier bezels are round. These rings were in fact pendants, as their loops were too small for a finger, and clearly belong to the family of seals.* They illustrate religious scenes with a real feeling for miniature, and offer at the same time masterpieces of art on a tiny scale and glimpses of a religion* still rather mysterious to us. These microscopic cult scenes, which include various figures along with altars* and sacred trees and enclosures, are a

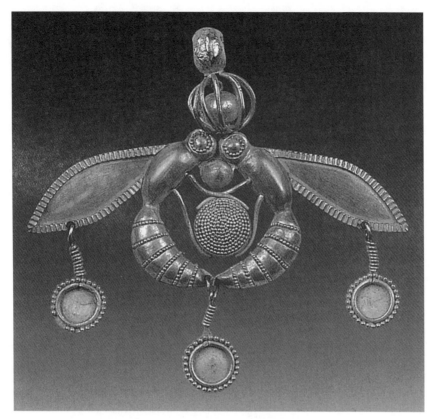

93, Bee pendant from Malia

major source of information for the archaeologist.

Beads were made of gold, silver or copper; also of different kinds of stone, such as cornelian, lapis lazuli and amethyst, and also of faience,* glass or paste (figure 94) that might be plated with gold; their shapes were extremely varied. From scenes on certain frescoes we may conclude that jewels were worn by both sexes.

Juktas (Mount). Mount Juktas, south of Knossos* and near Archanes,* with an altitude of 811 metres (2661 feet), had a peak sanctuary* on the highest summit, with a Minoan road supported on a terrace wall leading up to the sanctuary from Knossos.* This sanctuary was one of the largest and had a massive wall of huge rough blocks, in some places consisting of nine courses, and enclosing a wide area (*temenos*), on which a large shrine building was excavated in 1909 by Evans.* The shrine had three rooms approached by an ascending ramp; the largest room–nine by six metres (29×19 feet)–was floored with white plaster. This Middle Minoan sanctuary continued to be a cult place into the Late Minoan III period, and some of the walls were perhaps built during this time. The deposits of the

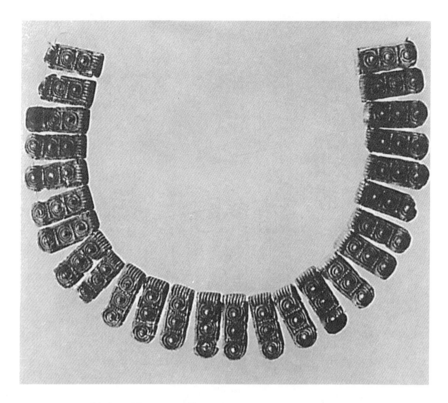

94. Late Minoan necklace of paste from the Mesara Plain

sanctuary have recently been further excavated by Ioannidou, yielding some excellent finds. The inaccurate old plan of the sanctuary has been improved.

Mount Juktas was the legendary burial-place of Zeus.* From some distance, e.g., from the palace at Knossos,* its shape resembles the bearded head of a reclining god. Byzantine and later scholars knew it as the "tomb of Zeus," a name which still survives today for the place on the summit.

Kainourio Fortress. Castel Nuovo, today in ruins, was built in 1206 by the Genoese Pescatore on a steep hill west of the village of Kastelli, near Moires in the Mesara Plain.* The fortress was called Kainourio Kastelli ("Castel Nuovo") by the Greeks, a name which was later extended over the whole province. Pescatore also built the Monofatsi Fortress.*

Kaloi Limenes see **Lasaia.**

KALYPSO see **Gaudos.**

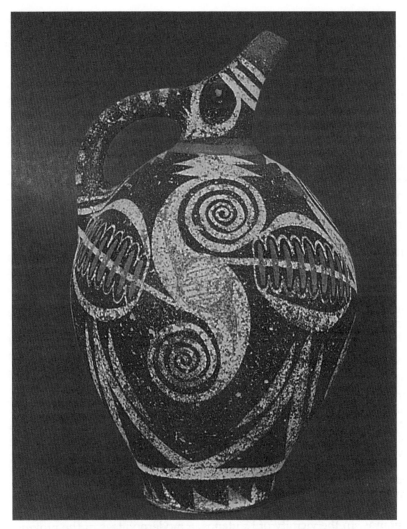

95. Kamares Ware jug from the Early Palace at Phaistos

Kamares Cave see **Caves; Kamares Ware.**

Kamares Ware. Surely the most beautiful variety of Minoan pottery*—by some considered the best of the whole Prehistoric world—is the so-called Kamares Ware, named after a sacred cave (see Caves*) of Mount Ida,* where quantities of this pottery were first found. Kamares Ware was exported as far as Cyprus, the Syrian coast and Egypt. This polychrome (many-coloured) ware, dated to the Middle Minoan I and II phases, or the period of the Early Palaces,* illustrates in a splendid way the Minoan love of movement and colour and an astounding wealth of imagination. The decoration—an evolution of the white-on-black of the previous phase—is

brilliant and delicate in the extreme (figure 95). The designs are formal-
ized but resemble vegetal forms and express a true dynamism, often
organized into twisting, interlocking and radiating patterns, developed
or repeated on the whole surface of the vessel.

The best examples were obviously made in palatial workshops for the
palaces,* since they are found chiefly at Knossos* and Phaistos.* Among
them are often drinking vessels of extreme thinness, the so-called eggshell ware, which with their fluted and embossed shapes imitate metal
vases, now lost. One example, as Pendlebury wrote, "is one of those airy
bubbles which seem to float in the hand." The shapes display great feeling for form and are perfectly executed. The patterns of the Kamares Ware
are made in white, brilliant red, orange or yellow, against a black ground
which is usually matt, with a lustrous metallic sheen in some outstanding eggshell pieces, recalling the glaze of Classical Greek pottery. The ornate motifs show spontaneity and inventiveness and are extremely varied: curvilinear abstract patterns including spirals of every shape, rosettes, twirls and coils rival each other in beauty with natural forms such
as fish* and other sea creatures, blossoms and palm-trees, or intricate
designs borrowed from the Cretan flora,* in a balanced relationship.

Kamilari. The tholos tomb at Kamilari, about two kilometres (1.2 miles)
from the palace at Phaistos,* has been excavated by the Italian, Doro Levi.
This tomb is the best preserved among the early tholos tombs* and one of
the largest. The walls are preserved up to a height of two metres (6.6 feet)
and show signs of vaulting. Some traces of burning on them were
perhaps caused by fumigation of the tomb during some new burial. A
complex of small rectangular rooms joins the tholos itself. The tomb was
built in Middle Minoan I times and was used for several centuries. Among
the finds, a clay model of a rectangular construction with human figures
inside is of utmost importance as evidence for the cult of the dead (see
Tholos Tombs*). Another outstanding object is a clay model depicting
four male dancers dancing in a ring, inside what we may conclude is a sacred enclosure, to judge from the sacral horns* standing on the wall (see
Dance*).

Kantanos. In the vicinity of Kantanos, a modern village of the province
Selino in Western Crete, is situated a Classical Greek city of the same
name. A Roman building was excavated here by Theophanides. A number of small Byzantine churches* with fine fresco-paintings are scattered
in the vicinity of the village; important among them is the Church of St.
Michael, painted in 1328. Kantanos was destroyed and many of its inhabitants executed during the Second World War by the occupation forces. A
bilingual inscription states: "Here was Kantanos." The village has been
rebuilt.

Karphi. The Sub-Minoan village of Karphi ("the Nail"), nearly 400 metres
(1300 feet) above the fertile plateau of Lasithi,* was perhaps already a
peak sanctuary* by the Middle Minoan period.* The founders of this

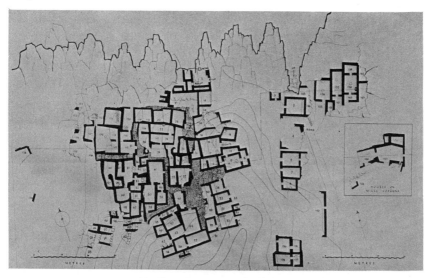

96. Plan of Karphi (*after Pendlebury*)

settlement, refugees of the old Minoan stock, obviously seeking to escape from trouble and to keep their freedom from the invading Dorians,* did build a poor substitute of a Minoan town like Gournia,* but on a high, desolate and inaccessible site exposed to almost unendurable cold and wind in winter but possessing great defensive value. The period of occupation perhaps lasted a hundred or hundred fifty years (1150-1000 B.C.). The population, estimated at about 3,500 persons, lived off the plain below, which was deserted, and at the end evacuated the place peacefully. The unwalled settlement shows no clear planning (figure 96). Some 150 rectangular rooms have been identified by J. Pendlebury. The houses,* usually of one storey only, were built of hard limestone without clay. Thresholds and doorjambs were made of well-cut blocks.

Karphi built its shrine* on the highest spot, an unpretentious construction consisting of three rooms; towards the north side of the largest of them there are the remains of an altar.* The clay cult statuettes and objects found here are especially interesting, demonstrating the survival of Minoan religion* and forms long after the fall of the Minoan state. The statuettes have their hands raised in a gesture of blessing. Some stand nearly a metre (three feet) high. The head of one of them is surmounted by birds* and disks. The feet were separately modelled and put inside openings in the cylindrical skirt. Among the cult object is a charioteer group and two altars* of unusual form; one of them has the shape of a tall rectangular building bearing sacral horns* and figures of animals on the four corners.

Two groups of small tholos tombs*—seventeen and four in each case—have been found at some distance down the hill.

Kato Symi see **Biannos.**

97. Wall-painting with Keftiu in the tomb of Senmut (*after Egypt. Arch.* 1)

Katsambas see **Egyptian Objects; Games; Harbours; Ivory; Neolithic Period.**

Kavousi see **Geometric Period.**

Keftiu. *Keftiu* is evidently the same word as *Kaphtor,* the Biblical name for Crete, related to the Anatolian name *Keptaru;* it was known in Egypt from the period of the Old Kingdom. Foreign emissaries who seem to have been Cretans, bearing as gift or tribute various objects of characteristically Minoan form, were portrayed on the walls of some fifteen tombs at Thebes in Upper Egypt belonging to high Egyptian officials and noblemen of the XVIIIth Dynasty. Among them is the tomb of Senmut (figure 97), the chief architect for the famous Queen Hatsepsut. Another tomb belongs to the Vizier User-amon.

The Cretans on the tomb of Rekhmire were originally painted wearing the codpiece, which after some years was overpainted into a short embroidered Mainland kilt (see Dress, Minoan*). This curious fact, a deliberate change of dress, probably reflects a change of Cretan fashions. In this tomb, which was begun at the end of the reign of Tuthmosis III and finished early in the reign of Amenophis II, the envoys are said to have come "from the land of Keftiu and the islands of the Green Sea." Among the offerings the Cretans bring, we recognize rolls of cloth,* perhaps dyed wool for court dresses, ingots,* palace amphorae, elaborate metal vases, tall fluted and engraved jars of gold and silver, the so-called "Vapheio cups" inlaid with silver, and bull's head rhyta (see Rhyton*) such as the one found at Knossos (see Little Palace*). The vases are depicted with such accuracy that archaeologists could easily date them as being from the Late Minoan IA period. The Keftiu wear their dark hair long with wavy strands over the shoulders. These paintings date to 1520-1420 B.C. As Renfrew remarked, "these scenes give a vivid and unexpected glimpse of a reality behind the rather scanty distributions of pottery which normally provides all our information."

Kernos. A multiple cult vessel called *kernos* by the antiquarian Polemon

98. Clay *kernos* from an Early Minoan tomb

who lived in the Hellenistic period,* and related to the goddesses Demeter* and Rhea, is a direct descendant of a class of Minoan composite vessels which had had similar cult functions—the offering of first-fruits and produce, an almost universal religious custom—and were named after it by modern scholars. Minoan *kernoi* show various individual forms, basically being a set of several small vessels, more or less independent, fixed upon a common base. Each of the smaller vessels contained a different kind of offering; some of these containers are covered with a lid while others take the form of simple cups or bowls. A series of interesting stone or clay *kernoi* (figure 98) have been recovered from tombs of the Early Minoan period* (see Platanos*). Vessels of a similar shape were also employed in predynastic Egypt, possibly for the same purpose. The famous stone table of offerings at the Central Court of the palace at Malia* is usually considered as a sort of huge *kernos.* * The offering of different kinds of first-fruits, grain or liquids such as wine* and olive oil* evidently expressed the wish of the devout to seek the blessing of the divinity upon his agricultural work and produce. This tradition survived in Cretan folklore-customs of a religious nature until the beginning of this century, and has been referred to as a good instance of the timelessness of ritual usage.

Khania see **Chania.**

Kilns see **Terracotta.**

Kisamos. This large city of the Greek period is situated at the location of modern Kisamos (former Kastelli Kisamou), a small coastal town west of

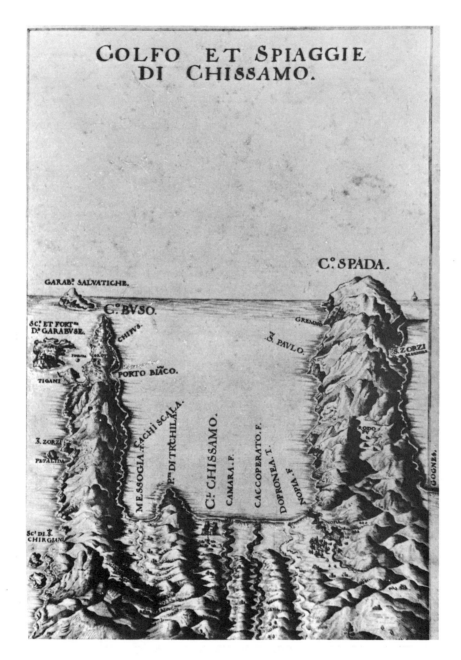

99. Gulf of Kisamos and Grambousa *(after a Venetian map)*

Chania,* and possesses a small and unimportant archaeological collection in provisional housing. Kisamos (figure 99) was a port of Polyrrhenia* but it was once independent and struck its own coinage.* The city is mentioned by Pliny and Ptolemy. It especially flourished during the Roman occupation,* which left a number of important buildings with mosaics, partly excavated in recent years. During the Byzantine period* Kisamos was the seat of a diocese, which later became a Roman Catholic one. The Venetians built a fortress here, today in ruins, which played a role during the Cretan revolts against the Turkish occupation.* Parts of the fortress are of Roman times. Here was perhaps situated a small Minoan settlement belonging to a harbour.*

A fine Venetian villa of the sixteenth century, known as Retonda (from rotonda, "a round building"), partly obliterated by modern constructions, can be visited at Kalathenes, a village near Kisamos. At the village Travasiana is another interesting Venetian building of the early sixteenth century, Villa Trevisan; the village had been named after this landlord.

Knossos (City of). The successor of the Bronze Age* Knossos (see Palace at Knossos*) was a Greek city-state of the same name, one of the mightiest and most important in Crete. Its territory extended from the Mount Ida* to the west to Lyttos,* its greatest rival during many centuries, to the east. The great extension of Knossos is referred to by the epic tradition: Homer describes it as "broad Knossos." During the Geometric period* Knossos was already flourishing again, as is shown by the evidence of extensive and richly furnished graveyards, mainly at the site of Fortetsa, which has yielded large collections of pottery.* Of importance was the sanctuary of Demeter (see Demeter*).

Knossos was among the first Cretan cities which issued a coinage.* Its silver coins were often very fine; among subjects depicted were such traditional ones as the Labyrinth in various standard forms and the Minotaur.* In 221-19 B.C. the Knossians, in alliance with Gortyn,* were able to control the whole of Crete except for Lyttos,* which stubbornly resisted. The Lyttian War was therefore begun and this traditional and notoriously warlike rival was captured and destroyed. During the second century B.C. the power of Knossos was dominant. The importance of Knossos is shown by the fact that the cities of Lato* and Olous* agreed to submit the arbitration of a dispute to a third party, Knossos. In 166/5 the Knossians, again in alliance with the Gortynians, overcame Rhaukos* and divided its territory between themselves. The cooperation between these two most powerful states, a condition for the subjection of the rest of Crete, was often interrupted by strife, which sometimes led to war.

After the Roman conquest, which Knossos resisted, the city lost its prominent place in Crete in favour of Gortyn.* Nevertheless it continued to flourish and was embellished by several public buildings. The Villa of Dionysos, of the time of Hadrian, is adorned with fine mosaic pavements. An important Knossian was the philosopher Ainesidemos, a Sceptic who wrote several books and taught in Alexandria. Knossos later became a major Early Christian center and possessed a fine basilica.

Knot see **Sacral Knot.**

Koinon. The Cretan *Koinon* was a loose federal organization of the Cretan city-states during the long Hellensitic period.* The *Koinon* had a Council of delegates of the member city-states, citizens of which formed a popular Assembly, but it possessed no federal magistrates, army or citizenship. The *Koinon* was convened from time to time in different cities and issued various decrees. Knossos* and Gortyn* were the leading member-states of this unstable federation, which failed to create a Cretan unity.

Kosmoi. After the abolishment of the monarchy in the sixth century B.C. by the aristocracies, the chief magistrates of a Dorian city-state in Crete were the *Kosmoi* ("Orders" or "Rulers"). They were leaders elected for a year and came from aristocratic families. They assumed political as well as military leadership of their communities, combining the functions of the Spartan kings and ephors. Their tenure of office served as a chronological definition in decrees and treaties inscribed on stone. These officals formed the most important political body and assumed the leadership in war. Aristotle informs us in the *Politics* at some length about their functions. The *Kosmoi* were not chosen from the whole people, but from certain important hereditary clans (see Social Structure of Dorian Crete*); indeed, the forms of Dorian tribal society were transformed into essential institutions of the city-state, the *polis*. The *Kosmoi* serving out their annual functions were included in a Council of Elders *(Gerousia)*, an important political body, and sat for life. These magistrates, Aristotle tells us, were sometimes overthrown by a conspiracy.

Kouloures. Three great walled pits in the west court of the Early Palace* at Knossos* were named *Kouloures* by workmen during their excavation, the word being accepted by Evans* as a term for these pits of uncertain purpose. In the two westernmost *Kouloures* were discovered traces of early houses,* one of which was of a religious nature and included a flight of red plaster steps which led down to a room with walls and floor coated with a similar plaster.* Two receptacles, evidently intended for libations, one round and one oblong, were formed on the floor. These *Kouloures* were paved over during a later arrangement while the eastern one remained open for a while. Similar but smaller *Kouloures* have been found in the west court of the palace at Malia.* These walled pits were possibly simple dumps dug to receive the broken pottery* and rubbish from the palace heaps, as Evans thought because of the rubbish found there, perhaps serving at the same time for drainage, since a pit near the "Theatral Area" of Knossos* possessed a stone drain. More probably they originally served as granaries, rather than cisterns, since their walls were not coated with plaster.* Rows of circular granaries were common in Egypt.

KOURETES. The nine Kouretes, sons of Earth and attendants of the young Zeus* in Crete, were said to be the first to gather sheep into flocks, to domesticate animals,* to rear bees and to discover the making of honey.* These benefactors of mankind also invented the bow and introduced archery* and hunting, and taught people how to live together in concord. The Kouretes, especially worshipped in Crete, were closely associated with the cult of the infant Zeus*: according to the myth, they invented the armed dance and danced around the baby a wild leaping dance,* clashing their spears and swords against their shields,* beating drums and shouting to drown out the noise of Zeus' wailing, lest his father Kronos might hear it from far off and come to swallow this child also. Rhea, the wife of Kronos, had taught the art of dancing to them. This weapon-clashing, of an orgiastic character, obviously reflects a custom intended to drive off evil spirits during ritual performances which included frenzied armed dances.

A fragmentary inscription of about 200 B.C. containing a hymn invoking Zeus in the name of the Kouretes was discovered at Palai-kastro.* The young Zeus is invoked annually, as the "greatest Kouros," to confer his blessings and give fertility and good fortune of every kind. This document seems to preserve some very ancient ritual. Because of the close association of the Kouretes with Crete, the island was also *Kouretis* in poetry. The Kouretes appear as the protectors of the simple life of hunters and herdsmen, and of the flocks. They were often identified with the Korybantes. Like the Daktyloi,* they played an important role in popular religion. They often were mentioned among the gods by whom the citizens of the Cretan city-states swore, but they tended to receive private rather than public worship.

Kritsa. Kritsa, one of the largest villages in Crete, is situated on an inland high place near Hagios Nikolaos.* The village enjoys a fine view over the Gulf of Mirabello and its traditional architectural character is interesting.

Kritsa is near the archaeological site of Lato* and the important Byzantine church* of Kera ("Our Lady"), which creates a profound impression. The southern nave dates from the end of the fourteenth century and is the earliest part of the church; its frescoes are among the best in Crete: they depict in bright colours contrasting with dark several scenes from the life of St. Anne and the Virgin Mary, taken from the *Apokrypha* (figure 100). The picture of St. Anne adorns the apse. These unworldly frescoes belong to the Macedonian School and show large figures drawn with clear lines in spacious pictures. The frescoes of the central nave are more severe and imposing. The Virgin is depicted in the couch of the apse (see Byzantine churches*). Above this is the Ascension. The vault includes the Twelve Prophets and the Four Angels, among other subjects. The northern nave was built and painted at the beginning of the fifteenth century. The style of the frescoes resembles that of the southern nave. The barrel vault is occupied by the Last Judgement and the apse by the figure of Christ. The nave is dedicated to St. Anthony.

Another interesting Byzantine church* with fine frescoes at Kritsa is that of St. John the Kavousiotis.

KRONOS see **ZEUS.**

100. Fresco in the church of Kera

KYDON. Kydon, son of Akakallis,* a daughter of Minos,* was the eponymous hero of the mighty city of Kydonia in Western Crete, modern Chania.* His father was Apollo or Hermes. Kydon as an infant was suckled by a
bitch; this scene was depicted on the coins of the city. The story reflects
the very old legend of a child being suckled by an animal, and is often
found in various myths, especially in Crete.

Kydonia. Kydonia, the *ku-do-ni-ja* of the tablets,* lay on the northwest
coast of Crete, facing the Peloponnese, where Chania* is now located. Its
mythical founder was Kydon,* grandson of King Minos.* The Kydonians
were referred to by Homer together with the Eteocretans* and possibly
were of pre-Greek stock. Herodotos tells us how the city was founded in
524 B.C. by Samians, who were reduced to slavery after a short period of
five years. The early importance of Kydonia is noted by Strabo, who reports that the greatest and most famous of all Cretan cities were Knossos,* Gortyn* and Kydonia, founded by Minos* in each of the three parts

into which he had divided the island after gaining mastery of the sea. Minoan remains in Kydonia go far back in time: an important site at Kastelli, inside the old town of Chania, has recently been discovered by Greek and Swedish archaeologists, underneath Medieval and modern constructions. The building had been destroyed by a violent fire. Among great quantities of pottery, the earliest seem to belong to the Neolithic period.* Most important was a rich archive of various clay sealings* and tablets* of the Linear A Script,* for the first time attested so far west in Crete. In other parts of Chania various antiquities have been found, such as a number of Late Minoan chamber-tombs* and a fine mosaic of the Hellenistic period, which shows Poseidon and the nymph Amymone.

A famous citizen of Kydonia during Classical Greek times was the sculptor Kresilas, a pupil of Pheidias. In 429 B.C., during the Peloponnesian War, the Athenians vainly tried to capture Kydonia by siege. During the Hellenistic period* Kydonia was a friend of Macedon, but later it joined the anti-Macedonian camp. During the Lyttian War (see Lyttos*) it was an ally of Knossos.* Kydonia was a rival of the neighbouring cities of Aptera,* Elyros* and Polyrrhenia* and often at war with them. In 171 B.C. the Kydonians attacked and captured Apollonia,* a city allied to them by treaty, but lost it at the end to Gortyn.* In 74 B.C. the Roman fleet lost a battle and was captured by the Cretans off the coast of Kydonia, but in 69 B.C. the city surrendered to three Roman legions and was consequently spared.

Labyrinth. The Labyrinth was the legendary maze-like dwelling of the Minotaur,* built according to Egyptian prototypes by Daidalos,* the skilled artist and engineer of King Minos.* The current theory is that labyrinth, a Greek word of pre-Greek origin, was derived from the word *labrys* ("double axe") and meant "the dwelling of the double axe." It has been further assumed that this place was the palace of Knossos* itself, as the *labrys*, the most eminent symbol of Minoan religion,* was cut innumerable times on the walls and especially on the sacred pillars* of the palace and was variously venerated inside it. A clay tablet of the Linear B script* from the palace unexpectedly revealed the existence of the cult title "Our Lady of the Labyrinth." The palace then, the religious character of which cannot be denied (along with its importance as the chief center of administration*), the dwelling of the "Priest-King,"* could have been the Labyrinth itself, the "House of the Double Axe." After the destruction of the palace, its ruins became more "labyrinthine" in character, and this meaning of the word, for a place full of intricacies or formed with winding passages, was passed on to the Greeks and Romans and then to modern European languages.

Among the Knossian frescoes* is one representing a labyrinth pattern, a series of mazes painted in a reddish-brown colour on an entrance passage of the palace. Another labyrinth pattern was recognized on a graffito on the rear side of a clay tablet from Pylos, scratched by some idle scribe quite independent of the tablet's text. The Greek city-state of Knossos* preserved the labyrinth pattern as an emblem on its coinage,* where it is portrayed as having a cruciform, rectangular or circular form.

The labyrinth has also been interpreted as a mimetic "maze" dance, or an arena—like the Theatral Areas of the palaces—in which such a ritual was performed. The dancer, masquerading as a bull, used labyrinthine convolutions to imitate the movement of the sun. The bull was also a symbol of the sun (see Dance*).

According to Paul Faure, the Labyrinth is to be identified not with the palace, but with the famous sacred cave of Skoteino near Knossos (see Caves*). An ancient subterranean quarry near Kastelli, not far from Gortyn,* with unending galleries where one can easily lose his way, has also been incorrectly associated with the Labyrinth.

An extremely ingenious association between the labyrinth and *labrys* has been recently made, quite apart from any linguistic speculation. The labyrinth pattern was directly connected to the stylized linear double axe sign, which was a regularized sign of both the Minoan scripts and the so-called masons' marks.* The true labyrinth pattern—that is one in which, beginning from a single entrance, one has to pass through all corridors only once in order to reach the center of the design—is a very difficult one to invent and cannot possibly be drawn from memory. It either has to be copied exactly or it may be drawn very easily, beginning from a basic design and following a certain order. Curiously enough, this basic design is the stylized double axe.* One simply adds four angle brackets to guide an encircling movement, as shown in the following drawing.

After completing the pattern, the basic double axe sign can be erased, leaving the labyrinth pattern as a glorified evolution of the original sign. Thus, the labyrinth derives from the *labrys*.

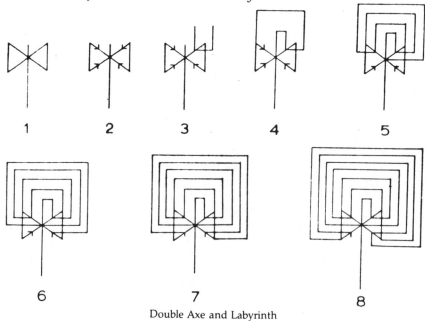

Double Axe and Labyrinth

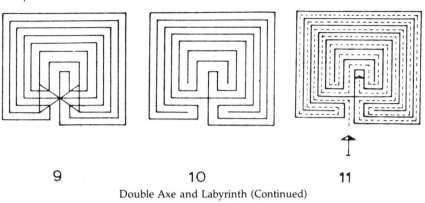

9   10   11

Double Axe and Labyrinth (Continued)

Lamps. Lamps burning olive oil* were indispensible furnishings for houses* in antiquity. They were already in use in Early Minoan times and examples have been found at places such as Myrtos,* Mochlos* or Koumasa. Minoan lamps of clay or stone had one or more troughs in the usually thick rims for one or more wicks, which were sometimes supported by long prongs extending sideways. Lamps of bronze were also made. Some stone lamps had tall pedestals and stood on the floor; their tops were ornate and evidently inspired by capitals of columns* or even small versions of them. A magnificent specimen of purple gypsum dating to Middle Minoan III times has been found in the South East House of Knossos*: the spirally fluted shaft with a winding, papyrus-like pattern in relief supports a capital reminiscent of that of an Egyptian palm-tree column. Another Egyptianizing "architectonic" lamp is formed like a double capital with buds and papyrus foliage on a quatrefoil pedestal. All these elaborate specimens probably were employed in the cult. Their ritual use has been associated with sympathetic magic: by creating light and heat one calls upon their source in nature. Most clay lamps were portable,

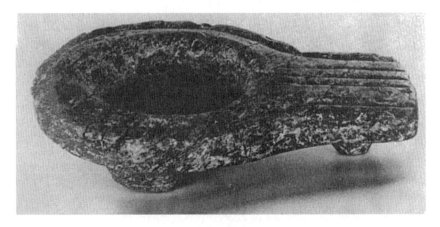

101. Stone lamp from Gournia

102. Late Minoan bathtub *larnax*

while some braziers* could have been used as lamps. Many pieces show traces of burning. An interesting example of a stone lamp standing on three small feet has been found by the author at Gournia* (figure 101). Wall niches were perhaps used as a place to put lamps.

Clay lamps of later Greek times in Crete do not differ from those on the Mainland. The earlier lamps are open above; eventually they become more closed, and in Roman times just a small hole is left on the upper surface, which is usually decorated in a moulded relief, sometimes with a gladiator, a cock, or an erotic scene. An outstanding example from Olous* now in the Hagios Nikolaos Museum* has seventy muzzles on its periphery.

Language (Greek) see **Greek Language.**

Language (Minoan) see **Linear A Script.**

Lappa. Lappa was a city-state of the Dorians* in Western Crete, near the modern Argyroupolis, west of Rethymnon.* The coins of Lappa portrayed a head of Apollo wreathed in laurel, or of Artemis. The city was an ally of Lyttos* and took part in the Lyttian War against Knossos.* It gave refuge to the Lyttians after the destruction of their city. Lappa was destroyed in 67 B.C. by the invading Romans. Later, during the battle of Actium, the Lappians helped the forces of Octavius against Antonius and were consequently favoured by Octavius, who permitted them to rebuild their city. Lappa flourished again for some centuries but was eventually destroyed by the Saracens (see Arab Occupation*). Its successor, Argyroupolis, became an important center during the Venetian occupation* and possessed several villas of Venetian landlords.

Larnakes. The use of larnakes or clay coffins appears in the Early Minoan III period and continues occasionally throughout Minoan times, disap-

103. Late Minoan chest *larnax*

pearing after the burial custom of cremation* became prevalent. The early larnakes, either plain or with a simple linear decoration, normally had an elliptical form and were very short: the dead were trussed tight and placed in them with feet drawn up, knees to chin, and the head raised, imitating an embryonic position. An almost universal use of larnakes painted in the style of the time becomes characteristic of the Late Minoan III period. A common type is the bathtub larnax of oval shape tapering toward the flat base and provided with a flat projecting rim and several horizontal handles (figure 102). Undoubtedly these larnakes provided with a hole just above the bottom, for emptying the water, were actually in domestic use as bathtubs before they were employed to contain the dead (see figure 127).

Most larnakes are in the form of rectangular chests with panelled

104. Late Minoan chest *larnax*

105. *Larnax* from Episkopi

sides. They have short thick legs and a gabled lid, with a ridge pole projecting at either end so that they can be lifted (figure 103). Occasionally the lid is flat. In contrast to earlier larnakes the whole construction of these coffins, as well as the imitation of certain details such as planks, betrays their origin as a wooden chest of household furniture* used for storing clothes and textiles. Occasionally wooden chests, perhaps resembling the clay larnakes, were used for burials; this seems to have been common in Western Crete. The larnakes were made of coarse clay and were decorated with abstract patterns, birds,* flowers, stylized trees, fish* and octopuses, the tentacles of which often extend in a very stylized manner to cover entire sides of the coffin (figure 104). Other motifs include double axes* or other sacred objects, sacral horns,* bulls and other animals, occasional ships,* or human figures, often in a stance of lamentation. Larger pictorial compositions are extremely rare. The best known example, from the village of Episkopi, with twelve panelled scenes which include chariots* and processions, is exhibited in the Archaeological Collection of Hierapetra* (figures 105, 145-47). Hunting scenes are depicted on several excellent larnakes found at Armenoi* in Western Crete. A unique limestone coffin painted with scenes of the utmost importance for the history of religion* is the famous sarcophagus* from Hagia Triada.*

Lasaia. The small town of Lasaia west of Lebena* on the south coast of the island was a secondary harbour of Gortyn.* Its ruins have never been systematically explored. Lasaia is a well-known place because of the landing of St. Paul at the neighbouring bay of Kaloi Limenes ("Fair Havens"), a site which had one of the finest landscapes in Crete before modern construction. In its vicinity several early tholos tombs* were explored by the author (see figure 185).

Lasithi. The large oval plateau of Lasithi between Central and Eastern Crete, thirty square kilometres (eleven and a half square miles) in area, surrounded by naked mountains over 2100 metres (almost 7000 feet) high, has an altitude of 817-850 metres (2680-2800 feet). Today it includes seventeen villages. This fertile area, cold in winter, produces among other things a great quantity of potatoes, unknown to the ancients, and apples. Ten thousand white-sailed windmills, which provide power to irrigate the soil, give the upland plain a very picturesque appearance at certain times of the year.

Inhabited since the Neolithic period,* Lasithi, thickly populated in antiquity, possesses a number of important archaeological sites, such as the caves of Psychro* and Trapeza (see Caves*) and the settlements of Plati* and Karphi,* which grew up towards the end of the Late Minoan period,* when the plateau below it was deserted. Later, the area of Lasithi belonged to the Dorian city-state of Lyttos.* Deep chessboard-like cuttings at the eastern part of the plain of unknown exact date—the so-called "linies"—are interpreted as having been Roman or Venetian drainage works. They have been cleaned out and are again in use as irrigation canals. During the Venetian occupation* this highland plateau (figure 106)

106. Plateau of Lasithi
(*after a Venetian map*)

became a center of the Cretan resistance movement; Venetian repression went so far as to evacuate the entire population from Lasithi in 1263 and forbid any cultivation and grazing. In the fifteenth century Venice, needing corn, allowed the resettling of the fertile upland. In the next century refugees from the Peloponnese, then conquered by the Turks, immigrated here. Lasithi again became a center of revolt during the Turkish occupation* and suffered two major destructions in the nineteenth century.

Late Minoan Period. The Late Minoan period (ca. 1500-1100 B.C.) is the last one of the Bronze Age* in Crete. Renfrew records 284 known sites or 34.7 sites per thousand square kilometres (9 sites per 100 square miles), a fairly dense population for ancient times. This period is divided in two by the great disaster of 1450 B.C., believed to have been caused by violent earthquakes* or even the eruption of the volcano of Thera.* During the first part of this age, the Late Minoan I phase, considered the Golden Age of Crete, the material prosperity and the subsequent zenith of Minoan civilization* achieved during the Middle Minoan period * reached its peak. Crete became a power in the known world (see map 5). Its population is calculated to have been more than 250,000. In pottery Floral* and

Marine* Styles prevail. Magnificent frescoes* were created in Knossos*
and Hagia Triada,* and the engraving of seals* reached a high degree of
perfection and delicacy.

After the disaster, historical changes occur: an Achaian* dynasty ruled
Knossos* for some fifty to seventy years, and settlers from the Mainland
gradually colonized the more fertile parts of the island. A new language,
Mycenaean Greek (see Greek Language*), and a new script, the Linear
B,* were introduced, as were basically the horse* and the chariot.* Knos-
sos* was again able to set the artistic standard for a while.

During the Late Minoan III phase (1400–1100 B.C.) Crete recovered
from the disasters and became a part of the Mycenaean world, but a rather
unimportant part, considering its great past. The palaces* lying in ruins
were abandoned, including the last of them, Knossos,* after about 1400
B.C. or a little later, and Crete ceased to be an organized unit under the
Mycenaean kings of Knossos.* The whole thirteenth century, still predominantly Minoan and not Mycenaean, seems to have been a period of
relative prosperity and peace for the island, as the density of population
demonstrates. Art, chiefly seen in pottery* manufactured in great quantity, becomes more and more stylized but never without artistic merit.

The end of the Late Minoan period, succeeded by a Sub-Minoan
phase, was characterized by a rapid decay of civilization and economy,*
as was true all over Greece. Cremation* of the dead gradually became the
prevailing burial custom.* The arrival of new Greek settlers, the Dorians,* coincided with an essential change in Cretan and Greek history, the
introduction of iron.* The Bronze Age* came to an end.

Lato. An important city-state of the Dorians* was Lato, in the east of the
island, near modern Kritsa* and Hagios Nikolaos.* Lato, perhaps the *ra-to*
of the tablets,* was named after Leto (Doric Lato), mother of Apollo and
Artemis, a goddess with strong Minoan associations. The cult of the goddess Eileithyia,* intimately connected with Leto, here enjoyed great
prominence. The city was a hereditary rival of its neighbour Olous* (modern Elounda) and often at war with it. Lato commanded a secondary harbour town, Lato pros Kamara, the present Hagios Nikolaos.*

The city, amidst a beautiful mountainous landscape, is undoubtedly
the most impressive example of a Dorian city of the first millenium B.C. in
Crete. It had a steep double acropolis with fortification walls and a fortified gateway. The city itself, erected mainly on the saddle between the
two peaks, comprises a large area. Excavations have been conducted by
the French. The town center (see following page) is formed by the so-
called *agora* (market-place), a spacious pentagonal area with a deep
square cistern **(3)** beside a small civic temple **(2)** consisting of a single
chamber—with no columns and probably hypaethral—in the center. The
north side is closed by a broad flight of steps, separated into three sections
by two rows of half-steps, which facilitated ascent **(7)**. This flight of steps,
dated to the fourth or third century B.C., imitates the rectilinear caveas of
the Greek mainland and was a place at wich people joined in public discussions, perhaps the *boule* or the Assembly of the city's Elders. On the
west are two small rooms **(6),** where perhaps the sacrificial animals were

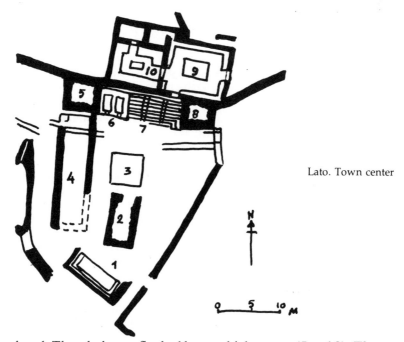

Lato. Town center

enclosed. The whole was flanked by two high towers **(5** and **8).** The steps led up to the *prytaneion,* in the west hall **(10)** of which was an *eschara,* the official hearth of the city, with a two-stepped bench around the walls supporting the place for several *klinai* (eating couches). This hall (*hestiatorion*) was used for the common meals of the magistrates and the reception of high visitors. The east room **(9)** has a bench along the walls and is now interprerted as a peristyle court with six columns. Along the west side of the *agora* runs a portico of the Doric order **(4).** Forming the south end of the *agora* is a rectangular *exedra* (a sort of open sitting room) **(1)** with two steps, partly hewn in the rock, datable to the Hellenistic period*. On a long terrace supported by a strong retaining wall in rustic ashlar masonry south of the *prytaneion* are the ruins of a temple, about 10 by 6.50 metres, which consisted just of a simple cella and an anteroom, having no columns. It dates from the end of the forth to the beginning of the third century B.C. Before its entrance stood an altar. East of the temple and below its supporting wall was a sort of theatral area facing north, which comprised tiers of steps beside an *exedra* or loggia with benches along its walls.

Law. Virtually nothing is known about law in Bronze Age* Crete. We may assume that the existing law system together with the administration had its center in the palaces,* the legislation being connected with the "priest-king'"* and divine right, as the later Greek legends about Minos* the law-giver and Rhadamanthys* "the just" or the Cretan Zeus* inform us. Aristotle in the *Politics* says that in later Greek times "the laws of Minos are still in force among the subject population of Crete." This unwritten law evidently formed a long traditional usage, psychologically stronger than a set of written legal rules. Of course it reflected the existing social structure* and the interests of the Minoan establishment.

After the introduction of the alphabet* in Crete, tribal custom yielded to written law, which became one of the main features of the Dorian society. Among the important surviving inscriptions are the one from Dreros* and especially the interesting Code* of Gortyn,* an invaluable document. In early times, the *Kosmoi*,* powerful aristocratic magistrates, also carried out judicial functions, which later became more general and supervisory, as a multitude of new laws were introduced. After a time special officials called *dikastai* ("judges") were assigned to different spheres of duty in the administration of justice, which reflected the increasing complexity of the social structure and existing legislation, such as cases involving pledges, inheritances, or the *hetaireiai* (see Social Structure of Dorian Crete*). The *orpanodikastai* were "judges of the affairs of orphans." Judges were assisted in procedural matters by special public officials, who also maintained records. The *dikastai* carried out their duties in the *dikasterion* ("law-court").

The Code* of Gortyn* is very informative about legal procedure and the duties of the judges. Divine blessing is invoked at the beginning of the Code. Other inscriptions reveal the constitutional status and legislative procedures of the various Cretan city-states, although our knowledge is often fragmentary and partial. Later, a sort of international law among the city-states evolved, and the authority of some special judges extended beyond the limits of their own states, as some decrees reveal.

Leather-working. Evidently leather-working played a certain role in Minoan economy.* Leather, like wood,* cannot survive for hundreds of years except in a desert, but we possess some indirect evidence about its use in Bronze Age* Crete. Some of the earliest tools,* like needles, cutters, awls and punches, must have been used for the manufacture of leather artifacts like bags, vessels, footwear, chariot* and stool surfaces (see Furniture*), and perhaps clothes. Leather was further used for shields* and animal harnesses, which we occasionally see painted on figurines of animals, such as the monkey of the Crocus-Gatherer Fresco (see Frescoes*). Corselets of leather also seem to have been used during Late Minoan times (see Armour*).

Lebena. Lebena (ancient Leben) on the south coast of the island was the harbour of Gortyn,* which flourished mainly during the period of the Roman occupation.* It possessed a famous sanctuary of Asklepios.* The site was partly excavated by the Italian Archaeological Institute.

The temple had a mosaic pavement, two columns and a podium; we know that the temple was restored by the Gortynians in the second to first century B.C. The sanctuary included a sacred spring (see springs, Sacred*); a cistern, a treasury, a monumental staircase of marble with eight steps; and a western portico. An eastern portico with a shrine of the Nymphs at its east end was used for "incubations" (see Asklepios*), which were a normal part of the cure. There were also rooms for the priests and the personnel of this eminent sanctuary, as well as for the crowds of pilgrims and patients. From the account of the visit of the philosopher Apollonios of Tyana in 46 A.D. we learn that the whole of Crete flocked to this famous Asklepieion, and many Libyans also crossed the sea to visit it.

In the area of Lebena some large tholos tombs* of the Early Minoan period* were explored in 1958-60 by the Greek archaeologist St. Alexiou, yielding among other things an abundance of quite interesting pottery,* which considerably enriches the existing material of this time. Some of the vessels show unique shapes; many belong to the Pyrgos Ware,* while others are painted with a reddish pigment and are considered by some scholars as forming a special "Lebena Ware," closely resembling the well-known Hagios Onouphrios Ware* but with the colours reversed. A clay vessel appears to represent a round hut: doorways and windows are indicated by rectangular holes in the walls, while a knob on the roof perhaps depicts the tied ends of thatching.

Leto see **Eileithyia; Lato; Phaistos.**

Leuke see **Islands of Crete, Satellite.**

Light-wells. The rectangular small open shafts or courtyards known as light-wells are a characteristic feature of Minoan architecture,* admirably suited to the Cretan climate.* They ran the full height of the building, sometimes several storeys high. By means of them, the Minoans were able to extend a building in any direction without depriving it of air and light. Exposed to the weather, they were constructed of hard materials. Around them were usually grouped the main living-rooms of a house (see Houses*), receiving only the reflected sunlight through columned peristyles, thus avoiding extensive outside exposure and affording protection from extremes of temperature. The light-wells, ensuring security and privacy, were a good solution for a period which possessed no window glass. Each of the great palaces* had a number of light-wells. At Knossos* they were usually placed at one end of the room but in Phaistos*· and Hagia Triada* they were sometimes situated in the middle of the room, something like a later *atrium*. Surely the most magnificent of all Minoan light-wells was the one flanking the Grand Staircase of the east wing of the palace at Knossos.*

Linear Script A. This form of writing, first appearing about the middle of the seventeenth century B.C. or even a little earlier, was current throughout Crete during the sixteenth and fifteenth centuries B.C., perhaps until about 1450 B.C. It was derived from the Hieroglyphic script.* Some curious similarities have been noted between it and the earliest scripts of Syria, Mesopotamia and Elam (Iran), which undoubtedly served as a model. It was a syllabic system, rather difficult to compose, which relied heavily on ideograms for intelligibility. Linear A, thus named by Evans*

107. Linear A inscribed stone vessel (*after Davaras*)

in order to distinguish it from the later Linear B script,* with which it shares a considerable number of signs (both being pre-alphabetic cursive scripts), is usually found on clay tablets* and ritual stone vases,* occasionally on bronze double axes,* and in one case on a gold signet. There are also two surviving inscriptions written in ink (see Writing*) on vases, perhaps incantations against evil spirits. Both scripts were named "linear" because their signs, in contrast to the earlier Pictographic script, are not pictures but symbols made just of lines. Most Linear A tablets, which seem to contain almost exclusively business documents or accounts (see Writing*), have been found at Hagia Triada,* in deposits assignable to about 1450 B.C. Others have been recovered from the palaces* at Malia,* Phaistos* and Zakros.* A number of Linear A examples have recently been found in the extreme west of the island, Chania.* Linear A inscribed libation vessels of stone are sometimes recovered from peak sanctuaries* (figure 107).

The number of all the Linear A inscriptions known to date is extremely limited, not much more than three hundred. This is perhaps the main reason that, despite enormous efforts on the part of an international array of scholars, the Linear A script, supposed to express the Minoan language, has not yet been deciphered. The symbols of numbers, which belong to a decimal system, are understood: units were indicated by straight vertical strokes, tens by horizontal lines, hundreds by circles, and thousands by circles with four short lines radiating from their circumferences. Quarters were shown by an L. Owing to its limitations, it is presumed that this script could not have expressed the full richness of the language, but only certain standard ideas exclusively concerning religion* and accounting, as other uses for this script are not known. The Cypro-Minoan script seems to have been inspired by the Cretan Linear A. There is a difference of opinion among specialists about the nature of the Minoan tongue: it is generally considered non-Indo-European and non-Semitic, and is more likely to be an offshoot of the languages of the Lycians and other ancient peoples of Anatolia.

Linear Script B. Linear A script* was supplanted about 1450 B.C. by another, named by Evans* Linear B. This script, although often found in Mycenaean centers of the Mainland (chiefly in the palace at Pylos which was destroyed in about 1200 B.C.), has been recovered in Crete almost ex-clusively at Knossos.* In both areas it is clearly not only the same script but also the same language. The Knossos tablets are the earliest known examples of the script. The sudden appearance of Mycenaean Greek at Knossos obviously reflects the existence of a new dynasty of Achaians,* a Mycenaean ruling class. Possibly this new dynasty was the reason for the invention of the new script, as Linear A, made for another language, was unsuited to Mycenaean Greek. The late date to which L.R. Palmer attrib-utes these tablets has raised criticisms which are generally considered as conclusive and convincing. Linear B shares with A a considerable number of signs (more than fifty), perhaps with the same phonetic value; both are pre-alphabetic cursive scripts.

Most of the texts are written on small clay tablets*—over 3000 frag-ments of them have been recovered from Knossos—from left to right be-tween parallel lines or from top to bottom (figures 108 and 181). Most or all of the tablets* seem to contain simple lists of people, some indicating their duties or the produce delivered by them; animals and commodities of various kinds; the contents of armouries; accounting notes of the palatial economy,* and daily business. The writing consists partly of words in a clumsy syllabic system, but also of ideograms, representing commod-ities, numerals and values. The sign groups are divided from each other by vertical strokes and probably stand for words.

In 1953 Michael Ventris, a young English architect—later killed in a car accident—in collaboration with the philologist John Chadwick, proposed an ingenious decipherment, claiming that the language is an early form of pre-Dorian Greek, allied to Classical Arcadian and Cyprian, the script be-ing chiefly a syllabary. He further claimed that by studying the way in which the syllabic signs are used (their frequency, position in the word, different combinations) and by inferring the content of the documents from certain signs which are not syllabic but ideographic, one can dis-cover the phonetic value of most of the syllabic values. The basic work on the subject, *Documents in Mycenaean Greek*, appeared in 1956. This script is an imperfect means of writing Greek (a dialect of Greek 500 years older than Homer) about seven centuries before the first Greek inscriptions, the imperfections evidently being an inheritance from Linear A, which had been formed for a different language. As a result of this decipherment and despite uncertainties and difficulties, it is now essentially possible to read and understand this clumsy syllabary, thus winning much definite his-torical information.

It seems that the purpose of this script was strictly limited to account-ing. Hence it has been supposed that a professional class of scribes ex-isted. Some scholars do not accept such a restricted literacy. According to the study of the handwriting, it has been claimed that the Knossos tablets were written by approximately 75 scribes. When the palatial economy* which had produced and supported this system of writing passed away, the writing ceased, and it was not until several centuries of illiteracy had passed that the Greek alphabet* emerged.

The decipherment proposed by Ventris—a brilliant landmark in re-

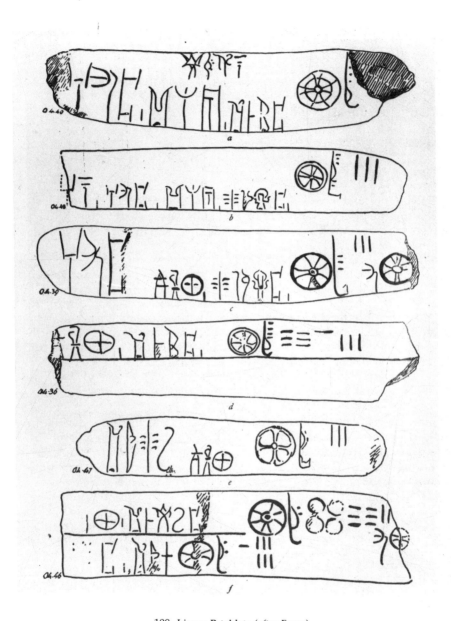

108. Linear B tablets (*after Evans*)

search—has been accepted by all scholars except for a small minority of sceptics, which is constantly diminishing. Some examples show the proposed decipherment; thus: *ko-no-so*=Knossos, *a-mi-ni-so*=Amnisos, *pu-ro*=Pylos, *a-ta-na*=Athene, *ai-ku-pi-ti-jo-*=Egyptian, *ku-pi-ri-jo*=Cypriot, *a-re-ka-sa-da-ra*=Alexandra, *te-se-u*=Theseus, *te-o-do-ra*=Theodora, *de-u-ka-ri-jo*=Deukalion, *a-ko-ra*=agora (market-place), *e-re-u-te-ro*=eleutheros (free), *ku-ru-so*=chrysos (gold), *ti-ri-po*=tripous (tripod), *ke-ra-me-u*=kerameus (potter), *ku-mi-no*=kyminon (cumin), *mi-ta*=minthe (mint). Sometimes it is possible to interpret a word in many ways according to the context: thus *pa-te*=pater (father) but also pantes (all).

Lions see **Animals (Wild).**

Liopetro see **Siteia.**

Liparite see **Shells.**

Lisos. A port of Elyros* and later an independent ally of Hyrtakina,* Lisos was the site of a rich sanctuary of Asklepios (*Asklepieion*), where healings were performed by his priests (see Asklepios*). An inscription reveals the existence of a temple of Diktynna.* The city was part of a monetary union with Hyrtakina,* Elyros* and Tarrha.*

The Greek archaeologist N. Platon excavated the sanctuary of the god, which includes a sacred spring* and a temple with a mosaic pavement, in 1957, in the middle of a fascinating landscape overlooking the Libyan Sea, and difficult to reach. The temple pavement featured animals and intricate geometric patterns. The temple had been destroyed by an earthquake. A considerable number of votive offerings, inscriptions and statues found here are now in the Chania Museum.

The ruins of two Early Christian basilicas can also be seen in Lisos. The city possessed an aqueduct, a theater and public baths (*thermae*).

Literature (Cretan). This term encompasses Greek literature during the period of the Venetian occupation,* a rather rich literature especially interesting for Greek-speaking people. After the fall of Constantinople, Byzantine cultural tradition continued to live—enriched with Italian influences—in the paintings of Cretan School* as well as in literature written in a contemporary vigorous Cretan Greek free of archaisms. Byzantine "religious" poetry was revived (Choumnos). Didactic poetry (Sachlikis, who is reminiscent of Rabelais, Defaranas, Falieros), sometimes very realistic, is a source of information as to the social conditions of the time. The "Apokopos," a long poem of Bergadis, is a vigorous creation influenced by Dante's *Inferno*. About the end of the sixteenth century Byzantine tradition died out and Italian influence became dominant in the works of the so-called Cretan School of Poetry.

The literary production of Crete reached its zenith with the fine works of the *Cretan Theater*, such as those of Vincent Kornaros from Siteia,* which include the famous "Erotokritos," a charming courtly story written in 1646 which became a classic and created the legendary figure of the "Fair Shepherdess," later popular folklore; and "The Sacrifice of Abraham," a religious drama.

Little Palace. The construction of the so-called Little Palace at Knossos is a

109. Little Palace and "Unexplored Mansion" (*after Popham*)

remarkable work of the transitional Middle Minoan III-Late Minoan I period. The building, in front of a paved road coming from the Theatral Area
of the palace, is noteworthy for the fine ashlar masonry of its exterior
walls. Much of it has disappeared. The main entrance is formed by a columned propylon, from which short flights of steps lead up into a paved
peristyle court, partly preserved (figure 109). The stately main hall next to
this court is divided into two halves by a pier-and-door partition; similar
partitions connect the hall with the court to the south and to a columned
portico to the east. West of this hall there was originally a Lustral Basin,*
converted into a shrine* in the latest reoccupation period of the building,
known as the "Fetish Shrine" and including a pair of sacral horns* and
four "fetish" natural stalagmitic formations vaguely resembling human
forms. Mud brick used between the wooden columns of the original Lustral Basin has preserved in the burned clay the impression of the convex
fluting of the columns,* destroyed in a fire. The Lustral Basin* had an
anteroom to the north. The northwest corner is formed by a paved lavatory communicating with a drain outside the building. From the southwest area of the peristyle court a great two-flight gypsum* stairway led to
an upper storey, now vanished. South of this, a narrow service stairway

led down to the pillar crypts of the basements at the south end of the building. The Little Palace was presumably occupied by some important Minoan official.

The best find of the Little Palace, which escaped looting by having been thrown into a well, is the famous bull's head rhyton,* a libation vessel cut and hollowed out of a solid piece of black steatite, originally fitted with wooden horns covered with gold foil. On its base the artist had made a summary sketch of the bull's head, important for depicting the spring of the horns. Inlaid shell* curves round the nostrils. One of the eyes is still preserved: the pupil of rock crystal is painted scarlet on the underside with a black iris, and is set in a border of red jasper which gives the frightening effect of the bloodshot eyes of a bull. As Evans* wrote, "the crystal lens of the eye both illuminates and magnifies the pupil and imparts to the whole an almost startling impression of fiery life."

Behind the Little Palace lies a large Minoan building named by Evans* the Unexplored Mansion, as he uncovered only its ashlar eastern facade. A bridge resting on two buttresses connected it to the Little Palace. In recent years the British School completed the excavation. The Mansion measures about 25 by 15 metres (82 by 49 feet), divided in three sectors. The central part is occupied by a pillar-hall, the most important room of the building, with four massive pillars.* South of it a stairway led up to the second storey. Some rooms had cists sunk in their floors. The Mansion was burned down in the Late Minoan II period, but its northern part has been reoccupied in later times. Extensive ruins of post-Minoan occupation have been cleared above the Mansion, belonging to every period down to Roman times.

Loincloth see **Dress (Minoan).**

Loom Weights see **Cloth.**

Lustral Basins. "Lustral Basins" was the name given by Evans* to sunken rectangular rooms of small dimensions, which may have been used for ritual functions such as purifications and anointings of some kind; steps led down into them. We see these peculiar rooms in Minoan palaces* and villas.* About twenty-five examples were found in all. The Lustral Basins were usually lined with gypsum* veneer and sometimes had a fresco decoration, or benches and occasionally niches in the wall. The more elaborate palatial examples had purely decorative colonnades resting on parapets. Some scholars have suggested that they might have been ordinary bathrooms, the movable tubs for water being made of clay or maybe of metal, although no trace of them was ever found. At Knossos* one basin is significantly attached to the so-called Throne Room. As Palmer asked, "Why should a throne room have so public a bath?" Evans* seems to have been basically right in his interpretation. These rooms were in no way connected to the elaborate drainage systems* which often run nearby. They were not only lacking any sense of privacy but they give the impression that spectators were expected or even welcome. The practical Minoans evidently built and decorated these sunken rooms of a characteristic architectural form exclusively for religious purposes. Besides, these basins often yielded sacral objects. Probably people purified themselves by means of sanctified water, either by bathing or sprinkling before taking part in religious ceremonies. Evidently only a small quantity of water was symbolically employed in the ceremony. It has been suggested that special libation vessels, often of an extremely elaborate manufacture, the rhyta (see Rhyton*), were employed among the cult paraphernalia, perhaps connected to an underworld divinity. The use of holy water for purification was among the rites of several Oriental religions, inherited by the Greeks and later by the Christians and the Moslems. Thus, we may accept that these rooms were, in fact, shrines.*

Luwians see **Destructions of Palaces.**

Lykastos see **Minos' Loves; Rhaukos.**

Lyttos. Lyttos—or Lyktos before the third century B.C., named after the son of Lykaon—was one of the oldest and most powerful city-states of Classical Greek times and a bitter enemy of Knossos.* It is referred to by Homer as "broad Lyttos." The city was colonized from Lakonia. Aristotle in his *Politics* informs us that Spartan institutions were pre-Dorian, transmitted to the great Spartan lawgiver, Lykourgos, by this Spartan colony when he visited Crete. Its large territory extended from the north to the south coasts, cutting the island in two halves, and including the harbour of Chersonesos,* Milatos* and the plateau of Lasithi.* Lyttos took part in the Cretan contingent under Idomeneus* against Troy. As Homer tells us, Koiranos, leader of the Lyttians, was killed attempting to rescue Idomeneus from the spear of Hector.

The history of Lyttos consists mainly of its struggle for supremacy against its mighty rival, Knossos.* Its neighbours, like Dreros,* feared the warlike character of the Lyttians and their sudden raids. In 346 B.C. the city was captured by 8000 mercenaries led by the Phocian Phalaikos and paid by Knossos, but was freed in a short time after Sparta's intervention. The so-called Lyttian War in 221-19 B.C. was caused by Lyttos, rebellious against the alliance between Knossos* and Gortyn,* each at the head of a group of allied cities. This war, which involved also forces from external powers such as Macedon, Rhodes and Aetolia, ended with the capture and utter destruction of Lyttos, the over-confident army of which was making an expedition against Hierapytna* leaving the city unguarded. The historian Polybios gives a vivid description of the destruction of Lyttos, which was burned and demolished, while the women and children were sent to Knossos. When the Lyttian army came back, these proud soldiers were so distressed at seeing their city in ruins and their beloved gone, that they did not enter the desolated city, but went weeping away to friendly Lappa,* where they asked for refuge.

The city was later rebuilt. It vainly resisted the Roman conquest and

110. Silver coins of Lyttos (*courtesy Mrs. M. Oeconomides*)

was captured by Metellus, but was able to flourish again during the Roman occupation.* No systematic archaeological exploration has been undertaken, but a number of statues and inscriptions were found here. Lyttian coins mostly bear an eagle and a boar's head (figure 110). The theater of the city, with an oval peristyle court in front, was perhaps the largest of the whole island.

Magasas see **Neolithic Period.**

Magazines. Each Minoan palace, being a redistributive point for the economic activities of a larger area, included on the ground floor several easily accessible storerooms or magazines, often in a considerable number of rows, stocked with huge jars. These magazines evidently were necessary for storing the products of the rich estates, as well as for tributes and taxes, which were all paid in kind. The magazines were conspicuous and characteristic of the role which the palaces* played in economy.* In the palace at Knossos,* between the cult rooms of the West Wing and the outside wall, the facade of the palace on the West Court, ran a long corridor with rows of long narrow magazines, containing a considerable number of pithoi*—originally perhaps as many as 420—and stone-built rectangular chests lined with stone slabs, designed to hold clothes and other valuable objects (figure 111). This has been the largest of all the storage complexes of Minoan Crete yet discovered. Their limestone doorjambs must have contained doors, which could be safely locked. These storerooms seem to have been lit chiefly by lamps.* Some of them have been restored completely with roofs.

Male God see **Divinities; Zeus.**

Maleme. West of Chania* on the Aegean coast is the village of Maleme, which already existed in Venetian times, widely known from the invasion of German parachutists in 1941 and the battle over the capture of a small airport. On a hillside near the village a plundered tholos tomb* of the Late Minoan period,* of a rectangular shape, mostly built of well-cut masonry,

111. Magazines of the West Wing at Knossos

with a relieving triangle behind an upright slab above the heavy lintel of the doorway and possessing an exceptionally long, lined *dromos* leading to it, was explored in 1966 by the author. Two fine seals* were discovered there: one of bronze, perhaps originally covered with gold foil, showing a cow suckling her calf and tenderly turning toward it, the other of agate with two running wild goats (figure 112).

Malevisi Fortress. The Venetian fortress Castel Malvisin or Malvicino, today in ruins, lies near the village of Keramoutsi in the prefecture of Herakleion.* This name, which was later given to the whole province and to its formerly famous Malmsey wine (see Wine*), was derived from the Medieval siege-machine known as "malvesin" or "mauvais voisin."

Malia see **Palace at Malia.**

Malla. The modern village of Malles in the province of Hierapetra* pre-

112. Seal with running wild goats from Maleme (*after Davaras*)

serves the name of the Greek city-state of Malla, which occupied a nearby hill to the east. Malla was a rather unimportant inland city. A decree of the second century B.C. reveals that Malla had fallen into internal disorder and was obliged to appeal to the cities of Knossos* and Lyttos,* which dispatched judges. No excavations have taken place but an interesting early Dedalic* relief representing a seated female figure was found in this area, which is now in the Herakleion Museum. The city's principal deity, Zeus Monnitios, was depicted on its coinage.*

Marine Style. The so-called Marine Style of pottery, belonging to the Late Minoan IB phase (ca. 1500-1450 B.C.), succeeds the equally famous Floral Style.* Both represent the triumph of naturalism in Minoan art,* but a certain ornamental stylization dominating the principles of decoration is always apparent. This Marine style uses a large repertoire of sea creatures painted in a black paint, often glossy, in an over-all decoration on a yellowish background. Various forms of marine life are delicately represented in a life-like way: octopuses, dolphins, sea anemones, argonauts or nautiluses, fish,* conch shells* and starfish swim round the vessel against a background of seaweed, sponges and rocks.

A splendid jug with argonauts of the best Knossian fabric, now in Marseille, had turned up in Egypt. A stirrup-jar from Gournia* is covered

113. Marine Style flask with an octopus from Palaikastro

with an octopus with glaring eyes. One of its erratically waving tentacles is gripping the neck of the vessel. A flask from Palaikastro* is decorated with a similar subject (figure 113). The decoration always is perfectly adapted to the form of the vessel. In later pottery these motifs degenerate or become stylized.

The Marine Style, perhaps an exclusive product of the royal workshops at Knossos* and obviously influenced by frescoes,* is one of the finest in the long history of Cretan pottery.* Marine Style vases had a wide distribution throughout Crete and were even exported. Many of these fine vessels were intended for ritual use, as their shapes suggest. The style itself seems to have had a special appropriateness to the marine aspect of the Minoan Goddess (see Divinities;* Shells;* Ships*), and the emergence of the style at the time of the presumed peak of Minoan navigation (see Piracy;* Ships*) perhaps is not a mere coincidence.

Masons' Marks. A class of symbols cut on the blocks of the Minoan palaces* and larger houses,* the so-called masons' marks, includes a variety of linear signs such as double axes,* stars, tridents, arrows, crosses,* stylized trees and distaffs. These signs range in size from the miniature to seventy centimetres (28 inches) and can be seen on more than twenty sites. In Knossos* alone there are 33 different signs (see Tree and Pillar Cult*). Earlier examples are deeper cut and more clearly seen. There is a certain affinity between them and the signs of the Linear A script,* but they are not identical. Most scholars feel that these marks must have had some cult significance rather than being of practical use as quarrymen's labels or builders' certifications or, like the masons' signs of the later Greeks, being useful in the process of assembling the blocks. Possibly they were intended to put the building under divine protection.

Master of Animals see **Animals (Wild).**

Matala. This picturesque fishermen's hamlet on the south coast of the island has recently become very popular with young people. The nearby site of Kommos was a harbourage for Phaistos* in Minoan times and later, and for Gortyn* after 220 B.C. According to Homer, who describes the place very accurately, Menelaos returning home after the sack of Troy was shipwrecked in this area. Some shipwrecks of Roman Imperial times and their cargo consisting of large wine jars have been located not far from the coast. On the steep cliffs of the coast were cut several elaborate tombs of the Graeco-Roman and Early Christian period. They often contain arched niches. The rock floors of some of them are now submerged almost two metres (six feet) below sea-level (see Geography*).

Matriarchy see **Woman (Position of).**

Melidoni Cave see **Caves.**

MENELAOS see **Matala.**

Mercenaries. Cretan mercenaries enjoyed a great reputation abroad in the Hellenistic period* as stone slingers and especially as archers,* the more poorly equipped sorts of mercenaries. In the unending wars of these times they were much sought after and were considered "invincible" for special aspects of warfare such as surprise attacks, the capture of prisoners, ambushes and night-fighting. Crete became a major source for the recruitment of mercenaries and supplied all the great powers in the Mediterranaean. Alexander the Great used them on various occasions, such as during the siege of Thebes, where their leader Eurybotas was killed, or in the battle at Issos. All Cretan mercenaries probably were citizens who had the means to provide their own arms and armour. They were recruited by foreign agents probably with the consent of the state's authorities. By chance of war, they often were enlisted in opposing forces and had to face each other in battle: as one example we mention the battle of Raphia in 217 B.C., where 3000 Cretans in the Egyptian army faced 2500 Cretans in the forces of Antiochos III.

Mesara Plain. In the south part of the prefecture of Herakleion* is found the long Quaternary alluvial plain of the Mesara, the largest, hottest and most fertile plain of the island. To the south the long ridge of the Ast-erousia Mountains—the highest peak is Kophinas, of an altitude of 1231 metres (4039 feet) with a rich Minoan peak sanctuary* excavated by N. Platon— separates the plain from the Libyan Sea, while to the north rises the majestic Mount Ida,* the highest of the island. The plain ends at the Bay of Mesara on the Libyan Sea. A small river, Geropotamos, keeps its water throughout the year.

Outside of the Knossos* area, the Mesara Plain was the most impor-tant and prosperous region of Cretan civilization in antiquity. Inhabited since early times and thickly populated, with a rich rural culture, it includes most of the tholos tombs* of the Early Minoan period,* such as those at Platanos,* Apesokari,* Kamilari* and others, the palace at Phaistos,* Hagia Triada* and a great number of other Minoan settle-ments, sanctuaries and cemeteries. In later times Gortyn* flourished as the capital of the Roman province of Crete and Cyrene (Libya). The largest village today is Moires between Gortyn* and Phaistos:* its name, meaning "allotments," reflects the fact that the land around it had been allotted to peasants during the Middle Ages.

Metallurgy. The first use of metals—the "metallurgical revolution" as it has been called—marks the transition from the Neolithic period* to the Bronze Age.* Unalloyed copper was the first metal worked. Later, copper was alloyed with tin or arsenic to make bronze, a discovery which led to the manufacture of finer yet stronger objects. Crete is an island rather poor in mineral resources* and much of the metal needed had to be im-ported (see Imports*). Nevertheless Minoan Crete was not totally de-pendent upon Cyprus for its copper, as some copper mines prove. Metal-lurgy, at the beginning influenced from the Cyclades, developed rapidly into one of the most important Minoan industries.* Minoan metallurgists created a great tradition and a legend, which survived in early Greek times. Some of their products, such as the double axes,* reached as far as Britain. Among their achievements were a variety of tools* and weap-ons,* toilet articles,* parts of defensive armour,* pieces of jewellery,* huge cauldrons* and impressionistically rendered statuettes (see Sculp-ture, Minoan*). Gold and silver or copper and bronze vessels are rarely found, but it is clear that many of the pottery shapes are imitations of metal vessels, now lost. A variety of bronze vessels and utensils employed for cooking and storage were manufactured at the beginning of the Late Minoan period.* A hoard of them has been found in a tomb at Zapher Papoura near Knossos.* The existence of a group of itinerant metallurgists, who travelled far and wide selling and manufacturing their products or teaching their craft, has been assumed.

A revival of metallurgical art occurs in the early Iron Age,* during the Orientalizing period,* with a series of splendid shields* and sphyrelaton* statuettes, cauldrons decorated with fine bronze attachments, tripods, elaborate belts, helmets and other parts of defensive armour,* and cut-out plaques for decorating wooden surfaces. It seems likely that metal-workers from the Near East had established themselves in Crete, creating workshops there. Already developed types of fibulae—brooches, often of the safety pin type—in both iron and bronze appear, with a coiled spring to the pin and a broad square plate in which the pin catches. This catch plate, in contrast to other parts of the Aegean, is not decorated. The earliest type was the violin-bow fibula. The close-fitting dress* of the Minoans had nothing of the kind. Pins with a knobbed end clearly show the emergence of a new type of garment kept up on the shoulder and depending on those pins and fibulae.

Metropolis see **Byzantine Period; Gortyn.**

Miamou Cave see **Caves.**

Middle Minoan Period. The Middle Minoan period (about 2200-2000 until 1580-1550 B.C.), which covers the period of the Middle Kingdom in Egypt including the Hyksos phase, saw two principal changes: the emergence of the palaces* and their economy,* and a more pronounced unity of culture with a centralized organization and strong authority. During this period Crete, with communities based upon large cities and towns (see Urbanism*) dominated by the unfortified palaces,* made a great forward stride and reached the stage of a major civilization. According to the 190 known settlements and their size Renfrew has calculated that the approximate population of the island was about 214,000, with a density of 26.1 per square kilometre (68 per square mile). Of course, new excavations may augment these numbers (see map 4).

Overseas relations and contacts became regularized and trade,* including both exports* and imports,* expanded. Because of its ships* the island dominated the sea routes and attained a degree of security astounding for that early time, the other Aegean states being as yet no match for it. The introduction of the fast potter's wheel* led to a technical mastery in pottery.* Vase-painting was dominated by the Kamares Ware,* perhaps the most beautiful style in the entire Prehistoric world, but towards the end of the period, the quality of pottery* became lower. Brilliant frescoes* came into existence, art* and economy* flourished. At the beginning of this period, Hieroglyphic script* was in use; from it evolved the Linear A script* towards the era's end. Thus, Minoan civilization became a literate one after the introduction of writing,* a necessary measure to ensure the evolution of a centralized and commercial state. A monumental rebuilding during the third phase followed upon a great catastrophe which destroyed the Early Palaces.*

Milatos. The modern fishing village of Milatos at the north coast of the Mirabello Province near Neapolis,* below Kadistos Mountain, preserves the name of the Dorian city-state situated here. Milatos, already settled in the Bronze Age,* was mentioned by Homer as the home town of Pandareos, the man who had stolen the dog of Zeus* and, according to Homer, was consequently killed by the god together with his wife, while their two daughters were given to the Furies. The city is also mentioned in the important inscription of neighbouring Dreros.* Milatos is the Doric equivalent of Miletos, the great Ionian city on the coast of Asia Minor, which, according to legend, was founded by Milatians under the leadership of the young Miletos (see Minos, Rhadamanthys and Sarpedon*) or Sarpedon,* Minos' brother. As a matter of fact traces of a Minoan settlement of early date have been located there. Milatos was destroyed and absorbed by Lyttos,* its dangerous neighbour, in the third century B.C., and many of its inhabitants emigrated to Miletos, near Hagios Phanourios.

Two chamber tombs* of the Late Minoan period* containing clay larnakes* and some interesting vases with a stylized decoration have been found in the vicinity of the city, which is still unexplored.

A rather famous large cave near Milatos was the place of refuge and the subsequent massacre by the Turks of 3700 women and children in the revolt of 1823.

Mineral Resources. Crete is not very rich in mineral resources. Among those found are some low grade copper (see Metallurgy*), rich iron ore, and small sources of lead, zinc, manganese, talc, lignite, and perhaps tungsten. Some of them were already exploited in antiquity. A number of ancient mines all over the island have been located by a tireless French scholar, Paul Faure.

Minoa see **Pachyammos; Souda Bay; Trade.**

Minoan Civilization. The term *Minoan* was adopted by Evans* for the whole Bronze Age* civilization in Crete, named after the legendary King Minos.* Its homeland was Crete, to which it was essentially restricted, although it had a broad range of trade* and a few island outposts or colonies. Homer refers to Crete as the home of ancient civilization. Partly a cultural offshoot of Anatolia, this great civilization which rivals the better known ancient civilizations of Egypt and Mesopotamia in interest, forms a single archaeological culture both geographically and stylistically. In fact it was the first European civilization. Subdivided into periods (see Chronology*), it lasted for something like fourteen hundred years, reaching maturity for a period of six hundred years from about 2000 B.C. to 1400 B.C., during which magnificent palaces* were the focal point of religion,* economy* and a really creative art* of an unsurpassed quality. Being the first naval power in history (see Ships*), Minoan Crete assumed the leading place in the Aegean, extended its trade* overseas and kept its peaceful people and unwalled cities secure. In its later stages it was intimately connected with the Mycenaean civilization of the Greek Mainland, to which it gave all essential cultural features. This great legacy was to survive—especially concerning religion—to a large extent into Classical Greece. The Minoan civilization—in its later phase politically dominated by the Achaians*—was followed by a period of decline and the subsequent Dark Ages,* during which a fruitful cultural fermentation took place, giving birth to the Greek civilization of the Dorians* and the Iron Age.*

MINOS. Minos was the legendary king of Knossos* according to classical Greek sources. Of divine origin as a son of Zeus* and Europa* (see Minos, Rhadamanthys, and Sarpedon*), Minos married Pasiphae* but had many amorous adventures (see Minos' Loves*). Queen Pasiphae* bore him many children, of whom Ariadne,* connected with the story of Theseus* and the Minotaur,* was the most famous. Minos, besides being a "Ruler of the Waves," was a great lawgiver (see Diktaian Cave;* Law;* Talos*) and the patron of the famous artist and engineer Daidalos.* After a long and magnificent reign, during which Crete became the mighty seapower of its time, Minos died in Sicily, killed by treachery. Diodoros of Sicily, the Greek historian who lived in the first century B.C., has left a rather gruesome account of the legendary death of Minos. When he arrived in Sicily, the local king Kokalos killed his guest by pushing him into a bathtub filled with boiling water.

In the fifth century B.C. Theron, the tyrant of Akragas, discovered what he believed to be the bones of Minos, and sent them back to Crete for reburial.

For the Greeks, Minos personified the ruler of Bronze Age* Crete, with which he was associated in their mythology; above all he was remembered as lord of the seas. He was much praised by authors such as Homer, Hesiod, Plato and Aristotle. The whole Cretan civilization was named after him by modern scholars. The chronological periods of the Minoan civilization* were also named after him (see Chronology*). It has been suggested that "Minos" was really a royal title, such as Pharaoh, Sultan or Tzar. Diodoros' genealogy mentions an elder and a younger Minos. He was possibly identical with the well-known Cretan "priest-king,"* whose tenure of office was probably restricted to an octennial period (see Calendar*). It has been correctly remarked that any attempt to separate the historical and mythical features of Minos is hopeless.

MINOS, RHADAMANTHYS, and **SARPEDON.** According to Greek mythology when Zeus* left Europa,* who had borne him three sons in Crete—Minos, Rhadamanthys, and Sarpedon—Europa married Asterios ("Starry One"), the reigning king, who adopted the three young brothers. When they grew to manhood, they quarreled for the love of a beautiful boy named Miletos, a son of Apollon and Akakallis,* who as a baby had been suckled by wolves in the forests. When Miletos chose Sarpedon, he was driven from the island by Minos, who was jealous and vexed. After killing Asterios, the gigantic husband of Europa, Miletos sailed with a fleet to Caria in Asia Minor, where he founded the city and kingdom of Miletos. Minos then claimed the Cretan throne, while Sarpedon fled to Cilicia in Asia Minor.

Rhadamanthys "the Just," the other brother, remained in Crete and was awarded a third part of Asterios' dominions. Renowned as a just lawgiver, inexorable in his punishment of evildoers, he legislated both for the Cretans and the islanders of Asia Minor. Every ninth year he would visit Zeus' cave and bring back a new set of laws, a custom afterwards followed by Minos (see Diktaian Cave,* Talos*). Rhadamanthys eventually went to the Mainland, to Boeotia, where he married Alkmene, Herakles' mother. His son was Gortys, the founder of Gortyn.* According to Homer, the blond Rhadamanthys was intimately connected with Elysium. Zeus appointed him one of the three judges of the dead, along with Minos and Aiakos.

MINOS' Loves. King Minos* loved many women, such as the nymph Paria, whose sons colonized the island of Paros in the Cyclades; Androgeneia, the mother of the lesser Asterios; Phronia, mother of Iasion (see Ida, Mount*); and Itone, who gave him a son, Lykastos, his later successor. He especially pursued Britomartis.* His countless infidelities so enraged his wife, Queen Pasiphae,* that she put a spell upon him: whenever he lay with another woman he discharged not seed but a swarm of noxious serpents, scorpions and millepedes, which preyed on the woman's vitals. Prokris, daughter of the Athenian King Erechtheus, visiting Crete, was seduced by Minos, who bribed her with a hound that never failed to catch his prey, and a magical dart that never missed its mark. Prokris accepted but wisely insisted that Minos should take a prophylactic draught to prevent him from filling her with serpents and insects. This draught had the desired effect. Minos also fell in love with the beautiful boy Miletos (see Minos, Rhadamanthys, and Sarpedon*). All these stories in a way reflect the mores and customs of society.

Minos and Pasiphae had four sons: Katreus, Deukalion, Glaukos* and Androgeos, as well as four daughters: Akakallis,* Xenodike, Ariadne* and Phaidra ("Bright").

His son Androgeos went to Athens to attend the games, and won every prize, but was then ambushed and murdered. Enraged by this event, Minos sought vengeance first by besieging Megara, an ally of Athens. There Scylla, daughter of King Nisos, betrayed and killed her father for the love of Minos, but was later forsaken by him. Minos then sailed against Athens itself. Each year after the fall of Athens—or each nine years according to another legend—seven youths and seven maidens were chosen by lot and sent to Crete as tribute to Minos, there to be fed to the Minotaur.*

MINOTAUR. The Minotaur ("Minos Bull"), whose name was Asterios or

Asterion, was a monstrous bull-headed man—the offspring of Minos'
wife Queen Pasiphae* and a white bull sent by the god Poseidon (see
Pasiphae;* Daidalos*). To the Minotaur, dwelling under guard in the
Labyrinth* were fed, according to the instructions of the Delphic Oracle,
seven youths and seven maidens chosen from Minos' tributary subjects
of Athens from time to time (see Minos' Loves*) in payment for the death
of Minos' son Androgeos, until Theseus,* prince of Athens, slew the
monster with a sword and escaped from the Labyrinth by means of a
magic thread given him by Ariadne,* daughter of Minos,* with which he
was able to find his way out of the maze.

Many scholars believe that the Minotaur was a representative or
embodiment of the sun-god. The myth is related to an assumed ritual
coupling ("Sacred Marriage", in a later cult a ritual concerning Zeus* and
Hera) of solar bull and lunar cow, which would have been performed by a
man and woman masquerading as bull and cow. Similar religious performances were enacted at the court of the Pharaoh.

Mirrors see **Toilet Articles (Minoan).**

Mistress of Animals see **Animals (Wild); Divinities (Minoan).**

Mitra see **Armour.**

Mochlos. Mochlos is a round tiny island separated from the northeast
coast of Crete by about a hundred and fifty metres (almost 500 feet) of
water. In the Bronze Age,* when the sea-level was lower (see Geography*), it was almost certainly a peninsula, being united to Crete by a narrow isthmus forming a good harbour* on either side, the one used depending on the prevailing wind. This fact, as well as the position of
Mochlos near some important seaways, accounts for its flourishing in antiquity. This now submerged spit of land has some two metres (six feet) or
less of water over it.

The place was excavated in 1908 in a hurry by the American archaeologist R. Seager, who discovered several collective tombs built about the
ground like houses* (see Burial Customs*), dating from the Early Minoan
period.* They stood on a wide ledge on a high cliff over the sea on the
west side of the island, which enjoys a splendid view (figure 114). These
tombs, of a type usually known as house-tombs because of their resemblance to the houses* of the living, had rectangular compartments,
and in some cases formed one complex. They belonged to important families to judge by the wealth of exceptionally beautiful gold jewellery* recovered in them, especially a number of diadems. A splendid diadem
adorned with high antennae and a dot-repoussé decoration consisting of
animal figures, now in the Hagios Nikolaos Museum, has been recently
found. The treasure of Mochlos is more or less contemporary with the
gold jewellery that Schliemann found in the second city of Troy. Among
the finds were also a number of fine seals* (figure 115), a silver cylinder

114. House-tomb complex at Mochlos

seal from Mesopotamia, assigned to the time of Sargon of Akkad, some especially fine stone vases,* and votive double axes.* An interesting find was a gold signet ring, portraying a goddess sitting in a curious boat in which the bow is the head of a horse, and the stern is the tail of a fish (see Ships*). On a burial jar were incised double axes* picked out with white dots.

On the south or landward side of the island a settlement of the Early, Middle* and Late Minoan period,* was partly explored. A narrow stepped road is visible alongside a large building. The ruins of fortifications seen at the north of the islet on the top of the hill are of Byzantine times.

On the land opposite the island of Mochlos some Late Minoan chamber tombs have been excavated on the slope and two rock-cut fish-tanks of Roman times have been located on the water-front (see Fish and Fishing*).

Moires see **Mesara Plain.**

Monastiraki. Near the village of Monastiraki west of Mount Ida* in the prefecture of Rethymnon,* part of a Middle Minoan II settlement was ex-

115. Seal with water-fowl from Mochlos

cavated by the German archaeologist E. Kirsten. The local ruler or governor lived in a sort of small "palace" not unlike that found at Gournia* in the east part of the island. The site was destroyed by fire. Among other finds a hoard of sealings* was discovered, today in the Chania Museum.

Monkeys. Monkeys were not native to Crete but were probably brought from Egypt as pets. They are sometimes depicted on Minoan frescoes* as on panels from the "House of the Frescoes" or on the well-known "Crocus-Gatherer" fresco from the palace at Knossos,* where a blue monkey wearing a harness of red leather had been wrongly interpreted as a boy by Evans.* Some scholars believe that the monkeys, painted blue according to Egyptian convention, were copied from Egyptian murals, but N. Platon has suggested that the scene represents a royal park at Knossos.* Blue monkeys are also depicted on a fresco from the island of Thera* of the sixteenth century B.C. Carved figures of monkeys already appear as handles on some Early Minoan seals.*

Monofatsi Fortress. The Monofatsi Fortress, today in ruins, was built before 1212 by the Genoese Pescatore and was named Castel Bonifacio after a fortress in Corsica. The Greeks called it Monofatsi, a name which later was extended over the whole province, which forms part of the prefecture of Herakleion.* Pescatore also built the Kainourio Fortress.*

Monsters. Minoan art* displays a limited variety of monstrous figures, especially on seals.* Demons*—or genii—are uniform in type and form a class which clearly has religious associations. Fabulous animals like sphinxes and griffins* imitate Oriental prototypes; they are not holy beings but merely solemn followers of the divinities and guardians of sacred places and objects. Minoan sphinxes were sometimes wingless. Of interest are the bulging steatite locks of a large composite head of a sphinx from Knossos,* and two complete figures of wingless sphinxes from Hagia Triada* and Tylissos,* perhaps imported. These creatures have been inherited by Greek mythology and art, where they played about the same role as in Minoan times.

On the other hand clay sealings,* such as the hoard from Zakros,* often show a great variety of composite grotesque monsters in fantastic combinations—winged imps, bats, bull's heads with boar's tusks, and the like, with added tails, buttocks and breasts. Perhaps they have no religious associations. As Evans* said, "the types shift and transform themselves like phantoms of a dream." All of them probably belong to the same hand, an artist who has been compared to Hieronymus Bosch.

Other compound monsters are of a more regular type and are anatomically less extravagant, with a human body and animal's head: thus, we see bull-men reminiscent of the Minotaur,* stag-men, eagle-women, lion-men and other creatures of a rare imagination, probably with no cult significance, unless they represent human attendants masked with the heads of some animal companions of the divinities or totems of some kind. Of these monsters the bull-men of course immediately recall the mythical Minotaur,* but it is quite uncertain whether there is any connection between them, or whether the similarity is purely fortuitous.

Mother-goddess see **Calendar; Divinities.**

Museums (Cretan). The main archaeological museum of Crete—the second largest in Greece but unique of its kind—is at Herakleion;* it was founded in 1883. All periods in Crete from Neolithic until Graeco-Roman times are richly represented. The greater part of the movable remains of the whole Minoan civilization* is housed here, including all the existing frescoes.* The collection of sculptures and figurines* of the Dedalic Style* is considered the best in Greece. The exhibition follows a chronological order. It comprises twenty rooms and galleries in two storeys. The museum now includes the rich Giamalakis Collection, where all periods are represented, as well as a special exhibition for scholars and students, almost as rich as the exhibition for the public.

Other smaller but interesting archaeological museums are at Chania,* Hagios Nikolaos,* and Rethymnon.* These museums house objects which have come from a large area. Hierapetra* has a small collection in provisional housing, while at Siteia* a museum is under construction. Exhibits of the Early Christian, Byzantine* and more recent periods, including objects of historical interest as well as Turkish inscriptions and fountains, some fine Byzantine and later jewellery, and a series of excellent icons and church items are displayed in the interesting Historical Museum of Herakleion. The museum includes the interior of a Cretan peasant house together with such articles of popular art as woven and embroidered materials. Of a similar character but rather limited is the collection housed in the Archives Library at Chania.* Important but not accessible to the public is the private Metaxas Collection of Minoan and later antiquities in Herakleion,* a very selective collection especially known for its Minoan seals.*

Music. Our information about Minoan music is very limited. The first music must have been made by the human voice. The Late Minoan sarcophagus* from Hagia Triada* shows a male minstrel in a long robe playing a seven-stringed lyre of the known Classical type with a tortoise-shell sounding board, presumably tuned to a double tetrachord, with the central note belonging to both tetrachords. This lyre, played either with the fingers or with a plectrum, is like the standard Greek lyre—the special instrument of Apollo—until the fifth century B.C., when one or two strings were added. But a lyre with eight strings and a simpler instrument with only four strings are also depicted. The seven-stringed lyre appears also as a sign of the Hieroglyphic script,* sometimes with four or eight strings, considered to imply perhaps a heptatonic scale. There are many other representations of lyres in Minoan art.* Later, Greek lyric poetry developed from songs sung to the accompaniment of the lyre. The later *phorminx* of the Geometric period* had four or five strings.

On the other side of the sarcophagus* from Hagia Triada* the sacrificial scene is ritually completed with a man playing long double pipes which bear a resemblance to the Greek *aulos,* while on a minature fresco* from Knossos* we see three pairs of flutes attached to one another by some kind of strings. A fine bronze statuette of a youth wearing a flat brimmed hat, perhaps from the Phaistos area and now in the Leiden Museum, most probably represents a flute-player, but the hands with the instrument are lost. Percussion instruments such as the cymbal and the *sistrum* (Egyptian rattle), which is seen on the famous Harvester Vase (see Stone Vases*), were known in Minoan Crete. This Minoan *sistrum* is of primitive form with a single bar instead of the three or four of the Egyptian examples. The bagpipe was perhaps also used.

During later Greek times music was intimately connected with dancing and lyric poetry. According to traditions several forms of musical performance were of Cretan origin (figure 116), introduced to the Mainland by Cretans: notable are the solemn *paean,* a choral hymn to Apollo performed to the accompaniment of lyres and flutes, and the *nomos,* the solo hymn to the same god, which was accompanied by the singer on a lyre, first performed at Delphi by Chrysothemis the Cretan. Both were also dances. The *hyporchema,* the choral song and dance (see also Dance*) executed at Delos to the accompaniment of instrumental music, said to be

116. Geometric bronze figurine of a lyre-player

invented by the mythical Kouretes* and introduced by the Gortynian or Knossian Thaletas, was considered Cretan by Simonides himself. Thaletas, who flourished in the seventh century B.C. and probably founded a school, went to Sparta as directed by an oracle of Apollo at Delphi to cure a plague by means of his music and introduced there Cretan rhythms and important musical reforms. He also became a teacher of the famous Spartan lawgiver Lykourgos in matters concerning the aristocratic social order. Music was part of the education received by the young Cretans in the *agelai;* their warlike exercises and combats, both armed and unarmed, were accompanied, as in actual warfare,* by the music of flutes and lyres.

Modern Cretan folk-music is rather different from that of the Greek Mainland. The songs of Western Crete known as "rizitika," of an austere character, are particularly remarkable. The main musical instrument is the Cretan *lyra,* a stringed instrument played with a bow, which accompanies songs and dances (see Dance*). A well-known kind of Cretan song of a uniform melody is the *matinada,* a word borrowed from the Venetian *matinata*. As Evans remarked, it often is "of impromptu composition, allusive, topical, with capping of rhymes and clever transitions of subject." Today Crete, as well as the whole of Greece, is submerged in cheap modern songs mostly of Near Eastern inspiration.

Mycenaeans see **Achaians.**

Myrtos. The village of Myrtos—the word means "myrtle"—on the south coast west of Hierapetra* occupies an unexplored Graeco-Roman site. The ruins of a public bath with mosaic floors can be seen to the west of the village just above the road.

A large Early Minoan II settlement (ca. 2600-2200 B.C.) destroyed by fire was completely excavated in 1967-68 by the English archaeologist Peter Warren at Phournou Koryphi, the summit area of a steep hill 3.5 kilometres (2.2 miles) east of Myrtos, above the sea shore. The settlement covers an area of 1250 square metres (three-tenths of an acre). The houses, built of unworked blocks of stone, were provided with small rectangular rooms like some houses* of the Neolithic period.* The walls sometimes of mud-brick in the upper structure, were covered with plaster,* sometimes painted brown or red, as in the contemporary houses* at Vasiliki,* with which they share several other technical similarities. Floors were of beaten earth. Roofing plaster* had been laid on to reeds over wooden beams. This architectural complex contained about eighty rooms belonging to two main periods of occupation and divided by passages; they were mostly of a small size, the largest being just over five by five metres (16.5 by 16.5 feet), with a central support for the roof. No separate houses existed. A room of the earlier period was used as a potter's workshop, containing eight primitive potter's wheels.* Some staircases built of slabs have been found on narrow ways between the houses,* which were packed together and had no upper storey. A complex of rooms at the north side perhaps has been used for the manufacture of cloth.* Other rooms, containing pithoi,* were for storage.

The whole building complex was probably defined by a continuous outer wall with two entrances and a sort of round bastion to protect the southern entrance. It is clear that the inhabitants felt the need for some elementary defense, a need which did not arise again until the end of the Bronze Age.* A sort of shrine,* the earliest known Minoan domestic shrine, had an altar* on which originally stood a unique clay vase in the form of a woman, interpreted as a domestic goddess, holding a jug in the crook of her arm: the extraordinary "Goddess of Myrtos" is now exhibited in the Hagios Nikolaos Museum together with the other finds, which include a collection of more than 700 vases (mottled Vasiliki Ware* etc.) and pithoi,* several seals* and clay sealings.* Some of the seals, which count among the earliest extant in Crete, were unfinished. One of the sealings* may have sealed the door of a room.

On Pyrgos, a hill to the west and near the village, an important country house was explored by Gerald Cadogan. This house belongs to the

Middle Minoan III period. Some of the rooms have a monumental appearance with their stuccoed walls and their large staircases. Among the finds was a broken tablet of the Linear A script.* The house was burned down in the Late Minoan IB phase.

MYSON see **Siteia.**

Navigation see **Piracy; Ships.**

Neapolis. A small agricultural town in Eastern Crete, west of Hagios Nikolaos,* Neapolis (3500 inhabitants) is next to the early Doric city of Dreros.* An important group of Neolithic pottery* has been recovered from a deep well at Phourni, a village between Neapolis and Elounda;* the well is considered the earliest technical work of Crete.

During Venetian times Neapolis was known as *Kares,* and after its destruction during some revolution, as *Chienurio Chorio,* ("new village"), a name used until recently. Here was born in 1340 A.D. Petros Philagros, who as an orphan boy was educated at a local Roman Catholic monastery and later in Padova, Oxford and Paris. Philagros converted the Lithuanians and their king to Christianity, and in 1409 became pope of Rome, as Alexander V.

Neolithic Period. A culture of hunters is presumed to have existed in Crete since the Mesolithic or even the Palaeolithic period (Old Stone Age). The first Neolithic or New Stone Age settlers seem to have arrived in primitive boats probably from Anatolia over the string of islands of the Dodecanese during the seventh millenium B.C., bringing seed and domestic animals* with them. Other people from the East followed in small groups, but the island was not really populated until the Late Neolithic period, that is, the latter part of the fourth millenium B.C. and a little later.

The chief characteristics of Neolithic cultures, which are by no means uniform, are the manufacture of pottery,* the making of polished stone celts, or axes* (figure 117), the domestication of stock, and the cultivation of cereals. All four are present in the case of Crete. Neolithic Crete has been rightly considered as an insular offshoot of Anatolia.

Beneath the Minoan palace at Knossos* was discovered not only the earliest Neolithic pottery of Crete but also an important settlement mound over seven metres (twenty-three feet) high, formed by the accumulated remains of ten successive habitations. This deposit, extending beyond the limits of the palace, can be subdivided into Early, Middle and Late periods. The lowest level yielded no pottery and no remains of houses, as the people probably lived in wooden huts.

In higher levels, the houses* were rectangular, built of mud-brick on stone socles; the roofs were probably flat, in a typically Mediterranaean way, with wooden rafters supporting branches covered by a layer of clay. The thresholds were raised and the floors were of beaten earth. Some houses feature stone benches, cupboards and plastered walls. Fixed

117. Neolithic axe-head

hearths of clay and small fire-holes were found in some rooms, often up against a wall, but cooking, as it has been remarked, was probably mostly done outdoors. The plan of the houses was rather haphazard, as rooms of various shapes and sizes were added when necessary. The earliest deposit here was dated by a carbon 14 sample to 6000 B.C. Two late Neolithic houses found below the Central Court of the palace are quite remarkable.

Another settlement existed at Phaistos.* The ruins of a rectangular Late Neolithic house have been found near a rock shelter at Magasas in the extreme east of the island, belonging to the type that the Scots called "but-and-ben," with an entrance living room and a fairly large inner sleeping and living room. The south side of thirteen metres (forty-three feet) was the longest one. Another Late Neolithic settlement was excavated near Katsambas, east of Herakleion.*

Rock shelters were simple overhanging ledges of rock giving an elementary protection to the space below, which was unevenly walled in. Perhaps shelters and caves*—also used for burials—were chiefly inhabited by hunters and shepherds. No cult places have been ascertained.

The hand-made Neolithic pottery,* usually dark-faced and often made on an open fire, is quite interesting; it often was tastefully decorated by incising and rippling, or burnishing for the finer examples. Rippling was done by means of a blunt bone instrument from the rim of the vessel downwards. The incisions consist of simple patterns of a severely geometric nature including zigzag and chevron bands, geometric figures formed in dots, fringed lines, chequered patterns, hatched rectangles and triangles often on a pointillé background; they were made on the exterior of the vessel and might be filled with a white chalky paste. They often were applied on strap handles. Storage vessels were left plain. Sometimes knobs or ribs were applied. Some vases had tubular or strap handles, or the characteristic shape known as wishbone handle. Among the shapes, which often are carinated, we see large open bowls, ladles, funnel-necked jars, miniature cups and rectangular trays with partitions. There are also stone vases.* A later shape is the chalice.

Obsidian* and other stones were shaped as tools, often mounted in wooden hafts. Polished stone celts—short and broad or longer and heavier (see Axes*)—and mace-heads have been found at Knossos.* Archery* was evidently already known. There were also bone implements, grinding-stones, loom-weights and terracotta* spindle-whorls, which imply the manufacture of cloth.* Some pierced toe bones of animals could possibly have served as whistles, as some scholars believe, an interesting item in the history of music.*

Little figurines* of clay or stone, often stumpy, steatopygous, and usually female in an obvious way, perhaps do not represent divinities* connected to the cult of the Mother Goddess as Evans* thought, but rather fulfilled a variety of purposes: they could have been dolls, or perhaps used for sympathetic magic. A usual figure is that of a fat squatting or sitting female. Relatively naturalistic is a remarkable, well-burnished female statuette of the Giamalakis Collection in the Herakleion Museum, with one leg crossed over the other and the arms bent at the elbows. This statuette, almost fifteen centimetres (six inches) high, which turned up at Epano Chorio near Hierapetra,* is considered one of the most important examples found in the whole Balkan Peninsula. The head on a long neck is well modelled, with incised eyes and an aquiline nose.

The steatopygous figures evidently have nothing to do with steatopygy, a racial characteristic of some Negroid tribes, but may be interpreted as simply representing very fat women. Many figurines are strongly stylized.

Outstanding is a unique white marble statuette from Knossos,* probably male and remarkably naturalistic. The figure is headless. There are also some birds and domestic animals,* such as goats, oxen and dogs. These Neolithic figurines often show considerable skill in detailed modelling. There is no paint on them, the decoration being restricted to incised patterns. Neolithic art generally shows a clear tendency to abstraction.

The small agricultural communities (see map 6) seem to have possessed religious beliefs and an elementary social organization: it has been assumed that women cultivated the land (allotted according to a tribal principle), ground cereals with millstones, cooked, and traditionally made cloth and pottery, while the men hunted and fished, built, cleared new lands for cultivation of cereals and fruits, and made stone tools and weapons. A closer professional differentiation at this time does not seem likely. The existence of an elementary trade may be presumed. The basic social unit was evidently the clan, united by a traditional kinship and common tribal ownership. Descent was obviously matrilinear (see Woman, Position of*). The island—living in peaceful conditions—already had connections with Anatolia and in a later period perhaps with Egypt. According to the 42 known settlements and their size Renfrew has calculated that Crete possessed an approximate population of almost 13,000 at this time (see Urbanism*). Of course these numbers may be augmented after new excavations. About 3000 B.C. or a little later, after four long millenia, the Neolithic period of Crete and the subsequent Sub-Neolithic phase ended, and the transition to the Bronze Age* followed.

Nirou. The remarkable villa* at Nirou (or Nirou Chani) in the small bay east of that at Amnisos,* near Herakleion,* is associated with a tiny harbour* possessing a mole. This villa (figure 118), excavated in 1918-19 by

118. View of the Villa at Nirou

the Greek Stephanos Xanthoudides, was erected at the beginning of the Late Minoan IA period and destroyed by a fierce fire. The main hall **(5)** (figure 119) opened through a two-columned propylon **(2)** onto a paved east court **(1)** and formed the center of the residential quarter, while the ground floor of the north side was occupied by magazines* **(26-32)** with rectangular corn-bins and pithoi.* South of the main part of the building ran a narrow yard with schist paving **(44)**. The building included a little room **(16)** with a corner bench and a light well;* behind it opened a small dark chamber **(15)** lit by artificial light, as several stone lamps* found inside it have shown. The south wing was stocked with ritual objects, such as four huge bronze double axes* for ritual use, reaching nearly a metre and a fifth (four feet) in breadth **(10)**, over forty clay tripod altars* with polychrome decoration stacked in piles against the walls **(18-19)**, stone lamps* and other cult paraphernalia. Because of their considerable number it has been suggested with much imagination that the villa and the neighbouring harbour formed a sort of central office for the propagation of the Minoan religion* among infidels abroad. Indeed, the pronounced religious character of the building cannot be denied. Furthermore, in the east court lay the remains of stone sacral horns* and in the main corridor has been found a fragmented fresco of sacral knots fallen from above.* The building presumably had at least one more storey built with crude brick and wood, as is shown by two stairways in both north **(26-27)** and south **(13-14)** wings.

Obsidian. A sort of volcanic rock, blackish and glass-like, obsidian is a hard material—harder than copper—but easily chipped into sharp blades

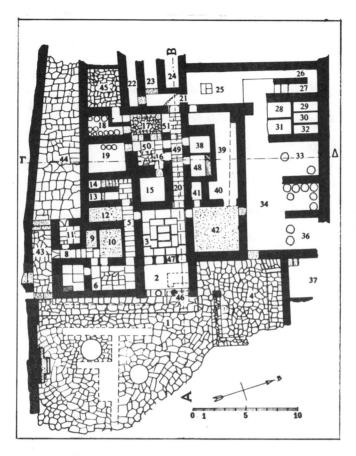

119. Plan of the Villa at Nirou (*after Xanthoudides*)

and flakes. In Crete finely flaked obsidian is found from Early Neolithic
deposits onwards. Narrow long obsidian blades are often found among
grave-goods,* usually still quite sharp: several hundreds of them were recovered at the cemetery of Hagia Photia,* a collection unique for Crete as
regards number, length and quality (figure 120). Many of them were still
sharp enough to be used as razors. Seal cutters and stone vase makers
sometimes used this fine material.

The main source of obsidian in the Aegean was the island of Melos in
the Cyclades, where it could be easily quarried; big lumps of it lie thick on
the surface of the island. A transparent and white-spotted variety is
found on the island of Yiali near Kos. This decorative variety has been
used for the manufacture of the splendid sacred communion* chalice
found at Zakros.* The presence of obsidian cores in Crete shows that the
material was imported and worked on the spot. Blades of obsidian occur
on prehistoric sites all over the Aegean.

120. Obsidian blades from Early Minoan tombs

Occupations of Population see **Industries; Social Structure.**

Olive and Olive Oil. The cultivation of the olive is attested for Minoan times, perhaps from the beginning of the Bronze Age* if not earlier. According to a Greek legend, it had been introduced to Olympia by the Cretan Herakles, one of the Daktyloi.* Olive may have been native to Crete and it decidedly played an important role in Cretan economy.* It may have been considered sacred (see Tree and Pillar Cult*). This tree is illustrated in a remarkable way on the Charging Bull Fresco (see Frescoes*); it is also depicted on the famous sarcophagus* from Hagia Triada.* Olive oil, always abundantly produced and highly estimated in Greece, was especially useful for cooking, (taking the place of butter in the northern diet, and considered healthier), lighting, and as a body cleanser. Oil lamps* have been recovered dating from the Early Minoan period on. In the Minoan palaces* many thousands of gallons of olive oil could be stored in the huge pithoi* of the magazines,* and the storage of such inflammable material apparently played a considerable role in the final destruction of the palace of Knossos* in the last great fire. Olive oil (probably transported in stirrup-jars*) was one of the chief exports* of the island; early evidence is represented by a sealing* of about 1700 B.C. from Knossos, depicting sprays of olive above a ship.

Crete today has olive trees yielding on the average more oil than any others in the Eastern Mediterranaean, as well as Italy. Each tree yields an average of 2.5 kilograms (5.5 pounds) of oil. The crop in Crete represents more than a third of the Greek crop as a whole. The fruit was first beaten

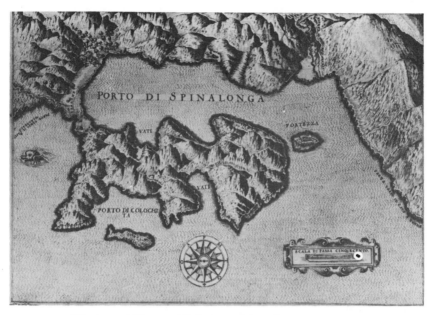

121. Area of Olous and Spinalonga (*after a Venetian map of 1614*)

off the tree with sticks and then winnowed from the leaves, drenched in hot water, crushed in a press to extract the oil, and placed in settling vats, where the oil rose to the surface, the water being drawn off through a spout at the bottom. In general this same procedure is followed today. Olive presses and olive separators have been found in excavations in various sites, although they are difficult to distingusih from wine* presses, perhaps being used for both purposes. Most impressive have been the olives found in a good condition inside a vessel at the palace of Zakros.* During the Late Minoan period* or even earlier oil perfumed with sweet-smelling herbs was also used. In the tablets* of the Linear A* and B* scripts we see ideograms for both olive and olive oil; these documents often record rations.

Olous. Olous was a city-state of Classical Greek times in Eastern Crete, whose name is preserved in the name of the modern village Elounda, which is situated at almost the same place (*Elounda* from *Olous*, genitive *Olountos*). The city lay about the isthmus between the mainland and the peninsula which ends at the fortress of Spinalonga* (figure 121). On this picturesque isthmus at the beginning of the twentieth century the French army dug a small channel connecting the Elounda Bay with the open sea. Part of the city is today submerged because of the rise of sea level since ancient times together with a local depression of the coast (see Geography*). Some ruins can be seen today below the surface of the water. Olous possessed a *xoanon* (Archaic wooden statue) of Britomartis,* a work of Daidalos.* Her festival, the *Britomarpeia*, is mentioned in an inscription. Several other inscriptions found here inform us about the history, the institutions and the festivals of the city. The presence of Pamphyloi, one of the three tribes of the Dorians,* is attested for Olous. The boundary treaty with Lato* is interesting as a detailed document preserving a number of place names otherwise unknown, and sometimes of pre-Greek origin. The treaty with Rhodes (200 B.C.) illustrates the effort of this city to gain control over Eastern Crete in order to supress piracy, which was supported by Olous and incited by Philip V, king of Macedon, then a great enemy of Rhodes. A joint decree of Olous and Lato* of about 120-116 B.C. concerns negotiations, with Knossos* as the arbitrator.

East of the isthmus at a small distance lay the ruins of an Early Christian basilica, excavated by A. Orlandos, the mosaic pavement of which shows vegetal or geometric patterns, various fish, and a dedicatory inscription of the seventh century A.D. In this same vicinity, a very rich deposit of Archaic and Classical times containing various clay votive offerings, such as figurines of goddesses, protomes, satyrs, pigs, tortoises and lamps,* exhibited today in the Hagios Nikolaos Museum, has been excavated by N. Platon. Most of the fifth century examples copy Rhodian types. Not far away are the ruins of still another basilica.

Near the hamlet Sta Lenika (Hellenika) between Hagios Nikolaos* and Elounda, lies the Aphrodision, a rectangular sanctuary of the second century B.C. erected on the place of a Geometric shrine, the "old Aphrodision" according to an inscription. The excavations of the French School of Archaeology brought to light two rooms, one dedicated to Aphrodite and the other to Ares, which had bench-altars and opened to a common vestibule. Underneath this vestibule was discovered the *eschara* (a low altar like that of Dreros*) of the old shrine. The sanctuary had been disputed between Olous and Lato,* and the rights of the latter were finally confirmed by the Roman Senate.

Omalos. An impressive view is obtainable from Omalos, an uninhabited plateau at an altitude of 1080 metres (3543 feet) in the White Mountains of Western Crete in the prefecture of Chania.* A place of refuge, which also saw several battles during Cretan revolts from the Turkish occupation,* Omalos is often referred to in folk-poetry and song. The well-known Samaria Gorge* extends from here down to the south coast.

Omphalion see **Zeus.**

Orientalizing and Archaic Periods. These periods—the impressionable years of Greece—cover the years from about 730 to 480 B.C. in Crete, as in the rest of Greece. The Orientalizing period in art, succeeding the Geometric period,* shows both the influence of Minoan survivals and that of Oriental models resulting from frequent interchange with the Near East. This influence includes figures of fabulous monsters* and strange animals and plants. In fact, study of Oriental models seems to have restored many of the lost memories of the Great Minoan heritage. On the other hand, a progressive Hellenization of the motifs is apparent. The succeeding Archaic period in Crete, which roughly covers the sixth century and first years of the fifth century B.C., is not a time of brilliant creations, as it is in

122. Orientalizing cinerary urn with griffin heads and painted sphinxes

other Greek areas, but marks the twilight of Crete from the cultural point
of view.

The architecture of these times can best be seen at sites such as Lato*
and Prinias.* The building of tholos tombs* died out; burials—cremations* were now in cinerary urns. Pottery* broke free from the Geometric tradition and created a true "renaissance" of the Minoan spirit,
which can also be seen in other forms of art. Floral motifs were introduced
in vase painting and the decoration became rich. Free curvilinear patterns
and decorative motifs of Oriental origin painted on a thick white slip
gradually evolved. Among these patterns are large cables, lotus garlands,
the Oriental "Tree of Life" with volute-coiled branches and sometimes a
palmette on top, as well as a variety of other floral designs, or panels with
Geometric motifs. Figures of birds, sphinxes and humans become common (figure 122), but a true figure style was never attained as it was in
contemporary Attica or Corinth.

A fine collection of vases was found at Fortetsa near Knossos* and another, more rustic but with a variety of techniques, at Arkades.* Important are the small polychrome funerary pithoi* which contained cremations* together with small grave-goods.* These exclusively Cretan
three-legged urns continue a Geometric tradition. Their decoration—red
and blue-black on a light ground—is charming but still rather Geometric
in spirit. Pithoi* decorated in relief were very popular during this time. In
the Archaic period vase painting declines and seems to die out.

Metallurgy* reached a high standard and with the help of immigrated
Oriental masters a number of excellent works of art in bronze was produced. The shields* of the Idaian Cave* and the sphyrelaton* statues

123. Pachyammos and the island of Pseira (*after a Venetian map*)

found at Dreros* are particularly famous. A number of cut-out bronze plaques have affinities with Assyrian plaques.

The seventh century was the time of creation of the so-called Dedalic series of sculptures and figurines* (see Dedalic Style*), in which the earliest Greek monumental sculpture finds its expression. During this century Crete was a leading part of the Greek world, not only artistically but also politically. Eventually the early kings were overthrown, replaced by the regime of the aristocratic *kosmoi*.* The Cretans took part in the Greek colonization, founding the city of Gela in Sicily together with the Rhodians in 688 B.C. With the beginning of the next century the island—under a heavy aristocratic establishment and a rigid conservative social structure—declined rather suddenly and fell into the backwater of the Greek history and civilization for years to come.

Ossuaries see **Burial Customs; Tholos Tombs.**

Ostrich Eggs see **Imports.**

Pachyammos. The modern village of Pachyammos ("Deep Sand") is situated on the site of the Greek town Minoa,* at the head of the Gulf of Mirabello and the Isthmus of Hierapetra,* very near Gournia* (figure 123). Here the American, R. Seager, the explorer of Mochlos* and Pseira,* excavated in 1914 a large cemetery belonging mainly to the Middle Minoan and the Late Minoan I periods. The dead were buried inside 213 large clay pithoi* of various types and six square or oval larnakes* in the sandy beach, accompanied by jars. In many cases pithoi* were found surrounded with large stones to hold them more securely in position. Many of them were unpainted while others were decorated with the "tricklepattern," or rarely with fine paintings including dolphins and sea foam (very reminiscent of the Dolphin Fresco at Knossos*), octopuses or floral designs.

At a small distance from this cemetery St. Alexiou excavated a Late Minoan chamber-tomb containing among other items a clay box which was decorated with two heraldically placed birds pecking a flower.

Painting (Minoan) see **Frescoes.**

Palace at Knossos. The palace at Knossos is the largest and most important of the Minoan palaces,* a vast labyrinthine complex (see Labyrinth*) some four kilometres (two and a half miles) from the north coast. It is the last phase of a succession of buildings rebuilt after each of the several destructions on the site of the main settlement of the Neolithic period* in Crete (see Early Palaces*). The plan of this last palace (figure 124) has been obscured in some places by alterations and erosions. It was roughly square, measuring about 150 metres (nearly 500 feet) on each side, and occupying an area of 20,000 square metres (about 5 acres).

West of the palace and past the modern entrance to the site is a large flagstone paved court, crossed by slightly raised walks ("causeways"), perhaps of a ceremonial nature. The West Court **(4)**, which includes two altars* **(1)** and **(5)**, some earlier ruins and three very large walled pits **(2)** (see *kouloures**), approached from the west by a broad ramp, is terraced

124. Plan of the Palace at Knossos (*after Evans*)

and supported by an outer retaining wall to the west, while to the east it is limited by the facade of the palace. This monumental facade has several set-backs or recesses (see Palaces*), with benches along its lower course, which is covered by gypsum* slabs still blackened by the last fire. Its upper parts have been reconstructed. Evans* thought that in front of this west facade ran the one of the Early Palace. Its foundations are still visible as a row of great flagstones among the pavement of the court. It has been assumed that the space lying between the earlier and the later facade became holy ground, and an altar was placed here **(5)**, perhaps in front of an earlier entrance, a passage between two "insulae" (see Early Palaces*) which allowed direct communication between the west and central courts, which was blocked when the later facade was built.

A causeway leads straight to the West Porch **(6)**, the state entrance, which was provided with a single wooden column on a huge alabaster base, having an original height of about 5.5 metres (18 feet), and on the east wall a fresco depicting the bull-games,* and next with a guard lodge and reception room possibly containing a throne for the official on duty. Behind a door with two leaves begins the long winding Corridor of the Procession

(7), a clearly ceremonial entrance with a raised causeway named after the fresco (see Frescoes,* *Cup-Bearer)* with the gift-bearing life-sized ritual figures of youths and maidens which adorned its walls. This corridor, perhaps unroofed, today partly preserved, connects the West Porch round the southwest angle of the palace with the majestic South Propylon (8), an elaborate columned structure having three entrances, each with a door (named after the monumental gates of the Classical Greek architecture), and the neighbouring Stepped Portico* (12). A replica of the original fresco was placed in the heavily restored Propylon, which originally contained a great part of the Procession Fresco as it is supposed. During the reoccupation or latest period of the palace, some pithoi* were placed in the Propylon, which was used as a storeroom.

At the north side of the South Propylon, the monumental Grand Staircase (9), flanked by colonnades resting on strong walls, leads up to the second floor of the west wing of the palace, named by Evans the Piano Nobile (an Italian Renaissance term), which is occupied by a suite of official rooms, reconstructed in concrete, great public halls conjecturally restored, including a Great Hall with two columns, a Central Tricolumnar Shrine, a Sanctuary Hall with six columns and frescoes, and other rooms. Some of the column bases were found on the ground floor below, as well as the fragments of the *Campstool Fresco* (see Frescoes*), found inside two magazines below the Great Hall. The main access to the Piano Nobile was through the Grand Staircase and the South Propylon in front of it. In its vicinity is the South Entrance. To the east of the Grand Staircase a later Greek temple, perhaps of the goddess Rhea according to the testimony of Diodoros, built on the ruins of the palace with materials taken from it, has been identified and dismantled. In its vicinity is the South Entrance (13), near which a replica of the famous Priest-King Fresco was placed (see Frescoes*).

The Central Court of the palace covers an area of 50×25 m. The ground floor of the west wing was mainly intended for cult purposes. At the north edge is the Throne Room. Passing through a pier-and-door partition one descends five steps into an antechamber with gypsum benches around the walls. Between the benches along the north wall a wooden replica of the stone throne from the Throne Room itself has been placed on the spot where a heap of charred material was found. A similar bench runs along the south wall. A large porphyry basin found nearby has been placed here in its presumably original position.

In the Throne Room (17), against the middle of the right-hand wall, stands a gypsum* throne—well modelled and comfortable (see Furniture, Minoan*)—quite intact and left where it was found. It is heraldically flanked by reproductions of frescoes representing crouching wingless griffins* (see Frescoes*) above a low bench running along the wall and returning at one end. Some sixteen people could sit here—a kind of *sacrum collegium*. The central part of the floor was coated with red plaster.* This dignified "oldest throne in Europe" with its high back and undulating outline imitating a wooden prototype may have been a cathedral chair intended for a high priestess, attendant of the Mother Goddess—the throne of Ariadne* rather than the throne of Minos.* Facing it is a sunken Lustral Basin,* some 60 centimetres (2 feet) below and approached by six steps **(18)**. The walls of the basin (which was also the bottom of a light-well) were faced with dadoes and coated with red plaster in the upper parts. Between the basin and the room is a low parapet with timber columns, which left charred traces in the parapet and the stone bench before it.

The Throne Room with its frescoes is supposed to be one of the latest parts of the palace, built during the period of the Achaian* dynasty of Knossos and reflecting the new rulers' tastes. There is evidence to believe that some ceremony was being held in the Throne Room during the time of the destruction, perhaps intended to avert it.

Next to this group of rooms which includes the so-called Inner Sanctuary, to the south and facing the court, comes an imposing columned stairway with twelve steps, the so-called Stepped Porch **(19)**, with one monumental central column and behind it another one, higher up. The stairway leads up again to the Piano Nobile, the second floor of the west wing, already described. We should remark that this modern reconstruction is quite useful for covering and protecting the original lower parts of the building and also for giving a clearer idea of it; nontheless it obliterates the genuine picture of the ruins as left by time, through the obvious interference of masses of modern materials. The same is true of excessive reconstructions of other parts of the palace, a legacy of last century's principles of reconstruction, which allowed a modern sculptor to replace the lost parts of an ancient statue.

Next to the Stepped Porch and opposite to the court's center are the lower parts of the facade of the Tripartite or Columnar Shrine **(20)** (see Shrines*), with a higher central section flanked by two lower ones, and crowned with sacral horns.* Beyond it a flight of steps leads down into a small paved court, known as the Lobby of the Stone Seat **(21)**. South of the Lobby's entrance a pillar portico faces the court. The Lobby itself is connected to the north with two rooms, of which the first **(27)**, known as the Room of the Tall Pithos, contained a cist and a large medallion pithos, while the second served as the Temple Repositories **(23)**. Here were stored in sunken cists the treasures of the Tripartite Shrine, including the famous Snake Goddess* and a splendid collection of other faience* objects (see Temple Repositories*). West of the Lobby are two dark Pillar Crypts **(24)** entered through two doors, with the sign of the double axe* incised at many places on each of the two stone pillars.* The pillar of the first crypt is flanked by two sunken shallow basins, while that of the west crypt is surrounded by a sunken square area, probably serving to receive libations (see Tree and Pillar cult*). A bench runs along a wall of the second crypt. To the north of the first crypt open out two other dark rooms, the eastern one being the Vat Room, which contained a row of rectangular receptacles, perhaps for wooden chests.

Beyond these official rooms of the west wing a Long Corridor **(25)** runs parallel to the Central Court and leads to a series of eighteen long narrow magazines* containing sunken chests and pithoi* on stone bases. When the palace was destroyed, the blazing olive oil* of overturned pithoi* soaked into the gypsum* slabs, leaving black, greasy traces. These maga-

125. Hall of Double Axes showing suspended shields. Restored view (*by Piet de Jong*)

zines are limited at their west ends by the external facade of the palace on the West Court. The Long Corridor was also provided with pithoi* and sunken chests coated with hard plaster,* perhaps for liquids; some shallower masonry-lined examples were faced with lead, perhaps to contain treasure. The Corridor originally had a wooden ceiling, with an upper long corridor at the second floor, probably unroofed.

Along the east of the Central Court is the East Wing or Domestic Quarters, the ground floor of which was at the bottom of a deep cutting inside the slope of the hill, two storeys below the level of the court, with two more storeys above it, or four in total, while the West Wing had two storeys above the ground floor. This residential quarter was entered by a splendid Grand Staircase **(42)**, indeed a monumental achievement of Minoan architecture,* with a double flight of broad, shallow gypsum* steps on each floor and a great light-well* to the east, to which each flight had a colonnade, resting on a stepped parapet, with corresponding galleries on two of the other sides of the light-well. This ingeniously built structure was found intact, as the mud-brick of the upper parts of the walls has dissolved and filled the interspace, thus replacing the decayed wooden parts which originally supported the whole structure, the columns* and beams. The staircase led down to the bottom of the light-well **(43)**, where the Hall of the Colonnades **(44)** was formed, an impressive construction with four massive columns* and a corridor behind it. Beyond this Hall lies a large rectangular room or a complex of rooms, the largest of the palace, named the Hall of the Double Axes **(45)** after the frequent occurrence of this symbol as a mason's mark on the blocks of a light-well to the west (figure 125). This Hall, divided by a pier-and-door partition, possessed two other similar partitions to the east and south, which gave access to a

126. "Queen's Megaron." Restored view (*by Piet de Jong*)

large portico **(46)** with a corner pillar.* Beyond it probably was an open
terrace enjoying a fine view, perhaps of the palace gardens, as has been
suggested. There was also a throne, perhaps under a canopy resting on
four small wooden columns,* as can be inferred from some impressions in
a mass of melted gypsum plaster at the north wall. The walls were covered
with decorated plaster above a high dado of gypsum veneer and perhaps
adorned with hanging oxhide shields,* as Evans presumed. The floors
were paved with limestone slabs.

Next to the Hall a winding narrow passage leads into the "Queen's
Megaron" **(48)**, which had a number of windows on the east and south
sides looking towards two light-wells* (figure 126). Benches below the
windows have been restored according to some evidence, but the restoration remains doubtful. Frescoes with vivid scenes of marine life and
others with charming dancing girls covered the walls (see Frescoes*: *Girl
Dancer; Dolphin Fresco*); a section was adorned with a spiral pattern of a
later date. Various phases of the floor construction can still be seen. A
small staircase leads up to the floor above. The small room to the west **(49)**
is separated from the Megaron by a doorway and a balustrade. This room
was thought to have been the bathroom (figure 127), but the clay bathtub
put here by Evans* was actually found elsewhere. According to another
interpretation, this place was rather a bedroom, well-sheltered from
draughts, or more probably an inner shrine, as some scholars believe today. A corridor leads to the so-called «dressing-room» and «toilet room»,
incredibly refined for the time with its wooden seet and arrangements for
flushing, directly connected to the elaborate dranage system* of the palace, as Evans thought: nevertheless this whole interpretation is today
disputed.

127. "Bathroom" of the "Queen's Megaron". Restored view (*after Evans*)

Farther on is a light-well known as the Court of the Distaffs **(47)** from the masons' marks* found here. Another winding passage with a service stair to the upper floor leads back to the Hall of the Colonnades. An inside windowless room may have been employed for the storage of valuables or clothes **(50)**. All these apartments on the ground floor, evidently with the plan reproduced on the floor above it, were sheltered from the cold in winter but were cool in summer.

To the south are several interesting rooms. A bathroom had a plaster* partition and a bathtub. Behind a similar partition in the adjoining room stand three pithoi,* one of which has a false spout. After the destruction of 1600 B.C. the whole suite was filled in and a new one was built above it. A small room to the south was converted into the Shrine of the Double Axes (see Shrines*) during the Post-Palatial period. Further south is a stairway and a light-well near a Lustral Basin.* This complex forms the end of the palace. Beyond it a number of private houses* were erected: the South-East House **(53)** and, west of it, the House of the Chancel Screen*

(51), the House of the Sacrificed Oxen, and the House of the Fallen Blocks (for both see Earthquakes*).

To the north of the Domestic Quarters and the long east-west corridor which divides the East Wing in two are several rooms devoted to the workshops of the palace. First comes the Lobby of the Wooden Posts, named after the posts which originally reinforced the walls. Near the Eastern Portico which had four columns,* a heap of natural blocks of basalt (lapis lacedaemonius) imported from the region of Sparta for the manufacture of stone vases* was found in the Lapidary's Workshop. Some of the lumps were half-worked. The room immediately above it yielded two unfinished stone vases.* Another room to the north, known as the School Room **(39)**, had benches on three sides and stone basins beside them, and has been variously interpreted as a potter's workroom, a schoolroom for apprentice scribes, or an atelier of fresco painters. A door to the north leads to the Court of the Stone Spout, named after a spout seen high up at the west wall. The so-called Corridor of the Bays **(40)** possesses three small magazines* just before the Central Court. Next to it comes the long Magazine of the Medallion Pithoi **(47)**, with some of them still in place, while inside neighbouring rooms some Kamares Style* pottery* and the famous Town Mosaic (see Houses*) were found. Inside a small room to the west some bronze locks of hair supposedly from a colossal statue (see Sculpture, Minoan*) were found, fallen from an upper floor together with masses of charred wood. To the north is the area of the Magazines of the Giant Pithoi **(36)**, a relic of the Early Palace.*

The east entrance of the palace was formed by the so-called East Bastion **(37)** which has the appearance of a strongly protected postern gate with a winding staircase—leading down to the valley of the Kairatos River—and an open conduit alongside the steps, displaying an elaborate method of automatically checking the rush of rainwater down the steep incline by use of a series of small waterfalls created by parabolic curves. At intervals are small settling tanks for the deposit of sediment. It has been supposed that below the East Bastion was the laundry of the palace, or the arena for the Bull-games.* Running north to south to the west of the Magazines of the Giant Pithoi is the Corridor of the Draught-board **(55)**, where the famous gaming board (see Games*) was found. Under the floor a part of the elaborate drainage system* of the palace is visible.

North of the Central Court is a group of rooms. The northernmost one, a spacious hall of two storeys **(31)**, with eight pillars* and two terminal columns* in two rows, was named the "Customs House," as it constitutes the sea gate of Knossos. Probably it was a waiting room or a banquet hall. At its west wall a gate opens to the outside of the palace. From this hall the long, narrow North Entrance Passage **(58)**, which was unroofed and flanked by bastion-like structures carrying porticoes at a level with the court, leads straight and steeply to the Central Court. The bastions of this passage were built later, making the passage narrower. Among the masons' marks* cut on them is often found the trident, perhaps having some connection with the sea gate of the palace.

The bastion to the west, accessible through a small staircase, covers

128. "Theatral Area" of the Palace at Knossos

the reproduction of the Charging Bull Fresco (see Frescoes*), a huge painting in relief which stood here. A similar picture—evidently of bull-leaping—might adorn the east bastion. It has been suggested that this fresco, which was probably still standing in later Greek times, must have lent some colour to the legend of the Minotaur.*

At the northwest corner of the Central Court a building complex with six very deep narrow cells, probably magazines,* is a relic of the Early Palace.* It was originally one of the "insulae," the independent units which formed the palace. Because of its appearance it was named the North Keep **(26)**. Later a shrine was built over its "dungeons," which were filled in. The North Lustral Area **(27)** is a small distance from here. It included a flight of steps with a columned stepped balustrade, and columned parapets on two of its sides, and was lined with dadoes above which were frescoes imitating sponge impressions.

To the northwest of the palace is a rectangular paved area framed on two sides with banks of low, step-like seats and a bastion-like platform at the junction, assumed to be the "Royal Box." Alongside the steps runs a drain to carry off the rainwater. This "Theatral Area" **(28)**, perhaps modelled on the earlier example at Phaistos,* was evidently designed for some performance or spectacle, where some 500 persons could assist (figure 128). From here a well-paved road, known as the "Royal Road" **(29)** and said to be "the oldest road in Europe," with houses of the town on either side such as the "Arsenal" and the "House of Frescoes," leads to the main road north and to the splendid Little Palace.* Among the dependencies of the palace are also the Royal Villa,* the South House* **(11)**, the Caravanserai* and others (see Index).

Palace at Malia. The palace at Malia, the third in size of the Minoan palaces and of somehow provincial character, occupying an area of 7,500 square metres (3.5 acres), is named after the modern village of Malia (often wrongly spelled with double l) which lies some four kilometres (two and a half miles) west on the north coast. Its ancient name is unknown, as it ceased to exist early in Greek times, but it has been suggested that it was possibly Milatos.* It has been assumed that the king of this palace was Sarpedon,* Minos' youngest brother. The palace was discovered by the Greek archaeologist Joseph Hazzidakis who began the excavation in 1915, but since World War I the work has been continued by the French School of Archaeology.

The site was occupied in the Late Neolithic and the Early Minoan period,* as some scanty remains prove. There are also some traces of a reoccupation during the Post-Palatial period, after the final destruction of 1450 B.C. The palace was completely unfortified and surrounded by a city, which is not fully explored, and was provided with a harbour.* The first palace dates from the Middle Minoan I period (see Early Palaces*). The later palace was similar to the first one in the main outlines of its plan. Unlike Knossos,* no large-scale restorations have been made (figure 129).

The triangular and well-paved West Court is bounded on the east by the facade of the palace, which is not rectilinear but displays several setbacks or recesses (see Architecture, Minoan*) and offers no entrance, the main entrance being to the south of the Central Court. A slightly raised ceremonial walk runs along this facade towards the so-called Hypostyle Crypt to the north.

The Central Court, focal point of the building (see Central Courts*) and a well-preserved relic of the first palace, has a hollow, sunken square altar* at the center with four mud-brick supports, and porticoes along its north and east sides. The east side portico, like that at Phaistos,* displays a rhythmical alternation of columns* and pillars.* The spaces between the columns of this portico were closed with a balustrade or low screen walls, perhaps for the protection of the spectators of a bull-game,* if this really was held in the court. The eleven columns of the north side portico were also screened. Originally two more columns existed further west, with their bases still visible between some later walls.

At the south end of the east side portico was the South-East Entrance to the palace, a simple direct passage with a propylon in front. Behind the portico are the East Magazines **(XI)**, a block of six restored magazines* with a parallel entrance passage and a long corridor in the east. The first magazine was shorter. Along the walls of each bay runs a bench for the placement of pithoi* on either side, provided with a carefully planned device to avoid the wastage of liquid: drainage furrows running to a central channel for the collecting of spilled olive oil* or wine,* which itself emptied into a jar sunk into the floor. A similar arrangement existed

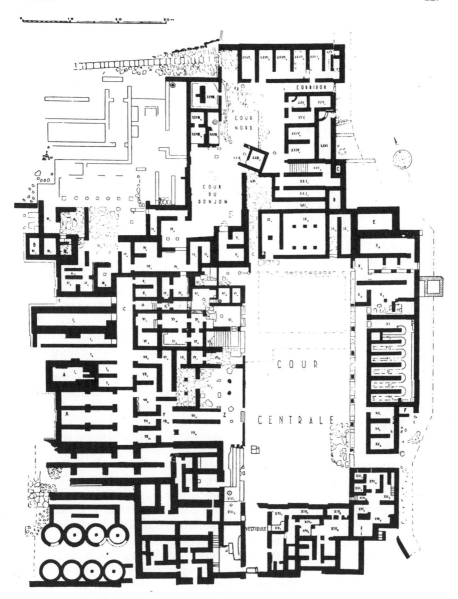

129. Plan of the Palace at Malia (*after Chapouthier and Demargne*)

in the corridor. Near the entrance is a bench for the guardian or overseer of the storerooms, who recorded everything.

On the west side of the Central Court is a group of rooms probably for some religious purpose. The northernmost room, a well paved Loggia placed higher than the court and obviously employed for religious ceremonies, is entered by a flight of four broad steps on either side of a pillar.

It had an altar* or table of offerings in the middle. A rectangular raised stone was surely not the base for a wooden throne. Behind the Loggia a narrow stairway between two columns leads down to a series of rooms employed for storing various cult objects evidently used in ceremonies held in the Loggia. Here was found, among other things, a magnificent long sword (see Weapons*) and inside a pithos the famous ceremonial stone axe (see Axes*) in the form of a leaping panther. Beside the Loggia is an imposing broad stairway with nine steps flanked by two other lateral flights of steps and provided with a door in front, possibly leading up to a Columnar Shrine in the second floor.

South of this group are several well-built rooms, including a large paved lobby with a stone bench along the south wall, and a light-well* to the east with two columns. An entrance to the opposite west side was formed in a later phase; here stood originally two columns,* now incorporated into the later masonry. This entrance gives way to a large and finely paved Pillar Crypt with different masons' marks,* such as double axes,* stars and a trident, carved on two massive pillars.* The walls probably were coated with red-painted plaster.* This Pillar Crypt seems to be associated with ritual practices, like its counterparts at Knossos.*

A double door to the west leads from the crypt through a series of rooms to a long corridor running from north to south and giving access to the West Magazines of the palace. The whole arrangement recalls the one at Knossos.* The west side of the Central Court ends at its south extremity with a very broad monumental stairway with four steps probably leading up to the public reception halls of the second storey, answering to the Piano Nobile at Knossos.* Perhaps this stairway corresponds to the "Theatral Areas" of the other palaces.* Close to it is the famous Table of Offerings, a sort of glorified kernos,* a large circular stone ninety centimetres (thirty-five inches) in diameter, with thirty-four small round depressions, one of which is a little larger than the others, arranged round the circumference, and one deep cavity in the middle. It has been assumed that in each cup was put a different kind of grain or first-fruit as an offering to the Fertility Goddess (see Divinities;* Kernos*), but some scholars believe that the table was a large gaming board (see Games*), a rather improbable interpretation unless the game had a religious or magical meaning.

The adjacent Quarter to the south is independent. Its only entrance from the south opens into a little room which served as a shrine to outside visitors. The shrine included a stone bench, a partition wall to the east, a stone altar* incised with symbols and some cult paraphernalia. The nearby South Entrance leads to the Central Court through a large and finely paved passage (Vestibule). Distributed about the palace are numerous magazines* and workshops. At the southwest corner of the palace were located two rows of four circular walled pits (see Kouloures*), which were cisterns or more probably granaries, with a central pillar.

North of the Central Court and behind the north side portico is a vast group of rooms. Among others is a spacious Pillared Hall (IX) having the bases of six pillars* in two unsymmetrical rows, preceded to the east by a long vestibule with a single pillar base. Perhaps a large columned hall for banquets was situated over the Pillared Hall, accessible through a double staircase to the east, where the guests would enjoy a fine view over the Central Court. Further to the sea is a columned court, the North Court, with porticoes along its north and east sides, surrounded by service rooms and magazines.* It was connected to the Central Court with a paved corridor west of the Pillared Hall. The north end of this corridor is blocked off with a later diagonal building **(XXIII)**, a shrine of the Post-Palatial period constructed among the ruins of the palace with materials taken from it. East of the shrine a flight of steps leads up to the second storey. Between it and the Pillared Hall are three long magazines* **(XXI)**. On the other side of the paved corridor, just at the north west corner of the Central Court, are the ruins of a strong towerlike square building known as the Keep or *"donjon"* **(V)**. The Keep contains two rooms and is accessible only by two steps leading down to the vast Court of the Keep *(Cour du donjon)*, which is connected to the North Court.

On the northwest corner of this court opens the North Entrance of the Palace, with a slightly raised walk before it. This "causeway" leads to a public area outside the palace, which includes a court and a building with magazines* and stuccoed rooms with benches along the walls, the well-known Hypostyle Crypt, which is thought to have been a civic building used by the magistrates of Malia.

At the northwest corner of the palace **(III)**, was located the Megaron thought to have been the royal Residential Suite, which includes a hall with a paved floor surrounded by pier-and-door partitions on three sides, a light-well* to the south, and a smaller paved hall with a Lustral Basin.* West of it the famous Acrobat's Sword was found (see Weapons*). Both halls shared a five-columned portico having a northern exposure facing the sea, a refreshing place in summer. The major private rooms were probably on the upper floor. South of the light-well* is another pillar crypt, a cult room which yielded a number of libation cups, and tablets* and disks of the Hieroglyphic script.*

The palace was surrounded by districts of houses,* like the Quarters **D** and **Z**, to the west and the east of the palace respectively. Well preserved is House **Da**, which includes a lobby, a main hall, a light-well* with a single column, a Lustral Basin* and a toilet, considered the best preserved installation of this kind from the Bronze Age.* This house has been restored at the level of the first storey. House **Za** is divided into two parts by a wall with a single doorway. The residential quarter has a main hall with a pier-and-door partition giving access to a single-columned light-well. There is also a Lustral Basin.* The rest of this house was used for work and storage purposes. House **Zb** has an irregular plan and comprises a central room with a single column, a stairway leading up to the second storey and a main hall opening on to a light-well.* An interesting feature of this house is a weaving room, where loom-weights (see Cloth*) were recovered. House **Zc** which belongs to the Middle Minoan I period, has a small open courtyard inside the main entrance, and several large and small rooms. The largest of all the private houses around the palace is House **E** to the south, sometimes referred to as the "Little Palace." Its plan

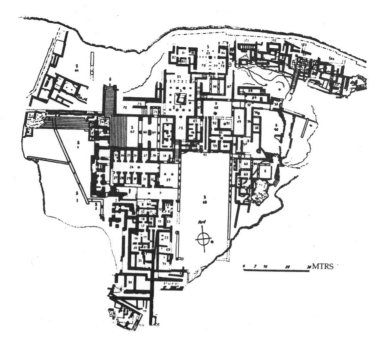

130. Plan of the Palace at Phaistos (*after Pernier*)

is peculiar and rather labyrinthine; among other rooms are included a paved vestibule, an L-shaped portico, an *impluvium*-like court and a Lustral Basin with two niches in its west wall, perhaps for lamps.* A large room was adorned with frescoes,* which featured horizontal bands, panels and stylized flowers. Perhaps this house had no second storey.

In the vicinity of the palace on the shore, at the site known as Chryso-lakkos ("the Gold Hole"), a large burial ground (?) (see Burial Customs*) was excavated, which has produced some of the finest existing Minoan jewellery, including the splendid Bee Pendant but not probably the so-called Aegina Treasure (see Jewellery*).

Palace at Phaistos. The palace at Phaistos is the second largest of the Minoan palaces,* occupying an area of 8,400 square metres (about 2 acres). The palace stood on a Neolithic and Pre-Palatial site on a steep hill at the end of the Mesara Plain,* from which it enjoys a superb view. It has been excavated since 1900 by the Italian School of Archaeology, mainly by Halbherr, Pernier and Levi. Most of what we see today belongs to the new or later palace, erected after the destruction of the first (see Early Palaces*), but with a slightly different plan and alignment (figure 130). Unlike Knossos,* no excessive reconstructions were made here. Some later buildings were constructed on the site. All around the palace on the slopes of the hill were Minoan, Geometric and Hellenistic houses. Along the west side of the palace are two courts, or rather one court laid out in

131. View of the Palace at Phaistos from the NW.

two parts because of the existing natural conditions, connected by a staircase; the southern one is on a lower level while the northern one is some six metres higher. Both are crossed by slightly raised ceremonial walks. A seventeen-columned shallow portico runs along the west side of the Upper Court, which is a relic of the Early Palace. The court was crossed by a ceremonial causeway. A considerable area of it is occupied by buildings of later Greek times, including one with inside columns,* benches and a central hearth. The West Court **(1)**, which belongs also to the Early Palace, was bounded on the north by a broad flight of eight steps (figure 131) or rather seats, probably used like the one at Knossos as a "Theatral Area" for some performance or spectacle **(4)**. Behind it rises a high ashlar wall, which buttresses the Upper Court. Only four steps were left in view when the level of the West Court was raised and enlarged during the construction of the new palace, which runs unpaved over the top of what was left of the earlier facade so that the new facade is set back seven metres (twenty-three feet). The later fill has been removed, leaving the original level visible. The West Court has several large walled pits (*kouloures**) at its western part, towards which a ceremonial causeway runs. One of the pits was rectangular and coated with plaster. A bottle-shaped cistern was used in later Greek times. The new court covered the lower parts of a tripartite shrine **(2)** (see Early Palaces*).

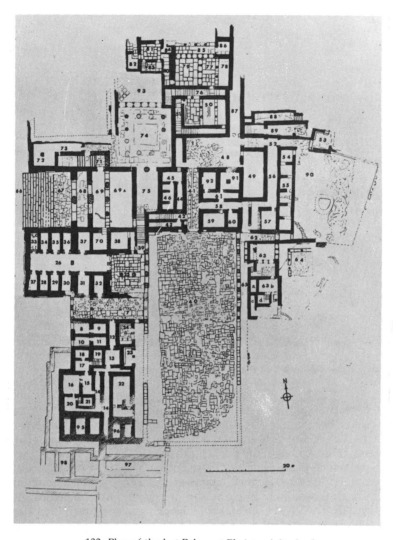

132. Plan of the last Palace at Phaistos (*after Levi*)

The main entrance of the later palace (figure 132) is formed by a broad open-air stairway of monumental proportions unique in Minoan architecture,* with steps slightly sloped to shed rainwater. This studied convexity gives life to the building and anticipates the architectural subtlety of the Parthenon. The stairway leads up to the Propylon **(67-69)** in the form of a double porch. A large oval column divides in two the outer opening, which leads to a pair of portals separated by a large pier. These

Fig. 132. Plan of the Palace at Phaistos

1. West Court
2. Protopalatial Tripartite Shrine
3. Protopalatial Propylon
4. "Theatral Area"
6. Monumental Staircase
7. Pillared Corridor
8-20. Southwest Group of Rooms
8-11. West Wing Shrines
19. Lustral Basin
21. Lustral Basin
22. Two-Pillared Shrine (?)
23-24. Rooms with Benches
25. Anteroom of Magazines (Room of Sealings)
26. Corridor of Magazines
27-37. Magazines
32. Guard's Lodge
33. Magazine with Pithoi
38. Anteroom
39. Staircase
40. Central Court
41. North Wing Entrance and Corridor
42-43. Staircase
45-46. Rooms with Cupboards
47. Neopalatial Room
48. North Court
49. Northeast Court
50. Room with "Atrium" ("Queen's Room")
51. Stairway
52. Corridor to East Court
53. Guard's Lodge (East Entrance)
54, 55, 57. Workshops
56. Corridor of Workshops

58 and 61. Rooms with Protopalatial Peristyle
62. Passage to East Court
63-64. East Suite
63. Hall
63d. Lustral Basin
63e. Toilet
64. Veranda
65. West Portico
67-69. Propylon
70. Protopalatial Lustral Basin
76. Staircase to Peristyle Court
77 and 79. Main Hall of Royal Suite
78. Light-well
80. Passage
81. Lustral Area ("Queen's Hall")
82. Toilet
83. Lustral Basin
85. Main Hall Portico
86. Main Hall Guard's Lodge
87. Corridor
88. Protopalatial Room
90. East Court and Kiln
93. Peristyle Court and Room with Rhomboidal Pavement
94. Upper Court
97. South Corridor
97-99. Southwest Quarter
100. Later Greek Temple of Rhea
101-104. Protopalatial Northeast Apartments
101. Phaistos Disk Building
102. Pillar Crypt
103. Northeast Peristyle Court
104. Pottery Storeroom

twin portals had no doors. Behind the Propylon there is a large light well* of ashlar masonry with three oval columns.* The whole arrangement is quite imposing. South of the Propylon extends the west wing of the palace, with a corridor running east-west **(26)** and magazines* **(27-38)** on either side, with stone-built benches and cupboards in the walls. The westernmost magazine **(33)** contained some pithoi,* a raised pathway and a pot sunk into the floor for spilled liquids like olive oil* and wine.* West of magazine **(38)** is a small Lustral Basin* with a window. A small stairway beyond the light-well* descends to the Central Court.

The Central Court (see Central Courts*), a relic of the earlier palace and focal point of the whole building (40), was regularly paved with lime-stone slabs and had porticoes running along the east and west sides, giving it a more monumental appearance than the slightly larger court at Knossos.* The east side portico displays an alternation of columns* and pillars,* a usual feature of Minoan architecture.* A similar portico on the west side was placed on a slightly higher level than an earlier colonnade. On the northwest corner of the court are the ruins of a stepped structure, probably an altar.* The southeast corner of the court has vanished down the sheer hillside.

Near the northern end of the west side, a monumental entrance with a column between two pillars* rising to a height of two storeys leads into a large room (25) with two columns* inside; the walls are lined with gypsum surmounted by painted plaster.* Below the pavement of this room a great hoard of splendid clay sealings* of early date was found.

South of this room and the magazines* beyond it is a large formal corridor (7) running east-west with a pillar and a causeway along the south side. Two adjacent (23-24) facing the Central Court have benches along the walls, while a room to the south (22) with two pillars, obliterated by a Greek construction, was perhaps a shrine, like the famous Pillar Crypt at Knossos.* The whole group of rooms behind them, which includes two Lustral Basins* (21 and 19) with parapets and descending steps, seems to have had a sacral character. On some walls several masons' marks were cut. Some scholars believe that they may have been apartments for guests. At the south extremity of this wing of the palace are the remains of a later Greek temple of Rhea.

The north side of the Central court is connected by the paved Corridor (41) with another court of small dimensions (48). The broad doorway to Corridor (41) facing the Central Court is flanked by wooden half-columns, partly restored, of which only the stone bases have survived. Perhaps they supported a decorative cornice over the doorway. Next to them, symmetrically arranged on either side, are deep niches decorated with frescoes* depicting lozenge patterns; they are thought to have been used by sentinels guarding the entrance to the Royal Quarter. A similar niche can be seen to the left of the entrance, guarding a stair leading up. The whole forms an imposing facade.

The Corridor (41), originally closed with a door and perhaps unroofed, is flanked on either side by small rooms with cupboards let into the walls. Rooms (58) and (61) contain the remains of a peristyle of the Early Palace. The Corridor leads to Court (48) where remains of an earlier pavement can be seen at a deeper level below the plaster floor, while a round cistern belongs perhaps to later Greek times. Court (90) on the east has in the middle the remains of a horseshoe-shaped kiln perhaps used for smelting copper, although two potter's wheels* were found there. To the north is a guard-lodge (53) at the end of Corridor (52), controlling the east entrance into the palace. The neighbouring long room (88), perhaps a Lustral Basin, provided with a few steps leading down, belonged to the Early Palace.

The royal residential suite, located at the north end of the palace, was reached by the open Peristyle Court with four columns on each side, through a long corridor. The court might have enclosed a royal garden. Probably an upper colonnade formed a loggia in the second storey. North of the Peristyle Court a pier-and-door partition leads into a large room (93) tastefully paved with gypsum slabs of a unique rhomboidal shape. The royal residential suite enjoyed a splendid panorama toward Mount Ida* and a northern exposure, very refreshing in summer. The main hall (77-79) had a four-bayed pier-and-door partition with two-leaved doors dividing the room into two parts; the eastern one (77) had a two-columned light-well* at the east end (78). A similar pier-and-door partition led to a three-columned portico (85) with a guard-lodge to the east (86). Gypsum* was used in abundance to decorate this hall; the joints between the gypsum slabs covering the floor were filled with red plaster* while the walls were adorned with frescoes* depicting floral and abstract motifs. The so-called Queens's Hall (81), the walls of which were decorated with frescoes,* has an elaborate sunken Lustral Basin* (83), while the toilet (82) comes next, against the outside wall of another room. Between the residential suite and the palace proper is a room (50) with a light-well* located unusually in the center of the room, enclosed by two pairs of columns. This arrangement brings to mind an *atrium* or *impluvium* of later times. Its splendid original pavement with red plaster in the interstices was restored. This room was provided with benches and dadoes. A band of painted rosettes decorated the walls above the alabaster dado. A narrow stairway to the west (51) led up to the second storey.

Behind the portico of the east side of the Central Court is another suite of rooms (63-64), which included a hall (63) with a small light-well* without columns and two pier-and-door partitions, the eastern one opening on an L-shaped columned veranda (64). Between it and the portico of the Central Court are two plastered cisterns with a bench along their south side. Next comes a small room (63b) provided with a sunken Lustral Basin* (63d) where a number of fine cult vessels were found, and possibly a toilet with a drain (63e). This group of rooms is independent and gives the impression of having been the apartment of some noble person, perhaps a prince.

Beyond the northeast area of the palace extends an independent complex of Protopalatial buildings. In the westernmost of them (101) was discovered the famous Phaistos Disk,* which had fallen from an upper storey. The sanctity of this area is denoted not only by a series of thin mud-brick partitions for the keeping of cult objects—recalling an example of similar receptacles in the palace at Zakros*—but also by the existence of a Pillar Crypt (102) to the east. The pillar shows a mason's mark.* A bull-shaped rhyton* has been found inside the crypt. The ruins of area (103), approached by a small L-shaped passage, with a paved peristyle court with pillars* and columns* perhaps belonged to a private house, probably originally two-storeyed. A staircase to the south leads to the guard-lodge (53), while a suite to the east (104) includes the so-called Potter's Storeroom.

Palace at Zakros. The fourth great Minoan palace (see Palaces*) is the one at Zakros (the harbourage and hamlet of Kato Zakros), the exploration of which was begun in 1961 by the Greek archaeologist Professor N. Platon. The palace, situated on a picturesque small bay (figure 133) at the east coast of the island still undisturbed by modern construction, possessed one of the more important harbours* of Crete, obviously the main gate of the island to the Orient. It has been presumed that the "Keftiu,'"* the Cretan gift-bearers painted in Egyptian tombs, sailed to Egypt from this eastern port. The palace, suddenly destroyed by fire at the time of the disasters of about 1450 B.C. (see Destructions of Palaces;* Thera*), was not plundered of its treasures. In its main features it is similar to the other great palaces, sharing with them a labyrinthine layout and probably a number of storeys. The palace was surrounded by an urban community. Some of its houses have been explored by Hogarth at the beginning of this century.

In front of the west facade was a court, originally paved. The rectangular Central Court (figure 134) is here also the focal point of the whole structure (see Central Courts*), although at 30 by 12 metres (98 by 39 feet) it is considerably smaller than those of the other palaces. Its orientation deviates slightly from the precise north-south alignment of the others. This court was not paved but floored with tamped earth. A square stone at its northwest corner might have been the base of an altar.* The large Room **(XXXII)** was obviously the kitchen and the dining quarters—for the first time found in a Minoan palace—with a storeroom **(XXXIII)** in a corner. The rooms **(I-VIII)** to the left were magazines,* with an adjoining reception lobby **(IX)**, while to the right a monumental paved portico **(XXXIV)** with storerooms behind it faces the court, connecting it with a stepped ramp **(LV)** leading to the north quarters.

Along the west side of the Central Court, the whole of the ground floor was occupied by the main state appartments **(XXVIII-XXIX)**, provided with panelled floors with stucco interstices and a paved light-well.* The large openings could be screened with curtains. The first room **(XXVIII)**, entered directly from the court and displaying a number of columns* along its axis, has been named the Hall of Ceremonies. Next to it, the square room **(XXIX)** perhaps was a banquet hall. Its walls were gaily adorned with painted plaster* reliefs showing a frieze of large spirals linked together. Behind them was a suite of rooms of ritual functions, such as a shrine **(XXIII)** with a ledge at the back and a niche in the south wall, and further on a large sunken Lustral Basin* **(XXIV)** provided with a sort of balustrade; a flight of eight well-preserved steps led down to it. The Archive Room **(XVI)** yielded several clay tablets* of the Linear A script:* these had been kept in wooden boxes of which only the bronze hinges had survived. A group of superb ritual vessels (see Stone Vases*) was discovered in one room **(XXV)**, a real treasury of the shrine, stored in eight contiguous bins along the walls, formed by thin partitions of mud brick, which had partly collapsed. The west wing also possessed a number of workshops **(XVII-XXI)**.

Along the east side of the Central Court lay the formal living quarters

133. Area of Zakros (*after a Venetian map of 1615*)

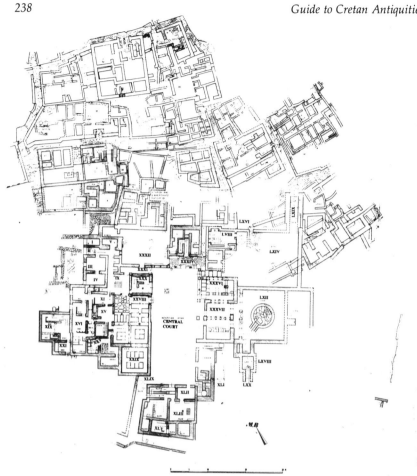

134. Plan of the Palace at Zakros (*after Platon*)

of the royal family **(XXXVI-XXXVII)**, spacious rooms provided with pier-and-door partitions. The throne room might have been here. A sunken Lustral Basin* to the north **(LVIII)** with three wooden columns along its walls was possibly the actual bathroom connected with them. Room **(XXXVII)** opened on to a portico and a large open rectangular court behind it. In its center a flight of eight perfectly-preserved steps led down to a paved circular spring chamber **(LXII)**, of an outer diameter of seven metres (23 feet) possibly with a roof above it, supported by wooden columns* round its edge. The walls, built of dressed stones, were coated with plaster.* The water was kept at a standard level. The excavator thought that this spring chamber might also have been used as an aquarium or for swimming. If so, he suggested, this would be the first instance of a private swimming pool in Prehistoric times. Another sunken spring chamber of rectangular shape could obviously be approached only from outside the palace **(LXX)**. The water came into the basin through an opening at the base of the north wall.

At the south east corner of the Central Court a stairway led down to a well **(XLI)**, probably used for offerings before the destruction of the palace. Many small clay vases were recovered, one of them full of olives* which the water had preserved in a charred condition. As the excavator wrote, the olives had even retained their fleshy parts, looking as if they had just been picked from the tree. A few minutes after they had come out of the water the skins wrinkled rapidly, and, despite much effort, never regained their original appearance.

A group of rooms **(XLII-XLVI)** to the south of the Central Court, originally two-storeyed, were probably used as workshops for stone, ivory* and faience,* and perhaps for making perfumes.* Among the finds here was a clay grill and a fine brazier.* Next comes a long corridor **(XLIX)** leading directly into the Central Court. Another entrance to the palace has been identified to the northeast **(LXIX)**, from which led a paved road with a central raised causeway. The palace possessed a drainage system* which formed an elaborate network. Near the palace proper, to the northwest, a large Protopalatial oblique building—later incorporated into the palace—was explored. This building, divided into two parts and possessing an upper storey, was perhaps the dwelling of some high official. Its floor had panels with plaster interstices. Outside it, to the west, ran a paved road, partly stepped. North of the palace several blocks separated by paved roads or stepped ramps turning at right angles were excavated. Among them was the Strong Building, named after the sturdy construction of its outer walls. It consisted of at least fifteen rooms.

The excavation of the palace yielded among other remarkable objects: two very long swords with golden nails, some complete elephants' tusks evidently from Syria, six bronze ingots* perhaps of Cypriot manufacture, lots of tools* including some huge saws, and an astounding variety of splendid vases; one of them shows in relief a tripartite shrine, a masterpiece of Minoan art* (see Stone Vases*). In the vicinity of the palace lay a number of tombs of earlier times. Many burials were located in caves* along the impressive "Gorge of the Dead," which leads up to the area of Epano Zakros, the main village of the district.

Palaces. Undoubtedly the palace was the central feature of Minoan Crete. The palaces were the focal point of a centralized social organization, in fact of the whole Minoan civilization* in its maturity. Both came into existence at about the beginning of the second millenium b.c. The three great palaces were at Knossos,* Phaistos* and Malia;* a fourth has more recently been uncovered at Zakros* in the extreme east. But each small plain or valley may have possessed its small "palace," where the local ruler or governor lived. Such palaces have been excavated at Gournia* and at Monastiraki,* or identified at Archanes* and at Kanli Kastelli and perhaps at Chania.* Possibly several more wait to be discovered.

The palaces suffered several destructions* but were rebuilt. They stood for about 600 years. After their final destruction—at about 1400 B.C. or a little later for Knossos*—they were not again rebuilt, although it is possible that they were reoccupied on a very limited scale. We distinguish two major phases (see Chronology*): the First or Early Palaces,* founded ca. 1900 B.C. or a little earlier, and the Second or Later Palaces, built on the same spot, the excavated ruins of which form most of that which can be seen today at the various sites.

The palaces have no fortification walls. Their architecture* shares an essential feature: the large rectangular central court (see Central Courts*) which was their focal point and held the whole together. These impressive spacious palaces, which possessed a number of storeys, share also a common plan, probably modelled on Knossos,* which in its turn owes certain limited features to Oriental models and is slightly indebted to that of the large palaces and temples of the Near East, including Egypt. They all have a central court, although the court of the Minoan palaces has a quite different relationship to the buildings surrounding it. The formal plan of an Oriental palace was restricted by its outer walls, which run on straight lines and met at right angles to each other, and, as far as possible, were without openings. The rectangular plan of these outer walls dictated the shape of the inner rooms of the central court as well. The plan of a Minoan palace—a result of an inventive and creative spirit—shows exactly the inverse principle: using space generously, it develops from within outwards, ignoring any restriction imposed by outer walls, thus following the Early Minoan precedents such as the houses* at Vasiliki.* Thus, the exterior facades often have several set-backs or recesses. We must also bear in mind that the final plan of the palaces was not conceived in every detail at one time but was the result of a long evolution and succession of buildings and architectural phases.

Usually the main entrance is to be found on the west side. The visitor was led to the state apartment by a circuitous route, which, being wisely designed and decorated, left a vivid impression on him. The architects evidently enjoyed considerable freedom of design; nevertheless they carefully planned their effects. The walls were covered with plaster,* often decorated with bright frescoes,* and a variety of colourful building materials* was used. Another feature is the abundant use of pillars* and columns* within the buildings to replace some of the walls and to create an impression of spaciousness. Space, light and refreshing air in summer was also the purpose of numerous light-wells* distributed in many places. The main walls of the palaces, reposing on heavy foundations of large stone blocks, were built with ashlar masonry covering a rubble core. Wooden beams were inserted to strengthen the walls and give them resilience against the frequent earthquakes.* The upper storeys were reached by broad flights of stairs, sometimes combined with light-wells* and with colonnades, or even frescoes* like those of the rooms. The palaces had a monumental facade on the west with another court in front. We must bear in mind that what survives of the palaces today is mainly the basement, often the service quarters.

These great palaces served a variety of purposes. Directly related to the surrounding urban community, they were not only the residences of the ruling families and their retinues, as well as the focal point of social life and the main offices of Minoan administration,* but also major centers of various industries* and of trade.* In fact they were distribution points for the economic activities of a larger area. Thus they included large-scale storage rooms not only for the goods to be consumed by the dwellers of the palace but mainly for the taxes and tributes, all paid in kind. Their west wings were especially devoted to the cult, but the whole was permeated with a religious element, so that they were at the same time shrines* and centers of religious life and its festivities. No political rivalry seems to have existed between the palaces.

Palace Style. The so-called Palace Style pottery belongs to the Late Minoan II period (ca. 1450–1400 B.C. or a little later). It was so named because it has rarely been found in Crete outside the palace at Knossos.* This style uses earlier naturalistic motifs of the Floral* and Marine* Styles but shows a certain grandiose and increasingly formal character as well as a precise tectonic organization and real sense of monumentality, for the first time seen in vase painting (figure 135). Nevertheless, it is often rather conventional and stiff, sometimes even a little pompous, without the originality of the earlier periods. As Evans* remarked, the aim of the artist now was not so much picturesque beauty as stateliness of effect. Clumps of stylized lifeless lilies and reeds, octopuses, successions of dolphins, elaborate double axes* surrounded by rosettes, and architectural motifs taken over from wall decoration are most popular, painted with competence and keeping much of their Minoan grace. Many decorative motifs reproduce details of metal-work models, sometimes in a literal way. The spirit of this style is rather foreign to Minoan Crete and probably reflects the presence of Achaians,* a Mycenaean ruling class, at Knossos,* who introduced an almost identical style evolved in the Greek Mainland, where it occurs at almost every known center. This Palace Style spirit can be also observed in other artistic creations of this period, such as wall-painting and seal-engraving.

Palaikastro. On the northern end of the east coast lay the Minoan town of Palaikastro, named after a modern village ("Old Castle") in its vicinity. The town flourished during the Late Minoan period.* It overlooked a small bay, possessing a good natural harbour—protected by the islet Grandes—which played an important role in eastern trade as it offered convenient harbourage at a place important for navigation. The site was excavated by the British School of Archaeology but was partly ruined during the Second World War, and more recently by a bulldozer. It also yielded remains of the Early and Middle Minoan period, mainly cemeteries, including finely built ossuaries, but also ruins of fairly large dwellings with stone walls.

The dense and continuous town-plan (figure 136) comprises a few main roads and several narrow winding streets, surfaced and often stepped, and many houses divided into a number of irregular extensive

135. Palace Style amphora from Knossos

blocks. No palace or public square has been discovered, but some shops
have been identified. The main road is broad and flanked by houses* with
impressive facades. The town possessed an elaborate drainage system.*
Most of the ruins are today covered with earth for protection and only a
part of the town can be seen. Originally the whole town perhaps covered
an area larger than 50,000 square metres (12.3 acres) without fortification
walls (see Urbanism*) and was densely populated.

A good example is House B. At the south part of the house lay an open
court with a veranda showing alternating columns* and pillars,* a characteristic feature of Minoan architecture.* A small guard-lodge is provided with a stone bench. The main hall has four column bases at the cor-

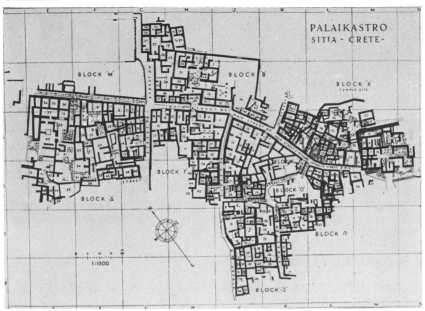

136. Plan of the town at Palaikastro (*after Bosanquet and Dawkins*)

ners of a slightly sunken square, a sort of *impluvium*, at the center of the pavement. The house includes a well, a typical Lustral Basin* approached through a double doorway, a small domestic shrine provided with plaster* sacral horns,* and several storerooms. A second storey was reached by a staircase. The house was built at the end of the Middle Minoan III period and was modified at the beginning of the next period.

The house on the opposite side of the road has a facade with recesses, which correspond to the rooms behind. Traces of a domestic cult have been located in some of the houses* of the settlement. In recent years new researches of a limited scale were undertaken by Popham, McGillivray and Sackett in a section of the town in order to clarify the stratification.

On Petsophas, a steep hill above Palaikastro, was excavated in 1903 by J. L. Myres of the British School and recently by the author one of the most important peak sanctuaries* which included a small shrine with plaster benches. The site yielded a huge number of votive offerings, some of which were extremely fine, including clay figurines* of people and animals, plaster sacral horns* in a unique combination, and libation stone vessels bearing Linear A* inscriptions.

The temple of Diktaian Zeus, a prosperous sanctuary belonging to the Dorian city-state of Itanos,* with a continuing cult from Geometric down to Hellenistic and Roman times, was situated at Palaikastro. The site of the temple was found at Roussolakkos, over two blocks of the Minoan town. From this temple which had been completely demolished come a number of antefixes in the form of a Medusa-like protome, and a clay *sima* of the sixth century B.C., consisting of several blocks all cast from the same mould and showing a warrior mounting a chariot drawn by two horses, below which runs a dog. Also interesting was a series of bronze objects including four shields,* tripods, bowls, miniature armour* and figurines.* Of special importance was an inscription containing a hymn (see Kouretes*) invoking the young Zeus* in the name of the Kouretes. The cult evidently had a mystical character.

Palaiochora. This pleasant large village on the south coast of the province of Selino in Western Crete is perhaps situated on or near the site of the Dorian town of Kalamyde. In 1282 A.D. the Venetian Duke of Crete built a fortress here against the Cretan insurgents, who were nontheless able to capture and demolish it. The fortress was known as Castel Selino. In 1334 it was rebuilt and a settlement was created around it. The famous pirate Barbarossa destroyed it in 1539 and despite some restorations the fortress has since lost its importance.

PANDAREOS see **Milatos.**

PASIPHAE. According to the Greek tradition, Queen Pasiphae ("She who shines on all"), a daughter of Helios ("the Sun") and the nymph Crete,* was the wife of Minos.* The mighty god of the sea Poseidon caused her to fall in love with the white bull which had emerged from the sea as a gift of the god to Minos but had been wrongly withheld by the king from sacrifice because of its exceptional value. To avenge this affront, Poseidon visited this utterly unnatural passion upon Minos' wife. Pasiphae confided her desire to the skilled artist of the king, the famous Daidalos,* who built for her a hollow wooden cow set on wheels and covered with a cow's hide which he had skinned. Daidalos placed the cow in a meadow near Gortyn,* where the white bull was grazing, after instructing Pasiphae how to slip inside with her legs thrust down into its hindquarters. Eventually the bull mounted the cow, so that the queen was satisfied. In consequence she later gave birth to the monstrous bull-headed Minotaur.* Nonetheless Pasiphae was very jealous of Minos' loves and, being an able sorceress as a daughter of Helios, put a spell upon him to prevent any further infidelities (see Minos' Loves*). Among Pasiphae's children by Minos were Akakallis,* Ariadne* and Glaukos.*

According to Pausanias, Pasiphae was the moon. This strange myth of Pasiphae perhaps reflects a religious belief about a sacred marriage of sun and moon. It has been supposed that the ritual coupling of solar bull and lunar cow would have been performed by a man and woman masquerading as bull and cow. Similar practises are known from Egypt. This sacred marriage was perhaps part of the ritual at Knossos,* in which the "priest-king"* participated.

In recent years the discovery of a papyrus fragment brought to light parts of a lost drama of Euripides, *Kretes* ("The Cretans"), the subject of which was the tale of Pasiphae and the bull. The great Athenian dramatist, who saw the deeply tragic aspect of this tale, describes the vigorous defense of the queen, who argues that her conduct was so utterly unnat-

137. Head of worshipper from Mochlos

ural as to be an involuntary act, the consequence of madness sent by a god.

Patsos Cave see **Sybrita.**

Peak Sanctuaries. From the beginning of the Middle Minoan period,* several peaks of high hills or mountains became places of worship and pilgrimage. Some were entirely without buildings, and in others little shrines* were built and sacrificial bonfires were occasionally lit. The devout climbed up these places of worship to pray, probably on certain fixed days. They brought offerings and also votive clay figurines,* thousands of which have been found (figure 137). The human figurines represented the worshippers themselves, perhaps simulacra constantly attending the divinity after the actual devout had left the place. Whole clay herds of domestic animals, possibly substitutes for sacrifices were offered. Clay

138. Woman with a swollen leg from a peak sanctuary

figurines of such wild animals as weasels, stoats, *agrimia* (ibexes), tortoises, hedgehogs, birds,* etc. have also been found. Figurines of rhinoceros beetles (*oryctes nasicornis*) are often found—the largest known specimen having recently been found at Prinias near Siteia,* modelled as a rhyton* (a cult vessel for libations), a fact demonstrating that these inoffensive beetles cannot any more be considered as pests, as some scholars

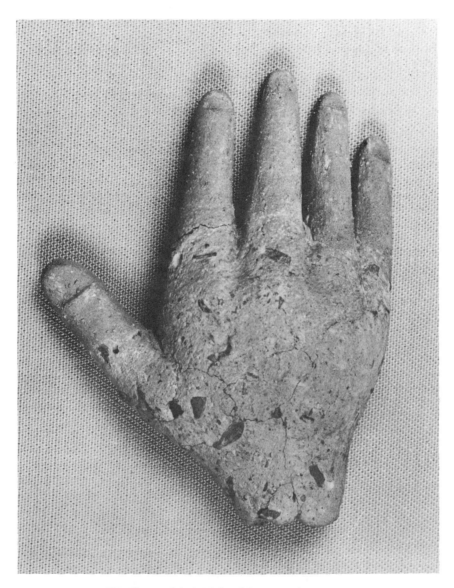

139. Clay model of sick hand from a peak sanctuary

thought. Perhaps their long horn was significant for the Minoans.

Individual limbs or other parts of the human body, sometimes deformed by illness (figures 138 and 139), or with an injured part indicated in some way, were either dedicated to the divinity as thank offerings or as special petitions for cures, a custom which still survives in the Greek Orthodox Church today. Among the finds in the sanctuaries are also some

The remains of these votive offerings are found in rock crevices. Some of
the peak sanctuaries continued to be in use as cult places into the Late Minoan I period and later. Some fine stone vases* are believed to be adorned
in relief with pictures of them, with the small shrines included, such as
the famous stone vase found in the palace at Zakros* (see Shrines*).

Among the best known peak sanctuaries are those on Mount Juktas,*
Petsophas near Palaikastro* (see Palaikastro*), Kophinas (at an altitude of
1231 metres or 4039 feet) on the Asterousia Mountains south of the Mesara Plain,* Prinias near Siteia* and Traostalos north of Zakros* (see figure
133, peak to the right). The majority of these sanctuaries are located in the
far east of the island, and some in Central Crete, but a few were found also
in the west like a very rich one on Mount Vrysinas south of Rethymnon.*
Many of them were identified by a tireless French scholar, Paul Faure.
Several peak sanctuaries have been excavated by the author; some of
them have yielded gold and bronze objects, including figurines. The nature of the deity or deities worshipped at the peak sanctuaries remains a
subject of discussion among the scholars (see map 7).

Perfumes. The Minoans paid extraordinary respect to cleanliness, as ample evidence shows, and they also probably used aromatic oils and ointments in bathing, like the Egyptians and later the Greeks. As elsewhere,
almond and bitter almond, as well as cedar and various native herbs were
probably among the materials employed for the manufacture of perfumes, ointments and aromatic oils, which were stored and exported
overseas in the characteristic stirrup-jars.* We may assume that animal
fats were also used, such as sheep and ox fat, as was true in Egypt. The existence of a perfume laboratory has been suggested for one of the workshops at the south wing of the palace at Zakros.* The clay tablets* of the
Linear B script* mention among other occupations of the population of
Knossos* that of the unguent boiler.

Phaistos see **Palace at Phaistos.**

Phaistos (City of). One of the Dorian city states of Classical Crete, Phaistos was among the seven Cretan towns which took part in the Trojan
War (see Idomeneus*). The eponymous hero of the city was probably a
son or grandson of Herakles, Phaistos, who was killed by King Idomeneus. According to legend, here reigned Rhadamanthys,* Minos' brother.
The famous seer Epimenides* was a Phaistian.

Some of the houses of the city have been excavated near the Minoan
palace. The early settlement was invaded by Dorians* from Argolis. The
city was independent, issuing its own coinage* (figure 140), until the second half of the second century B.C., when it seems to have been absorbed by
its powerful neighbour, Gortyn,* along with its harbourage on the Libyan
Sea, Matala.*

Among the divinites of the city was Zeus Welchanos* and Lato Phytia,
mother of Apollo. The goddess was celebrated with a festival known as

140. Silver coin of Phaistos (*courtesy Mrs. M. Oeconomides*)

the Ekdysia, during which the young men put aside their boyhood clothes. This festival, probably reflecting some old fertility and initiation ritual, commemorated the myth of Leukippos ("he who rides white horses"), who was changed from a girl to a boy with the consent of the goddess.

Phaistos Disk. The famous and still mysterious disk of baked clay was discovered in 1903 inside a small room at Phaistos* in a Middle Minoan III context (ca. 1600 B.C.) together with a tablet of the Linear A script.* Some scholars believed that the disk may have been made in Anatolia, while more recently on the basis of some strong evidence others consider it probably Cretan. The roughly circular solid disk, with a diameter of about sixteen centimetres (six inches) is completely covered on both sides with a spiraliform inscription of an unrelated ideographic script (figure 141). Each sign has been separately sharply impressed on the wet clay by means of a stamp, probably of metal or even wood. This is, in fact, a real anticipation of a printed inscription, several millenia before Gutenberg. There are 241 signs in all, arranged in 61 groups inside an incised spiral from the circumference to the center, to guide the reader's eye. The sign groups are separated by vertical lines. Among them are figures of standing or running men, women and children, heads with feather crowns, fish,* birds,* insects, vessels, shields,* boughs, ships,* tools,* parts of animals and others. The text, possibly a religious hymn, has not yet been successfully deciphered, although much work has been done on it. Various languages have been suggested, some of which are rather unprobable, such as Basque or Finnish. According to one scholar the text is a list of soldiers; to another it is a hymn to the "rain lord"; another believes that here the king speaks about the construction of the palace at Phaistos.*

Phalasarna. A neighbour of Polyrhenia* and its traditional enemy, Phalasarna was a Greek city-state on the picturesque west coast of Crete. Its secure close harbour, once accessible through a channel, is today completely dry because of the considerable rise of the coast over sea-level since ancient times (see Geography*). The city, named after a nymph, developed into a wealthy and commercial center. The Ptolemies, the Macedonian kings of Egypt, had a strong influence here. In the beginning of the third century B.C. Phalasarna concluded a treaty with Polyrrhenia, with Sparta as mediator. The city was captured in 184 B.C. by Kydonia*

141. Phaistos Disk: Face A

but was evacuated after diplomatic pressure from the part of Rome. Phalasarna was among the thirty-one Cretan cities which in 183 B.C. made an alliance with Eumenes II, king of Pergamon. The city still possesses the ruins of Byzantine fortification walls.

Phoinix see **Anopolis.**

Pillars. Square pillars, distinguished from circular columns,* were a common feature of Minoan architecture.* Pillars were supports for rectangular cross-sections and purely utilitarian in function, but often they were alternated with columns* in porticoes. Wooden pillars were also used. Larger pillars were built with dressed stone blocks, or with rubble held together by a wooden frame consisting of posts at the four corners. A cult of pillars (see Tree and Pillar Cult*) seems to have evolved in the Minoan religion.* A special veneration was obviously paid to the pillars of the dark Pillar Crypts of the Palace at Knossos.*

Pins see **Metallurgy.**

Piracy. The great Greek historian Thucydides tells how Minos did his best to suppress piracy after establishing a navy: "Still more addicted to piracy were the islanders....But when the navy of Minos had been established, navigation between various peoples became safer—for the evildoers of the islands were expelled by him and he proceeded to colonize most of them—and the dwellers of the sea-coast now began to acquire property more than before, and to become more settled in their homes..." Indeed, piracy has been a constant activity of sea-going peoples from remote antiquity until recent times, practised upon passing merchant vessels as well as upon any accessible settlements, not only by ordinary pirates but also by lords, sometimes being a form of struggle between nations. From the Bronze Age* onwards the maritime powers of the Mediterranean were able to suppress piracy to a certain degree, at certain times. Obviously the centralization of Minoan administration* and the emergence of the palace economy* were decisive factors as far as Crete was concerned. When one examines the location of the settlements in Crete throughout antiquity one can demonstrate that their distance from the coast was directly related to the degree of potential danger from the sea. While most of the Minoan settlements were less than a hundred metres (328 feet) above sea-level, vulnerable coastal lands were abandoned and occupied areas were removed to higher and safer levels when piracy was unchecked in post-Minoan times. Crete with its extensive and remote coasts has often been a dangerous nest of pirates during unstable times such as during the long Hellenistic period* and the Arab occupation* in the ninth century A.D., when the Aegean was infested by the Saracens.

Cretan piracy was a widespread and profitable business especially in Hellenistic times, as Strabo informs us. Cretan pirates succeeded the Etruscans and other Italians as the principal marauders of this period, to be replaced by Cilician pirates after the Roman conquest. Piracy was usually practised with state protection and authority, and piratical forces often were systematically used, especially in time of war (see Olous*). Even neutral cities were sometimes raided by them. Piratical enterprises were very profitable, especially for large-scale raiding and kidnapping. Prisoners were ransomed or sold to the slave-market. During the second half of the second century B.C. there was a marked diminution of Cretan piracy because of the prolonged counter-measures taken by Rhodes, and despite the efforts of Macedon.

Venice wiped out piracy when it included Crete in its sea-empire, as the Romans under Pompey the Great and Metellus Creticus had done in the first century B.C. During the Turkish occupation* piracy flourished again, with extensive depopulation as a direct result. The small fortified island of Grambousa* in the far west was a pirate lair. As Miller observed, "piracy has in all ages been the curse of the Aegean, and at this time the corsairs of every nation infested that beautiful sea."

142. Typical pithos with trickle pattern

Pithoi. The gigantic store-jars have been manufactured in Crete since Minoan times. They are still made in some villages today, especially at Thrapsano near Herakleion.* They were used to store various items such as olive oil,* grain, honey* and other things—even clothes. They often stand well over the size of a man. Glaukos,* son of Minos,was drowned in such a pithos, according to myth. In the palace at Knossos* there was room for some 400 of these jars, placed in a row inside the narrow magazines* (see figure 111). The aggregate capacity of these pithoi has been estimated as over 240,000 gallons (908,400 litres) or even more.

Early pithoi were usually decorated with the simple "trickle-pattern," favoured over a long period. This ornament, applied at the top of the jar and allowed to trickle down on the buff clay (figure 142), evidently imitated natural stains of the olive oil* stored inside the jars which occasionally spilled on the outside. Other ornamentation was sometimes used.

Usually numerous handles were arranged in zones; sometimes there were two sets, one around the shoulders and one above the base. Their mouths were covered either with flat clay or stone lids, or with fabric tied round their short necks. Minoan pithoi were usually decorated with patterns in added clay, such as round "medallions," an early pattern, knobs, bands of applied and thumb-impressed decoration, broad, flat, wavy bands and the "rope pattern," a moulded imitation of the actual ropes with which they were bound for purposes of transport and reinforcement. From the Late Minoan II period onwards this "rope pattern" is abandoned, replaced by raised incised bands running around the body. Decorative handles in friezes were sometimes added. There is evidence that pithoi made of stone actually existed in Knossos.* Some late Bronze Age* pithoi are almost barrel-shaped.

The manufacture of pithoi continues into the Iron Age.* Some examples of the Orientalizing period* were adorned with figures or various ornaments in relief. These relief pithoi, often counting among the best artistic creations of the time, were characterized by stamped Oriental motifs such as sphinxes and lions, or sometimes horses.* A pithos from Prinias shows the *Potnia theron* ("Mistress of the Wild Animals").

Pithoi were also used in different periods for burials (see Burial Customs*). The large Minoan cemetery at Pachyammos* contained 213 pithoi. Sometimes previously damaged pithoi were employed for burial purposes.

Plaster. Minoan walls were usually coated either with a fine lime plaster, or gypsum* veneer. Of course ashlar masonry was left exposed. Lime plaster, essentially composed of pure caustic lime free of inert materials, was applied on an undercoat of clay plaster, which was used alone in poorer constructions. Plaster was freely employed as a revetment of walls. Some floors were also plastered, especially in unroofed areas, such as light-wells* and courts, sometimes with embedded small rounded pebbles. Benches, steps and niches were often coated with plaster. A special water-resistant plaster was used for cisterns during the Late Minoan period.* Plaster was often painted, at first usually in dark red. The painting of simple geometric designs such as interconnected running spirals eventually evolved into frescoes.*

Platanos. Near the village of Platanos in the Mesara Plain,* the Greek archaeologist Stephanos Xanthoudides excavated in 1915 two free-standing Early Minoan tholos tombs,* which are among the largest of this kind of funerary architecture: Tholos A has an interior diameter of thirteen metres (43 feet) and the circular wall has a thickness of about two and a half metres (8 feet). The tombs yielded a number of excellent vases and seals.* Among the stone vases* were a number of oblong "pepper-and-salt" trays with cups sunk in them, resembling *kernoi*.* Most important for the fixing of the Minoan chronology* was a cylinder seal of the period of the famous Hammurabi, founder of the First Dynasty of Babylon, which was recovered from Tholos B, the smaller of the tombs, along with three Egyptian scarabs* of the XIIth Dynasty.

Plati. A small Minoan settlement near the modern village of Plati on the Plateau of Lasithi* was excavated before the Second World War by the British School of Archaeology. The buildings are datable to the Late Minoan I and III period. A number of rather nondescript small rooms possibly belonging to three houses were explored around an open area possessing a hearth, possibly a central court of a single unified complex or the public court of a town. The site was resettled in later Greek times.

PLATO. Plato's late and rather utopian work, *The Laws*, of the first part of the fourth century B.C., incorporates certain features of social life of contemporary Crete, which is the scene of this dialogue. Here the old Cretan Kleinias takes part in the discussion, together with an Athenean and a Spartan, during a walk from Knossos* to the Idaian Cave.* The argument concerns the ideal state and the formulation of a new set of laws for a colony to be found under Kleinias. The great Athenean philosopher praises Minos* as a lord of the sea and Rhadamanthys* "the Just," idealizes the Cretan way of life and admires its conservative and aristocratic institutions and their stability, comparing it to the collapse of democratic Athens. Plato probably had accurate information about the conditions of Cretan society.

Plough see **Agriculture.**

Polyrhenia. An important Classical Greek city-state in Western Crete, at first colonized from Laconia, Polyrhenia ("rich in lambs") had a vast territory extending from the north to the south coast. Both coasts can be seen from its high acropolis, which rises over a steep and naturally fortified place. The ruins of the city walls have parts dated from every period from the Greek to the Venetian, including the Byzantine. One of the more interesting remains of the city is the aqueduct, perhaps a work of the time of Hadrian. Polyrhenia was an enemy of Knossos* and Kydonia* and took part in the Lyttian War (see Lyttos*). It also was the traditional rival of neighbouring Phalasarna.* An inscription datable to 69 B.C. refers to a statue made by the polyrhenians in honour of the Roman conqueror of Crete, Quintus Metellus Creticus, referred to as a "saviour and benefactor of the city." Polyrrhenia did not take part in the resistance against the Romans and was consequently spared from destruction.

Poppy see **Flora.**

Popular Art. Cretan popular art is generally of good quality, especially in embroidery and weaving. Cretan embroidery reached its zenith during the eighteenth century but did not develop further thereafter because of the extremely troubled history of the island. Embroidery shows a great variety of colours, motifs and stitches. Among the basic motifs are the

143. Popular chest of the 18th century; Historical Museum, Herakleion

flower pot and the traditional two-headed eagle, the emblem of the Byzantine Empire. More recent than embroidery, Cretan weaving is perhaps the best in Greece, with various bright colours extracted from the island's rich varieties of flora.* The decoration, which shows a great sense
of style, is either abstract and geometric or figured, with birds, flowers
dancing girls or even recent historical subjects in a "naif" style. A well-
known artifact is the woolen *vouria* or *vourieli*, a sort of small rucksack.
Another item is the *prosomi*, a narrow shoulder band for carrying a jar. A
special kind of weaving is the *kouskouses* or *skoulato* with a curly surface. A
fine exhibition of popular art can be seen at the Historical Museum at
Herakleion (see Museums*); of importance is a collection of woodcarvings, which includes a number of elaborately carved chests with
painted interior lids (figure 143).

Population see **Urban Revolution.**

Potter's Wheel. The first attempts to escape from the labour of making
pottery by hand led to the use of a primitive tournette, "slow-wheel" or
turn-table, in which the revolving disk was supported on a pivot. The
earliest examples in the Aegean have been found at Myrtos* in Eastern
Crete; they were flat on one side, convex on the other. Several had
painted crosses. The largest is almost 26 centimeters (about 10 inches) in
diameter. In this process the vases were turned by hand while being
shaped, while later, after the introduction of the freely rotating fast potter's wheel, the vases were thrown and built up, with the force coming
from the rotary motion itself.

The invention of the fast wheel—one of the chief instruments of ancient man—was a major innovation which led to technical mastery in pottery* and allowed the forms of the vessels to become more graceful. Its mythical inventor was Talos.* In Crete it was introduced—perhaps from the Near East—or invented independently during the Middle Minoan IB period (ca. 1800 B.C.), as attested by Knossian vases with concentric striations on their interiors and string-cut bases. Towards the end of the Bronze Age* there are wheel-made figurines* of humans and animals. The wheel was a heavy disk of clay, set upon a wooden wheel which was fixed to a free-turning vertical pivot or spindle. A hollow in the center of the underside of the disk, sometimes surrounded by striations, made it adhere better to the surface of the wooden wheel. Many wheels have been found at various Middle Minoan III-Late Minoan III sites, such as Gournia,* Phaistos,* Kritsa,* Tylissos* and Vathypetro.* Sometimes they bear incised signs such as double axes.*

Pottery (Minoan). Pottery, with its ubiquitous sherds, is a principal element for fixing chronology.* Its importance is stressed by the fact that terracotta* is practically imperishable and able to withstand the passage of time. Thus pottery becomes not only the main artistic expression of ancient times left to us, but also a major source of archaeological knowledge and classification.

Pottery of the Neolithic and Early Minoan periods was made by hand (see Neolithic Period*). The shapes of the earliest Bronze Age* vases are often complicated and extravagant but always attractive. During the Early Minoan I phase round-bottomed jugs with beaked spouts appear as well as other shapes including bowls on high pedestals, decorated with simple linear patterns in a red or brown semilustrous paint on a yellowish background (Hagios Onouphrios Ware*). Other vessels such as suspension pots are decorated with simple but expertly drawn incised patterns, or with simple dots over the whole surface of the vase. Some vessels belong to the so-called Fine Gray Ware. Another characteristic shape of this time is a tall chalice with a burnished decoration, which belongs to the well-known Pyrgos Ware.*

The best achievement of the pottery of the Early Minoan II phase (ca. 2600-2300 B.C.) is the attractive mottled Vasiliki Ware.* There are also monochrome vessels. The jugs of this period have a flat bottom. The decoration is dark—a dull red or brown varnish—on a light background. Among the patterns are hatched triangles, concentric semicircles, the "butterfly" pattern or lattice work. Some vessels are in the form of a man or an animal. The next phase sees the evolution of a reverse system of decoration, light-on-dark (figure 144). The patterns, in a thick creamy white, are now mostly curvilinear. This important innovation includes running spirals and interlocked curves. Other patterns are cross-hatched circles and lozenges, zigzags and other motifs often linked to each other. Horizontal designs are the general rule. Animal figures appear for the first time, and polychromy is introduced before the end of the period. There is a great variety of shapes. Spouts are now shorter, handles round or al-

144. Middle Minoan I vessel with light-on-dark decoration

most round in section, and bases flatter. The commonest shape is a rounded "tea-cup," often without a handle.

During the Middle Minoan I period, both dark-on-light and light-on-dark decoration exist. A typical vessel of this period is a small jug with a short cut-away neck, as well as a handleless cup, often with a pedestal, which a little later shows a ribbon handle and straight or slightly out-curving sides. The introduction of the fast potter's wheel which succeeded the primitive turn-table (see Potter's Wheel*) was a major innovation which led to technical mastery in pottery.

The earliest clay vases made with the wheel are assignable to the Middle Minoan IB phase. It is generally thought that until then women were the potters. Now, together with the Early Palaces* appears the most exquisite Cretan pottery, the famous polychrome Kamares Ware,* surely without peer. The torsional principle, essential in Cretan decoration, is here at its best. A variety is the so-called Barbotine decoration.*

The pottery of the early stages of the second palaces (Middle Minoan III: ca. 1700-1550 B.C.), uses much the same forms of decoration as in the previous period, but there is a clear decline, perhaps because art now uses a greater variety of materials. Sometimes the decoration is very elaborate but it certainly lacks the earlier spontaneity and inventiveness. Elaborate flowers and leaves and very often spirals and rosettes are painted in white on a black background. From the cemetery at Pachyammos* comes a fine vessel decorated with dolphins. Nevertheless, a falling off from the standard can be seen. The decoration is chiefly white on black, while the red paint is abandoned. Later, dark-on-light decoration becomes increasingly popular. A typical shape is the cup but now with a larger handle and more spreading rim, which becomes flaring for the handleless examples, with a swelling body above a rather sharp base. Later the cups become shallower and rest on a low pedestal. Another common shape is a small

145. Larnax from Episkopi: Side B (*courtesy Professor N. Platon*)

elongated store jar, often with an oval mouth and variously placed handles or a beaked spout and three handles meeting the rim.

Now a forthright naturalism becomes a characteristic feature of the art of the second palaces. The dark-on-light decoration—a dark red-black paint, often glossy, with occasional white paint as an auxiliary for details, over a fine yellowish background—gradually prevails over the light-on-dark style and becomes universal, then and for the years to come. The quality of material is improved and the baking finer. The Late Minoan I period (ca. 1550-1450 B.C.) also sees the triumph of naturalism: the Floral Style* and later the Marine Style* are developed, both outstanding achievements of Minoan art,* showing the Cretan love of purely natural subjects. The decoration of the vessels always is well adapted to their form. Rhyta (see Rhyton*) and jugs in various shapes are very popular. Contemporary frescoes* lend not only their naturalistic motifs to the Floral Style* but also the geometrical patterns of their borders to other vases. A common pattern is one consisting of rows of joint thick-rimmed spirals with a solid center. The shapes of the vases show elegant curves and are very expressive. The potter delights in slender forms.

During the Late Minoan II phase (ca. 1450–1400 B.C.), a tendency to stylization and increasing formalization of the natural forms leads at Knossos* to the so-called Palace Style,* which is decorative and monumental. This style of decoration was originally virtually confined to the

146. Larnax from Episkopi: Side C (*courtesy Professor N. Platon*)

Knossos area, but during the earliest phase of the next period it spread throughout the island.

After 1400 B.C. and the coming of Achaian* settlers, the long Late Minoan III period begins, during which the pottery of the Mycenaean Empire dominates. This pottery, manufactured in great quantities, is standard over the whole area of Mycenaean influence, including, to a certain extent Crete. Technically, the manufacture is of the best quality. The clay is now better refined. The pottery is fired at a higher temperature, an achievement which gives certain practical advantages to the vase. Designs are made in a lustrous paint ranging from black to brown and red with occasional white colour for details. The background is a well-polished smooth chalky slip. The field of the vessel is often divided into

147. Larnax from Episkopi: Side D (*courtesy Professor N. Platon*)

zones or juxtaposed panels. The decoration is dominated by a sense of real monumentality and its composition is tectonic and disciplined. On the other hand there is a tendency to rigidity and lack of imagination. The naturalistic motifs of the earlier periods become more and more stylized, abstract and linear: for instance flowers now consist of arcs and dots. Nevertheless, good taste is never absent. The painting of horizontal stripes—made mechanically as the vessel revolved on the wheel—is very common.

The Cretan pottery of this time did not forget its glorious ancestry and was rather nonconformist, in fact predominantly Minoan, and at variance with the uniform Mycenaean style, showing a spirit less monumental and disciplined but more creative. This spirit, unlike anything truly Mycenaean, has its roots in the older tradition of the Minoan legacy which had partially resisted the Mainland style. A very characteristic shape is the stirrup-jar.* A class of libation vessels are the bird vases (see Birds*). Other shapes are the *kylix* or tall-stemmed shallow drinking goblet, and the *krater*, a large wide-mouthed mixing bowl. Figures of birds,* especially waterfowl, are much favoured. The human figure is rarely depicted. Large painted surfaces can be seen in contemporary terracotta* coffins (see Larnakes*). The chest form becomes most common (figures 145, 146, and 147). During the last phase of this period (see figure 33), the ever-increasing stylization and abstraction of motifs oversimplifies them and often makes their original forms unrecognizable. The octopus motif is much used. Often the tentacles are reduced or increased in number and symmetrically prolonged much beyond the normal, sometimes becoming straggling lines or disconnected series of loops. The body of the octopus is sometimes omitted.

Praisos. Praisos was one of the most powerful city-states of Classical Greek times in Eastern Crete. It was the city of the Eteocretans,* the descendants of the old Minoan population. An interesting religious custom of the Praisians was the giving of offerings to a sacred pig, a customary sacrifice before marraige. This animal evidently was a totem, the ancestor of an early clan, in the earliest religious beliefs of the Minoans, and the later Cretans continued to have a taboo on pork, as Moslems were to have later. According to Athenaios, this custom had its origin in the belief that a sow had suckled Zeus in the Diktaian Cave.*

The city was surrounded by a fortification wall. Its territory extended over the whole east extremity of the island—which corresponds to the modern province of Siteia*—except the area belonging to Itanos.* Priasos continued to be independent until 146 B.C., when it was finally devastated by Hierapytna,* its powerful western neighbour and old rival. The Praisians found a refuge in their harbour on the north coast, Siteia.

Many interesting terracottas, including a number of large painted figures of lions, were found on the Altar Hill. On the slopes of the so-called First Acropolis a large house of the Hellenistic period* built on a terrace was excavated by the British School of Archaeology. The outer walls are of fine masonry with uneven courses. The residential quarters occupied the north and east sides. A workroom on the south side contained a stone *impluvium* and an olive* press in one of the corners.

Prehistory see **Bronze Age.**

Preveli Monastery. This monastery on the south coast of the prefecture of Rethymnon* was built in the sixteenth or seventeenth century and because of its remote position played a role in the Cretan revolts against the Turkish occupation.* The monastery lies in the center of a splendid landscape. The British Admiral Spratt wrote about it in the middle of the nineteenth century: "It is the paradise of Crete in one of the most happily chosen spots for a retreat from the cares and responsibilities of life."

"Priest-King." Not much is known about the functions of the Minoan "priest-king"—thus termed by Evans* after the divine "priest-kings" of the great religious centers of the Near East—of whom the legendary King Minos* is the familiar prototype. Perhaps the term "king" is misleading and "prince" would be a more appropriate one. Nonetheless, we may assume that coexisting with other kings he was not at all an absolute despot in the sense of the Oriental monarchs, or a god incarnate, or even that he was succeeded by his son. Furthermore, there are reasons to believe that his tenure of office was probably restricted to an octennial period (see Calendar*). His sacral functions seem to have been primary to his political functions, although he probably was the head of Minoan administration.*

The Throne Room of the palace at Knossos,* connected with a Lustral Basin,* clearly was designed for cult functions, while the palaces* themselves had a strong religious character. According to Evans,* the emblems of spiritual and temporal power of the "priest-king" were the sword and the lustral sprinkler (see Stone Vases,* *Chieftain Cup,* figure 179). As Willetts noted, the "priest-king" of Knossos was in no position to reflect all the forces of his society so as to appear before that society overwhelmingly as god manifest, as the divine abstraction of all social forces. It would seem then that in a way his fellow-merchants were his social peers, his counterparts in the other palaces were his religious peers. He appears to have ranked first among equals *(primus inter pares).* However, our ideas about him are necessarily rather vague. One of the best Minoan frescoes,* *("Priest-King")* was wrongly supposed to represent him.

In the Mycenaean Mainland, the temples of the later Greek divinities were sometimes characteristically built upon the ruins of the palace of the Mycenaean king. Besides, after the introduction of democracy in many Greek cities, as in Athens the title of king *(basileus)* continued to be held by some high sacral officals, who evidently had assumed the religious offices of the old kings.

Prinias. The Greek city-state of Rhizenia, near the modern village of Prinias in the prefecture of Herakleion,* was erected on a natural acropolis, first settled at the end of the Bronze Age*, obviously as a city of refuge like Karphi* and Vrokastro* in the east. The Italian archaeologist Luigi Pernier here excavated two early Greek temples, the earlier of which was constructed about the middle of the seventh century B.C. and measured about 8 by 15 metres (25 by 50 feet) externally. The pronaos of this important temple—named "Temple A"—is entered from the east and has a Minoan-like appearance with its pillar between the *antae* (side posts) of the porch, instead of the pair of columns which would be normally expected in a *templum in antis,* the simplest form of Greek temple.

As in Dreros,* in the middle of the *cella* there were probably two wooden axial columns with round stone bases flanking a central sacrifical hearth lined with slabs of limestone and containing burned bones. These columns supported a flat roof. The entrance was flanked on the inside with wooden half-columns resting on semicircular stone bases. The central post of the entrance supported a limestone transom with female figures carved in sunk relief on the soffit and with a frieze of animals on the front side of the transom. Two female figures, probably goddesses, also in the Dedalic Style,* were placed above the transom at each end, seated facing each other, and seem to carry the true lintel on their heads. The temple was adorned with reliefs representing a frieze of mounted spearmen, with traces of painting, presumably set up as a parapet *sima*. All these fine sculptures are today exhibited in the Herakleion Museum. "Temple B" is similar but not well preserved.

From the Prinias area come several archaic tombstones. These early *stelai* depict exquisite figures of women or heavily armed warriors incised in the soft stone.

Pseira. Pseira is a small hilly island at the eastern part of the Gulf of Mirabello, today uninhabited and barren (see figure 123). It can be visited by boat either from Hagios Nikolaos* or even from Mochlos.* A sheltered cove at its east coast near some important seaways offers an excellent harbourage for small craft, a fact which accounts for the flourishing of an isolated but prosperous settlement in the Early Minoan II period. Pseira, home of sailors and evidently an important station of transit trade, developed particularly in Late Minoan I times. Sponge-diving and murex-shell fisheries were probably local industries here.

The settlement covers an area of about 15,000 square metres (3.7 acres). The small houses are clustered along a narrow rocky tongue of land projecting into the sea and there are steps at intervals descending to the harbour below on the south side. The main road runs through the long axis of the settlement, with smaller streets meeting it at right angles. Most of the streets were just cleared rock surfaces. The houses* were built of large, roughly squared boulders of local limestone, while natural slabs of schist covered the floors. No brick seems to have been used. The excavator of the site, the American Richard Seager, remarks that the houses* were built in terrace fashion, thus permitting a single house to contain a number of floors and yet never stand more than two storeys high at any one point, a form still common in Cretan popular architecture.*

No palace was discovered at Pseira but there are some large houses. A public square has been found during the recent excavations of Ph. Betancourt and the author. Three rooms of one building were filled with beach pebbles, identified as slingstones belonging to a primitive arsenal. One room was perhaps a domestic shrine. One house was even adorned with a fine relief fresco of late date, the only known example outside Knossos,* a fact interpreted as an indication of a close and friendly relationship between the island and the capital. The fresco–reminiscent of the Ladies in Blue–illustrates two female figures in richly embroidered dress with bared breasts, sitting on the rocks, perhaps by the seaside.

The settlement yielded great numbers of fine pottery.* A splendid jar shows facing bulls' heads with double axes* between the horns and between each head, on a background of sprays. On a rhyton of the Marine Style* we see dolphins which seem to be enclosed in the meshes of a net.

The settlement was also occupied in later times. Perhaps a beacon

148. Plan of the upper Psychro Cave *(after Hogarth)*

station along with a military camp were installed on the highest point of the island.

Psiloritis see **Ida (Mount).**

Psychro Cave. The famous cave of Psychro, named after a modern village nearby, on the Plateau of Lasithi,* was explored by different scholars at different times during the end of the nineteenth century. The initial assumption that this cave could be identified with the Diktaian Cave,* the birthplace of Zeus,* has gained ground in recent years. The cave, which lies at a height of 1025 metres (3363 feet) has an upper chamber and a steep slope of about 60 metres (200 feet) leading down to a pool and several stalactite halls (figure 148), one of which contains an altar-like structure about one metre (three feet) high. The innermost area was separated by a wall and roughly paved. The cave, one of the most impressive caves* of Crete, was a cult place from the Middle Minoan until the Geometric and Archaic periods. The cave was still visited in Roman times.

The rich votive offerings, partly taken to the Ashmolean Museum at Oxford, include fragments of libation stone vessels and tables with Linear A* inscriptions, seals,* different vases and lamps,* bronze swords and daggers, knives and arrow-heads, double axes,* various bronze dress and toilet articles,* and bronze figurines* of men, women and animals. Of interest are some seals* and fragmentary relief pithoi.* Notable also are a bronze model of a two-wheeled cart drawn by an ox and a ram; a small clay mask painted with ochre; a bronze votive tablet depicting a cult scene with a bird, the sacred tree, several pairs of sacral horns* with a bough in the middle, a fish and a votary, the sun's orb, and the moon sickle at the upper edge. The whole picture has been interpreted to represent the essential elements of a cosmogony.

Pyrgos Ware. This pottery, dated to the Early Minoan I period, is named after a settlement and burial cave (see Caves*) near Nirou Chani,* not far from Knossos,* but found on several places all over the island. A common shape of this ware is a chalice on a high pedestal (figure 149). Decoration consists of a pattern burnish, in which the burnishing instrument either is used with varying pressure or makes a design in burnish on the smooth matt surface of the vessel. This surface is usually black to dark grey. The pattern takes the form of burnished lines around or down the side of the vase. The inside surface of chalices very often shows a horizontal burnishing. Many chalices have a short neck between the bowl and the pedestal. Perhaps this pattern-burnish is intended to imitate wood grain; if this suggestion is true, these Pyrgos chalices are imitations in clay of a wooden original which disintegrated long ago.

Racial Characteristics of the Minoans. The physical appearance of the Bronze Age Cretans was basically the same as that of other Mediterranean people now and then: dark hair and eyes, sallow complexion, of medium height, and with slender bones and slight build. They were also small waisted, although this might have been somewhat idealized in art.* Their skulls as found in excavations were predominantly dolichocephalic or long-headed, with a cranial index falling below 75, while a minority were brachycephalic and mesocephalic, belonging to another, taller racial element which is known as Tauric. Considerable research has been done on this subject by various scholars and especially by the Greek anthropologist A. Poulianos, who has concluded that the present racial type has not changed since the Bronze Age.* Hawes and von Luschan also agreed that later invaders such as the Arabs, Venetians and Turks had not had much influence on the existing racial types. Pendlebury writes: "Many a village boy might be the direct descendant of the Cup-Bearer or the Priest-King, and who can deny the possibility that he may be?"

149. Pyrgos Ware chalice from Eastern Crete

Razors see **Toilet Articles (Minoan).**

Religion (Minoan). The religion of Bronze Age* Crete has been the subject of a considerable number of studies. It is generally considered to be of an ecstatic nature and a distant relative of contemporary Oriental religions. Our knowledge about Minoan religion is, however, limited and, as it has been pointed out, rather like a gallery of pictures totally deprived of the explanatory texts which are such a precious and detailed source of information for other religions. Thus, the reconstruction and interpretation of Minoan religion, still rather heavily veiled to us, is no easy task. We may accept that its roots were in totemism, magic and popular beliefs. Especially concerning magic, either as a part of the official cult or as a folk custom and practice, we may infer its existence and forms only because of what is known from other ancient religions and beliefs.

Apart from the monuments themselves, such as the excavated peak sanctuaries,* sacred caves* and various shrines* with their rich cult furniture, much can be guessed about belief and ceremonies from the pictures on frescoes* and relief stone vases,* seals* and sealings* and some gold rings (see Jewellery*). Certain classes of seals* are considered to have had value as talismans or amulets.* Nevertheless, there is now a fair idea about Minoan divinities* and demons,* which can be interpreted with the help of what is known about the social structure* of Bronze Age* Crete and also of what has survived in later Greek ritual, poetry, legend and religion, although many of the interpretations given are necessarily tentative. Of course a certain degree of evolution inside the broad chronological range of Minoan religion must be presumed, partly reflecting changes in social history.

It is felt certain an anthropomorphic female divinity, the Mother Goddess, is the central figure and the main feature of Minoan religion. The "priest-king"* seems to be the head of the priesthood. No animal-worship is attested with certainty, but the bull, (see Bull-games*), the snake (see Snake Cult*) and the dove appear often in a religious connection. The bull was certainly sacrificed, as may be seen on the painted scenes of the famous sarcophagus* from Hagia Triada.* Its horns seem to have been gilded, a custom which survived in later Greek and Roman times. The possibility of the existence of a bull-cult like those of certain Oriental religions has been discussed, but is considered as rather inconsistent with the sacrifice of the bull and with the pictures on seals showing a bull being devoured by a lion.

Perhaps the tool of sacrifice or at least of its initial phase was the double axe,* a religious symbol of the utmost importance. Other important symbols were the sacral horns,* often crowning the shrines,* and the sacral knot.* Doves frequently accompany the goddess and are seen perching on objects considered as holy, such as double axes* mounted on stepped bases, columns,* pillars* and trees (see Birds in Religion;* Tree and Pillar Cult*). Among the cult paraphernalia were also altars* and small basins, incense-burners (see Braziers*), sprinkling vessels for purifications and various vessels made especially for ritual purposes (see Rhyton*). Other vessels with special functions were the kernoi* for offering the first fruit and produce, as well as the sacred communion* chalices. Stone hammers seem to have been emblems of the priesthood (see Tools*).

Rituals and ceremonies were held in the open as at the peak sanctuaries* or inside unroofed sacred enclosures, and also perhaps by the sea during the procession of the sacred ship (see Ships*). Probably the chief ceremonies and initiations took place inside the specially designed halls of the palaces,* which could be also observed through spacious openings from the central courts.* The mystic character of the Cretan religion is well illustrated by the existence of dark crypts and caves,* and probably of the sunken Lustral Basins,* where the devout purified themselves. Burial customs* of the Minoans are also instructive and yield some valuable evidence about religion and beliefs concerning the after-life.

Although controversial, the evidence from the decipherment of the Linear B script,* if proved correct, supplies us with a list of Mycenaean divinities who were worshipped in Crete after the coming of the Achaians* in the Late Bronze Age. Among them are Zeus,* Hera, Demeter,* Poseidon, Dionysos and Athena with the title *potnia* ("Lady"). Even before the tablets* bore witness to this, it was known that the Greek religion had its roots in Bronze Age Crete, with its chief divinities, as well as lesser deities such as Britomartis,* Eileithyia* and Welchanos,* being survivals of Minoan ones, although transformed and integrated in the Greek mythology. In fact an amalgamation of the two religions took place as early as the second millenium B.C., especially concerning fertility and nature cults. Even in Roman times some cults were peculiarly Cretan. The best account is the one given by the Greeks themselves; thus Diodoros of Sicily writes:

> The inhabitants of Crete have left the following evidence that divine cults, sacrifices and mystery rites were carried from Crete to other peoples; the dedication rites which were performed by the Athenians in Eleusis perhaps the most famous of all, as well as the rites in Samothrace and those that are practised among the Kikones, whence the inventor of rites, Orpheus, comes—these were all secret, but in Knossos it was an old custom to perform these rites openly, and that which among others is done in secret is not hidden by them from anyone who desires to know about it. They say that most of the gods have gone out from Crete as benefactors of mankind, giving to each and all a share in their useful discoveries.

Repoussé Technique see **Jewellery.**

Rethymnon. The third largest city in Crete is Rethymnon with slightly more than 15,000 inhabitants, the capital of a prefecture of the same name. Here, on the place of a Late Minoan settlement, was situated the small Greek town of Rithymna: the name is pre-Greek. This city was rather unimportant but independent and issued its own coinage,* which depicted a pair of elegant dolphins. Just south of Rethymnon rises Mount Vrysinas of an altitude of 858 metres (2815 feet) where one of the richest peak sanctuaries* of the Middle Minoan period* was recently excavated. Rethymnon, known as Rettimo to the Venetians, flourished mainly during the Creto-Venetian era (figure 150), which left a number of interesting houses and fountains isolated amidst cheap modern constructions. Important is the Loggia, a rectangular building of the end of the sixteenth or the beginning of the seventeenth century, which served as a club for nobles (figure 151). Today the Loggia houses an interesting local Archaeological Museum. Among other buildings of this time are the Fountain Rimondi with four columns and three spouts, and the elaborate Porta Guora. Rethymnon during this period became a major center of cultural life in Crete. The large fortress Fortetsa on a hill by the shore, which dominates the town and the picturesque little Venetian harbour, was built in 1573, after the destructive raids of the pirates Barbarossa in 1538 and

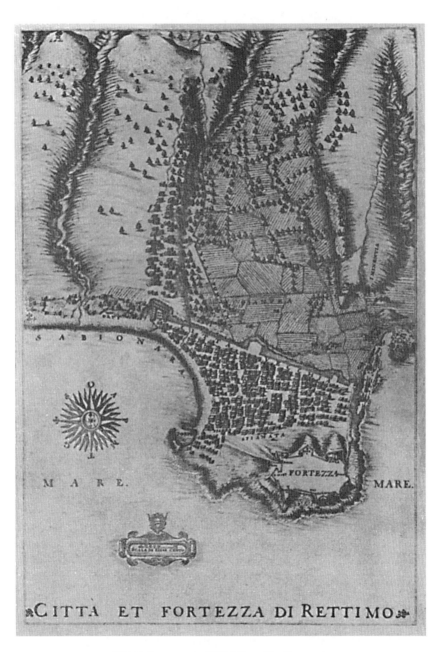

150. Rethymnon in 1619 (*after a Venetian map*)

151. Loggia of Rethymnon (*after Gerola*)

Oulouch Ali—a fearsome Italian renegade who took part in the sea-battle of Lepanto—in 1567. The fortress and the town were captured by the Turks in 1646 after a short siege. During the Turkish occupation Rethymnon was inhabited mainly by Turks, who left some unimportant mosques which sometimes were converted churches. The interesting mosque on the Fortetsa has a huge dome.

Rhaukos. Rhaukos, near the modern village of Hagios Myron in the prefecture of Herakleion,* was a Greek city-state. Homer reports that Rhaukos took part in the Trojan War (see Idomeneus*). As an ally of Gortyn* and Lyttos* it conquered Lykastos, but in 184 B.C. was forced by the Romans to give it back to Knossos.* Rhaukos was one of thirty-one Cretan cities which made an alliance with Eumenes II, king of Pergamon. About 166 B.C. the city was destroyed by the Gortynians and ceased to have an independent coinage.* Its coins bear dolphins and tridents. The site is still unexplored.

RHEA see **DAKTYLOI; Phaistos; ZEUS.**

Rhizenia see **Prinias.**

Rhyton. Rhyton was the Greek name for a vessel especially perforated at the bottom—or other place—for the pouring of libations. The aperture was small for the gradual trickling out of the liquid. Minoan rhyta have various shapes such as the Middle Minoan "peg-top" form and an ovoid variety, or a typical conical form of rather large dimensions, which first appeared at the very beginning of the Late Minoan period* in stone and

later was copied in clay, sometimes brilliantly decorated in the Marine
Style.* The famous "Cup-Bearer" is holding one of these conical rhyta.
The stone examples were often adorned with fine reliefs (see Stone
Vases*). Many of them take the form of a human or of an animal: the
"bull's head rhyton" from Knossos* (see Little Palace*) is famous, as is a
similar one from the palace at Zakros.* Interesting is an early human-
shaped rhyton from Mochlos,* which has the form of the upper part of a
woman holding her breasts, which are perforated so as to form spouts.

Two magnificent rhyta found in the Treasury of the Sanctuary at
Knossos,* real pieces of sculpture, represent the heads of a lion and lioness. They were made of alabaster* and white translucent marble-like
limestone with inlay work. Ostrich eggs were often transformed into
rhyta or imitated in stone or clay. Some clay rhyta recovered from the
peak sanctuaries* are in the form of a bull, sometimes with the forepart
doubled and taking the place of the hind part of the animal. A unique rhyton in the shape of a large rhinoceros beetle has been discovered in the
peak sanctuary* of Prinias in Eastern Crete. Another unique specimen of
clay has the form of a hammer, a tool which sometimes is seen in the
hands of priestly persons as a symbol of their authority.

Rithymna see **Rethymnon.**

Rock Shelters see **Burial Customs.**

Rodovani see **Elyros.**

Roman Occupation. The Romans acted as arbitrators in the quarrels of
the Cretan city-states as early as the beginning of the second century B.C.
Later, they often played a role in the internal affairs of the island. The Cretans, accused of supporting piracy* and of backing King Mithridates, who
strongly opposed the Roman expansion in Asia Minor, became involved
in war with Rome and successfully resisted a first invasion, obliging
Rome to accept a peace on unfavourable terms in 71 B.C. Later Quintus
Metellus (afterwards called Creticus), in a ruthless campaign conquered
the island, the last remaining center of Greek independence, in 67 B.C. As
Willetts remarked, the Roman occupation can easily be invested with an
air of doomed inevitability, a final act in a protracted drama of crisis and
decay. But the fierce resistance of the Cretans against the Roman invasion
can be considered as the first episode in a long struggle for independence
which lasted until the end of the Turkish occupation.*

Crete was incorporated with Cyrene (Libya) in Africa into a single Roman Province, and the large city of Gortyn* in the Mesara Plain* became
the provincial capital. The island was exploited by the conquerors mainly
for its grain. On the other hand, with the ending of wars and incessant
strife between its cities, under the *Pax Romana* Crete entered a period of
prosperity reminiscent of the old Minoan days.

Greek civilization continued to exist and flourish, and several cities
destroyed during the Roman campaign were rebuilt. Emperor Hadrian

152. Coloured glass gem with an erotic scene
of Roman times from Eastern Crete

was a great patron of some of the Cretan cities. Public buildings, often
with fine mosaics, embellished a number of cities, especially the capital,
Gortyn,* and some others such as Hierapytna,* Aptera,* Knossos,* Lyttos* and Lebena.* Engineering works like roads and aqueducts were constructed. Gortyn* also possessed the Roman mint, which issued a coin for
the whole island (see Coinage*). Some interesting jewellery from this
period has been found (figure 152).

As Pendlebury wrote, Crete was fortunate in being in the backwater of
history and in lying well away from the storm where emperors rose and
fell.

"Rope-pattern" see **Pithoi.**

Royal Villa. A building of outstanding quality in the immediate vicinity
of the palace at Knossos* is the so-called Royal Villa, erected in the Late
Minoan I period. It was directly connected with the palace by a paved
road and was obviously some important dependency of it. The most interesting feature of the Royal Villa (figure 153) is the throne, set in a sort of
apse behind a heavy balustrade supporting two columns on either side of
a three-stepped opening, at the back of the main hall of the building. This
apse communicates through a light-well* with a room above. It seems evident that some very important rite or ceremony took place here. The nearby staircase divides into two separate wings after the first landing—a
unique arrangement in Minoan architecture*—to reach the upper storey.
To the north of the main hall a door opens into a pillar crypt, which had
three huge roof beams of cypress and a single pillar, around which are
sunken channels and basins to catch liquid offerings poured before the
sacred pillar (see Tree and Pillar Cult*). The crypt's walls are of gypsum*

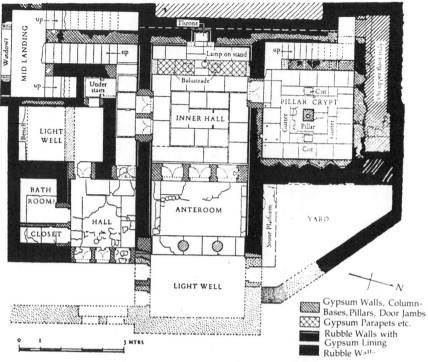

Gypsum Walls, Column-
Bases, Pillars, Door Jambs
Gypsum Parapets etc.
Rubble Walls with
Gypsum Lining
Rubble Walls

153. Royal Villa at Knossos *(after Evans)*

coursed masonry and the floor of gypsum* slabs. The southeast corner of
the villa, which included a paved room, a closet, and a light-well,* seems
to have had a more private character.

Sacral Horns. A very distinctive feature of Minoan religion* are the so-
called sacral horns—or Horns of Consecration as Evans* called them—a
symbol resembling a pair of bull's horns. This symbol has been variously
interpreted; the assumption that it represents stylized versions of bull's
horns and skull *(bucranium)* has gained ground. The symbol has been connected to the sacrificial victim (see Bull-games;* Religion*). Examples are
known in the Near East as far away as Mesopotamia. These sacral horns
appear in Crete from the earliest times as an implement of the cult, in clay,
stone or white-coated alabaster, sometimes recovered from peak sanctuaries,* or seen in pictorial representations, but from the Middle Minoan III
period onwards they become a consistent and characteristic feature—perhaps as a religious element of an architectural decoration—of Minoan
altars* (see figure 160), and roofs of shrines* (see figure 166), thus marking
a place of consecration, as known from several representations (among
which the sarcophagus* from Hagia Triada* is an outstanding example),
often combined with figures of votaries. Sometimes they are found inside
a shrine (see figure 165) among the cult paraphernalia, often used as bases
for the shaft of a double axe or a sacred bough, thus denoting the sanctity
of the subject. In some rare cases they also are associated with the snake
tubes (see Snake Cult*), or are seen on moulds and relief pithoi.* In repre-

154. Ivory sacral knot from a house at Knossos

sentations on seals* we sometimes see the sacral horns combined with a libation jug. Near the South Propylon of the palace at Knossos* a colossal pair of limestone horns over two metres (nearly seven feet) high probably originally crowned the south facade of the building. Another large example, of plaster,* was found at Nirou Chani,* and a tiny one of the same material was recently recovered from the peak sanctuary of Petsophas in Eastern Crete. This latter example is in fact a double pair of horns, a small pair inside a larger one. This unique example is reminiscent of the "quadruple" double axe, where the edges are redoubled in emphasis.

Sacral Knot. The so-called sacral knot, a rigid band of cloth with a loop, a knot and two free-hanging ends, sometimes with a fringe below, is one of the symbols of the Minoan religion* (figure 154). We often see its representation decorating the altars* and columns* of shrines* or vases of a cult character combined with the double axe.* Sometimes it is imitated in faience* or ivory.* As a distinctive sacerdotal sign it is used on the dress of the priestesses, as in the case of the well-known fresco of the "Parisienne" (see Frescoes*), although some scholars consider this a mere ornament. On other frescoes it is independently depicted. It is a ritual symbol of wide magical implications, which are known in folklore, also in Classical Greece; well-known is the Gordian Knot and the "Knot of Herakles," the *nodus Herculeus*, endowed with magical virtues. Its significance was perhaps mainly prophylactic, as can be deduced from the corresponding knot of the Egyptian goddess Isis.

Sacred Marriage see **EUROPA; MINOTAUR; PASIPHAE.**

Saint PAUL see **Lasaia; ZEUS.**

Saint TITUS see **Chersonesos; Gortyn.**

Samaria Gorge. The longest and most beautiful gorge in Crete is that of Samaria in Western Crete, in the prefecture of Chania* (18 kilometres or 11 miles). This canyon, one of the natural wonders of Europe, is in several spots 600 metres (nearly 2000 feet) deep and six metres (about 20 feet) wide. A stream flows through it, easily forded in summer. It penetrates the heart of the impressive White Mountains from the Plateau of Omalos* till the south coast, where ancient Tarrha* (modern Hagia Roumeli) was situated. The Samaria Gorge is quite famous for its dramatic scenery, still unspoiled by man. The Cretan ibex (see Animals, Wild*) still lives here in limited numbers.

Samonion see **Itanos.**

Saracens see **Arab Occupation.**

Sarcophagus from Hagia Triada. This famous limestone coffin, dated to the end of the Neopalatial period, about 1400 B.C., was found inside a small tomb at Hagia Triada near Phaistos.* This unique monument of Cretan painting bears on all four sides panelled and brightly coloured scenes painted on plaster in fresco. These religious scenes, which unlike the wall frescoes* are practically complete, constitute a major source of archaeological information and the most important document of Minoan religion,* after-life beliefs, and cult practices. Among other scenes are sacrifices, processions, and libations, in all probability connected with funerary rites. No attitude of mourning is shown. Each panel is framed with bands of elaborate ornamentation, which includes rosettes and running spirals.

The dead man, or rather his spirit, in a long dappled robe which does not show his arms, stands motionless in front of the elaborately painted doorway of his tomb, while three priests dressed in tailed skins (see Dress, Minoan*) bring him a pair of calves and a model boat with a high prow, perhaps for his after-life voyage (see Ships*). Next to him is a tree. According to one interpretation, the spirit is beginning to sink beneath the ground on its way to the afterworld, like the ghost of Patroklos in the Iliad.

155. Sarcophagus from Hagia Triada: side with bull-sacrifice

In the next panel of this side, two women pour libations or liquids such as wine and water, perhaps for the funerary toast, into a bucket set between two elaborately incised double axes* with redoubled edges, on which birds are perched, evidently symbolizing the presence of divinity (see Birds in Religion*). Behind them a man in a long priestly robe plays a lyre (see Music*), perhaps summoning the Divinity.

On the other side of the sarcophagus (figure 155) is a scene of the sacrifice of a bull (see Religion, Minoan*), which lies bound on a table; its throat has been cut and the blood drips into a bucket-shaped vase. Below the table crouch two frightened animals. The officiating priestess in a short jacket and a baggy tailed kilt, perhaps representing the mottled skin of some animal, touches ritually at an altar, to the music of double pipes. A libation jug and a basket of fruit are represented in the space above the altar. Behind the flute-player come five women whose upper parts have vanished. Only the first woman, who wears a diadem, is complete. Beyond the altar is another double axe with a bird perching on top, and behind that is a much decorated shrine surmounted by sacral horns* and apparently surrounding an olive tree* (see Tree and Pillar Cult*).

Each end of the sarcophagus illustrates two goddesses riding in a chariot, one drawn by horses* (as many scholars think) or rather wild goats with faintly visible horns, the other by winged griffins,* above which hovers a fantastic bird. The goddesses are probably escorts for the after-life voyage.

The scenes of the coffin, unique in Aegean funerary art, raise many problems of interpretation and have been much discussed, but obviously relate to the worship of the dead, the admission of the spirit to the afterworld in a happy after-life, and perhaps indirectly to the vegetation cult.

SARPEDON see **MINOS, RHADAMANTHYS and SARPEDON.**

Scarabs. Among the Egyptian objects found in Crete are many scarabs (beetle-shaped seals). A certain number of them have been recovered in early tholos tombs,* in places such as Lebena,* Gournes, Platanos* and Hagia Triada.* Some of them belong to the Middle Kingdom (XIIth Dynasty), while another example from Knossos* might belong to the next Dynasty or even to the Hyksos period. These scarabs were imitated by Cretan craftsmen. Among the rich votive offerings of the sacred cave of Eileithyia* at Inatos* on the south coast were a number of Egyptian scarabs datable to the Saite period.

Script see **Writing.**

Script (Greek) see **Alphabet.**

Sculpture (Greek) see **Dedalic Style.**

Sculpture (Minoan). No large statues have survived from the Bronze Age,* although their existence can be deduced from some oversize bronze locks of hair embedded in masses of carbonized wood found in the Corridor of the Bays in the palace at Knossos,* thought to belong to a colossal wooden statue of a goddess. These curling locks—originally covered with gold foil or plating—are elegantly modelled. The statue is calculated to have been about 2.80 metres high. Today this interpretation is challenged. Some small stone heads may have belonged to wooden statues. Otherwise, no real stone sculpture is known from Bronze Age Crete, and probably no need for it was felt. Evidently the artist had little taste for large works, being fond of his splendid miniature studies–most sensitive statuettes in bronze, ivory* and faience*–as well as clay figurines,* sometimes very large, and plaster* relief frescoes* of large size. The figures represent goddesses or priestesses, vötaries and athletes. Nevertheless we must bear in mind that a suspicion has been cast on many of them, especially on some ivory pieces, as their provenance–either some illicit excavation or some forger's workshop–is unknown.

The stone and ivory figures were made in several pieces (see Ivory*). Statuettes cast solid by the *cire perdue* (lost wax) process become common after the sixteenth century B.C.: a wax model was coated with clay, which was then heated. The wax melted and ran out of a hole left for that purpose in the clay, and was replaced by molten bronze which thus took exactly the shape of the original wax model, the negative of which was preserved in the inner surface of the clay. The surface of the bronzes was not smoothed off and polished but intentionally left rough, giving an impressionistic effect with the features often blurred and small excrescences left. This surface was effectively copied by Rodin in the nineteenth century. These exquisite Minoan statuettes usually represent worshippers at attention with the right fist ritually raised to the brow (see figures 27, 28, and 45). The pose is not really stiff but with its supple curves makes the

156. Bronze statuette from Western Crete: back view

figure graceful and renders the impression of an instantaneously recorded movement. It has been remarked that anatomy and proportions are ignored or distorted, but distorted to effect (figure 156). Some good examples—in fact among the best achievements of Minoan sculpture in general—were found at Tylissos* by Hazzidakis and in the sacred cave of Skoteino (see Caves*) by the author. Another statuette perhaps represents a flute-player (see Music*). The great age of Minoan sculpture undoubtedly was the transitional Middle Minoan–Late Minoan period, where probably the best pieces belong. A unique find comes from a Middle Minoan II context at Phaistos*: the clay coating for a bronze hand slightly smaller than life-size.

Sea-level (Changes in) see **Geography**.

Sealings. In Minoan times a lump of wet clay could be placed on a cord fastening a door, box, chest, jar, cupboard, document or some other article and then stamped with the owner's seal, who thus could secure ownership or access, and consign goods. Of course the sealing could not be removed or replaced without being destroyed. A great number of these sealings—accidentally hardened by fire—have survived until today, portraying Minoan seals* now lost and thus increasing the repertoire of their designs and pictures. Many of the earlier sealings were additionally countermarked with incised signs of the Linear script in use. A great hoard of sealings—many thousands—was recovered in a Middle Minoan II deposit at Phaistos* under the floor of the later palace; the majority of the designs are still abstract. About 280 types can be classified. They probably belonged to an inventory made after the control of the suppliers and the registration of sealed goods delivered to the palace, probably inside boxes which were fastened with cords wound around pegs.

Important sealings from Middle Minoan Knossos* are those found in the Hieroglyphic Deposit and those from the Temple Repositories.* Among them are whirl compositions, animal studies and two pieces representing real portrait heads of a man and a young boy, perhaps a ruler and a prince. Most interesting is a vivid scene of a man on the deck of a boat trying desperately to beat off a monster, perhaps a hippopotamus, whose head appears out of the waves. Elsewhere a fish stalks an octopus among coral-like reefs.

Other interesting hoards of sealings were found at Zakros,* often depicting fantastic monsters of a rare imagination (see Monsters*), and recently at the other end of the island, in Chania.* Among the subjects of the sealings from Hagia Triada* we see a battle scene, or the goddess who is offered a chalice in front of her shrine. Sealings found at places distant from each other, like Gournia,* Zakros,* Hagia Triada* and Sklavokambos,* show impressions from identical seals,* a fact which proves an exchange of correspondence between these centers.

Seals. Seals form an essential feature of Minoan civilization* and the most characteristic form of its art.* Their use had been introduced from Babylonia and Egypt for the practical purpose of marking identification, preventing access and securing property, all at a time before there were locks. The owner's seal could be impressed upon a lump of wet clay, the sealing, which secured the strings of doors, boxes and others (see Sealings*). It was also used for the authentication of written documents. The purpose of the seal was therefore a utilitarian one, but evolved rapidly into the art of gem cutting. Obviously the seal, being essentially a sign, led to a form of writing.* Among grave-goods* there are often seals; this burial custom shows how the idea of personal identification is attached to the seal.

At first, as early as the latter half of the third millenium B.C. and before the emergence of the palaces,* softer and more easily carved materials such as bone, ivory,* serpentine and steatite were used for the manufacture of large seals, which are almost exclusively found in the early tholos tombs* of the Mesara Plain.* Later on, after the copper tubular drill and the cutting-wheel, used with crystalline carbon abrasives, had been invented, important improvements in engraving techniques were made, leading to a technical mastery of cutting the intaglio. The Minoans could then use the harder and more beautiful stones which they preferred, such as orange carnelian, red and green jasper, banded agate, amethyst, quartz, chalcedony, obsidian* and rock crystal, which have been able to withstand the passage of time. Some Middle Minoan seals were made of bronze, gold or silver. A few seals were made of terracotta* and, later, of glass. A seal cutter's shop of Middle Minoan I–II times with a hoard of some 150 seals has been discovered in the town area of the palace at Malia.*

Shapes show great variety: some of the Early Minoan seals are shaped as cones, pyramids, rings, cylinders engraved on the ends, often naturally shaped pieces of elephant tusks. Other seals take the form of animals* or parts of animals and birds* or animal and bird heads with engraving on their bases. A favourite shape was the signet with an elegant stalk which had a string hole through it, perhaps derived from the shape known as stamp or button. This latter shape, first appearing in the Middle Minoan period,* had a pinched top which served as a flat handle. The cylinder seal, common in Mesopotamia and later in Syria, seems to have been first modified in Crete, having the designs on the flat ends and not on the curve which was left plain, while the eastern seals, following the reverse practice, were rolled to make a continuous impression. This shape dies out after the Middle Minoan period.* There were also scarabs.* Bead seals could be worn round the neck or the wrist. In the Later Bronze Age circular lentoid (lens-shaped) and amygdaloid (almond-shaped) seals were worn like wrist-watches, as we see on frescoes.* Both had two convex sides but normally only one was engraved. The former had developed from the discoid shape; it became the dominant form after the Middle Minoan II period.

The motifs engraved on these earliest seals were usually decorative torsional patterns and compositions, or interlocking all-over patterns

157. Maned lioness attacking a bull on a seal (*after a cast*)

showing varying degrees of complexity; there were also animal friezes, representations of insects such as scorpions (see figure 3) and spiders, and occasionally men or monkeys.* The art of gem-cutting reached its peak during the Late Minoan I period, showing great technical virtuosity. Designs are extremely varied, never failing to stir the imagination, and are usually of unsurpassed artistic value, forming a fascinating world on a tiny scale. These designs follow an artistic evolution, the steps of which can be rather clearly defined. As Kenna remarked, in the hundreds of different motifs exquisitely treated on the seals, a record of the ebb and flow of Minoan culture is mirrored. He notes that "the work on the seals shows a preoccupation not only with the formal qualities of objects and their relationship, but the problem of light, surface planes and movement. These are much the same problems with which modern art and aesthetics are concerned." Some smooth small pieces of rock crystal in the approximate form of a modern magnifying glass from a Middle Minoan tomb at Knossos* have been interpreted as such, which is very likely if we consider the necessity of some help for the eye of the seal-engraver in his fine work.

Some of the subjects are abstract, but mostly they portray different subjects, including purely decorative or lively naturalistic studies of animals such as lions or lions' masks, bulls or bulls' horns, boar, dogs, cats, birds,* stag or goats (see figure 112). Often very complicated poses are depicted, including lions galloping, or leaping on a bull (figure 157), or wounded and twisting to claw an arrow protruding from the body.

158. Minoan seals (*after Evans*)

Wounded bulls attempt to extract the arrow with their hoofs. In these tiny pictures the Minoan principle of torsion is always apparent. Very often we see the animal in the characteristically Minoan "flying gallop" position, with all four legs at full stretch. Each of these exquisite animal studies is a personal creation differing from the next. Anatomical detail is transcended by some dominant feature of the animal which impressed the artist, such as muscle power, swiftness or graceful curves.

We also see butterflies, symbols of vegetation, studies of people and demons,* facades of buildings and other architectural motifs, fabulous monsters* like sphinxes and griffins.* Various secular or religious scenes are portrayed: a fisherman proudly carries a large fish in one hand and an octopus in the other (figure 158, left); an ibex standing on a rock ledge is ready to defend himself with his sweeping horns against a collared dog which barks below; two dancers or acrobats in plumed head-dress are balancing on their hands in a field with lilies—the bodies of the dancers are engraved as lily fronds. Scenes from the bull-games* are often found. Marine life is richly represented by various fish (see figure 3), such as dolphins (figure 159), octopus and flying fish (figure 158, right) or by ships.* The drilling technique and especially the tubular drill which cut circles neatly often determined the nature of the decoration.

In later times black or gray serpentine became the most common material and the lentoid the most common shape. The engraving repeats the subjects of the earlier periods, but there is a tendency even in the best seals for these subjects to become formal in pattern and detail, and still later to become linear. The bodies seem less substantial and there is a minimum of modelling. In the last phase the subjects tend to disintegration.

Early seals, often in the shape of three-sided prisms, have decoratively stylized inscriptions in the Minoan Hieroglyphic script.* There is also a four-sided prism variety. These seals eventually became less formal in arrangement and of a character more decorative than semantic.

One special class of seals ("talismanic") seems to have been magical amulets* and talismans, or lucky charms possessing qualities of a mag-

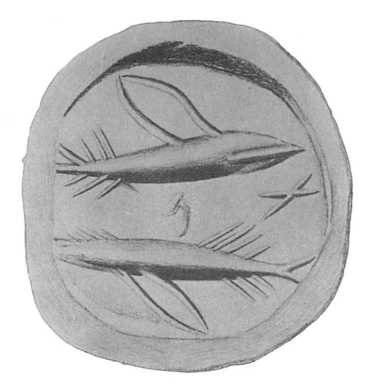

159. Pair of dolphins on a seal from Mochlos (*after Davaras*)

ical nature according to the shape, design and material of the seal. Thus, designs with spouted jugs or other ritual vessels and branches have been interpreted as rain charms. Prisms may have had a talismanic character. All of them have a strange stylization. From this class of talismanic stones no sealings* have been found.

Shells. The Minoans, surrounded by the sea and partly living off it, were fond of sea-food (see Fish and Fishing*) and evidently consumed quantities of cockles, as attested in excavations of settlements. They also used to make amulets* and ornaments of the shells, or to imitate them in clay, faience* and stone. Shells were also employed in pottery* as motifs of painting (see Marine Style*) or as moulds for impressed decoration, or as inlay for some Early Minoan II stone vases.* Murex shells were exploited for their purple dye (see Fish and Fishing); heaps of crushed specimens associated with Middle Minoan pottery have been found. The Minoans often strewed the floors and altar ledges of their shrines**with shells and shore-pebbles, a religious custom most natural for islanders. Already in a Neolithic deposit at Phaistos* a clay female idol was found together with shells. Painted shells—mostly cockles—have been recovered in abundance from the Temple Repositories* at Knossos;* they had been

160. Seal with a religious scene from the Idaian Cave (*after a cast*)

streaked and banded with a variety of brilliant tints such as orange, crimson, black, green or red (see figure 169). The triton shell (conch shell), perforated on top, was used as a trumpet in certain religious ceremonies perhaps for summoning the divinity: on a seal from the Idaian Cave* we see a woman blowing such a trumpet before an altar (figure 160). A triton shell was found in a shrine at Phaistos. Models of shells were sometimes made; an especially impressive copy is carved out of a block of liparite, a volcanic glass obtained from the Aiolian Islands near Sicily.

All this evidence points to the marine aspect of the Minoan divinities and especially that of the Great Mother Goddess, an aspect also demonstrated by other finds, such as the faience flying fish and other sea creatures of the Temple Repositories,* and the connection of ships* with the cult.

Shields. Minoan full length body shields were rectangular or had a characteristic form with a figure-of-eight outline. They consisted of a wooden base covered with an entire ox-hide, cut to shape and several folds deep, stretched over two staves placed at right angles. This great tower shield gave head to foot protection to the warrior, who is thought to have been brought to the battlefield by chariot.* They evidently were employed only by heavily armed troops. None of them has survived but from about 1600 B.C. onwards pictorial representations of them appear on seals,* amulets,* ivory* boxes and frescoes,* such as the great wall painting from the Upper Hall of the Colonnades of the palace at Knossos,* (figure 161), representing them hanging in a row, in a military spirit, a restoration based on a miniature copy of a similar subject found at Tiryns on the Mainland.

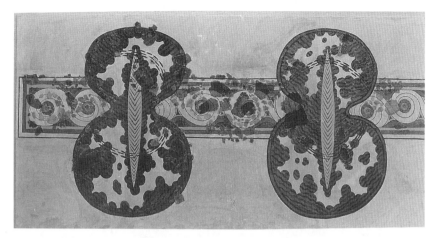

161. Reconstructed Shield Fresco from the head of the Grand Staircase at Knossos

They are 1.63 metres (3.3 feet) high. The dappled bull's hide is conventionally depicted, showing that the hair of the hide was retained. The stitches for the double thickness in the middle are shown. Various evidence, including the existence of amulets* in miniature shield form, suggests that the figure-of-eight shield probably had some religious aspect. Sometimes we see it as an attachment on metal and alabaster* vases.

There also were small rectangular shields. A semi-cylindrical shield with a curved top appears later on seals,* probably introduced by Mycenaean Greeks. The manufacture of shields must have been an important part of Minoan leather-working.*

The shields of the Iron Age* were usually round. The examples found in the Idaian Cave,* dating from about 750 to 650 B.C. are famous. Dedicated as votive offerings, they were made of thin bronze sheet attached to a leather-covered wooden base. Of course they were too flimsy for actual warfare,* but probably they were employed in a ritual dance* or ceremony celebrating the birth of the Cretan Zeus,* in accordance with the story about the Kouretes.* The most characteristic shape is convex. They were decorated in relief covering the whole surface usually in concentric zones around a central boss, sometimes representing a lion's head (figure 162), a bird of prey and so on.

Another shield form has no central boss and is comparatively flat. These have a hammered out or more sparingly incised decoration showing a strong Oriental influence and a progressive Hellenization of the style (see Idaian Cave*). The same designs, such as palmette or lotus chains, lotus flowers, rosettes and volutes, animal friezes, sphinxes and groups with monsters,* occur on the Orientalizing pottery. The decoration includes cult and hunting scenes. The "Hunt-Shield" depicts the nude goddess between lions. The "Shield of Horus" is the largest, reaching 0.68 metres in diameter; the central boss bird stretches its wings across

162. Orientalizing votive shield from the Idaian Cave

the shield, crossing two horned snakes. Four other important shields have been recovered from the sanctuary of Diktaian Zeus at Palaikastro.*

Ships. In the Mediterranaean there were no strong currents or tides to hinder the early seaman when the weather was fair. The first Neolithic settlers arrived in Crete by sea, as did of course all other waves of immigration. The first direct evidence is given by clay models of boats assignable to the Early Minoan period,* recovered at Mochlos* and Palaikastro;* the former may have been a dug-out while the latter shows a high projecting stern and low bow, as Dorothea Gray has recently shown.

By the beginning of the second millenium B.C., a number of seals* (figure 163) illustrate tiny representations of large vessels, with slender rounded hull and high prow to breast the waves of the open sea, and a stern identical or nearly identical. A single ponderous mast supported by stays fore and aft carried a broad square sail relatively high. Some seals seem to depict ships with three masts, but in fact they were one-masted, the outer vertical lines perhaps representing halyards. A magnificent flat-

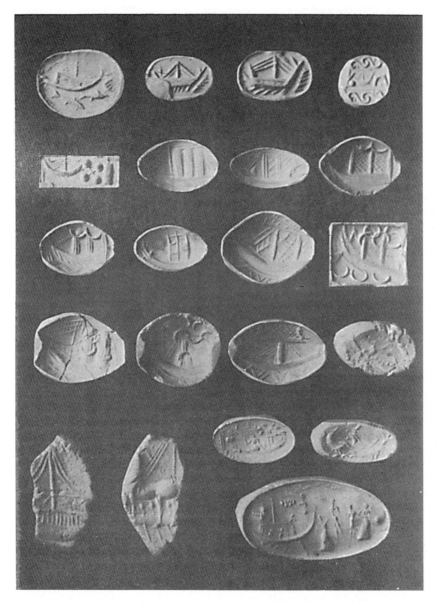

163. Seals, sealings and impressions of gold rings with ships (*after casts*)

tened cylinder from the Knossos* district depicts a ship under full sail; the vessel has a long forked projection. On other representations on seals the hull is so rounded that it seems almost crescent-shaped. Often the stern ends in a pronged ornament.

The construction of these ships, really suited for long sea journeys, re-

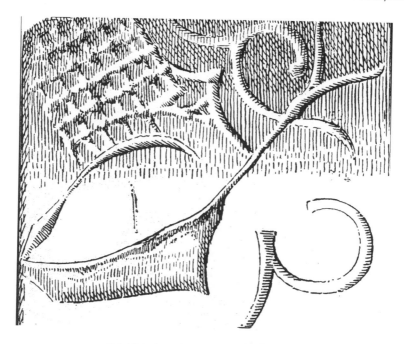

164. Ship in a storm on a seal (*after Evans*)

quired adequate timber, which was amply available in the Cretan forests.* These ships had ten or fifteen oars on one side apart from the steer-
ing sweeps. Oarsmen would be necessary during calm weather, when
working into wind or for manoeuvring. There are also clay models of
mastless boats. One marble model has been found at Hagia Triada.*
Larger merchant vessels were decked, and deck cabins or shelters were
sometimes represented. It has been estimated that the probable
maximum size for Minaon vessels would have been about 23 metres (75
feet) long, or even up to 30 metres (100 feet) and more, according to
others. Some unique frescoes* representing Minoan ships in an overseas expedition have been recently discovered at Thera.*

Minoan ships could carry trade across the open sea, even directly to
Egypt, and were not obliged to follow the coastal route. Evidently they
always took advantage of the prevailing winds. The Minoans are considered the first builders of oared ships with sails (figure 164), which were
able to face the difficult conditions of a rough open sea. This type of ship
was later imitated by the Mycenaeans and the Phoenicians. The importance of navigation becomes more clear when we consider the fact that
most of the transport* between the different areas of Crete was done by
sea. Some important Minoan centers such as Mochlos,* Pseira* and
Zakros* offer good harbourage near some main seaways, a fact accounting for their flourishing. A number of harbours* is known. Perforated
heavy stones were employed as anchors. A magnificent pyramidical royal
anchor from Knossos,* at first thought to be a talent,* is decorated with

octopuses in relief, the tentacles of which are arranged over the entire surface of the reddish stone.

The great Greek historian Thucydides states that "the earliest ruler known to have possessed a fleet was Minos. He made himself master of the Greek waters." Minoan Crete developed a merchant marine and, perhaps, a navy of its own, repressing piracy* and assuring its isolation and security. It became the first naval power known to history with no rival of equal rank on the sea routes. Nevertheless, the legendary thalassocracy (sea-empire) of Minos perhaps has been a little exaggerated, although the other states, being land-powers, had no interest in disputing the Cretan supremacy on the sea. Recent researches in Aegean places like Thera,* Kythera, where a colony had already been founded at the end of the Early Minoan period, and further Kea, Skopelos, Rhodes and the coast of Asia Minor, where Minoan "colonies" or outposts existed, have documented this legend to a great extent. These colonies were mostly founded from about 1650–1500 B.C. Among the occupations recorded in the Linear B* tablets* from Knossos* are those of carpenter and shipbuilder.

The connection of ships with the cult, attested from dedications of ship models in shrines,* carvings of ships on altars,* or from the famous sarcophagus* from Hagia Triada* where a boat is presented to the dead, point to the marine aspect of the Minoan divinities. Furthermore the existence of ceremonial sacred barges has been presumed ever since a gold signet-ring representing a boat, which terminates in a horse's head and carries the Goddess, turned up at Mochlos.* Clear evidence has been demonstrated by a seal found by the author, at Makrygialos in Eastern Crete, where we see on board a votary or a priestess in a characteristic stance of adoration before an altar and a sacred tree.

Shrines (Minoan). Minoan civilization lacks the large palace-like temples found in the contemporary Orient, a fact with certain historical implications (see Social Structure of Minoan Crete*), although the palaces* played this role to some extent. Instead there are small shrines of little architectural importance, sometimes independent as were those of the peak sanctuaries,* but usually within a town, a palace or a private villa. The cult of the Household or Snake Goddess* was practiced here. The simplest type of shrine is a small crypt or a single room with a bench running along one wall for the deposition of cult images and paraphernalia, as well as votive offerings. Sometimes there is a pillar in its center (see Tree and Pillar Cult*) or a shallow porch in front. The exact function of these shrines is not clear. It is an open question whether these tiny domestic shrines were accessible only to priests, as some scholars believe, or to every devout person, as places of public worship. This latter assumption would perhaps seem more probable, at least on certain occasions or for some of the shrines, as for instance the late Civic Shrine at Gournia.* The earliest example of a domestic shrine came to light in the Early Minoan II settlement of Myrtos* in Eastern Crete. Other domestic shrines of larger houses may be seen at Knossos* in the House of the Chancel Screen* and that of the High Priest.*

165. Shrine of the Double Axes at Knossos (*after Evans*)

The shrine of the Double Axes near the southeast corner of the palace at Knossos,* a small room of Middle Minoan III date, 1.5 metre (about 5 feet) square, converted into a shrine during Post-Palatial times is an important one (figure 165). It is divided into three parts at different floor levels, with a shallow anteroom in front. On the foremost level a number of vases probably used to contain offerings has been found. The central level supported a round tripod altar or table of offerings. In the background to the north a ledge ran from wall to wall; on it stood several cult articles, including two pairs of sacral horns* made of plaster,* with small sockets, possibly for the insertion of double axes* as Evans* thought, or branches and a number of bell-shaped figurines* representing divinities and votaries, sometimes having birds* associated with them. A figurine of the goddess, wearing many necklaces and bracelets, with the arms raised in the customary manner, is shown. There is a seal on each wrist. A dove perches on her head. A small steatite double axe, after which the shrine was named, had redoubled edges.

Some of the clay models of shrines are interesting because they reveal details of construction lost today. Other shrines were more complex with several rooms, often pillared. It can be assumed that there were walled open-air sanctuaries or sacred enclosures around sacred trees. Other types of shrines were the country sanctuaries, such as that at Kannia near Phaistos. Among the shrines we should probably include as a special class the so-called Lustral Basins* of the palaces* and villas.*

166. Mountain tripartite shrine on a stone vase from Zakros (*after Platon*)

The best of the stone vases* found in the palace at Zakros* shows a tri-partite shrine (figure 166) consisting of a high structure flanked by lower wings, which are crowned by sacral horns* and have poles on either side, reminiscent of the flagstaffs in front of some sanctuaries in Egypt. This shrine perhaps represents a regular building and the mountainous back-ground of a peak sanctuary, to judge from some goats sitting on top of it. On the other hand it may be just an elaborate facade, similar to those erected by the Central Court of the palace at Knossos,* Vathypetro* and elsewhere, as depicted on the miniature frescoes.* Below the central part of the Zakros shrine a small altar is represented. Of a similar tripartite character is a sanctuary near the West Court of the first palace at Phaistos* (see Early Palaces*).

The cult furniture of the Minoan shrines usually includes statuettes of goddesses or priestesses, such as the famous Snake Goddesses* from the Temple Repositories* at Knossos,* or the large clay idols with hands up-raised (see Figurines*), such as those from Knossos* and Gournia* which have been previously discussed, and further from Gazi and Karphi.* Other cult objects found in shrines (see figure 72) are tripod altars* or of-fering tables, double axes* mounted on stepped stone bases, and splayed tubes, sometimes with snakes in relief (see Snake Cult*). In the "Fetish Shrine" of the Little Palace* at Knossos,* of the very latest Minoan period, some natural concretions were found (see Little Palace*). Floors and altar ledges of the shrines often were strewed with sea shells.* In many cases religious constructions were crowned with large horns,* models of which were also among the cult paraphernalia. Usually no votive offerings, at

167. Siteia in 1614 (*after a Venetian map*)

least to any considerable extent, seem to have been dedicated in these shrines.

Siteia. This pleasant town in Eastern Crete (about 7,000 inhabitants), capital of a province of the same name and the easternmost one of Crete, is situated on the site of ancient Etis or Eteia or Setaia, a harbour of Praisos* on the north coast. Eteia, already inhabited in the Bronze Age,* especially at the site of Petras to the east of the modern town, perhaps the *se-to-i-ja* of the tablets,* became the refuge of the Praisians in 146 B.C., after the destruction of their city by Hierapytna.* Here was born Myson, one of the seven sages of Classical Greece.

An excellent series of clay heads of the Dedalic Style* (today in the Hagios Nikolaos Museum) have been recovered from a deposit found in the foundations of a modern house. Of interest are some curious rock-cut fish tanks (see Fish and Fishing*) and pool of the Roman period, on the water front near the Customs House.

Siteia continued to flourish in Roman, Byzantine and Venetian times until 1508 (figure 167),when it was severely damaged by an earthquake. In 1538 the great pirate Barbarossa sacked it and burned it down. From this time onwards the town declined and in 1651 was completely abandoned. The population was transferred to the neighbouring Liopetro— today a large ruined fortress at a high altitude, of Classical Greek and later Byzantine date, overlooking the north coast near Chamaizi*—and the fortress of Siteia, a square structure, today in ruins and known as "Casarma," which was partly demolished by the Venetians.

Modern Siteia practically dates from 1870, when it was rebuilt according to the town-planning of a progressive Turk, Avni Pasha, and resettled. A small archaeological museum is now constructed.

Sklavokambos. In a high valley to the west of Tylissos* a large Minoan villa* of about 1500 B.C. was excavated before the Second World War by Sp. Marinatos. The villa was entered by a double door near the southeast corner. One of the rooms was possibly a small domestic shrine. Beside it a staircase led up to a second storey; in another room, under the staircase, a small toilet was found. In the middle of the building is a small court with four pillars* and traces of a hearth. The southern half of the villa, isolated from the other part of the building and provided with a separate entrance, was used for storage and service. A broad pillared veranda faced the north. A number of interesting sealings was found here (see Sealings*), among other things. The villa was destroyed by a violent fire. Its excavated ruins were damaged during the last war.

Skoteino Cave see **Caves.**

Slavery in Dorian Crete. After the coming of the Dorians* to Crete, the establishment of their aristocratic domination (see Social Structure*) and the rise of the city-states all over the island, the slave system became important. The early traditional form of patriarchal slavery, which was in fact a serfdom, with the peasants tied to the soil and paying tribute to the landlords but enjoying at the same time certain privileges, persisted for a considerable length of time in conservative Crete after the later form of slavery, commercial chattel slavery, had become the main form of servitude elsewhere.

The Code* of Gortyn* is a precious document which, among other problems deals in those concerning slavery. The peasant serfs had some rights which placed them above chattel slaves. They lived under quite favourable conditions and held a recognized social and legal status comparable with that of the Spartan helots, but in contrast to Sparta and other Greek cities there is no evidence of revolts by Cretan serfs. They could contract a legal marriage—and divorce—even with a free woman, and make a family protected by law. They had the right to possess private property including their own houses and cattle, as well as money. They even had an interest in the property of their master, who was called *pastas,* if he happened to die childless. On the other hand they were excluded from gymnastic exercises and the right to possess arms.

There were two kinds of serfs, the *mnoitai*—a name perhaps connected to the survivors of the older Minoan population—belonging to the state, and the *aphamiotai* or *clarotai* ("lot-men"), attached to the lots of the citizens. The Code of Gortyn has two servile terms, *woikeus* or serf, attached to the *oikos* ("household"), and *dolos* or slave. The chattel slaves had practically no legal rights and were considered as commodities to be bought and sold in the market place (see Social Structure*).

Slings see **Weapons.**

Snake Cult. The most prominent Minoan domestic cult was that of the snake, which was believed to be a symbol of eternity, immortality and reincarnation, and further of the chthonic (underworld) divinities. This widespread belief was in fact based on the snake's ability to cast its skin and to renew itself. Characteristic of this belief is the Cretan myth of Glaukos,* son of Minos,* in which the snake is a symbol of resurrection. In several Minoan shrines,* such as those of Gournia* and Koumasa, clay "snake tubes," often bottomless, were found among the cult furniture (see figure 72). On these the snake is represented in a very summary fashion by plastic loops down the side of the tube. The "snake tubes" from Gournia* bear sacral horns* in relief. The exact use of these tubes in the cult is a matter of conjecture, but it seems unlikely that they offered an actual shelter to snakes.

The earliest representations of snakes in Minoan art* can be seen on seals.* From Knossos* come ritual vessels with perforations all over their bodies, which have been interpreted as honeycombs, with moulded figures of climbing snakes feeding on them (figure 168). Recently Karageorghis, bringing new evidence from Cyprus, suggested that the perforations were intended for the circulation of the air inside the vessels, which would then be actual shelters for snakes. A tripod table has a ring for a vase in the center—perhaps to put milk in—and four grooves leading

168. Clay honeycomb with sacred snake from Knossos

to it from the circumference; Evans* thought it to be a table for a *parti carré* of snakes, an ingenious hypothesis if we can accept that the Minoan priests knew how to control these creatures. The snake cult was associated with the so-called Snake Goddess* or Household Goddess.

The later Greek and Roman snake worship is based on conceptions of the Minoans, who considered the snake as a beneficent spirit looking after the welfare of the house, and an object of reverence. As a beneficial force it became the attribute of Asklepios,* the healing divinity of the Greeks, through whom it still survives as the emblem of the medical profession. The house snake is well known in folklore not only in Asia and Africa but also all over Europe, reaching as far as Sweden, where it is called *tomtorm*. In Indian tradition the snake represents eternity as well as a mysterious force of nature known as *kundalini*. A pair of heraldically posing snakes adorns the head of the ceremonial sceptre of a Bishop of the Orthodox church.

Snake Goddess. The so-called Snake Goddess or Household Goddess, one of the Minoan divinities,* is closely associated with the snake cult.* This most popular goddess was worshipped in the small household shrines* of the palaces* and villas* from the Middle Minoan II period onwards as the special domestic goddess. These shrines include the Shrine

169. Faience Snake Goddesses and shells from the Temple Repositories

of the Double Axes at Knossos (see Shrines*) and the Civic Shrine at Gournia,* and latest of all the small shrine at Karphi.* Among the characteristic features of the cult of the Household Goddess are not only the "snake tubes" (see Snake Cult*) but also double axes,* sacral horns,* models of birds* identified as doves and stone offering tables. It has been assumed that before the construction of these shrines the Snake Goddess was worshipped in the peak sanctuaries,* but without her later household character.

From the Temple Repositories* of the palace at Knossos* were recovered two faience* ritual statuettes and fragments of a third, representing either the Snake Goddess or her human attendants, probably the former, assignable to about 1600 B.C. (figure 169). These brightly coloured figures are very decorative and show some degree of naturalism and elegance. They are extremely instructive about the elaborate formal dress* of the Minoan woman. Perhaps they are the best-known Cretan artifacts. The tallest figure, measuring 34 centimetres (14 inches), wears a tall tiara with a spotted snake coiled around it, a necklace, a tight-waisted short-sleeved bodice richly embroidered, with a laced corsage, leaving the large white breasts bare, and a long skirt with a kind of short double apron over it. The hair falls down behind on to the shoulders. Her eyes are black. Her arms are stretched out in front of her. The snake's tail interlaces with another snake which coils around her body and with its head appearing at her girdle. She holds a third snake which coils over her shoulder. One of the snakes is continued in a festoon in front of the apron. The snakes' bodies are greenish. The features of the goddess' face are added in black, while other details are purple or brown on a milky white ground. Parts of the statuette are restored.

The other figure, smaller and more fragmentary but skillfully restored, is similarly dressed but her skirt is flounced. She has a slim waist and bare prominent breasts. Her arms are extended and she grasps a snake in each hand. The hair falls down behind to the hips. Her flat cap with its raised medallions has a miniature spotted cat or leopardess on top.

Besides these figures from the Temple Repositories there are in Minoan art other statuettes representing goddesses or priestesses with snakes, like the one in Boston (see Ivory*), and another of bronze, today in Berlin, with a triple coil of snakes behind her neck.

The Classical Greek deity who embodied the spirit and the attributes of the Minoan Snake Goddess was Athena, with her sacred snake living on the Acropolis of Athens.

Perhaps the earliest representation of the goddess is a rhyton* from Koumasa. This libation vessel takes the form of a woman with bare breasts and a snake coiled around her neck and draped over her shoulders. The snake, with its extremities reaching down to the woman's waist, has red painted rings around its body.

Social Structure of Dorian Crete. The Dorian aristocratic society, existing in Crete during the greater part of the first millenium B.C., was comparable with other Dorian societies of the Greek world, such as that of Sparta. The great Spartan lawgiver Lykourgos is considered to have borrowed much from Crete. The Cretan city-states, self-governing political units occupying a closely settled area, failed to achieve democratic institutions and were relatively conservative as a matter of fact, both politically and economically. They remained at the second of the four traditional stages of development, which can be normally observed in other Greek city-states—monarchy, aristocracy, tyranny and democracy (four English words borrowed from the Greek). Aristotle, dealing with Crete in the second book of his *Politics*, attributed to Minos* the Cretan caste system, while Plato,* a notorious conservative, admired the Cretan institutions and their stability.

Although the primitive tribal society had passed away, to be succeeded by the *polis*, the city-state, the various tribal customs and institutions of the Dorians,* which were considered to have been kept purer in Crete, continued to play an important role in social life. Not only their influence but also their form and terminology survived, although they extensively evolved, adapting themselves to the changes and needs of a new social system. The Code* of Gortyn* is a legal and social document of the utmost importance. The peasants of the island, who "followed the laws of Minos," were evidently descendants of the older population held in servitude under Dorian aristocratic masters. Trade was restricted, and there is no evidence of the rise of a merchant class on a large scale.

The ruling citizen class enjoyed extensive social privileges. Many of them used to hire out their war skills abroad as mercenaries.* In this aristocratic society the citizens had the right to gather in general assemblies (*agorai*) and hear the resolves of the *kosmoi** and the Council of Elders (*Gerousia*), eventually voting but with no right to propose or even to discuss. Society was organized according to the old tribal system into organically related units, the clan (*genos,* corresponding to the Roman *gens*), the phratry (*phratria,* a group of clans, the Roman *curia*) and the tribe (*phyle,* a group of phratries, the Roman *tribus*). The totality of the citizen class seems to have been maintained by common funds, in the frame of the system of *syssitia* ("communal meals"). The real establishment consisted of the privileged clans who had the right to choose the *kosmoi,** these powerful magistrates who were the counterparts of the Spartan kings and ephors taken together. In fact the regime of Sparta is considered by modern historians as more liberal than that of the Cretan cities: the former has been characterized as a limited democracy, and the latter as a close aristocracy.

Usually no class of *perioikoi* existed as in Sparta, but it has been assumed that when a city-state was dominated by another, its citizens held a somewhat similar status to the Spartan *perioikoi*.

Marriage, as in tribal society, as a rule was still a collective ceremony, in which those young men who had finished their education in the *agelai** participated. Tribal endogamy was a rule.

In addition to the free citizens there were three other main classes of the population: the *apetairoi,* free persons inferior to full citizens, not belonging to one of the *hetaireiai,* the close associations of the male citizens, and excluded from political rights and privileges, and further the peasant serfs, and the slaves (see Slavery in Dorian Crete*).

Social Structure of Minoan Crete. Having no history records from Minoan times, we can only guess from indirect evidence certain features of the structure of Minoan society. A tribal system must have been established in the Neolithic period,* which evidently survived down into Dorian Crete. Among the burial customs* the early collective tholos tombs* perhaps are indicative of a tribal organization or of the existence of individual clans. Cretans followed communal life and urbanism* developed easily. The palaces* came into existence together with a centralized organization. Head of the state must have been the "priest-king",* of whom the legendary Minos* is the familar prototype. It has been remarked that our ideas about the Minoan state and monarchy are at best vague.

The palace at Knossos* was surrounded by several villas* or in fact minor palaces, usually dependencies of it, such as the Little Palace,* the Royal Villa,* the South House* and others, all provided with Lustral Basins* and presumably occupied by important members of a class of nobles or officials, possibly law* administrators, perhaps leaders of the priesthood, or relatives of the king, or both. The palace stood at the center of town. As George Thomson remarked, the very pleasantness of these Minoan towns bears witness to the greater freedom and flexibility of social relations. It has been thought that the many palaces imply many kings, but with no evident political rivalry between them, and probably enjoy-

ing a certain independence under the hegemony of the king of Knossos,*
which might be chiefly of a religious nature. In any case, the prominent
role of centrally placed Knossos* in religion as well as in administration*
and legislation seems evident.

The development of the economy* was an important factor in the formation of this highly stratified society. We may suppose that the social life
and tribal institutions of villages, as developed from the Neolithic period,* eventually were modified but not disrupted; it can also be assumed
that common people had to contribute, at certain times, labour service for
public works (see Architecture, Minoan*) and a tribute for the ruling
classes. When a systematic division of labour becomes necessary, specialized craftsmen of different industries* appear. A class of wealthy merchants is supposed to have fostered the expansion of trade,* even if that
was partly carried out by the heads of the palaces* and generally controlled
by the central authorities. The differences in size and richness of the
houses* as well as the variety in value of the grave goods* often must suggest unequal economic status. Despite the lack of any factual knowledge
about the organization of labour, a class of domestic servants or even slaves
employed in domestic work and industry may be assumed, but no slave
labour on a scale as in Classical antiquity and especially Rome can be
deduced.

The existence of small shrines* instead of large temples suggests the
absence of a theocratic domination of the Minoan religion* in the sense of
the Egyptian or Mesopotamian example. On the other hand the prominent position of the woman* and the existence of matrilinear traditions is
one of the most remarkable features of Minoan society.

In later times, when the Achaian* regime was established in Knossos,
we learn from tablets* of the Linear B script,* containing lists of men and
women with their occupation, that there existed a high specialization of
labour. The tablets themselves must have been the work of a class of
scribes. The system at Knossos like those of the Mycenaean Mainland
probably was an autocratic monarchy relying on a bureaucratic administration.

Souda Bay. One of the largest and most secure bays in the Mediterranean, surrounded by Minoan and later sites, Souda Bay was a lair of
pirates in the Middle Ages; today it is the harbour of Chania* as well as an
important naval base. On the small island at its entrance a large Venetian
fortress was built in 1560 (figure 170), a perfect fortification work for its
time. Indeed, the fortress was able to resist the Turkish attacks for a very
long time, until it surrendered in 1715. The ancient city of Aptera* over-
looks the bay which in Classical times possessed a port named Minoa (see
Trade*).

South House. The so-called South House was an important building of
the transitional Middle Minoan III–Late Minoan I period near the south
side of the palace at Knossos* (figure 171). It has been suggested that the
house, which was at least four storeys high, belonged to some important

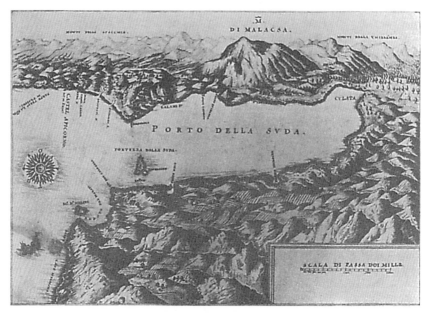

170. Souda Bay (*after a Venetian map*)

official or noble, as it was allowed to encroach on the line of the old Stepped Portico* of the palace. Evans calls the house the "best normal idea of a good burgher dwelling of the beginning of the New Era." The house includes a light-well,* a reception room and a small sunken Lustral Basin,* perhaps decorated with frescoes.* West of the main hall, which has the usual pier-and-door partitions, lies a pillar crypt, measuring 4 by 5 metres (13 by 16 feet), of a clearly religious character. On one side of the pillar (see Tree and Pillar Cult*), which has a height of two metres (about 6 feet), a conical double axe base of stone was found, while on the other side was a base with three sockets for sacral horns* and a double axe.* Below the ground floor there were storerooms constructed as pillar crypts.

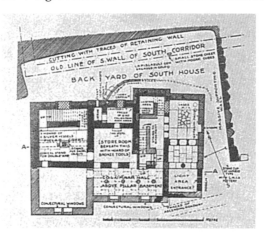

171. South House at Knossos
(*after Evans*)

Here one of the doors could be locked from both inside or outside by inserting a bronze pin into the wooden bolt. This bolt has perished but the pin was found still in position in its diagonal slot. In a small room a hoard of bronze tools* was found.

Sphakia. A large mountainous province on the south coast in Western Crete in the prefecture of Chania,* including most of the White Mountains and the famous Samaria Gorge,* Sphakia (figure 172) is known for its wild landscapes and the proud, independent and conservative character of its inhabitants. The anthropological type of the Sphakiots is at some variance with that of the other Cretans; statistically they, together with the Swedes, are the tallest Europeans. A widespread custom, today fortunately almost extinct, was the *vendetta*, the blood feud. The Turks feared these mountaineers and never inhabited this area. During their occupation* the Sphakiots were famous as pirates; they also possessed a substantial merchant fleet. The main village is Chora Sphakion, a picturesque small port with a ruined Venetian fortress. Other villages are Anopolis* and Aradena.* Francokastello* belongs also to Sphakia, as well as the upland plain of Askyphou.

Sphinxes see **Monsters.**

Sphoungaras see **Gournia.**

Sphyrelaton. The sphyrelaton technique—exclusively Cretan—is a type of bronze work done on small statues during the earlier part of the seventh century B.C., an achievement of metallurgy* of the Orientalizing period.* The word means *made by hammering* (i.e., a bronze sheet over a wooden core). The plates were joined with short pins. The earliest and most famous of the small statues which were made using this technique are a group of three, evidently representing Apollo, Artemis and Leto, their mother, found in the temple at Dreros* (figure 173). Apollo, reaching a height of eighty centimetres, has a domed head with long hair in relief ending in hook-like curls. The women show a characteristic cylindrical headdress, the *polos*.

Spinalonga. The small coastal island of Spinalonga, one of the satellite islands* of Crete which had a high strategic value, was originally the site of a fortress protecting the harbour of the Greek city-state of Olous.* In 1579 the Venetians built here one of their strongest fortresses in Crete (figure 174), able to resist the Turkish attacks long after the capture of Crete, in fact until 1715 when its garrison finally surrendered. The name of the island comes from the expression *stin Elounda* ("to Elounda"), which later became "Spinalonga" according to a small island of this name near Venice. The fortress is still relatively well preserved. Its strongest bastion, Mezzaluna Barbariga, a high crescent-shaped construction provided with a number of cannon-holes, faces Elounda. In 1903, after the emigration of

172. Area of Sphakia in 1615 (*after a Venetian map*)

173. Pre-Dedalic sphyrelaton statuette of Apollo from Dreros

the Turkish population, and for the following half century, Spinalonga became a leper colony.

Spindle Whorls see **Cloth.**

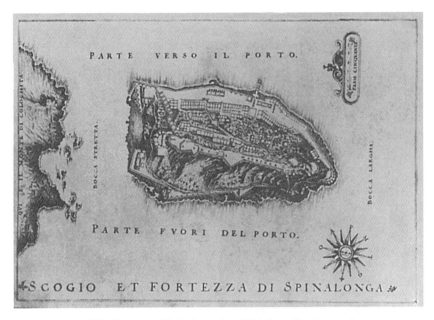

174. Fortress of Spinalonga in 1626 (*after a Venetian map*)

Sports (Minoan). Beside the exciting and dangerous bull-games,* which surely required good physical condition, severe training, and acrobatic ability, wrestling and boxing seem to have been quite popular in Minoan times. The representations of boxers in miniature frescoes* or in relief on stone vases* (the well-known rhyton* from Hagia Triada*) show them wearing heavy bronze helmets with cheek-pieces (see Armour*), necklaces, short kilts, leggings and knuckle-dusters or leather boxing gloves of the classical cestus type. This fact suggests that Minoan Crete was the source of Greek and Roman boxing traditions. The boxers show an over-emphasized muscular development. These vivid scénes often betray a violent match. Boxing and wrestling may have been considered not mere secular athletic contests but possibly forming part of initiation ceremonies of some sort.

After the introduction of the horse* in the fifteenth century B.C. we may suppose that riding was among the sports but evidently in a limited way, this being before the invention of saddles and stirrups.

Springs (Sacred). A characteristic feature of Minoan religion* was the existence of springs considered as sacred. A small spring shrine constructed over the outflow of the spring at the so-called Caravanserai south of the palace at Knossos* can still be visited today. The spring chamber had a little niche; it was constructed together with the whole Caravanserai* but survived much longer than it, being in use as a place of worship almost until the end of the second millenium B.C. (see Caravanserai*). Another sacred spring has been found in the palace at Zakros.* A fresco fragment from the House of the Frescoes at Knossos was interpreted by Evans* as illustrating a fountain in a garden. According to more recent opinions the scene depicts a natural waterfall in a flowered landscape; it probably has no religious significance.

This cult form survived into Classical Greece when the deities of the springs were worshipped as Nereids and Nymphs. The modern Greek word *Neraides* is used to mean "fairies."

State (Minoan) see **Social Structure of Minoan Crete.**

Statuettes (Minoan) see **Ivory; Sculpture.**

Stepped Portico. The imposing entranceway in the palace at Knossos* near the South House* known as the Stepped Portico led up to the south entrance of the palace. Most of it has vanished. This construction, assignable to the period of the Early Palace and used until about 1600 B.C. originally carried on massive foundations a monumental stepped approach with columns* and a succession of open balustrades only on the west side, while the other side was formed by a high blank wall. It has been supposed that the visitors from the south came through the Stepped Portico over a large viaduct after resting and refreshing themselves at the Caravanserai.*

Stirrup-jar. This kind of closed vessel—characteristically Minoan and Mycenaean—was so named in English because the false thin neck with a vertical handle on either side bears a vague resemblance to a stirrup (figure 175). The true spout, which is tubular, rises vertically beside the stirrup-shaped handle. The vase, invented in Crete in the later sixteenth century B.C., also became extremely popular on the Greek Mainland, mostly for the storage and overseas export of olive-oil,* often perfumed (see Perfumes*), and perhaps for wine,* from 1400 B.C. onwards. The earliest examples are more slender in their proportions. Later they become more uniform in shape. Some examples are extraordinarily large. The body was usually globular or pear-shaped. After 1200 B.C. the stirrup-jar had a small air-hole near the handle, and the small disk over the false neck rose to a conical shape.

Stone Vases. Imported stone vases appear in Crete as early as the end of the Neolithic period,* but their local manufacture, persisting throughout the Bronze Age,* was developed during the Early Minoan II period. The shapes of some of the earliest are evidently derived from Egyptian prototypes, while other forms are of Anatolian origin, but mostly they may be related to the Cycladic examples.

The stone vases required large amounts of labour and represented skill and craftmanship of a very high order. The technique for drilling the inside of the vase included the use of a simple drill and later of a tubular drill rotated at high speed by a bow and worked with water and an abra-

175. Stirrup-jar decorated with double axes. View from above

sive powder such as sand or emery imported from the island of Naxos; the
vase was finished to a smooth surface by means of hard grinding and pol-
ishing with abrasives. More complicated shapes were made in several
pieces adroitly joined together.

The objects were carved in different stones of various colours, at the
beginning easily worked ones such as soft chlorite, serpentine and
steatite (soapstone), but soon harder stones like mottled breccia, rock
crystal, obsidian,* orange stalactite, marble, limestone, alabaster* and
others, with their veins and colour possibilities adroitly exploited in order
to get a remarkable decorative effect (figure 176). The patterns of the
variegated stones were often imitated in painting. Some of the earlier
vases were decorated with spots of white shell* inlay.

The vessels show a great variety of sizes and graceful shapes, from
miniature to small pithoi,* and from the simplest to the most elaborate,
including goblets, chalices, bowls, cups, jars (figure 177), beaked jugs,
pots and libation vases. One of the most common shapes is a graceful
bowl resembling a bird's nest, tapering towards the base; a variety of this

176. Miniature stone box from the Gournia house-tombs

type, engraved on the outside to represent petals, which appear first in the Middle Minoan period* but are especially fashionable during Late Minoan times, is known as a blossom bowl. Some of the shapes are peculiar to stone, while others also appear in pottery.* Only a few of these vessels were found in settlements; it seems that most of them were never intended for practical use.

Very important is the bull's head rhyton* from Knossos* (see Little Palace*), as well as the series of vessels found in the palace at Zakros,* including several elegant chalices (see Communion*) and other types of stone vessels, by far the best collection ever found in Crete, including a magnificent two-handled jar of marble, and a rhyton showing a tripartite shrine (see also Shrines*). Among the Zakros vessels the famous rock crystal rhyton of an elongated shape is unique (figure 178). It was found crushed in more than 300 fragments. Its graciously curved handle consisted of crystal beads through which ran a bronze wire. At the base of the neck was a movable ring made of crystal and gilded ivory.

177. Stone bucket-jar from the Gournia house-tombs

A fine series of serpentine vases shows miniature pictures in relief. These vases, belonging to the later palaces, obviously were for ritual use. Sometimes, coated with gold sheet which left some traces, they were apparently intended to replace gold vessels.

Three well-known masterpieces of astonishing realism were found in Hagia Triada.* The first is the spirited *Harvester Vase,* a peg-top rhyton with a vivid procession of twenty-seven peasants in headcloths, shouting, singing, laughing in good humour and carrying winnowing forks over their shoulders and bags of seedcorn. They are shown in profile except for the upper parts of the bodies. They advance in close ranks, led by an elderly man wearing a curious quilted cloak and holding a stick. Among the people is a thick-set singer in a skull-cap waving a rattle resembling an Egyptian sistrum (see Music*), who is followed by a choir of three. All four have thick lips. A man has tripped and fallen on to the heels of the man in front. The whole scene is surprisingly lifelike and vivid.

The *Chieftain Cup* illustrates a young man in a graceful pose, with very long hair flowing loose and a jewelled collar, majestically holding a

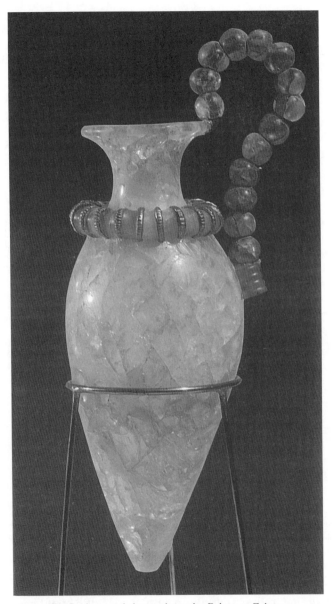

178. Rock crystal rhyton from the Palace at Zakros

sceptre or staff at arm's length, probably a ruler standing outside the gate of his palace (figure 179). He is faced by an officer in a similar pose, with his head slightly bowed and long sword resting on his right shoulder, holding with the left hand an object with a stiff handle and flexible tail, sloped over the left shoulder. This was interpreted as being a lustral

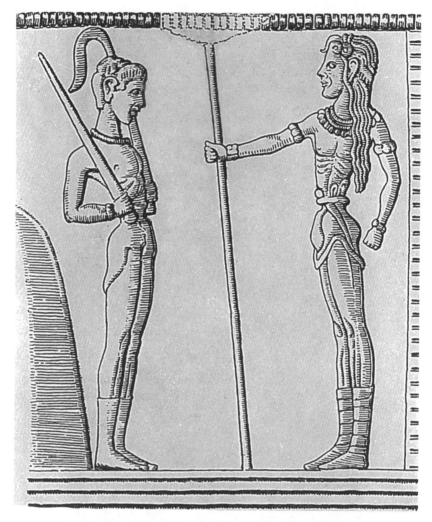

179. Chieftain Cup from Hagia Triada (*after Evans*)

sprinkler similar to the aspergillum employed by the pontifices of Rome, and later by Christian priests. Evans* thought that the sword and the lustral sprinkler were emblems of temporal and spiritual power, ceremonially carried by the "priest-king"* or held out in front of him. The officer is attended by three men carrying hides perhaps to be made into shields.* Evans* suggested they may be elephants' skins, spoils of hunters returned from Africa. Today the *"Chieftain"* is interpreted as a god.

The third vase from Hagia Triada,* of conical shape, is the *Boxer Rhy-*

ton, with vigorous scenes of boxing in four zones. The muscular development of the boxers is overemphasized (see Sports, Minoan*). There is also a scene of bull-leaping in one of the zones.

Stones (Semiprecious) see **Seals.**

Stylos. Stylos is a village near Chania,* to the south of ancient Aptera.* In its vicinity are two Byzantine churches:* a large one called Monastira, assignable to the eleventh or twelfth century, and the chapel of St. John, dated 1271–1280, the narthex of which is the original building.

   A tholos tomb* of the Late Minoan period* with a steep *dromos* was excavated between the village and Aptera* by N. Platon and the author. To the east a contemporary settlement is under exploration by the author on behalf of the Archaeological Society of Western Crete. A mason's mark* cut on a stone represents a trident. Among other remains a rather well-preserved pottery kiln (see Terracotta*) and a building of a rare oval shape were discovered.

Sun-god see **MINOTAUR.**

Swords see **Weapons.**

Sybrita. Sybritos or Sybrita, possibly the *su-ki-ri-ta* of the tablets,* was a Greek city-state situated near the village of Thronos, to the southeast of Rethymnon.* The city was built on a hill. Its ruins are still unexplored. It was among the thirty-one Cretan cities which in 183 B.C. made an alliance with Eumenes II, king of Pergamon. The principal divinity of the city was Hermes, appearing on its coinage as Hermes Kranaios. His cult was practised until Roman times in the Cave of Patsos in the Mount Ida,* which had been sacred since the Bronze Age.* Several clay and bronze figurines* of humans and animals have been found among the votive offerings, including a bronze one of the Syrian lightning-god Resheph and a clay pair of sacral horns.*

   Seat of a diocese during the early Byzantine period, Sybrita was eventually destroyed by the Saracens. Its original territory included the modern provinces of Amari and Hagios Basilios. Its port was Soulia, modern Hagia Galini, on the south coast. In its vicinity a Roman shipwreck was explored, yielding an interesting collection of Hellenistic and Roman bronzes and coins, today in the Rethymnon Museum. Probably the cargo of this ship consisted partly of antiquities looted from Phaistos* and Gortyn* to be sold in Rome.

Syia. A picturesque fishing harbour on the south coast of western Crete, Souyia is situated on the site of ancient Syia, a port of the Greek city-state of Elyros.* The town was eventually destroyed by the Saracens. Orlandos excavated here a large Early Christian basilica with three naves separated by colonnades. The central nave and the narthex were adorned with magnificent mosaic pavements featuring birds, fish, stags, and amphorae, as

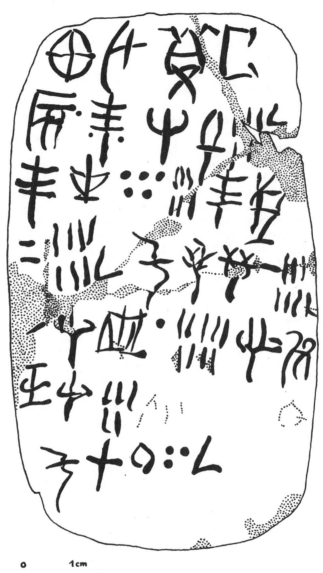

0   1cm

180. Linear A "page" type tablet (*facsimile after Raison*)

well as floral and geometric patterns. Two other basilicas are located to the east of the village.

Tablets. In Minoan Crete clay tablets were used for writing from the nineteenth century B.C. onwards. The oldest of them have been found at Phaistos.* The idea of writing on clay tablets, unknown in Egypt, reached Crete perhaps from Mesopotamia, where tablets were employed from

181. Linear B "palm-leaf" type tablets

Predynastic times, via Syria. In Crete tablets, usually found in palace archives, contained lists and numbers, the records of royal financial administration. Being matters of daily business, they evidently were considered as temporary. Clay tablets, originally simply dried in the sun, are unlikely to survive unless baked by fire; thus they are recovered from .fire-ravaged buildings. The front of the tablets was flat, while the back was more convex and sometimes bore traces of fingerprints. The tablets reveal redistributive operations, recording inventories and receipts or disbursements of goods; sometimes they include rations or tribute assessments. Later, they offer the names of gods, in which sometimes Classical Greek divinities can be recognized. Tablets are in both Linear A* and B* scripts. Two shapes are distinguished: the "palm-leaf" type (figure 180) and the rectangular "page" type (figure 181). The former often has a single line of writing, while the latter is often divided all over by horizontal cross-lines.

Talents see **Ingots.**

Talismans see **Amulets; Seals.**

TALOS. The Cretan Talos, the "bronze man," was, according to the Greek tradition, a gigantic guardian who ran around the island three times a day, patrolling it and throwing rocks at any foreign ship which approached. He was given by Zeus* or Hephaistos to Minos.* He belonged to a bronze generation. A single vein extended from his neck throughout his body to one of his heels, stopped by a bronze nail. Instead of blood the vein contained a divine fluid *(ichor)* identical with that in the veins of the gods. This is obviously a mythological transformation of the *cire-perdue* ("lost wax") process of bronze-casting (see Sculpture, Minoan*). According to Plato,* Talos' other task was to go three times yearly through the villages of the island, displaying Minos' laws inscribed on bronze tablets. He was further regarded as the mythical inventor of the potter's wheel* and personified the technical aspect of the Bronze Age.* He was variously connected to Zeus* and the sun. Talos was represented on the coins of Phaistos* (figure 182) as a youthful winged figure striding rapidly along and hurling stones as he went.

When the Sardinians tried to invade Crete, Talos destroyed them grinning fiercely; hence the expression "a sardonic grin." Jason, the leader of the Expedition of the Argonauts, as he was returning from the Black Sea with Medea and the Golden Fleece, tried to land his ship in Crete, but was driven off by Talos. But Medea, versed in the magical arts and knowing the secret of Talos' construction, extracted the bronze nail and allowed the divine fluid to flow off. Thus Talos, the first robot in history, collapsed.

182. Talos on a silver coin of Phaistos
(*courtesy Mrs. M. Oeconomides*)

Tarrha. This small but independent Greek city was situated at modern Hagia Roumeli, a picturesque fishing hamlet with some Byzantine churches,* on the Libyan Sea at the southern extremity of the Samaria

Gorge.* According to the myth, Apollo and Artemis came here for purification after the killing of Python at Delphi. Apollo then loved Akakallis* in the house of the seer Karmanor, who had won the prize in the first musical contest at Delphi.

The town was a religious center possessing a number of temples with rich votive offerings. The cult of Apollo Tarrhaios was prominent. Coins of the city show the head of a goat. Tarrha founded a colony in the far-off Caucasus area. This town had important workshops for the manufacture of glass. In 1959 the American S. Weinberg partly explored the site on behalf of the Corning Museum of Glass. The town was eventually abandoned in late antiquity.

TEKTAMOS see **Dorians.**

TELCHINES. The nine dog-headed, flipper-handed Telchines of Greek mythology originated in Rhodes and migrated to Crete, becoming its first inhabitants and famous bronze smiths. The word was derived by the Greek grammarians from *thelgein,* to enchant. They were supposed to be able to control the weather and to produce rain, snow and hail. According to Strabo, of the nine Telchines who lived in Rhodes, those who accompanied Rhea to Crete and nourished the young Zeus* were named Kouretes.* Because of the close association of the Telchines with Crete, the island was also named Telchinia in poetry. One of the Telchines, Kyrbas, was the mythical founder of Hierapytna.*

Temenia see **Hyrtakina.**

Temple Repositories at Knossos. Of utmost importance are the Temple Repositories in the west wing of the palace at Knossos,* near the central palace shrine or Tripartite Shrine. Inside a small chamber two sunken stone cists about 1.5 metres (5 feet) deep are built either of massive blocks of masonry or of thick interlocking slabs. Their shape is quadrangular. Along them a superficial cist of later date can still be seen. The cists have yielded a real treasure of finds. Those of the western cist included masses of gold foil, crystal plaques decorating a decayed treasure-chest, ritual stone hammers, a number of vessels, mostly amphorae and pitchers, a hoard of 150 clay sealings* of the Middle Minoan IIIB phase, and several steatite libation tables. An equal-armed cross of veined marble is unique (see Cross*). Painted sea-shells* were found here as well as in the eastern cist, which yielded several excellent faience* objects: among them were various elaborate vessels, imitations of fruits and flowers, flying fish, the well-known plaques depicting an ibex with her young and a cow with a suckling calf, and the famous statuettes of the "Snake Goddesses" (see Snake Goddess*). The middle part of the largest of them was, oddly enough, found in the other cist. Of importance are the faience models of sacral robes and girdles, which evidently represent the sacred wardrobe of the goddess. The finds of the

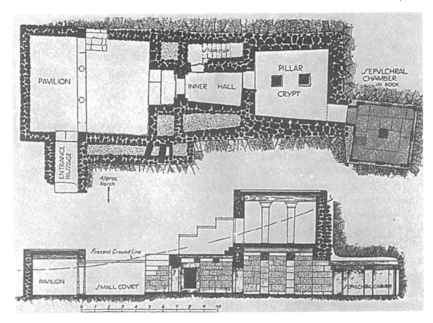

183. Temple-Tomb at Knossos (*after Evans*)

Temple Repositories are assignable to about 1600 B.C., the date of a severe destruction, after which these cists fell into disuse and were filled in.

Temples see **Shrines.**

Temple-Tomb. The great royal "Temple-Tomb" at the southern limits of the city of Knossos* was erected during the transitional Middle Minoan III–Late Minoan I period in the slope of a hill (figure 183). The entrance leads into a single-storeyed pavilion with a stairway leading up and a two-columned portico fronting on an enclosed open paved court. Behind the court a gateway with a massive bastion at either side leads into an inner hall with a door which was locked from within, and a pillar crypt. Here the two massive pillars* and the walls are incised with the double axe* sign. A kind of ossuary at the south side had walled compartments containing the bones of some twenty dead. Evans* thought that they belonged to the devout who fell as victims of a great earthquake, while other scholars consider them as earlier burials.

The northwest corner opens into the funerary chamber, a room cut into the cliff 3.6 metres (about twelve feet) square with a single gypsum pillar in the middle and paved with slabs of the same material. The original rough rock ceiling was painted a deep blue as if to imitate the sky. The larnax was perhaps of wood and left no traces (see Larnakes*). At the end of the Late Minoan II period a short middle-aged man and a child were buried here in a small pit at the northeast corner; perhaps this man was the last Minos of Knossos, as Evans had thought.

184. Pottery kiln of Roman times in Eastern Crete

From the inner hall before the pillar crypt and outside the locked door a stairway ascends to the open terrace above, to the outer ground level. Here a two-columned sanctuary was built directly above the pillar crypt. The whole arrangement bears a striking resemblance to the tomb of Minos* at Heraclea Minoa in Sicily as described by Diodoros: an underground tomb below and a temple to Aphrodite above. A cult of the dead was evidently practised in this tomb until the final destruction of the palace or even later.

Terracotta. In antiquity terracotta filled most of the needs of man for utensils as it is easily made, inexpensive, and the materials were always at hand. We must bear in mind that metals were then expensive and difficult to find and to process. In Minoan Crete terracotta was used for objects as diverse as cooking pots and house chests, hearths and storage jars (see

Pithoi*), elaborate drinking vessels and coffins (see Larnakes*), loom-weights (see Cloth*) and potter's wheels,* bathtubs and figurines,* olive oil* and wine* presses, boxes and all kinds of pottery.*

Terracotta was processed in kilns (figure 184) which were circular and domed structures having a perforated firing-platform of clay above the fire chamber and its flues. The kilns seem to have been fired normally to temperatures of about 900°C. A rather limited number of kilns has been found in Minoan sites, such as Knossos,* Phaistos,* Vathypetro* and recently Stylos.*

Terracotta objects are invaluable for the archaeologist because they do not deteriorate while buried in earth; otherwise we would be deprived of objects forming the greatest part of the Minoan heritage in painting and sculpture.* Terracotta objects and their ubiquitous fragments also yield prime evidence for fixing chronology.*

THALETAS see Music.

THEOTOCOPOULOS, DOMENICOS see Fodele.

Thera. The tremendous volcanic eruption in the small island of Thera (also known as Santorini), one of the Cyclades, which has the only active volcano in Greece, about one hundred kilometres (seventy miles) to the north of Crete, exceeded that which occurred in 1883 at Krakatoa in Indonesia. It destroyed in Late Minoan IA times—ca. 1500 B.C. or a little earlier—the existing settlements of the island. A *caldera* or sea-filled crater was formed after the eruption. In the 1860s historians first realized that this great natural event had taken place. Much later, serious attention was paid by the Greek archaeologist Sp. Marinatos to the possible effects of this explosion on Minoan Crete. It has been assumed that a second cataclysmic eruption of the volcano some fifty years later caused the violent destruction of the chief Minoan centers, which is attested for the time of Late Minoan IB, around 1450 B.C. The blast from the eruption, assumed as equaling that of many H-bombs, was supposed to have overwhelmed the coastal and inland settlements of Crete, and the clouds of ash rising from the exploding crater to a stratospheric height and driven by the wind must have imposed total darkness over the island for some days. Titanic tidal waves, named *tsunamis* by the Japanese, caused by the inrush of water after the collapse of the crater, swept down upon the exposed coasts no more than half an hour later, followed by earth-quakes and fires, while the wind spread a thick layer of volcanic debris and poisonous ash over Eastern Crete, destroying all vegetation, pol-luting the soil and making a desert out of it for a long time thereafter. Springs dried up or were polluted. The Krakatoa eruption, with its much smaller crater, caused tidal waves twenty-seven metres (89 feet) high and resulted in the loss of 36,000 lives.

According to some scholars, this cosmic destruction of Crete is re-flected in the Bible, described as "a day of wrath, a day of distress and desolation, a day of darkness and gloominess, a day of clouds and thick darkness'' (Zephaniah 1:15; 2:5). The plagues of Egypt as described in the Bible have also been connected to the eruption of Thera as they include the three-day darkness, the violent winds, the sudden epidemics of illness and other phenomena. The dating of the Exodus is placed some 480 years before the beginning of Solomon's reign in 970 B.C., that is about 1450 B.C.

Nevertheless, this dramatic picture of the catastrophe of 1450 B.C. leaves many questions, as the existing archaeological evidence still is rather ambiguous. According to Sinclair Hood, earthquakes* and tidal waves are unlikely to have caused fires in such a wholesale manner, and a blast from Thera can hardly have been responsible for the destruction of well-sheltered places like Sklavokambos,* Phaistos* and Hagia Triada,* while Knossos,* on a low spot near the exposed northern coast, seems to have been spared, suffering less serious damage. On the other hand, the eruption of 1500 B.C. seems to have wrought havoc in Crete, causing some destructions in the northern and eastern parts of the island, including Knossos,* as well as terror to the population, although the damage was repaired.

In 1885 A. Nicaise suggested, followed by Frost, Marinatos and other scholars, that the catastrophe of Minoan Crete might have formed the historic basis for the legendary lost island of Atlantis known to us by Plato's account. According to the tale told to Solon, the Athenian sage, by the Egyptians, Atlantis, a rich and populous island with a wonderful culture, disappeared beneath the sea during a terrifying onslaught of nature. Nevertheless, Plato himself did not identify Atlantis with Crete.

Marinatos and his successor Christos Doumas led increasingly spectacular excavations at Thera itself, uncovering a Bronze Age settlement buried under a thick layer of some thirty metres (98 feet) of volcanic debris, the position of which was known from small-scale excavations made in 1867 and 1870. The culture of this site is Cycladic in character but has many affinities to Minoan Crete, from which much pottery* was imported. A number of excellent frescoes were probably made by Minoan painters and their pupils. Evidently a Cretan colony or outpost was installed here.

THESEUS in Crete. According to the Greek legend, when the Athenians, then tributary subjects of Minos (see Minos' Loves*), for the third time had to draw lots to choose seven virgins and seven youths as victims for the monstrous Minotaur* of Knossos,* Theseus, son of the Athenian King Aegeus, volunteered to go as one of them, vowing that he would slay the monster and bring his companions home. Aegeus consented, but begged his son, if successful, to replace his black sails with white ones. Reaching Crete, Theseus retrieved the ring of Minos* from the sea, thus proving to Minos that he was a child of Poseidon. The king's daughter Ariadne* fell in love with him at first sight and promised to help him if he would take her with him when he left Crete. She gave him both a sword and a magic ball of woolen thread, instructing him how to fasten the loose end to the entrance door of the Labyrinth,* so that he could go inside and kill

185. Early Minoan tholos tomb near Kaloi Limenes

the Minotaur,* and retrace his steps by winding up the wool to find his way safely out. Then Ariadne guided the entire Athenian party to the harbour of Knossos* and they all—including Ariadne—fled on a ship after fighting a sea-battle. Some days later, after disembarking on the island of Naxos, one of the Cyclades, Theseus treacherously left Ariadne asleep on the shore and sailed away. Ariadne was soon avenged: Theseus, reaching the Attic coast, forgot his promise to hoist the white sail to signal his safe return. King Aegeus, his father, who stood on the cliffs watching for him, saw in the distance the black sail and threw himself in despair into the sea, which was hence named the Aegean.

Tholos Tombs. *Tholos* is the ancient Greek word for any circular building; the word is so used as a term in archaeology.

The most distinctive type of tomb in Crete during the Early Minoan period,* still constructed during the Middle Minoan period,* was the tholos tomb or circular tomb. These huge communal or family graves are found particularly in the Mesara Plain* vicinity such as those of Platanos*, Lebena,* Kamilari* near Phaistos,* Hagia Triada* and Apesokari.* They are circular structures of roughly dressed stones leaning slightly inward, with bonding clay and smaller stones in the interstices. They were built on the flat bedrock above ground and stood completely free, with a single low entrance, usually about one metre high, with monolithic side-posts and a heavy lintel (figure 185). The entrance always faces east, a fact indicative of some special funerary belief. In front of it to the outside there is often a shallow pit, a kind of stone-lined antechamber. The smaller of these tombs, with an interior diameter of about four metres (thirteen feet) seem to have been domed in stone; the larger were domed in stone or possibly in mud or mud-bricks as Hood has suggested. Perhaps they had a simple brushwood roof. In any case, the stone walls, sometimes reaching a height of at least two metres (six and a half feet) are all that now remains. These large vaults contained hundreds of burials and often were in use for centuries. The thickness of the walls grows with the diameter of the tomb (see Platanos). Complexes of enclosures and rectangular rooms were added to the circular construction, employed as ossuaries for the earlier burials as well as for the deposition of various grave-goods,* including clay and stone vases* which contained offerings of food and drink for the dead. Some of these rooms seem to have been intended for the cult of the dead, as the existence of elaborate funerary rites is often evident (see Burial Customs*). Two characteristic altars* are found at Apesokari.* A unique clay model of a rectangular structure open on three sides has been found in the tomb of Kamilari:* inside two couples are represented, with altars* or tables in front of them, accepting offerings of food and drink from the two living people who stand before them. This model is probably not earlier than the Middle Minoan III period. Evans thought that the origin of the tholos tombs is Libya, where parallels can be seen, but this opinion is disputable.

These tombs are perhaps the ancestors of the later tholos or beehive-like tombs of the Mycenaean Mainland, which nonetheless are rather different, being cut into the slope of a hillside, lined with stone masonry in horizontal courses. They are approached usually by a rather steeply sloping open-entranced passage, leading down from the natural surface level, sometimes of a considerable length, the *dromos* (figure 186). The entrance (*stomion*) was shaped like a deep doorway, framed in larger blocks of stone to make an ornamental facade, and instead of an actual door it was closed with a rubble wall, demolished and built each time a new burial was made. The roof was built in corbelled rings of stones, usually roughly worked in place, and smoothed toward the top, where a keystone was placed. Outside the filling of earth was replaced, buttressing the whole construction.

In Crete several tholos tombs of the Mycenaean Age have been found. The chamber is round, oval, or occasionally square (tombs at Damania,

186. Late Minoan tholos tomb at Maleme in Western Crete

Praisos* and Maleme,* see figure 186), but the roof is almost always vaulted. Sometimes there is a relieving triangle above the heavy lintel over the door. This is a Mainland feature. The *dromos* was often unlined with masonry, as in the case of the tomb at Apodoulou.* The elaborate tomb at Achladia near Siteia,* excavated by N. Platon, dating to about 1300 B.C., showed a peculiarity: the chamber possessed a blind door for the communication of the dead with the upper world. The tomb at Damania featured a door dividing the *dromos* into two parts, each with a different lining. The earlier tomb at Isopata between Knossos* and the sea, built in splendid ashlar masonry for some eminent person about 1500 B.C. but utterly destroyed during the last war, showed a peculiar pointed keel vault with Oriental affinities, some eight metres high, which was formed by projecting ashlar layers of stone over the rectangular chamber. The *dromos* had the usual form but with a long rectangular anteroom with two shallow side niches before the chamber. The late tombs near Karphi* displayed a quite unusual feature: they were either wholly or partially free-standing. A special type of tholos tomb was in use during the Dark Ages* (see Geometric Period*).

Thunder-weapon see **Double Axe.**

Toilet Articles (Minoan). Various toilet articles of the refined Minoan civilization* have been found. Well-polished bronze disks were used as mirrors, as they were throughout antiquity. Ivory* combs—sometimes elaborately carved as were the ivory or wooden mirror handles—appear often in the Late Minoan period* among grave-goods,* but we may suppose that ordinary combs were made of wood* and have not survived. Perhaps the oldest bone comb of the Aegean was found in a tomb at Archanes.* Bronze tweezers with the two ends widened were also used for removing hair as far back as the Early Minoan period.* The Cretans were clean-shaven, although beards and mustaches seem to have been worn occasionally. Sharp obsidian* blades obviously served for shaving in early times, but from the Early Minoan period* onwards bronze razors of various forms appear, usually leaf-shaped with a wooden handle. A razor resembling a chopper was employed during Late Minoan times, in imitation of a contemporary Egyptian type. Cosmetics and perfumes* seem to have been used freely. Some early stone vases* with two or more round compartments perhaps served for cosmetics. Paint for the eyes and face was employed, probably ground in stone bowls.

Tombs see **Burial Customs; Chamber-tombs; Tholos Tombs.**

Tools. During the Neolithic period* or New Stone Age, the Bronze Age,* and the Iron Age,* common tools and weapons* were made respectively of stone, bronze and iron. Thus, an Age is primarily named after the material of which its common tools and not its other objects are made. The oldest stone tools in Crete have been recently assigned by A. Zois to the Mesolithic or even to the Palaeolithic period. During the Bronze Age* the Minoans employed a great variety of bronze tools, cast in double moulds.

For work in the fields different tools were used, such as ploughs (see Agriculture*), picks (mattocks) and double adzes (hoes), the last two of which were also used in quarries. A standard tool was an axe-adze provided with a shaft-hole for mounting on a wooden handle: the axe blade was employed for cutting wood and clearing undergrowth, the adze for hoeing and weeding. An axe has the edge parallel to the handle, while an adze's edge is across it. Single-bladed axes, double adzes and especially the popular double axes were also much in use for various purposes (see - Double Axe*).

Other efficient tools at the disposal of the mason and the carpenter were chisels of various sizes, awls, scrapers, punches, borers and fine-toothed saws, invented by Talos* or Daidalos* according to the Greeks, often of great dimensions, up to one and a half metres (about five feet) in length. They were shaped by hammering. A number of them have been recovered from the palace at Zakros*: the longest of them had handles on both ends so that two men could work together. Hammers seem to have also been used as symbols of authority of the priesthood, according to some representations. Ritual specimens of stone and one of clay (see Rhyton*) of a distinctive type with expanded ends and a round shaft-hole have been found. For the former some practical use has been also suggested. Chisels usually were flat in section, with the butt-end being much narrower than the cutting-edge. Evidently daggers were not exclusively weapons* but also found an everyday use in the fields. There were also single-edged knives. For finer work including ivory* and seal cutting (see Seals*), there were miniature saws, drills, cutters and needles, and eventually bone or chipped stone tools even during later ages.

All these tools were made with apparent care and taste. As it has been remarked, Minoan Crete belongs to those happy ages when even everyday utensils were in their simple way objects of art.

Toplou Monastery see **Itanos.**

Trade. The peaceful Minoans were great merchants. We may assume that extensive local trade was carried on with the existing means of transport* between different areas of Crete to exchange their surplus production, either in agriculture* and fishing* or in exploitation of forests* and mineral resources.* The exports of the island covered a large area in the Mediterranaean, while imports* supplied it—although it was basically self-supporting—with a variety of articles. The palaces* were at the same time major storage places, workshops and commercial centers. The construction of palaces and other large-scale works of the Minoan architecture* implies that trade and materials were under some control of the central authorities who ruled the palaces. Besides, an active class of private merchants seems to have existed as in Egypt and other countries of the Near East (see Social Structure of Minoan Crete*).

The ships* that carried trade overseas could voyage across the open sea, even directly to Egypt, with which there was an extensive intercourse. This intercourse can be implied from various evidence, such as a number of affinities in art, the presence of Cretans in Egypt, known there as Keftiu* and represented in art, or the discovery of Egyptian objects* and other foreign materials and artifacts in Crete, and of objects of Minoan manufacture abroad. The Minoans had close relations with the Phoenician coast and Syria, where there is perhaps evidence of a Cretan settlement at Ugarit (Ras-Shamra), and naturally with Cyprus and the Cyclades. Melos was the chief source of obsidian,* which is found in early Bronze Age* deposits in Crete; besides, strong affinities between Melian and Early Minoan pottery are attested; at Phylakopi Minoan vases were imitated. The island might even have been dominated by Crete, like Kythera and Thera.* Minoan "colonies" or outposts seem to have existed all over the Aegean (see Ships*). Cretan merchants appear to have made their way westward as well; several features of early Italian cultures, including that of Malta and Sardinia, seem to reflect Minoan prototypes. This can be seen in the form of the earliest Italian daggers. With the decline of Minoan authority, trade with the Near East continues in the hands of Mycenae.

The Classical Greek tradition reflects this extensive Minoan presence on the sea by giving the name "Minoa" to a number of naval outposts and trading stations all over the Aegean, in islands such as Amorgos and

187. Clay model of four-wheeled cart from Palaikastro (*after Evans*)

Siphnos, and also in Kerkyra, Sicily, Arabia and Palestine, where Gaza bore the name "Minoa." On Crete itself such ports existed at Pachyammos* in the east and Souda Bay* in the west.

Transport. Because of the mountainous character of Crete, land transport since Early Minoan times must have been by pack animals, such as donkeys and perhaps oxen. A clay model recovered from Phaistos,* dating to about 1200 B.C. or even later, represents a donkey or horse (see Horses*) loaded with two large water jars. The man-carried loads were evidently slung on long poles balanced on the shoulder, or with a number of bearers at each end of the pole.

A clay model wagon with polychrome decoration of the Middle Minoan I period has been recovered at Palaikastro;* it probably represents a square-cut heavy vehicle drawn by oxen, with apparently solid wheels and the front axle fixed. Evans considered it the earliest European wagon, reminiscent of a modern railway truck or motor lorry in build (figure 187). It is supposed that wheeled vehicles had been introduced to Crete about 1900 B.C. or even earlier. This introduction revolutionized transport. Solid wheels are quite efficient for the slow transport of goods, and survived until recent times. Spoked wheels, which offer speed and manoeuvrability to the vehicle but demand a skillful craftsman and a lot of labour, appear for the first time on a seal attributed to the Late Minoan I period which shows two ibexes drawing a chariot.* The chariot was probably also used for travel, but on a very limited scale.

A road system joined the Minoan centers. Several retaining walls which supported roads, some even suitable for wheeled traffic, have survived near Knossos* and elsewhere. It has been suggested that the ancient and modern Greek word for a bridge, *gephyra*, may be of Minoan origin. Riding was also practised but probably on a limited scale. A form of luxurious passenger transport, evidently for ladies of the upper classes or for priestly persons, was the open litter or sedan chair (figure 188) attached to two carrying poles, which we see illustrated in a Middle Minoan II miniature clay model, with lattice design, and the fragmentary "Palanquin Fresco" of Late Minoan I date, both from Knossos.* Nevertheless, we may safely assume that travel and transport were essentially by sea

188. Clay model of sedan chair from Knossos

(see Ships*) as was always true until the construction of asphalt roads over the rugged surface of Crete.

Trapeza Cave see **Caves.**

Tree and Pillar Cult. A characteristic feature of Minoan religion* was the worship of trees and pillars,* which may have been the sacred places where the Goddess appeared. This dual cult perhaps was an identical form of worship. The worship of sacred boughs and trees was customary in antiquity all over Europe, as by the Druids, for example. In Classical Greece the olive tree of Athena on the Acropolis, the laurel of Apollo, and the oak of Zeus in the oracle at Dodona were famous. In Crete this worship was obviously related to the divinity of fertility (see Divinities, Minoan*), probably practised in country shrines.*

In one scene on a recovered gold ring the Goddess is sitting under the sacred tree. In other scenes devout men and women adore and venerate the tree, touching or shaking its branches, or dancing ecstatically before it. Demons* often appear as ministers of the cult. Sacred boughs are often painted on vases and larnakes* or engraved on seals* in combination with sacral horns* or libation jugs. Sometimes the tree is depicted inside a sacred enclosure or connected to an altar. In two instances it is carried on board a ceremonial boat or sacred barge. A seal from Makrygialos shows a ceremonial boat containing an altar, a sacred tree and a votary or priestess (see figure 189).

In the case of the pictures on the sarcophagus* from Hagia Triada* and elsewhere, the sacred tree is the olive,* a tree which can achieve an incredibly long lifespan, and the fruit of which offers both nourishment and

189. Seal from Makrygialos in Eastern Crete

fuel. Probably date palms were also considered as holy. The sacred tree was connected to the sacred stone (*baetyl*, defined by Hesychios as "living ·stone") and the column, which in some cases may have been hewn out of it. The later Greek myth of the Tree of Life which grew in the Gardens of the Hesperides is probably derived from the Minoans.

The functional role of the square pillar in Minoan architecture* is clear and we may not assume that every pillar was an object of veneration. Nevertheless, pillars occur often in rooms of the palaces* and villas* which are obviously shrines.* Among them are the pillar crypt of the South House* at Knossos,* where the stand of a double axe* was found on one side of the pillar, and that of the Royal Villa,* where receivers for liquid offerings were built around the pillar. Many pillars show various masons' marks* incised on them. The dark Pillar Crypts of the west wing of the palace at Knossos* possess two massive pillars with the double-axe sign carved no less than twenty-nine times upon them. This fact, as the majority of scholars feel, denotes the sanctity of these pillars and the religious character of the crypts. Graham attributes to these pillars a purely religious role, believing that in this case they do not serve any structural purpose.

The worship in pillar crypts possibly has associations with the worship in caves,* which is older; as a matter of fact, a pillar crypt might be considered an artificial domestic cave. On the other hand, the veneration paid to pillars could be associated with the fact that pillars were essential and conspicuous elements of stability in a country where houses* could be unpredictably damaged by frequent and often severe earthquakes.* The pillar is considered a form of aniconic worship, a place of habitation of a divinity. A scene of women adoring pillars inside structures perhaps representing pillar crypts is depicted on a Mycenaean vase from Cyprus.

"Trickle-pattern" see **Pithoi.**

Turkish Occupation. In the sixteenth century the Turks, having already conquered all the Balkan countries including the Greek Mainland and the Aegean islands, made various probing expeditions against Crete, in accordance with their policy of expansionism and of mastering their old enemy in the Mediterranaean, Venice. The Turkish conquest began in 1645 with the capture of Chania* by an invading army—50,000 strong. The next year they took Rethymnon* and two years later they had occupied most of the island except for Chandax (Herakleion*) and the fortified small coastal islands of Spinalonga,* Souda Bay* and Grambousa.* The great siege of Chandax began in 1648 and lasted for more than twenty years, until 1669, writing one of the most remarkable pages of military history (see Herakleion*). Venice retained for a while only the three island fortresses.

Under Turkish domination, completed in 1670, Crete was badly governed, and endured an intensive exploitation and heavy political and religious oppression. Large numbers of Cretans under strong pressure became Moslems but never lost their language. The French Tournefort informs us that in his time, thirty-one years after the fall of Chandax, most of the "Turks" in Crete were renegades or children of renegades. As a matter of fact, the same is true of the population of Asia Minor, where the majority of the Greeks and the other ancient peoples who lived there became Moslem, and racially assimilated the small number of original Turks, who had come from Central Asia (Turkestan, today in Soviet Asia). These Turks had racial affinities with the Mongols and linguistic affinities with the Japanese, the Finns and the Hungarians.

The Turks had periodic and unpredictable outbreaks of savagery. An abominable custom was the violent recruiting of small Christian boys for the large army of Janissaries, who were especially trained to become fierce oppressors of the Christians and the spearhead of the Turkish establishment. According to Pashley, the population of the island was 500,000 when the Venetians came, reduced to 250,000 in the sixteenth century and dramatically dropped to 80,000 a few years after the Turkish conquest. Forests* were destroyed and agriculture neglected; trade as well as culture declined rapidly. Only the area of Sphakia* in the west kept a kind of semi-independence.

The island was divided into three administrative compartments, the Pasha of Herakleion* being the general governor. Land was divided into that owned by the Sultan, that owned by the Moslem religious establishment, and private property, allotted in fief to the Pashas, Beys and Agas, whose rapacity and administrative inadequacy became legendary. The former proprietors were kept as serfs. All Christians paid the Kharatch, a capitation tax, the payment of which entitled them merely to stay alive. The population suffered gross poverty and insecurity of life. The church-

190. Bembo Fountain and Validé Mosque at Herakleion during the Turkish occupation

es were converted into mosques, baths, or store-rooms (figure 190). The Christian religion was tolerated although churches were forbidden to ring their bells.

There was much resistance to the Turks and a great number of minor and major revolts, such as the great upsurge in 1821, the year of the outbreak of the Greek Independence War, followed by massacres and oppression, partly by the Egyptians, who were then subjects of the Sultan. The population was reduced to half between 1821 and 1834.

As Turkish power declined, revolts in Crete became constant. The great revolt of 1866 was again ferociously repressed. The wanton atrocities shocked Europe and focused the attention of the Great Powers on the Cretan situation. In 1898 the last Turkish soldier left Crete, after the principal ports had been occupied by troops of the Great Powers (England, until then the traditional friend of Turkey, Russia, its hereditary enemy, France, and Italy) and after the Turks had unsuccessfully attacked the British in Herakleion. At the end of the year Prince George Glucksburg, a younger son of the king of Greece, became the High Commissioner of an independent Crete until the final union with Greece in 1913, which was formally acknowledged by Turkey in the Treaty of London.

Tylissos. Beside the remains of some Early Minoan houses, three important Minoan villas* were excavated in 1909-13 by the Greek archaeologist Joseph Hazzidakis at Tylissos (figure 191), the *tu-ri-so* of the tablets,* a village west of Herakleion* which still preserves its ancient name. These large houses* were destroyed with the palaces* about 1450 B.C.

House A is a good example of a town villa (figure 192). It was at least two storeys high, a fact attested to by the existence of several stairways.

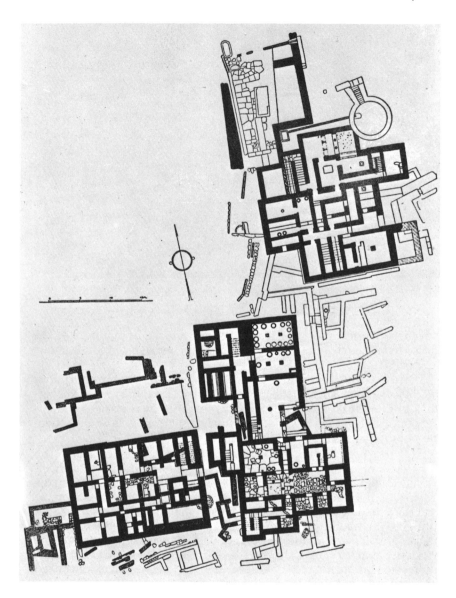

191. General plan of Tylissos (*after Hazzidakis*)

The main entrance, with two pillars* and a deep L-shaped portico behind **(15)**, was in the middle of the east side. The southern part, which contained the living quarters, had a main hall **(6)**, irregularly paved with flagstones. The floor of the hall included two slightly raised rectangular platforms of uncertain purpose. The hall opened through a pier-and-door partition to a colonnade which flanked a light-well.* A possible toilet **(7)**

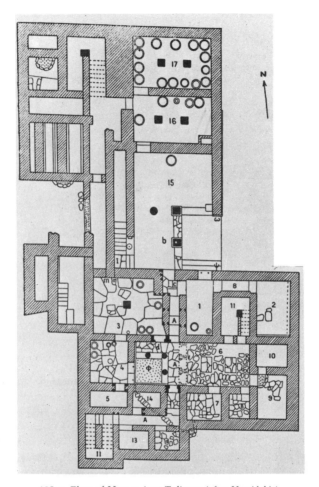

192 a. Plan of House A at Tylissos *(after Hazzidakis)*.

3. Pillar Crypt
4. Room of Cauldrons
5. Room of Ingot and Tablets
6. Main Hall
7. Lavatory (?)
8-10. Back Rooms (Sleeping-Rooms?)
11. Lustral Basin

14. Room with Drain
15. Entrance Portico
16-17. Pillared Magazines
I-II. Stairways
A, B. Corridors
Φ. Light-well

with a drain in a corner opened to the south. On the north side of the hall
was a sunken Lustral Basin* **(11)**. The pillar crypt **(3)** was probably a
domestic shrine, where a pyramidal stand for a double axe was found,
while the neighbouring rooms were employed for storage. Room **(4)**, with
a window opening on to a light-well, yielded three huge bronze
cauldrons,* while a bronze ingot was recovered in Room **(5)**. The neighbouring small rooms were perhaps sleeping-places, while the large
rooms at the north end of the house **(16-17)**, each with two axial pillars,
were used as magazines* containing pithoi. The existence of a banquet

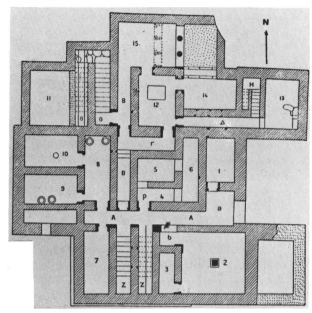

192 b. Plan of House C at Tylissos *(after Hazzidakis)*.

1. Entrance Lobby	13. Toilet Room
2. Pillar Crypt	14. Women's Room (?)
3. Secondary Cult Room	15. Main Hall
4-6. Rooms of Uncertain Use	a. Entrance Hall
7. Room of Frescoes	A-A, B-B, Γ, Δ. Corridors
8-10. Magazine Complex	Z, H, Θ. Stairways
12. Remodelled Lustral Basin	

hall above them has been presumed.

House B, the smallest of all, includes a main hall, a paved room and a staircase leading up to a second storey. The plan of this house forms a more perfect rectangle than that of the others.

House C, rebuilt in the Late Minoan III period, is well preserved. Various groups of rooms, served by an intricate system of corridors **(A-B)**, form projecting wings. A pillar crypt **(2)** was probably connected with the cult. The main hall **(15)** of the residential quarter has a pier-and-door partition leading to a light-well* with two columns* and a broad window on the adjacent side. A Lustral Basin* **(12)** was later remodeled. Room **(14)** has been considered as possibly reserved for the women, while the stairway **H** led up perhaps to the sleeping-places. Room **13** had a toilet provided with a drain through the outer wall, while Rooms **8-10** perhaps with a hall above, served as magazines.

In Classical Greek times Tylissos was an independent city-state, an ally or perhaps a vassal of Knossos,* its powerful neighbour. In 450 B.C. the two cities concluded a treaty, with Argos as an arbitrator. This Peloponnesian city traditionally had close bonds of language and cult with both of them.

Tzermiado see **Caves.**

Ugarit see **Trade.**

Unexplored Mansion see **Little Palace.**

Urbanism. Already by the Neolithic period* people had begun to live in
village communities, sometimes fairly large as in the case of Knossos.*
Farming villages became proto-urban communities during the Early
Minoan period,* and population steadily increased. The settlements at
Myrtos* and Vasiliki* in Eastern Crete are very important. After this first
urban stage, a true urban revolution appeared early in the second millenium B.C. and developed, along with the economy,* with astounding
rapidity. Large towns with splendid palaces* were erected, marking the
entrance of Minoan Crete into a high form of civilization, in the development of which the urban revolution was a major factor. The more important towns were clustered around the multipurposed palaces,* centers of
administration,* religion* and economy.* Not much is known about the
towns, as the palaces* themselves have attracted most of the attention of
the excavators. Again the eastern part of the island, with towns such as
Gournia,* Pseira* and Palaikastro,* yields the clearest picture about an urban settlement at the time of the peak of the Palatial era. All of the towns
were founded at the same time as the Early Palaces,* or even earlier, on
low hills near a good harbour,* close to important sea routes.

Town planning was limited to simple principles and never included
the totality of a town in such a clear way as was done in contemporary
Egypt. Surfaced and stepped roads had already been built in the Middle
Minoan settlements, a fact implying the existence of some central organization. The same is true of the elaborate drainage systems* which were
later developed. There was a tendency for the main roads to be laid in
such a way that they could serve most of the houses.* At Gournia (see figure 69) we see the settlement clustered around a public place and an
important building, a minor palace, with streets radiating out and united
laterally by roughly concentric streets, true ring-roads. Palaikastro* in the
far east has a different town plan (see figure 136). Here as well as at Pseira*
the main road follows the axial principle, running along the main axis of
the town, with smaller streets meeting it at right angles. Few areas inside
the densely set settlements were left open. The street system divided the
town into a number of great irregular units. In the case of Gournia we see
six of them, of various sizes and shapes, each including a number of separate houses.* There were no city walls, and settlements up to the end of
the Bronze Age* were unfortified, a fact probably associated with the existence of palatial centers and internal peace, and demonstrating that
people were entirely at their ease and felt a security from piracy* or
foreign invasion unknown elsewhere in the Aegean. Myrtos* is the single
possible early exception. The position of the towns near the sea-shore
during the entire Bronze Age also demonstrates that no danger from the

sea was expected. Outside the towns the land was dotted with villas* and farmhouses, either isolated or in small groups.

C. Renfrew has given a highly relevant table concerning the settlement continuity from one period to the succeeding one in Crete: according to his calculations the majority of settlements of each period remains inhabited during the next one, while a minority is abandoned; on the other hand new settlements appear according to the increase of population. A total of 379 settlement sites were calculated for Neolithic* and Bronze Age* Crete, but this number steadily increases, following an intensive archaeological research. The same scholar gives figures for the approximate population in Crete during the different periods: Neolithic* = 12,600; Early Minoan* = 75,000; Middle Minoan* = 214,000 and Late Minoan* = 256,000 inhabitants. The approximate population density in each case would respectively be 1.53, 9.18, 26.1 and 31.3.

Vai. This beautiful, extremely popular and still reasonably unspoiled beach on the east coast between the ancient sites of Itanos* and Palaikastro* possesses a palm grove, unique for Greece. Legend tells us how this grove had pushed up accidentally from the kernels of dates eaten by Phoenician merchants, who had anchored here. Some Minoan ruins have been located in its vicinity. The area together with the whole peninsula north of Palaikastro belongs to the rich Toplou Monastery (see Itanos*).

Varsamonero Monastery. Near the village of Voriza in the prefecture of Herakleion* are the ruins of the Varsamonero Monastery with a church of the fourteenth century. The church has two naves built in different periods. The walls are adorned with important and rather well-preserved frescoes. Interesting are some graffiti, the oldest of which dates to 1332. The north nave, the older of the two, is dedicated to the Virgin Mary and the frescoes are mainly referring to her iconographic cycle. The south nave, dedicated to St. John, was painted in 1400–1428, while the frescoes of the third nave across the church's axis (St. Phanourios), painted by Constantine Eirikos, give the impression of being icons instead of wall-paintings.

Vasiliki. Near the village of Vasiliki at the isthmus of Hierapetra* in eastern Crete, an important Early Minoan II and later settlement was excavated in the early 1900's by Richard Seager, the explorer of Mochlos* and Pseira.* The so-called "House on the Hill" is in fact a large mansion, a true small palace. It might be considered as the prototype, on a small scale, of the Minoan palaces.* Its orientation, with its corners pointing toward the cardinal points, is possibly influenced by Oriental architectural practises. The ruins of the house show rectangular rooms of all shapes and sizes, sometimes united by long passages. The existing wings are impressive. The southwestern wing is the largest. Some of its oblong rooms can be identified as magazines, while others could be personal quarters. To the west of this wing is a paved courtyard of unknown original dimensions.

The southeastern wing includes the largest rooms of the whole mansion. A rock-cut well is inside a small courtyard or a sort of light-well.* The existence of two original storeys seems very probable. The inner surface of the walls of the houses was covered with plaster* painted red, which dried very hard, thus helping to preserve the walls and providing the right surface with finished appearance for internal decoration. Some of these walls on a foundation of small stones and clay bonded with straw were held together by an interlacing framework of square-section and circular timbers. Bricks were used in the upper structure. This building was destroyed by fire but the hilltop was afterward reoccupied.

House A, built into the slope, belongs to the Middle Minoan I period and is a good example of Minoan "agglutinative" architecture, with rectangular rooms added when needed. Hutchinson remarked that the house had grown over the ground like an ivy plant; nevertheless, there is a certain regularity of construction. One narrow doorway gives on to the stepped street.

Recently the site has been further explored by A. Zois in behalf of the Archaeological Society of Athens. Several other houses of the settlement were discovered, belonging to various periods. The old excavation was cleared and stratigraphically examined.

Vasiliki Ware. This red-brown mottled pottery, of high quality and ingenuity, first appearing at Vasiliki* in Eastern Crete, belongs to the Early Minoan II period (figure 193). These vases, of various shapes such as the characteristic tall beak-spouted jug, the beaker or the "tea-pot," sometimes with a fantastically long horizontal spout, are so well made that their shapely forms almost appear to have been made with the potter's wheel.* They have a fine hard clay and are covered all over with a semi-lustrous slip showing a deliberately mottled surface, obviously achieved by means of uneven firing. The mottling was accidental at first, caused by baking the vases in an open fire. Later, mottling, imitating contemporary variegated stone vases, was probably achieved by carefully applying a burning twig to different points of the surface while the vase was still hot from the kiln, and by using slips of a different colour on the same vessel. Basically the patches are red shading to orange and brown, with black spots and lighter areas. The ornamental effect with its brilliant hues was extremely varied and very attractive. This ware, perhaps imitating metal prototypes as the metallic textures of the slip suggest, was very fashionable in the eastern parts of the island, but spread to the west as far as Chania.*

Vathypetro. South of Herakleion* and Archanes* a large Minoan country mansion of the sixteenth century b.c. was excavated by the Greek archaeologist Sp. Marinatos (figure 194). The villa, situated in a high place enjoying a fine view, is thought to have controlled a large rural estate. The villa includes an elaborate tricolumnar shrine facade (see Shrines*) by an open court (16); a small domestic shrine (2); a storeroom (4) with a pair of pillars,* in which sixteen large pithoi* were recovered; and a spacious pil-

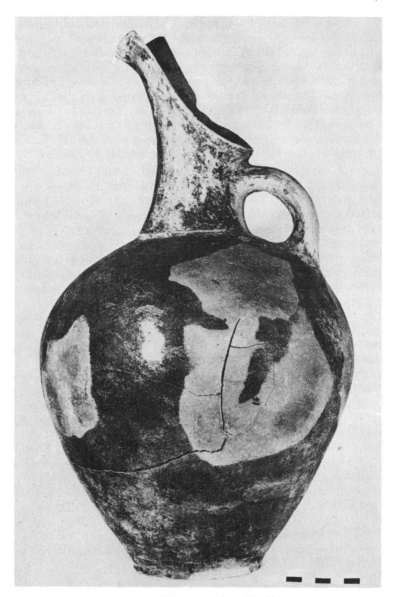

193. Vasiliki Ware jug from Vasiliki

lar room **(7)** with four pillars* in the middle. The main entrance of this wing is at its southwest corner, at the end of a paved road. Of particular interest is a splendidly preserved installation of a wine press in Room **13,** which was paved and had two pillars* in irregular positions; at its north-west corner was placed a large clay jar with a spout at the bottom (figure 195). The grapes would have been placed in the jar and trampled by a

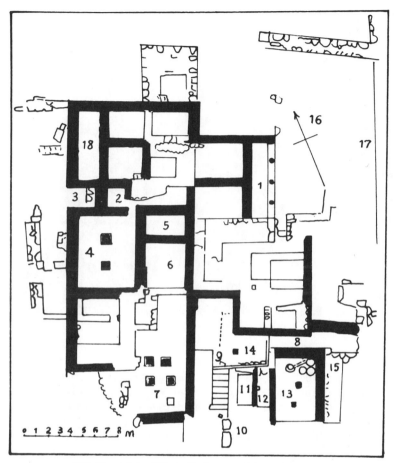

194. Plan of the Villa at Vathypetro (*after Marinatos*)

1. Tricolumnar Shrine Façade	7. Hypostyle Room	14. Court with Stone Drain
2. Domestic Shrine	8. South Corridor	16. Court
3. Lodge	9. Stairway	18. Veranda (?)
4. Pillared Storeroom	13. Wine Press Installation	

single person, in a way practiced until today, the juice flowing through the spout into a jar placed below it. Near the building were found traces of a large pottery kiln with exceptionally long flues (see Terracotta*). The site seems to have been destroyed by earthquake in the Late Minoan IB period.

Venetian Occupation. Captured in 1204 by Crusaders, Crete was lost to the Byzantine Empire and sold for 10,000 silver coins to Venice, the great Mediterranaean naval power of this time by Boniface, Marquis of Montferrat. The Genoese rivals of Venice, who occupied some parts of the island including Chandax (Herakleion*), were driven out. A Venetian governor, with the title of the Duke of Crete, elected every two years, was

195. Wine press installation at Vathypetro

appointed by 1210, but Cretan resistance was so stubborn that the greater part of the island was not completely occupied until 1434. In later times rebellions were common but were ferociously repressed (see Lasithi Plain*). For the Venetians Crete was important for its exports* as well as a base for controlling the east Mediterranean trade routes and a bastion against the Turkish expansionism. Feudal dues were huge. Land was divided into State, Roman Catholic Church and private property, the last of which was divided in six *Sexteria* and allotted in fief to 545 noble Venetian families. The native population was intensely exploited, while the Jews lived in ghettos. Society was divided in feudal classes. The upper class included the *Nobili Veneti* and the lower *Nobili Cretensi,* both titles given by the Venetian administration. Byzantine-Cretan noblemen also existed. Gradually some of the Venetians intermarried with Cretans, took Greek as their mother-language, were culturally absorbed and even joined the Orthodox Church—the same happened in the Ionian Islands—going so far as to unite in 1363 with Cretans to rebel against the Venetian Republic and form a short-lived independent state, the Republic of Titus. In the fourteenth century the island was divided into four administrative *territoria*, which roughly correspond to the prefectures or nomes existing today.

The Creto-Venetian era left several important monuments. Among them are fine country villas such as those at Etia* and Kalathenes (see Kisamos*), churches and fountains still preserved at Herakleion,* Chania* and Rethymnon,* magnificent city fortifications and strong fortresses against rebels and pirate raids such as Spinalonga,* Grambousa,* Franco-castello* and others. Greek Byzantine civilization flourished, enriched with Italian influences. Cretan literature* produced some fine works and the remarkable Cretan School* of painting was able to influence the Greek Mainland and Cyprus. Some famous institutes of scholars were founded in Candia (Herakleion*) and Rethymnon.* The rulers of the Venetian Republic, able diplomats anxious to avoid unnecessary rebellions in their "Stato del Mar," of which Crete was the more substantial part, after the intransigence of the first centuries became more tolerant and did not openly impose the Latin rite upon the Greeks. In the sixteenth century there were 376 Latin monasteries on the island. On the other hand an important Cretan colony flourished in Venice; among its members were some eminent editors, such as Markos Mousouros who published Greek authors in the Aldine Press. The first Mediaeval scholar to show an interest in Cretan archaeology was the Florentine monk Buondelmonti, who visited the island in 1415.

The Turkish invasion and the subsequent occupation* began in 1645.

Venice see **Venetian Occupation.**

VENIZELOS. Eleutherios Venizelos, the great statesman of modern Greece, was born at Chania* (1864–1936). He was a lawyer of immense learning. He played a leading role in the union of Crete with Greece, against the policy of the authoritative Prince George, the High Commissioner of the island (see Turkish Occupation*). In 1910 he became prime minister of Greece and made an alliance with Bulgaria and Serbia which was instrumental in the defeat of Turkey in 1913. During World War I, Venizelos brought Greece into the Allied side in direct opposition to the pro-German King Constantine I, a cousin of the Kaiser. A skilled diplomat of international caliber, Venizelos won many areas for Greece. He was leader of the Liberal Party. As prime minister he proceeded to serious political, economic and cultural reforms, and came to an understanding with Turkey. Venizelos is a much respected historical personality in Crete.

Viannos see **Biannos.**

Villas (Minoan). Minoan buildings comprise not only palaces* and ordinary houses* but also a number of large villas, usually two-storey buildings, which often possessed on a small scale all the essential elements of Minoan architecture,* including columns,* pillars,* light-wells* and Lustral Basins.* Some of these villas were within the limits of a town such as the three villas at Tylissos,* or were directly related to a palace such as the Royal Villa* at Knossos,* while the majority seem to have been isolated country mansions evidently controlling large rural estates, such as the villas at Sklavokambos,* Vathypetro* and those in the province of Siteia.*

Vinegar see **Wine.**

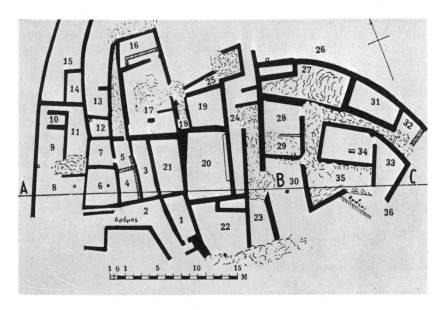

196. Plan of the houses at Vrokastro (*after Hall*)

2. Street with Drain to the NW
6. Room with Column Base
8,9,12. Rooms with Pithoi
12. Room with Pithos-Burial of Child
17. Room of Clay Head
17,18,19. Rooms with Cut-Out Rocks
24. Room, perhaps Original Road

25. Room of Chariot Model
26. Room, perhaps Original Road
26,27. Rooms with Middle Minoan
     Pottery
30. Cairn
34. Room with Rectangular Column Basis
36. Scarped Rock

Vrokastro. Vrokastro is the modern name of a steep hill of 300 metres (nearly a thousand feet) overlooking the Gulf of Mirabello in Eastern Crete, east of Kalo Chorio. Here a settlement enjoying a fine view as at Karphi * was built in the early twelfth century B.C. in a high and easily defensible site by people wishing to escape from trouble and unwilling to live under the domination of the Dorians.* The place has been continuously occupied until the Geometric period.*

The houses,* excavated by the American archaeologist Edith Hall, are tightly packed together (figure 196), still in the "agglutinative" manner of the architecture of Minoan towns; thus, with no clear plan, it is hard to distinguish where one house ends and another begins. Some long rooms here possibly reflect an Achaian* influence. The streets had a drainage system* along one side. In all probability the houses were built, like those on the island of Pseira,* in successive terraces. Some of the walls do not enclose rooms, but shut off the rocks where these emerge above the surface. The floors of the houses were made of beaten earth. Column bases,

197. Captain of the Blacks Fresco (*detail*)

one of them rectangular, occurred in three rooms. The site yielded some very interesting finds.

A number of quadrangular tholos tombs* and bone-enclosures has been excavated at various neighbouring sites, which yielded fine Geometric and earlier pottery.* The burial custom of cremation* was observed here.

Vrontisi Monastery. The monastery, founded in the fourteenth century, lies between the villages of Voriza and Zaros, in the prefecture of Herakleion.* It enjoys a fine view over the Mesara Plain.* It had been a center of religious education during the Venetian occupation.* Some good frescoes are still preserved. A fifteenth century marble fountain is outside the entrance of the monastery, depicting in relief God, Adam and Eve, and four figures serving as spouts and symbolizing the rivers of Paradise.

Warfare (Minoan). It is generally accepted that the Minoans were peaceful and more disposed to trade* than to war. The evidence concerning their defensive armour* is rather scanty. Their weapons,* sometimes found in excavations, show that although Minoan society possessed arms, they were rather unwarlike as a whole. Minoan palaces* and towns were unfortified and situated in places difficult to defend and usually not

198. Early Minoan dagger from Hagia Photia

far from the sea, a fact illustrating the existence of internal peace and of navigation safety as well as of suppression of piracy.* In Minoan art* representations of fights or of warriors are very few and of little prominence. Once we see a presumably historical scene showing a walled town under attack, but it is assumed that this town may lie outside Crete, perhaps having been related to some Minoan colony. The fragmentary miniature fresco (figure 197) from Knossos* (see Frescoes*), known as the Captain of the Blacks, represents a Minoan officer leading a file of black soldiers on the double; it has been assumed that these might be well-drilled Sudanese mercenaries serving as royal guards or police. Another military scene is on one of the best stone vases from Hagia Triada* (see Stone Vases:* *Chieftain Cup*) while two seals* depict lines of marching warriors with shields.* Some military spirit can be seen at a later time, during the Achaian* domination of Knossos,* when splendid weapons appear in the Warrior Tombs and chariots* were used in warfare, after the introduction of the horse.*

Weapons. Bronze Age Crete displays a variety of weapons. The essential weapon seems to have been the dagger and later the sword. The daggers of the Early Minoan period* often are of the so-called triangular type, usually with a medial rib and a tang with rivet holes for hafting, or a rounded base with two or more rivet holes. There are also longer daggers of Cycladic inspiration. The longest dagger of this period ever found, over thirty centimetres (one foot) long, a real shortsword, has been recovered from a tomb in Hagia Photia* (figure 198). Of special interest is a silver dagger with a midrib from Koumasa. Of course the handles of these daggers, made of bone or wood, are not preserved. Several types of daggers were developed. They were the favourite side-arms of the Minoans, probably being part of everyday attire (see Dress, Minoan*). Perhaps they were knives for everyday use as well as weapons, as the two functions became distinctly separate only after the Late Minoan period.* They are often found in tombs among the grave-goods* or depicted in art. A dagger from the plateau of Lasithi* is engraved with hunting scenes, with the incisions probably filled originally with gold wire.

Eventually the dagger evolved by progressive lengthening of the blade to form the rapier or sword, reaching a length of 0.9 metre (three feet). Such swords of the eighteenth century B.C. are illustrated in some splendid ceremonial examples from the palace at Malia.* One of them was about one metre (one yard) long and had a rock crystal pommel cut in eight facets. Another had a wooden hilt covered with gold foil, with a bone pommel beneath which was a circular gold disk bearing an embossed representation of a youthful acrobat bending his body backwards in a complete circle so that his feet touch the top of his head. It is one of the masterpieces of Minoan art.* These bulky pommels besides having decorative value were useful in balancing the weight of the long blade. Eventually long guardless rapiers appear with pronounced midribs and rounded shoulders. These weapons were designed only for thrusting.

A series of excellent swords has been found in the cave of Arkalochori (see Caves*). The weak point of the rapier, its short handle tang, was later improved by changing it into a long flat plate perforated with several rivet holes and flanged at the edges so that the inlaid wooden or ivory handle could be encased. The rivet heads often were goldplated. On the more luxurious specimens the midrib of the blade and the flanges of the hilt sometimes were decorated with double lines of running spirals in relief. Daggers follow the same general pattern.

Another improvement made at the beginning of the Late Minoan period* was the addition of a characteristic horned guard for the protection of the hand. The horned sword with the flanges of the tang and shoulder projecting upwards later became universal. Eventually the horns became more horizontal and were projected laterally, giving the weapon a cruciform shape. The pommel, sometimes of ivory,* agate or rock crystal, usually was sharply carinated, while the actual hilt often was goldplated. Still later the cut-and-thrust swords and daggers appeared, with the blade much reduced in length and the hilt attachment strengthened, permitting slicing attacks as well as puncturing ones. Pictorial designs of these swords with a characteristic leaf-shaped blade are often seen as ideograms on the so-called Sword Tablets of Knossos.*

Still later, just before the coming of the Iron Age,* another slashing type of sword became fashionable all over Greece, perhaps introduced from the north. This type, known as Naue II, was heavy and rather long.

Other weapons of the Minoans were the bow (see Archers and Archery*), the javelin or throwing-spear, and perhaps the sling, presumably with simple pebbles playing the role of the leaden almond-shaped sling bullets of Classical times in Crete and elsewhere; these missiles were inscribed with the abbreviated city-state's name such as Kno(ssos), or an exhortation to the bullet—"swiftly"—or the maker's name and device, and had a notch to fit the sling. A great number of such pebbles was recovered in a presumed arsenal at Pseira.* Bronze spearheads attest to the existence of spears since early times. Some early flat blades of considerable width might have been spearheads. At first the spearheads had circular perforations in the blade. Later, in Middle Minoan times, the addition of a socket was an important improvement in hafting. The *cire perdue* (lost wax) process was evidently used for manufacture of the spearheads (see Sculpture, Minoan*). The extremity of the socket was encircled by a ring of metal. A specimen found inside a tomb near Knossos* was more than thirty-four centimetres (over one foot) long and had been considered as a weapon both compact and penetrating.

The double axe* cannot be counted among regular weapons, as several scholars had originally thought.

WELCHANOS. The Cretan Zeus Welchanos was evidently a survival of the Minoan youth-god of fertility (see Divinities, Minoan*). His name is of pre-Greek origin. His temple was built upon the ruins of Hagia Triada.* A number of tiles bearing his name was recovered. The month-name of the god in Knossos,* Gortyn* and Lyttos* was *Welchanios,* and the name of his spring festival in Lyttos,* associated with this month, the *Welchania.* Coins of Phaistos* of the Classical period depict the god as a youthful beardless figure seated among the branches of a leafless tree, with a cock in his lap. On the reverse side of the coins is a bull.

Wheel see **Transport.**

Wine. The Greeks were fond of wine, which nevertheless they always drank freely mixed with water. Dionysos, god of wine, fled from Mesopotamia in disgust because its people were addicted to beer. Wine was obtained from the grapes of the vine which, like the olive,* may have been indigenous to the island. Grape pips have been found at Myrtos* and several other Minoan sites; they were possibly the remains of raisins, as the practice of drying the grapes in the sun may be taken for granted. A wine press installation in a very good state of preservation was found in the villa of Vathypetro. The grape juice was expressed from the grapes by pressing with the feet. The pressor stood upright inside the open vat on the pedestal, from which the juice ran into the container put on the floor beside it. The fermentation of the grape-juice took place inside jars or vats placed in cool cellars.

The Cretans probably cultivated both light and dark grapes to produce white and red wine; an alcohol content of about 14 per cent could be reached. Wine appears in the tablets* of the Linear B script.* It seems probable that the drinking of wine had some religious significance and played a role in the cult, perhaps in the sacred communion.*

Vinegar was obviously prepared by allowing wine to turn sour. It must have been quite useful since it was the strongest acid then known. As a solvent for drugs it was widely used in antiquity.

During the Middle Ages Cretan strong red wine was much appreciated, especially that made in the province of Malevisi* (Malvicino, Malvoisie) near Herakleion,* perhaps exported to England as Malmsey wine, also known as Malvasy or Malvaise wine, although Monemvasia in the Peloponnese has the same claims. The island of Madeira was stocked with Cretan vines when colonized in 1441. The famous Cretan wine is mentioned in Milton's *Paradise Regained.*

Woman (Position of). In Minoan art* and especially in frescoes* we see elegantly garbed women mingling freely with the men at the public meetings and festivities, usually occupying all the front seats. These good-mannered women seem to be the focal point of the gay and sophisticated palace life. The frescoes* show girls dancing in public and taking active part in the dangerous bull-games,* wearing the male dress for the purpose. According to Evans,* these acrobat girls were of gentle birth. The absolute prominence of female divinities* in religion* and especially their reigning over a traditionally female sphere of life, the household, as shown by the dominant aspect of the Mother Goddess (see Snake Goddess*) as the household deity, and further the existence of priestesses appearing in cult scenes, having obviously fundamental ritual functions, which survived in Classical Greece along with the cult of some goddesses, is very indicative of the position of woman in society. Perhaps the queens themselves had priestess duties analogous to the presumed ritual functions of the kings (see "Priest-King"*).

In Neolithic and later times the role of woman, especially in economy* (e.g., pottery* making is considered to have been one of the traditional female tasks), seems to have been quite important. It has been inferred that matriarchy (Mother Rule, female control of society) persisted in Bronze Age* Crete; it seems certain that Minoan society was in some undefined sense matriarchal. Matrilinear traditions and customs, implying succession and inheritance—including the royal family—through the female line, appear in primitive societies at the time when the role of the male in procreation was unsuspected and a child seemed to have a single parent, the mother, and was named after her. The matrilinear tradition in Crete was so strong that it partly survived into Dorian Crete, as the Code* of Gortyn* reveals. A clear survival of a similar tradition is attested for Western Asia Minor in Classical times among the Lycians and the Carians, both peoples with possibly close relations to the Minoans.

Wood. Wood, from the rich forests* which existed in the Bronze Age* Crete, was not only one of its exports but was also extensively used in Minoan architecture* for beams of roofs and ceilings, for columns,* window-and door-frames and doors, and also for timber framework tying the fabric of the walls together in order to make them stronger and more resilient (see Houses*). Wooden coffins and household chests served as the exact model for the clay larnakes.* Wood was also used for the manufacture of house furniture,* boxes, cooking utensils, toilet articles* such as combs, posts, and the handles of daggers and mirrors. It was also used for mounting the shaft-hole tools.* It seems likely that the Minoans knew the techniques of woodworking developed by the Egyptians. Some of the pottery* shapes, like the Pyrgos Ware* chalices, are probably imitations of wooden vessels. Great quantities of wood were used for the construction of ships* and carts. The carpenter had a variety of efficient tools* at his disposal. Some charred masses of a colossal cult statue found in the palace at Knossos* (see Sculpture, Minoan*) show that wood was also used by sculptors, as was the case for the earliest Greek statues (*xoana*) of the Geometric period* and later.

Wooden objects can survive only in deposits submerged in water, or under totally arid conditions, such as in the Egyptian desert; thus, wooden artifacts found in Minoan or later deposits in Crete are extremely rare.

Writing. For several centuries the only existing script in Crete was the Hieroglyphic* or Pictographic. The earliest datable examples, belonging to the beginning of the Middle Minoan period,* are sealings* of this script. Some simplified form of script—distinguishing marks and a numerical notation—may have been in use from the earliest times. In this sense seals,* sealings* and marks on pots or on building-stones (see Masons' Marks*) could be considered a sort of script. Because of the intimate affinity between the two activities, it has been suggested that the use of seals* led to the emergence of script.

It seems evident that a considerable amount of writing might have been done in dark cuttle-fish ink on perishable materials: on papyrus imported from Egypt or on palm leaves or even on parchment. Nonetheless, the only surviving ink inscriptions are on two clay cups written on their inner side by means of a brush or a soft reed pen (see Linear A Script*). Ink could be kept in objects like a serpentine sphinx from Hagia Triada* with a hollow on its back, possibly an inkwell as Evans* thought, and variously interpreted as Anatolian, Syrian or even Cretan. In fact the shapes of the signs of both Linear A and B scripts indicate that basically they were not designed for scratching on clay. The famous and mysterious Phaistos Disk* remains a solitary monument. A deposit at Phaistos,* containing the earliest clay tablets* known in Crete, incised with a linear version of the Hieroglyphic script, is assignable towards the end of the Middle Minoan period,* to ca. 1700 B.C. A mature version of linear script was named Linear A* to distinguish it from the later Linear B,* which was already Greek, introduced in the course of the fifteenth century B.C. The writing was done from left to right with the fine point of a stylus. The extinguishment of this script probably along with the class of scribes and the need for them in the bureaucratic palatial economy* towards the end of the Bronze Age* was followed by centuries of illiteracy, until the Greek alphabet* was introduced.

Writing in Minoan Crete was limited to very short texts—mainly on clay tablets*—of a practical nature, containing almost entirely daily business documents, matters difficult to remember, and simple accounting notes of the palatial economy,* such as entries concerning receipts of goods delivered, or contents of the armouries. Very rarely some inscribed objects such as altars* contained something different, perhaps a short dedication. Literacy must have been very limited. No real public inscriptions were put up on walls or carved on slabs, recording wars, laws, treaties, long religious texts, expeditions, the reception of tribute, or the might and glory of the king. In other words there are no Minoan monumental inscriptions recording history, as we see them in contemporary Egypt or in later Greece. In those countries, in contrast to Minoan Crete, the decorative value of inscriptions on large or smaller surfaces was extensively used and appreciated.

Zakros see **Palace at Zakros.**

ZEUS. The story of Zeus' birth in Crete, familiar to the entire ancient Greek world, is reflected in the specific epithet *Kretagenes* ("Cretan-born"). According to Hesiod's version, written in the eighth century B.C., Kronos, the youngest of the Titans, married Rhea who gave birth to five children—Hestia, Demeter,* Hera, Hades and Poseidon. These children were swallowed by their father, afraid that one of them would rob him of his kingship and the position of the supreme divinity, as he had robbed his own father, Ouranos (the "Heaven"), after castrating him with a sickle. When Rhea was about to give birth to Zeus, she came to Crete to conceal the birth. The baby Zeus, born in the Diktaian Cave,* was taken by his grandmother, Gaia ("Earth") and hidden in a deep cave on the wooded mountain Aigaion ("the Goat's Mountain"). The infant god was nursed there by the goat-nymph Amaltheia* and guarded by the nine Kouretes.* Kronos was given a stone wrapped in swaddling bands instead of the baby, and swallowed it, but later he vomited up this object together with his other immortal children and eventually lost his throne to Zeus. This story is in fact a Minoan and later a Greek version of a Hurrian tale as accounted by Hittite texts of the second millenium B.C. A place near Knossos* was called Omphalion because the Zeus-child was said to have lost his navel-string there. Among other places Zeus was worshipped at Amnisos* as Zeus Thenatas and at Phaistos* as Zeus Welchanos.* His cult in Crete, evidently a survival of Minoan religion,* had a mystic character related to Orphism (see Idaian Cave*) which was totally foreign to Zeus as worshipped in Greece proper.

It seems obvious that the Achaians* after their arrival in Crete gave the name of their sky-god (Zeus is an Indo-European name) to the youthful Minoan god, secondary among the divinities* and related as son or husband to the Great Mother Goddess. After this amalgamation the importance of the god became increasingly prominent. This fertility god of the Minoans, evidently intimately connected with the bull, represented the growth, decay and renewal of the vegetation cycle; hence he was a god who annually died and was reborn, and an annual festival was held in his honour. An analogy has been drawn between him and the Oriental gods Adonis and Tammuz, and the Egyptian god Osiris. The cult of the Cretan Zeus had a strong mystical character connected to the traditional mystery cults of Crete. Thus, the special Cretan Zeus was different from the Greek Zeus, the sky-god and Lord of men and the world, and a legend about his death and tomb (see Juktas*) was created, lasting until relatively recent times. This belief in a dying Zeus was regarded as downright blasphemy by the other Greeks and brought censure upon the Cretans for being liars. This is reflected in the poem of Epimenides,* who was nevertheless a Cretan, which was quoted by St. Paul. A fragment has been restored and translated by Rendel Harris as follows:

> The Cretans carved a tomb for thee, O Holy and High,
> Liars, noxious beasts, evil bellies,
> For thou didst not die, ever thou livest and standest firm
> For in thee we live and move and have our being.

CHART OF CRETAN HISTORY

I

APPROX. DATE (B.C.)	HISTORY	CULTURE
7000 (?)	Arrival of the first settlers. Fixation of the clans and installation in villages.	Hand-made Neolithic pottery and figurines.
3000	Arrival of new immigrants. Beginning of the Bronze Age and the Urban Revolution.	Pyrgos Ware, Hagios Onouphrios Ware.
2600	Rapid evolution of metal-working and other industries.	Vasiliki Ware. Gem-cutting and gold jewellery.
2300		White-on-dark decorated pottery.
2200	Beginning of the Middle Minoan period.	Kamares Ware. Worship in peak sanctuaries. Introduction of the Hieroglyphic script.
2000	Construction of the First Palaces. Regularization of overseas relations and trade.	The fast potter's wheel in common use.
1700	Destructions of the First Palaces. Construction of the New Palaces.	Beginning of fresco-painting.
1650		Appearance of the Linear A script.
1550	Transitional period (Middle to Late Minoan). Construction of the Little Palace, the South House and the Temple-Tomb at Knossos.	Floral Style pottery. Naturalism in art.
1500	Eruption of the volcano of Thera.	Marine Style pottery.
1450	Destruction of palaces and towns on a tremendous scale. Arrival of the Achaians and introduction of the horse and the chariot.	Introduction of the Greek language and the Linear B script. Palace Style pottery.
1400	Beginning of the third Late Minoan period. The last Knossian palace burned down a little later. Submission to the Mycenaean world.	Cretan Mycenaean pottery. Sarcophagus from Hagia Triada. Gradual stylization in art.
1050	Invasion of the Dorians. End of the Bronze Age and beginning of the Dark Ages. Subsequent gradual formation of the city-states.	Rapid decay of civilization. Cremation of the dead.
800	Development of the Dorian society.	Maturity of the Geometric pottery.
735	Intercourse with the Near East.	Orientalizing art.

II

DATE (B.C.)	HISTORY	CULTURE
700	Expansion of trade. Development of the personality of the citizen. Growing social unrest.	Sphyrelaton statues from Dreros. Gradual development of the Dedalic Style and the monumental sculpture.
650	Extensive intercourse with Egypt.	Colossal statue from Astritsi.
524	Foundation of Kydonia by Samians.	Archaic period approaching its end.
500-480	Many city-states issue a coinage. Stabilization of a conservative society.	Beginning of the Classical period. Beginning of the written law: Code of Gortyn.
323	Incessant strife between the city-states.	Beginning of the Hellenistic period.
221-19	The Lyttian War.	
200	Piracy unchecked. Treaty of Olous with Rhodes.	Many cities imitate the Athenian tetradrachm.
183	Alliance of thirty-one Cretan cities with Eumenes II, king of Pergamon.	
171	Destruction of Apollonia.	
166	Destruction of Rhaukos.	
140	Destruction of Praisos.	
121/20	War between Lato and Itanos against Olous and Hierapytna.	
67	Roman campaign and conquest of Crete. Gortyn becomes the capital of Crete and Cyrene (Libya).	Beginning of the Graeco-Roman period.
66	Destruction of Hierapytna.	

DATE (A.D.)		
324	Attachment of Crete to the Byzantine Empire.	Beginning of the Early Christian period.
823	Arab conquest and destruction of several cities.	
961	Liberation of Crete by Nikephoros Phokas.	Development of Byzantine art and culture.
1182	Emperor Alexios II sends twelve noble families.	
1204	Conquest of Crete by Crusaders and subsequent appointment of a Venetian governor. Beginning of Cretan resistance.	
1239		Construction of the St. Marc Basilica.

III

DATE (A.D.)	HISTORY	CULTURE
1263	Evacuation of population from Lasithi.	
1271-7	Revolt of the brothers Chortatzis.	
1283-99	Revolt of Alexios Kallergis.	
1340		Birth of Petros Philagros, Pope of Rome.
1363-4	Rebellion of Venetian noblemen against Venice and proclamation of an independent Republic.	
1365	Revolt of John Kallergis and destruction of Anopolis.	
1415		Visit of Buondelmonti, first scholar interested in Cretan archaeology.
1434	Venetian occupation completed.	
1462	Beginning of fortification of Candia.	
1500		Frescoes at Kera Church of Kritsa.
1545		Birth of Domenicos Theotokopoulos (El Greco).
1559		Death of Theophanes "the Cretan."
1579	Construction of the Spinalonga and Grambousa fortresses.	
1587		Construction of Baroque Church at Arkadi.
1628		Loggia and Morosini Fountain at Candia.
1645	Turkish invasion and capture of Chania.	
1648	Beginning of the siege of Candia.	
1669	End of siege and sack of Candia.	
1670	Last Venetian forces evacuate Crete.	
1690		Death of the painter Tzanes.
1715	Surrender of the Spinalonga garrison.	
1770-1	Insurrection of Daskaloyiannis in Western Crete.	
1821	Crete takes part in the Greek Independence War.	
1823	Massacre in the Milatos Cave.	
1830-40	Egyptian occupation.	
1841	Revolt ending by intervention of the Great Powers.	

IV

DATE (A.D.)	HISTORY	CULTURE
1866	General Cretan revolt and destruction of Arkadi.	
1869	Revolt ferociously repressed.	
1878		Preliminary excavation at Knossos by Minos Kalokairinos.
1897	Last Cretan revolt.	
1898	Turkish forces evacuate Crete. Prince George Gluecksburg appointed High Commissioner.	
1900		Beginning of the main excavations at Knossos by Evans, followed by Greek, American and Italian excavations.
1905	Movement at Therisos against Prince George.	
1912	Cretan deputies accepted in Greek Parliament.	
1913	Official union of Crete with Greece. Treaty of London.	
1941	Battle of Crete. German occupation.	
1944	German forces evacuate Crete.	
1961		Beginning of the excavations at Zakros.

CONCORDANCE OF ILLUSTRATIONS, MUSEUM INVENTORY NUMBERS AND PROVENANCE

(HM: Herakleion Museum, HNM: Hagios Nikolaos Museum,
CM: Chania Museum, RM: Rethymnon Museum)

3: HNM 3296 (Excavation 1972)
4: HNM 2466 (Phatsi, near Liopetro)
5: HM
6: HM 16569
7: HM 822-3 (Hagia Triada)
9: HM (Apesokari, Tholos B)
11: HM (Fortetsa Cemetery)
12: HM 175 (Zapher Papoura Cemetery)
13: HM (Tomb V)
14: HM
15: HM 2339
16: HM
17: HM (Sykia, near Gouves)
18: HNM 5047 (Phatsi, near Liopetro)
19: HM
20: HM 4126 (Koumasa)
23: HM (Arkalochori)
26: HM 593
27–28: HM 2573
30: Province of Siteia
33: HNM 173 (Kritsa)
36: HM 3903
37: HM 407 (Artritsi, near Herakleion)
38: HM 47 (Eleutherna, Rethymnon)
39: HM 2404 (Vorou Monofatsiou)
40: RM 148 (Hellenes Amariou)
41: HM 2416
42: HM 116 (Palaikastro)
44: HM 3405
45: HM 1762
46: HM (fig. 137)
47: HM 13261
49: HM 69
50: HM
51: HM 16465
52: HM
53: HM 9305
54: HM 18502
55: HM 16494
58: HM
65: HM 13492 (Atsalenio)
71: HM
76: HNM 4890 (Hagia Photia, Tomb CCXVI)

77: HNM 2674 (Hagia Photia, Tomb LXXI)
80: HNM 3617 (Hagia Photia, Tomb XCVI)
85: HNM 3114 (Cf. fig. 115)
88: HM 725
89: HM
90: HNM 4313
91: HNM 4352–55
92: HNM 3109
93: HM
94: HM (Kalochoraphitis)
95: HM
98: HNM 3168 (Hagia Photia, Tomb CLXXXI)
101: HNM 4412 (Room H26. Cleaning 1972)
102: HM 9500 (Pachyammos)
103: HM (Stavrakia, near Herakleion)
104: HM (Stavrakia, near Herakleion)
107: HNM 2470 (Petsophas 1971)
112: CM
113: HM 3383
115: HNM 3114 (Cf. fig. 85)
116: HM 2064
117: HNM 4650 (Hagia Photia)
120: HNM (Hagia Photia, various tombs)
122: HM 7944
135: HM
137: Fig. 46 (Traostalos)
138: HM 16443 (Traostalos)
139: HM (Traostalos)
142: HNM 6178 (Near Vasiliki)
144: HM 5267
149: HNM 4157 (Hagia Photia, Tomb CXXXIV)
152: HNM 2313
154: HM
155: HM
156: HM 2314 (Grivila, Rethymnon)
157: HM 124 (Monastiraki, near Knossos)
159: HNM 3113
160: HM 24
162: HM
164: HM (Near Knossos)
166: HM

168: HM 8131 (West Court Houses)
169: HM 63 and 65
173: HM 2445
175: HNM 2316 (Siteia)
176: HNM 4399 (Excavation 1972)
177: HNM 440l (Excavation 1972)
180: HM (Hagia Triada)
181: HM (Knossos)

184: Kalo Chorio (Ancient Istron)
187: HM
188: HM
189: HNM 4653
193: HM 3699
198: HNM 4670 (Hagia Photia, Tomb CCXVI)

PREHISTORIC CRETE

Approximate Chronological Table

7000–3000	Neolithic period
3000–2800	Early Minoan I A
2800–2600	Early Minoan I B
2600–2300	Early Minoan II
2300–2200	Early Minoan III
2200–2000	Middle Minoan I A
2000–1900	Middle Minoan I B
1900–1800	Middle Minoan II A
1800–1700	Middle Minoan II B
1700–1600	Middle Minoan III A
1600–1550	Middle Minoan III B
1550–1500	Late Minoan I A
1500–1450	Late Minoan I B
1450–1400	Late Minoan II
1400–1300	Late Minoan III A
1300–1220	Late Minoan III B
1220–1050	Late Minoan III C
1050–970	Sub-Minoan

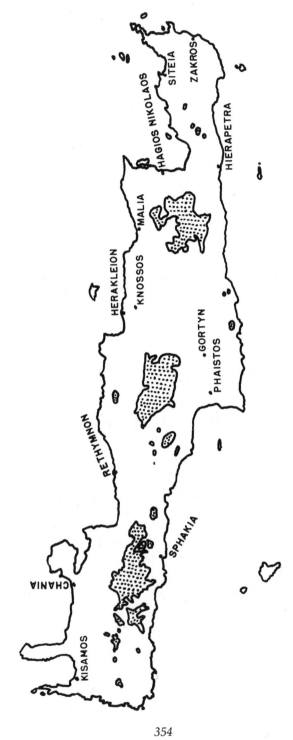

Map 1: Map of Crete with Mountainous Areas (1000 m. above sea level)

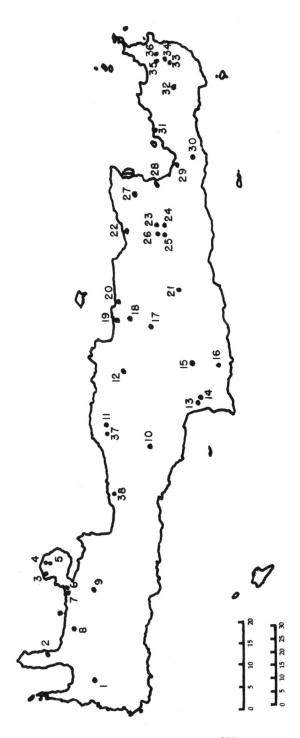

Map 2: Map of Crete with Important Neolithic Sites

1. Topolia
2. Hellinospilios
3. Lera
4. Arkoudiotissa
5. Koumarospilios
6. Hagios Ioannis
7. Chania
8. Myloniana

9. Platyvola
10. Hellenes
11. Melidoni
12. Gonies
13. Hagia Triada
14. Phaistos
15. Gortyn
16. Miamou

17. Stravomyti
18. Knossos
19. Katsambas
20. Rouses
21. Partira
22. Malia
23. Trapeza
24. Kastelos

25. Argoulia
26. Skaphidia
27. Phourni
28. Hagios Nikolaos
29. Sphoungaras
30. Epano Chorio
31. Mochlos
32. Sitanos

33. Karydi
34. Magasas
35. Xerolimni
36. Hagios Nikolaos
37. Perama
38. Gerani

Map 3: Map of Crete with Important Early Minoan Sites

1. Koutsochera 2. Hagia Eirini 3. Koumasa 4. Salame 5. Miamou 6. Hagia Triada 7. Marathokephalo 8. Phaistos 9. Knossos 10. Gazi 11. Amnisos 12. Pyrgos 13. Stravomyti 14. Partira 15. Arkalochori 16. Malia 17. Krasi 18. Trapeza Cave 19. Kastelos 20. Sphoungaras 21. Vasiliki 22. Gournia 23. Mochlos 24. Hagios Ioannis 25. Hagia Photia 26. Petras 27. Hagia Photia 28. Hagios Nikolaos 29. Palaikastro 30. Zakros 31. Hagios Antonios 32. Priniatikos Pyrgos 33. Hagios Onouphrios 34. Platanos 35. Kala-thiana 36. Hellenes 37. Pseira 38. Siva 39. Pachyammos 40. Vorou 41. Drakones 42. Tylissos 43. Kamares Cave 44. Christos 45. Linares 46. Myrsini 47. Kephali Hodigitrias 48. Megaloi Skinoi 49. Kaloi Limenes 50. Lebena 51. Rotasi 52. Viannos 53. Hagios Kyrillos 54. Melidoni 55. Vryses 56. Therisos 57. Maronia 58. Psychro Cave 59. Chania 60. Platyvola 61. Melidoni 62. Viran Episkopi 63. Myrtos 64. Topolia 65. Hagia Marina 66. Hagios Nikolaos 67. Arkoudiotissa 68. Chamaizi 69. Apesokari 70. Karydi 71. Adromyloi 72. Arvi 73. Hagia Pelagia 74. Damasta 75. Apodoulou 76. Rouphas 77. Gournes 78. Giophyrakia 79. Plati 80. Gaudos

356

Map 4: Map of Crete with Important Middle Minoan Sites

1. Christos
2. Porti
3. Drakones
4. Koumasa
5. Platanoi
6. Phaistos
7. Hagia Triada
8. Marathokephalo
9. Kalathiana -
10. Vorou
11. Kamares Cave
12. Tylissos
13. Giophyrakia
14. Knossos

15. Amnisos
16. Juktas
17. Arkalochori
18. Gournes
19. Malia
20. Krasi
21. Trapeza Cave
22. Kastelos
23. Pseira
24. Mochlos
25. Sphoungaras
26. Gournia
27. Vasiliki
28. Pachyammos

29. Hagia Photia
30. Petras
31. Palaikastro
32. Petsophas
33. Zakros
34. Elounda
35. Rouses
36. Skoteino Cave
37. Hagia Marina
38. Chamaizi
39. Gaudos
40. Avgousta
41. Marmaketo
42. Hagios Georgios
43. Mochos
44. Kouses
45. Apodoulou
46. Gazi
47. Archanes

48. Vathypetro
49. Kalamavka
50. Gortyn
51. Patsos Cave
52. Anopolis
53. Kasteli
54. Dia
55. Kanli Kasteli
56. Petrokephalo
57. Skinias
58. Stavromenos
59. Arvi
60. Kommos
61. Megali Vrysi
62. Makrygialos
63. Amiras
64. Vrachasi
65. Sphaka
66. Vistagi

67. Ampelos
68. Traostalos
69. Kalamaki
70. Chania
71. Vrysinas
72. Apesokari
73. Etia
74. Prinias
75. Myrtos
76. Ziros
77. Xykephalo
78. Galatas
79. Koumarospilios
80. Stylos
81. Nochia
82. Thrimbokambos
83. Melidoni
84. Misiria
85. Chamalevri

86. Monastiraki
87. Chondros
88. Viannos
89. Trochaloi
90. Drepanokephala
91. Asprosykia
92. Kouphotos
93. Lebena
94. Valis
95. Hagios Myron
96. Piskokephalo
97. Kophinas
98. Hellenes
99. Hagios Vasilios
100. Chrysoskalitissa
101. Dragonara

102. Axos
103. Hagia Pelagia
104. Tsoutsouros
105. Chochlakies
106. Rouphas
107. Hagios Onouphrios
108. Kritsa
109. Vasiliki
110. Kophinas
111. Choudetsi
112. Samba
113. Gonies
114. Kavrochori
115. Maza
116. Hagios Nikolaos
117. Skloka

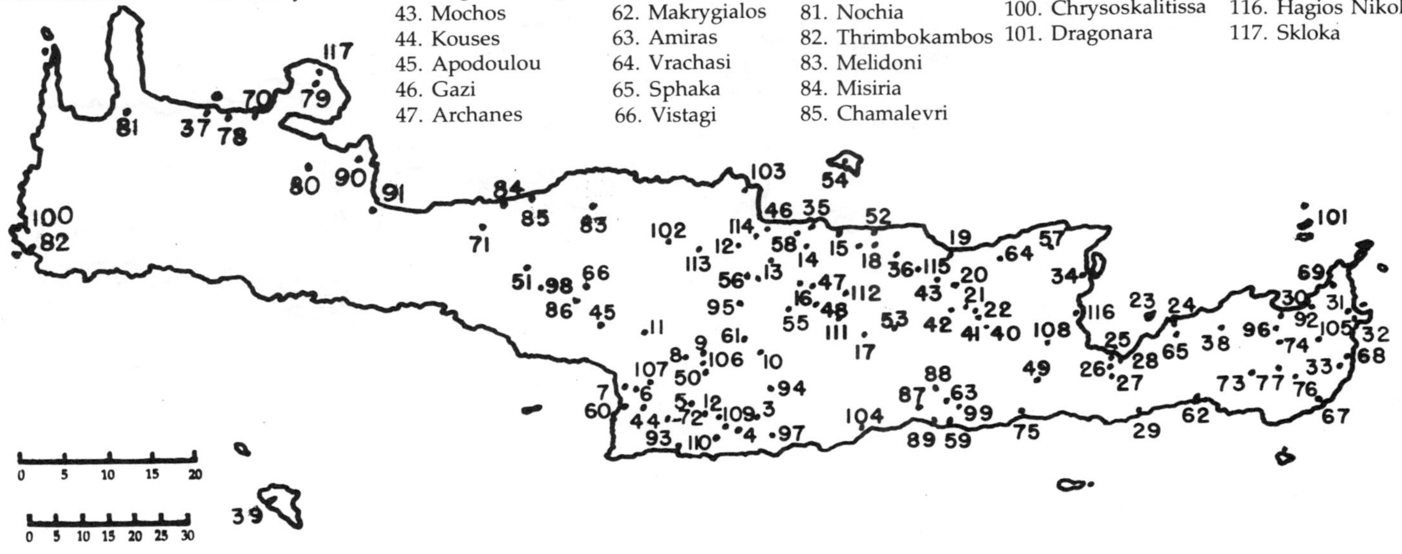

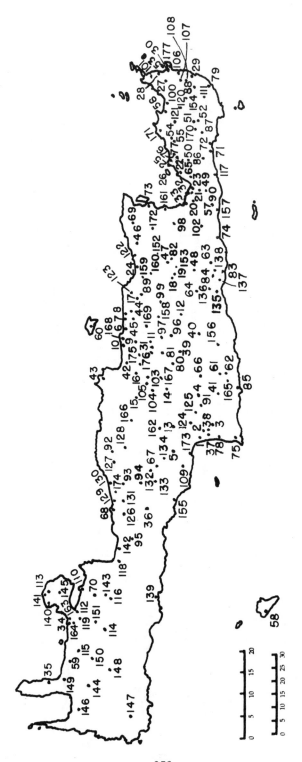

Map 5: Map of Crete with Important Late Minoan Sites

Map 5: Map of Crete with Important Late Minoan Sites

1. Hagia Triada
2. Phaistos
3. Kouses
4. Gortyn
5. Apodoulou
6. Amnisos
7. Hagioi Theodoroi
8. Nirou
9. Knossos
10. Herakleion
11. Archanes
12. Arkalochori
13. Kamares Cave
14. Prinias
15. Gonies
16. Tylissos
17. Skoteino Cave
18. Plati
19. Psychro Cave
20. Vrokastro
21. Gournia
22. Hagios Antonios
23. Pachyammos
24. Malia
25. Mochlos
26. Pseira
27. Hagios Nikolaos
28. Palaikastro
29. Zakros
30. Petsophas

31. Juktas
32. Sphoungaras
33. Priniatikos Pyrgos
34. Chania
35. Helliniospilios
36. Atsipades
37. Logiadi
38. Liliana
39. Damania
40. Ligortyno
41. Anogeia
42. Gazi
43. Hagia Pelagia
44. Gournes
45. Anopolis
46. Milatos
47. Trapeza
48. Erganos
49. Episkopi
50. Avgo
51. Skales
52. Praisos
53. Kouremenos
54. Chamaizi
55. Mouliana
56. Siteia
57. Hagioi Theodoroi
58. Gaudos
59. Maleme
60. Dia

61. Hagia Eirini
62. Koumasa
63. Kato Symi
64. Emparos
65. Kavousi
66. Valis
67. Monastiraki
68. Rethymnon
69. Skinias
70. Stylos
71. Makrygialos
72. Diaskari
73. Elounda
74. Myrtos
75. Vathy
76. Myrsini
77. Tourloti
78. Kommos
79. Ampelos
80. Pyrgos
81. Kanli Kasteli
82. Marmaketo
83. Arvi
84. Amiras
85. Trypiti
86. Stavrochori
87. Adromyloi
88. Epano Zakros
89. Kalo Chorio
90. Kentri

91. Moroni
92. Melidoni
93. Pangalochori
94. Patsos
95. Zouridi
96. Klisidi
97. Choudetsi
98. Kritsa
99. Kasteli
100. Petras
101. Vai
102. Kalamavka
103. Stavrakia
104. Krousonas
105. Pentamodi
106. Karoumes
107. Azokeramos
108. Chochlakies
109. Sachtouria
110. Kalami
111. Ziros
112. Souda
113. Arkoudiotissa
114. Therisos
115. Vryses
116. Melidoni
117. Hagia Photia
118. Asprosykia
119. Tsikalaria
120. Zou

121. Achladia
122. Sisi
123. Gouves
124. Kalochoraphitis
125. Galia
126. Armenoi
127. Perama
128. Choumeri
129. Misiria
130. Stavromenos
131. Prases
132. Thronos
133. Hellenes
134. Vizari
135. Viannos
136. Chondros
137. Vigla
138. Hagios Vasilios
139. Sphakia
140. Lera
141. Nerospilios
142. Dramia
143. Samonas
144. Zymbragos
145. Hagia Triada
146. Kato Palaiokastro
147. Phournakia
148. Nea Roumata
149. Grimbiliana
150. Koupho

151. Skourachlada
152. Kastellos
153. Kaminaki
154. Katsidoni
155. Kerames
156. Rotasi
157. Hierapetra
158. Samba
159. Mochos
160. Avdou
161. Hagios Nikolaos
162. Idaian Cave
163. Chalepa
164. Mameloukou
165. Tsingounia
166. Axos
167. Sarcho
168. Katsambas
169. Episkopi
170. Sklavoi
171. Liopetro
172. Choumeriakos
173. Hagia Galini
174. Pigi
175. Phoinikia
176. Athanatoi
177. Plaka

359

Map 6: Distribution Map of Excavated Peak Sanctuaries

1. Petsophas 2. Modi 3. Kalamaki 4. Traostalos 5. Ampelos 6. Juktas 7. Vigla 8. Ziros 9. Xykephalo 10. Prinias 11. Etiani Kephala 12. Maza 13. Kophinas 14. Vrysinas 15. Karphi 16. Koumasa 17. Pyrgos 18. Gonies

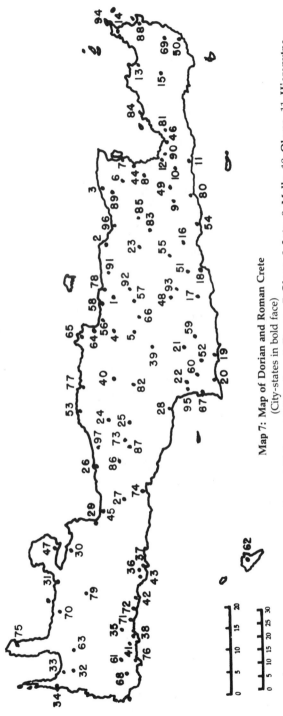

Map 7: Map of Dorian and Roman Crete

(City-states in bold face)

1. **Knossos** 2. **Chersonesos** 3. Milatos 4. Tylissos 5. Rhaukos 6. Dreros 7. Olous 8. **Lato** 9. **Malla** 10. **Oleros** 11. **Hierapytna** 12. **Istron** 13. Setaia 14. **Itanos** 15. **Praisos** 16. Biannos 17. Rhytion 18. Inatos 19. Lebena 20. Lasaia 21. **Gortyn** 22. **Phaistos** 23. **Lyttos** 24. **Eleutherna** 25. **Sybrita** 26. **Rithymna** 27. **Lappa** 28. Soulia 29. Amphimalla 30. **Aptera** 31. **Kydonia** 32. **Polyrrhenia** 33. Kisamos 34. **Phalasarna** 35. **Elyros** 36. Anopolis 37. Phoinix 38. Lisos 39. Rhizenia 40. **Axos** 41. **Hyrtakina** 42. **Tarrha** 43. **Araden** 44. Lato Pros Kamara 45. Hydramia 46. Minoa 47. Minoa 48. Pyranthos 49. Larisa 50. Ampelos 51. **Priansos** 52. Pyloros 53. Panormos 54. Arbis 55. **Apollonia** 56. **Arkades** 57. Acharna 58. Herakleion 59. Bene 60. Boibe 61. Kantanos 62. Kaudos 63. **Keraia** (?) 64. Kytaion 65. Dion (?) 66. Lykastos 67. Matalon 68. Pelkis 69. Dragmos 70. Bergamos (?) 71. Syia 72. Poikilassos 73. Phalanna 74. Phoinix Lampaion (?) 75. Diktynnaion 76. Kalamyde (?) 77. Astale 78. Amnisos 79. Polichna (?) 80. Myrtos 81. Kavousi 82. Idaian Cave 83. Psychro Cave 84. Mochlos 85. Trapeza 86. Onythe 87. Patsos Cave 88. Palaikastro 89. Anavlochos 90. Vrokastro 91. Gournes 92. Hagies Paraskies 93. Ligortyno 94. Samonion 95. Hagia Triada 96. Malia 97. Allaria (?)

361

INDEX TO SITES
(In bold letters when a visit is recommended)

(VI) Beautiful Landscapes

Agios/Agia, Ayios/Ayia, see Hagios/Hagia
Aptera
Araden Gorge see Araden
Arkadi Monastery
Chamaizi
Chrysoskalitissa Monastery
Elounda see Olous
Francocastello
Gournia
Gouverneto Monastery
Grambousa
Hagia Roumeli see Tarrha
Hagia Triada
Inatos
Itanos
Karphi
Kritsa
Lasaia
Lasithi Plain
Lato
Lebena
Lisos

Malla
Matala
Mochlos
Myrtos
Olous
Omalos
Palaikastro
Palaiochora
Phaistos
Phalasarna
Phoinix
Preveli Monastery
Pseira
Samaria Gorge
Souya see Syia
Sphakia
Syia
Tarrha
Vai
Vathypetro
Vrokastro
Zakros

SELECTED BIBLIOGRAPHY IN ENGLISH

Alexiou, S., *Minoan Civilization*, Herakleion 1969.

Alexiou, S., *A Guide to the Minoan Palaces*, Herakleion 1970 (?).

Alexiou, S., Platon N. and Guanella H., *Ancient Crete*, New York 1968.

Boardman, J., *The Cretan Collection in Oxford, Iron Age Crete*, Oxford 1961.

Branigan, K., *The Foundations of Palatial Crete*, London 1969.

Branigan, K., *The Tombs of Mesara*, London 1970.

Brock, J.K., *Fortetsa*, Cambridge 1957.

Demargne, P., *Aegean Art. The Origins of Greek Art*, London 1964.

Evans, A.J., *The Palace of Minos at Knossos* I-IV, London 1921-36. Reprinted 1964.

Graham, J.W., *The Palaces of Crete*, Princeton 1962.

Higgins, R., *Minoan and Mycenaean Art*, London 1967.

Hood, S., *The Home of the Heroes. The Aegean before the Greeks*, London 1967.

Hood, S., *The Minoans*, London 1971.

Hutchinson, R.W., *Prehistoric Crete*, Harmondsworth 1962.

Jenkins, R.J.H., *Dedalica*, 1936.

Kenna, V.E.G., *Cretan Seals*, Oxford 1961.

Levi, D., *Early Hellenic Pottery of Crete*, Amsterdam 1969.

Marinatos S. and Hirmer M., *Crete, Mycenae and Thera*, London 1974.

Matz, F., *Crete and Early Greece*, London 1962.

Nilsson, M.P., *The Minoan-Mycenaean Religion*, 2nd ed. Lund 1950.

Pendlebury, J.D.S., *The Archaeology of Crete*, London 1939. Reprinted 1964.

Pendlebury, J.D.S., *A Handbook to the Palace of Minos*, 2nd ed. 1954.

Platon, N., *Crete*, London 1966.

Platon, N., *Zakros*, New York 1971.

Rutkowski, B., *Cult Places in the Aegean World*, Warsaw 1972.

Warren, P., *Minoan Stone Vases*, Cambridge 1969.

Willetts, R.F., *Aristocratic Society in Ancient Crete*, London 1955.

Willetts, R.F., *Cretan Cults and Festivals*, London 1962.

Willetts, R.F., *Ancient Crete. A Social History*, London-Toronto 1965.

Willetts, R.F., *Everyday Life in Ancient Crete*, London 1969.

Index of Alphabetical Entries